Kris Lamb

A GUIDE TO

DB2

THIRD EDITION

A user's guide to the IBM product
IBM DATABASE 2 (a relational database
management system for the MVS environment)
and its major companion products
QMF, AS, CSP, etc.

C. J. DATE

with

COLIN J. WHITE

Codd and Date International

ADDISON-WESLEY PUBLISHING COMPANY

Reading, Massachusetts • Menlo Park, California • New York •
Don Mills, Ontario • Wokingham, England • Amsterdam • Bonn •
Sydney • Singapore • Tokyo • Madrid • San Juan

Library of Congress Cataloging-in-Publication Data

Date, C. J.
  A guide to DB2. / C. J. Date with Colin J. White—3rd ed.

  Bibliography: p.
  Includes index.
  1. IBM Database 2 (Computer system)
2. Relational data bases. I. White, Colin J.
II. Title.
QA76.9.D3D369 1989   055.75′65 88–35002
ISBN 0–201–50113–9

ABCDEFGHIJ-DO-89

To Ted, for obvious reasons

Preface to the
First Edition

The subject of this book, DB2, is an IBM program product for the MVS environment. More specifically, it is a relational database management system for MVS, which means that it is a product that allows users in that environment (both end-users and application programmers) to store data in, and retrieve data from, databases that are perceived as collections of relations or tables. It provides access to those databases by means of a relational language called SQL ("Structured Query Language").

As a name, "DB2" can scarcely be said to display much distinction— it does little to suggest the nature of the product—and the full name ("IBM DATABASE 2") is not much better. Specifically, it does not make it clear that the product is relational, or that it supports the SQL language, or that it runs on MVS. (Furthermore, it is not even particularly accurate. The product is not a database at all, it is a database management system.) This inauspicious start cannot however conceal the fact that DB2 is a highly important product. Its announcement in June 1983 was a significant event: It placed IBM's final seal of approval on what has come to be known as *the relational approach* to database management. That approach, first proposed in 1969–70 by E. F. Codd (at that time a member of the IBM San Jose Research Laboratory), has slowly but steadily been gaining acceptance, both inside and outside IBM, ever since that time. DB2 is now the leading member of a family of mainline products from IBM, all of them relational, all of them based to a greater or lesser extent on the SQL language, and all of them running on one of the major IBM operating systems (MVS/370, MVS/XA, MVS/ESA, VM/SP, VM/XA, DOS/VSE, PC/DOS, OS/2 Extended Edition, and OS/400).

As just mentioned, the relational approach was first proposed in 1969–70. The SQL language was proposed in 1974, and a major prototype implementation of that language, called System R, was built and evaluated by IBM over a period of approximately five years (1975–79). The technology developed in that prototype was then incorporated into SQL/DS, IBM's first fully supported relational product (announced for DOS/VSE in 1981, for VM/CMS in 1983, and for VM/XA in 1987). Following the success of the SQL/DS product, the same technology was subsequently incorporated into the following products:

- DB2 (announced for MVS/370 and MVS/XA in 1983 and MVS/ESA in 1988)

- The OS/2 Extended Edition Database Manager (announced for OS/2 Extended Edition in 1986)

- The OS/400 Database Manager, SQL/400 (announced for OS/400 in 1988)

All of these various products (and the System R prototype) have very similar externals; in particular, the SQL language is very similar across the different systems. Thus, although this book is specifically concerned with DB2, much of it applies with little change to the other systems also.

The major purpose of the book is to present a detailed (and not wholly uncritical) description of the DB2 product: what it is and is not, what it is intended for, and how it can be used. The book is aimed at DP management, end-user management, database specialists (including database and system administrators, database designers, and database application programmers), DP students and teachers, and end-users or DP professionals who wish to broaden their knowledge of the database field by studying a state-of-the-art system. The emphasis throughout is on the *user* (where by "user" we mean, principally, either an end-user or an application programmer); treatment of user-oriented material, such as the SQL language, is very thorough. By contrast, details that are of interest only to system programmers or operators, such as details of system commands, are generally omitted or at best treated only rather sketchily. Readers are assumed to have at least a general appreciation of the overall structure, concepts, and objectives of database systems in general; however, prior knowledge of relational systems per se is not required.

ACKNOWLEDGMENTS

First and foremost, it is a real pleasure to acknowledge the friendship and support I have received from Ted Codd, not only during the writing of this book but throughout my professional activities over the last several years. Like so many other people in this field, I owe my career and very livelihood to the work that Ted originally did in the late sixties and early seventies, and I am delighted to be able to acknowledge that debt in public here. It is only fitting that this book should be dedicated to him.

Second, I would like to thank the following friends and colleagues for their assistance and encouragement throughout this project and for their constructive criticism of early drafts of the manuscript: Jnan Dash, Walt Roseberry, Phil Shaw, and most especially Sharon Weinberg. Third, I would like to express my gratitude to my erstwhile colleagues on the DB2 design and development team for their patience in dealing with my numerous technical questions; there are too many individuals involved to name them all here, but I would especially like to mention (in addition to those already identified above) my coworkers in the DB2 technical planning department: Sandy Eveland, Paul Higginbotham, Roger Reinsch, Dan Wardman, and George Zagelow. Finally, I am very pleased to acknowledge the hard work put in, at Addison-Wesley and elsewhere, by the many people directly involved in the production of this book. I hope the result does justice to their efforts.

Saratoga, California   C. J. Date
1983 (revised 1988)

Preface to the
Second Edition

DB2 is a highly successful product. Consider the following:

- There are believed to be well over 2,000 DB2 customer licenses at the time of writing (early 1987). Whatever the actual figure is (and 2,000 is probably not too wide of the mark), there can be no doubt that it will have increased significantly by the time this book appears in print. What is more, that 2,000 (?) figure was reached in only 30 months or so of general availability of the product, a fact that surprised many people (including some within IBM). *Note added in third edition:* In late 1988 the number of licenses is believed to be well in excess of 3,500.

- The product has gone through several releases and has proved itself in production environments as well as in ad hoc query applications. (Relational systems were always strong in the ad hoc query area but are only now beginning to show their strength as transaction processing systems also.) Transaction rates have been achieved with DB2 that are in the same league as all but the fastest nonrelational systems, and the end is not in sight.

- There are numerous DB2 application success stories. IBM itself has stated that DB2 is "strategic" and is developing applications on DB2.

- In fact, IBM now considers DB2 to be a key member of its "Systems Application Architecture" (SAA) product set. SAA was announced in March 1987. It consists of a set of IBM standard interfaces, conventions, and protocols that are collectively intended to provide what IBM calls "cross-system consistency"—i.e., the ability to develop applications in and for all major IBM computing environments in a consistent, compatible, and portable manner. The SQL language is defined as the common database interface within SAA, and of course DB2 is the provider of that interface in the MVS environment.

- IBM has developed (and continues to develop) a wide range of auxiliary products to work with DB2, both brand new products such as QMF and extended versions of existing products such as CSP. Collectively, these products form "the IBM Relational Productivity Family." All of the IBM products discussed in this book—SQL/DS, QMF, CSP, AS, DXT, DBRAD, ECF, etc.—are members of this family.

- Other vendors are doing likewise; there are many new products on the market that are specifically designed to run on or with DB2 (e.g., DB2 ALTER from BMC Software), and many older products are being extended to provide some kind of DB2 interface (e.g., FOCUS from Information Builders Inc. now runs on DB2).

- In fact, the entire database market has "gone relational." No one now doubts that relational technology is the way to go. The stories regarding ease of application development, ease of maintenance, improved productivity, etc., really do have a significant basis in fact. Relational systems such as DB2 are beginning to dominate the marketplace—and will continue to do so, moreover, for as far out as anyone can see.

- Independent DBMS vendors (e.g., Oracle Corp., Relational Technology Inc.) are beginning to discuss the possibility of a distributed database system in which their own proprietary product running at one site in a computer network will be able to access data stored under DB2 at another site.

- Finally, there is now an official (industry-wide) standard interface for dealing with relational databases, namely the American National Standards Institute (ANSI)/International Standards Organization (ISO) dialect of SQL, and that standard is quite close to the IBM dialect of SQL as implemented in DB2. In fact, certain features of DB2 Release

3 (the first release after the formal ratification of the ANSI/ISO standard) were explicitly added in order to bring the DB2 dialect a little closer into line with the standard.

Some of the foregoing points bear a little elaboration. The fact is that the widespread acceptance of DB2 is inextricably bound up with the widespread acceptance of two other items, namely relational technology in general and the SQL language in particular. To some extent, the success of each of these three has contributed to and reinforced the success of the other two:

- As a concrete realization of the abstract concepts of the relational model,* the SQL language has made the advantages of relational technology readily understandable, and hence acceptable, to a large and diverse collection of people;

- As a robust, well-supported, and well-publicized implementation of SQL, the DB2 product has lent both general credibility and (not just incidentally) the specific weight of IBM's own endorsement to that language; and

- As the technological base on which DB2 is founded, the relational model has provided the necessary set of guiding principles that have enabled that product to achieve as many of its goals as it has done.

It is also undeniable that it is the fact that IBM has supported SQL that has led to numerous other vendors doing likewise, which in turn has led to the acceptance of a dialect of that language as an official ANSI/ISO standard.

DB2 does have its shortcomings, of course; we will identify several of them in this book. Nevertheless, it is still probably fair to say that DB2 represents the de facto standard in the commercial relational world (at least in the large mainframe environment). Of course, this is not to say that there are no other relational products that are as good as DB2—indeed, there may be some that are better; but DB2 is unquestionably a market leader, and (as pointed out above) it has the good fortune to bear the IBM imprimatur. As a consequence, DB2 is important now, and will continue to remain so for the foreseeable future. Hence this book.

The following remarks apply to the second edition specifically:

---

*Or some of them, at any rate. Regrettably, SQL in its present form does not include support for all aspects of the relational model. See Appendix A (Section A.2) and Appendix B for further discussion, also Appendix F ("An Annotated Critique of the SQL Database Language") in my book *A Guide to the SQL Standard* (2nd edition, Addison-Wesley, 1989).

- First (as already suggested above), it seemed appropriate at the time of that edition to extend the coverage to include a significant amount of material on the principal auxiliary products (QMF, AS, CSP, etc.) in addition to the discussions of DB2 per se. That material, which appears in Part III of the book, was written by my friend and coauthor Colin White, and I believe it enhances the value and usefulness of the book considerably.

- The second edition overall was at the DB2 Release 3 level; thus there were many new topics for discussion, and many revisions to the discussion of older topics, compared with the first edition (which was of course at the Release 1 level). I also took the opportunity to expand or otherwise improve the presentation in many places and to correct a number of minor errors from the first edition. *Note added in third edition:* The third edition is at the level of DB2 Version 2, Release 1 (it also incorporates some material on Version 2, Release 2). See the Preface to the third edition, later.

- The only major item from the first edition that was dropped in the second edition was the appendix discussing database design. That appendix was superseded and made obsolete by Chapter 19, "A Practical Approach to Database Design," of my book *Relational Database: Selected Writings* (Addison-Wesley, 1986).

ACKNOWLEDGMENTS

Most of all, I would like to thank my coauthor Colin White for his major contribution to this edition. I would also like to acknowledge the many comments I have received from friends and students on the first edition, which allowed me to make many improvements in the present version. I would also like to thank the reviewers of this edition—Marc Descollonges of Codd and Date International and Jim Doak, Roger Miller, and Phil Shaw, all of IBM—for their many constructive criticisms. Thanks too to Bob Engles, Nick Nomm, and Ueli Wahli, also of IBM, for helping with technical questions. Finally, I cannot do better than repeat the following from the preface to another of my books: I am (as always) grateful to my editor, Elydia Davis, and to the staff at Addison-Wesley for their assistance and their continually high standards of professionalism. It has been (as always) a pleasure to work with them.

Saratoga, California   C. J. Date
1987 (revised 1988)

Preface to the Third Edition

I am a little embarrassed at producing a third edition of this book so hot on the heels of the second—but consider the following facts:

1. In April 1988, IBM announced a very significant new version (Version 2) of the DB2 product. That announcement included:

- Support for primary and foreign keys (a *major* functional improvement, in this writer's opinion)

- Significant performance enhancements in several discrete areas (online transaction processing, ad hoc query, sort, utilities, etc.)

- Various operational improvements (improved security facilities, auditing, a governor facility, new storage structures, etc.)

2. Version 2 of DB2 became generally available in September 1988. At that time, IBM announced additional enhancements to the product, including:

- C language support
- Further performance improvements

3. Almost immediately after releasing DB2 Version 2, IBM announced another significant new release (DB2 Version 2 Release 2, scheduled for general availability in the third quarter of 1989). Version 2 Release 2 provides DB2's preliminary support for distributed database. In a simultaneous announcement, IBM also added distributed database facilities to its Systems Application Architecture, SAA.

The foregoing developments, taken together, seemed more than enough to justify a revision of this book; hence this third edition. (Perhaps I should say that I do not expect the next few releases of DB2 to have such a dramatic impact as the last two—but I have been wrong before! IBM is clearly taking the DB2 produce very seriously indeed and is devoting a great deal of energy to it.)

The major differences between this new edition and its predecessor can be summarized as follows:

- An important new chapter (Chapter 12) has been added on *integrity*. This chapter explains the relational primary and foreign key concepts in detail and describes the DB2 Version 2 support for these concepts— including the IBM implementation restrictions—in considerable depth. The chapter also includes an extensive set of exercises and answers.

- Compensating changes required by the new support for primary and foreign keys have been made in several other places throughout the book.

- Chapter 9 on the DB2 catalog has been significantly revised, and a new appendix (Appendix E) summarizing the tables of the catalog has been added.

- Material has been added on security improvements, audit facilities, locking improvements, and the new "segmented" tablespace structure.

- A new chapter (Chapter 17) has been added on DB2 system and database administration facilities. This chapter retains the discussion of the DB2 Interactive interface (DB2I) from the second edition but incorporates much new material on DB2 utilities, service aids, the Boot Strap Data Set, etc.

- A new chapter (Chapter 26) has been added on distributed database.

- The chapter on QMF (Chapter 19) has been significantly revised to incorporate material on the newest release (Version 2 Release 3). Minor revisions have also been made to other chapters in Part III of the book to incorporate various product release changes.

- The appendix summarizing differences between the DB2 SQL dialect and the ANSI/ISO SQL standard has been updated to take account of the recent integrity extensions to both DB2 and the standard.

- The only item of any significance in the second edition that has been removed from the third is the rather general discussion of relational performance in the old Chapter 25. The fact is that that discussion has been more or less overtaken by events. The intent of the discussion was to demonstrate that there was no reason, at least in principle, why relational systems should not be able to achieve good performance (and indeed to argue that, again in principle, relational systems in the future might generally *out*perform nonrelational ones). There seems no point in preserving that material in this book any longer, given the announced DB2 performance figures from IBM. This is not the place to get into details; let me simply quote the following "laboratory performance measurements" from the IBM DB2 Version 2 Announcement letter (April 19, 1988) and the DB2 Version 2 General Availability letter (September 20, 1988):

Standard DB2 workload:	270 TPS
	(TPS = transactions/second)
"High volume transaction	300 TPS (debit processing)
processing" workload:	438 TPS (credit check)

For details of exactly what processing the transactions entailed, the hardware configuration, the software options in effect, etc., the reader is referred to IBM; the point here is not to get into such details, but merely to show that DB2 is certainly capable of reasonably high transaction rates. A fair general statement would be that DB2 in its current release is somewhere in the range of 80 to 90 percent of IMS Full Function in terms of the transaction rates it can handle.

As usual, of course, I have also taken the opportunity to make a large number of minor improvements and corrections throughout the text. One further point: The product discussions in Part III are once again all at the level of the most recent release of the product in question. For convenience those release levels are summarized below:

QMF	Version 2 Release 3
AS	Version 1 Release 5 Modification Level 1
CSP	Version 3 Release 2 Modification Level 2
ADF	Version 2 Release 2
DXT	Version 2 Release 3
HDBV	Version 2 Release 1 Modification Level 1
ECF	Version 1 Release 1
DBRAD	Version 1 Release 1

ACKNOWLEDGMENTS

Once again I would like to thank my coauthor Colin White for his contribution to this book. As with the second edition, I would also like to acknowledge the variety of comments received from friends and students on the previous edition, which have enabled me to make a number of improvements in the present version. In particular, I would like to thank Nagraj Alur of Codd and Date International for numerous helpful discussions, especially with respect to the material of Chapter 12. And, last but not least, I must record my gratitude once again to my editor, Elydia Davis, and to Addison-Wesley for their usual top-quality assistance and support. As always, it has been a pleasure to work with them.

Saratoga, California   C. J. Date
1988

Contents

PART II   THE DB2 DATABASE MANAGEMENT SYSTEM

**PART III   THE IBM RELATIONAL
PRODUCTIVITY FAMILY**

PART IV   FUTURE DIRECTIONS

APPENDIXES

PART

I

AN OVERVIEW OF DB2

C H A P T E R

◆ 1 ◆

DB2: A Relational System

1.1 INTRODUCTION

"DB2" is an abbreviation for "IBM DATABASE 2." DB2 is a subsystem of the MVS operating system.* More specifically, it is a *database management system* (DBMS) for that operating system. Even more specifically, it is IBM's long-awaited, and by now (1989) highly successful, *relational* DBMS for MVS; it is a system that allows any number of MVS users to access any number of relational databases by means of the well-known relational language SQL ("Structured Query Language"). IBM's product line prior to DB2 included a nonrelational (actually hierarchic) DBMS for MVS, namely

---

*Version 1 of DB2 ran on both the original MVS/370 system product ("Multiple Virtual Systems/370") and the extended version MVS/XA ("MVS/Extended Architecture"). Version 2 runs on MVS/XA and the new MVS/ESA ("MVS/Enterprise Systems Architecture"). References in the text to the term "MVS" should be interpreted accordingly.

3

IMS, and a relational DBMS for VM and VSE, namely SQL/DS, but did not include a relational offering for MVS. (We shall have more to say about IMS and SQL/DS later.) In June 1983, however, the MVS relational system DB2 was finally announced. The purpose of this book is to describe that system.

What does it mean for a system to be relational? To answer this question properly, it would unfortunately be necessary to discuss a good deal of preliminary material first. Since any such discussion would be out of place at this early point in the book, we defer it for now (see Section 1.2 and Appendix B for the details); however, we give a rough-and-ready answer to the question without that discussion, in the hope that such an answer will help to allay any apprehensions the reader may be feeling at the outset. Briefly, a relational system is a system in which:

(a) The data is perceived by the user as tables (and nothing but tables); and

(b) The operators at the user's disposal (e.g., for query) are operators that generate new tables from old. For example, there will be one operator to extract a subset of the rows of a given table, and another to extract a subset of the columns—and of course a row subset and a column subset of a table can both in turn be regarded as tables themselves.

Fig. 1.1 illustrates these two points. The data (see part (a) of the figure) consists of a single table, named CELLAR, with three columns and four rows. Two sample queries—one involving a row-subsetting operation and

(a) Given table:

CELLAR	WINE	YEAR	BOTTLES
	Zinfandel	81	10
	Chardonnay	86	6
	Cabernet	80	12
	Riesling	86	9

(b) Operators (examples):

1. Row subset:

```
SELECT WINE, YEAR, BOTTLES
FROM    CELLAR
WHERE   YEAR = 86 ;
```

Result:

WINE	YEAR	BOTTLES
Chardonnay	86	6
Riesling	86	9

2. Column subset:

```
SELECT WINE, BOTTLES
FROM    CELLAR ;
```

Result:

WINE	BOTTLES
Zinfandel	10
Chardonnay	6
Cabernet	12
Riesling	9

Fig. 1.1 Data structure and operators in a relational system (examples)

the other a column-subsetting operation—are shown in part (b) of the figure.

Note: The two queries of Fig. 1.1 are in fact examples of the SELECT statement of the Structured Query Language SQL mentioned earlier. SQL (usually pronounced "sequel," though the official pronunciation is "ess-cue-ell") is the database language supported, not only by DB2, but also by IBM's SQL/DS, OS/2 Extended Edition Database Manager, and SQL/400 products, and also by numerous nonIBM products. A dialect of SQL was adopted by the American National Standards Institute (ANSI) in 1986 and by the International Standards Organization (ISO) in 1987 as an official standard for relational systems. The DB2 dialect of SQL is reasonably close to that standard (see Appendix F).

The purpose of this book, then, is to provide an in-depth tutorial and reference text on a specific relational system, DB2 (also on its principal companion products QMF, AS, CSP, etc.—see Chapter 3). It is intended for end-users, application programmers, database administrators, and more generally anyone who wishes to obtain an understanding of the major concepts of the DB2 system. It is not intended as a substitute for the system manuals provided by IBM; but it *is* intended as a comprehensive, convenient (single-volume) guide to the use of the product. As stated in the Preface to the first edition, the emphasis is definitely on the user, and therefore on product externals rather than internals, although various internal aspects are discussed from time to time. The reader is assumed to have an overall appreciation of the structure and objectives of database systems in general, but not necessarily any specific knowledge of relational systems in particular. All applicable relational concepts are introduced in the text as they are needed. In addition, Appendix B provides a more formal summary of those concepts, for purposes of reference.

In this preliminary chapter, we present a brief overview of the DB2 product. In particular, we give some idea as to what is involved in creating and accessing data in a DB2 database, and we briefly discuss the DB2 database language SQL. These topics, and of course many others, are amplified in subsequent chapters.

1.2 RELATIONAL DATABASES

DB2 databases are relational. *A relational database is a database that is perceived by its users as a collection of tables (and nothing but tables).* An example (the suppliers-and-parts database) is shown in Fig. 1.2.

As you can see, this database consists of three tables, namely S,P, and SP.

S	S#	SNAME	STATUS	CITY		SP	S#	P#	QTY
	S1	Smith	20	London			S1	P1	300
	S2	Jones	10	Paris			S1	P2	200
	S3	Blake	30	Paris			S1	P3	400
	S4	Clark	20	London			S1	P4	200
	S5	Adams	30	Athens			S1	P5	100
							S1	P6	100
P	P#	PNAME	COLOR	WEIGHT	CITY		S2	P1	300
							S2	P2	400
	P1	Nut	Red	12	London		S3	P2	200
	P2	Bolt	Green	17	Paris		S4	P2	200
	P3	Screw	Blue	17	Rome		S4	P4	300
	P4	Screw	Red	14	London		S4	P5	400
	P5	Cam	Blue	12	Paris					
	P6	Cog	Red	19	London					

Fig. 1.2 The suppliers-and-parts database (sample values)

- Table S represents suppliers. Each supplier has a supplier number (S#), unique to that supplier; a supplier name (SNAME), not necessarily unique; a rating or status value (STATUS); and a location (CITY). For the sake of the example, we assume that each supplier is located in exactly one city.

- Table P represents parts (more accurately, kinds of part). Each kind of part has a part number (P#), which is unique; a part name (PNAME), not necessarily unique; a color (COLOR); a weight (WEIGHT); and a location where parts of that type are stored (CITY). For the sake of the example, again, we assume that each kind of part comes in exactly one color and is stored in a warehouse in exactly one city.

- Table SP represents shipments. It serves in a sense to connect the other two tables together. For example, the first row of table SP in Fig. 1.2 connects a specific supplier from table S (namely, supplier S1) with a specific part from table P (namely, part P1); in other words, it represents a shipment of parts of kind P1 by the supplier called S1 (and the shipment quantity is 300). Thus, each shipment has a supplier number (S#), a part number (P#), and a quantity (QTY). For the sake of the example, once again, we assume that there can be at most one shipment at any given time for a given supplier and a given part; thus, for a given shipment, the combination of S# value and P# value is unique with respect to the set of shipments currently appearing in the SP table.

This example is of course extremely simple, much more simple than any real database that you are likely to encounter in practice. Nevertheless, it is adequate to illustrate most of the points that we need to make in this book, and we will use it as the basis for most (not all) of the examples in the following chapters. You should therefore take a little time to familiarize yourself with it now.

Note: There is nothing wrong with using more descriptive names such as SUPPLIERS, PARTS, and SHIPMENTS in place of the rather terse names S, P, and SP; indeed, descriptive names are generally to be recommended in practice. But in the case of the suppliers-and-parts database specifically, the three tables are referenced so frequently in the chapters that follow that very short names seemed desirable. Long names tend to become irksome with much repetition.

There are a few points arising from the example that are worth calling out explicitly:

- First, note that *all data values are atomic.* That is, at every row-and-column position in every table there is always exactly one data value, never a set of multiple values. Thus, for example, in table SP (considering the first two columns only, for simplicity), we have

```
         S#   P#
         --   --
          .    .
         S2   P1
         S2   P2
          .    .
         S4   P2
         S4   P4
         S4   P5
          .    .
          .    .
```

  instead of

```
       S#     P#
       --     ---------------
        .      .
       S2    ( P1, P2 )
        .      .
       S4    ( P2, P4, P5 )
        .      .
        .      .
```

  A column such as P# in the second version of this table represents what is sometimes called a "repeating group." A repeating group is a column that contains *sets* of data values (different numbers of values in different rows), instead of just one value in each row. *Relational databases do not allow repeating groups.* The second version of the table above would not be permitted in a relational system.

- Second, note that the entire information content of the database is represented as *explicit data values.* This method of representation (as explicit values in column positions within rows of tables) is the *only* method available in a relational database. Specifically, there are no "links" or pointers connecting one table to another.* For example, there is a connexion (as already pointed out) between the S1 row of table S and the P1 row of table P, because supplier S1 supplies part P1; but that connexion is represented, not by pointers, but by the existence of a row in table SP in which the S# value is S1 and the P# value is P1. In nonrelational systems such as IMS, by contrast, such information is typically represented by some kind of physical link or pointer that is explicitly visible to the user. Some consequences of this difference will be discussed later in the book.

- Third, note that each of the tables in the example has a *unique identifier*—that is, a column (or combination of columns) whose value in any given row is unique with respect to the set of all such values appearing in the table. The unique identifier for table S is S#; for table P, it is P#; and for table SP it is the combination (S#,P#). For example, values of the S# column of table S can be used to pinpoint individual supplier rows within that table.

The formal relational term for such a unique identifier is *primary key*. DB2 does not fully enforce the primary key discipline (that is, it does not actually require every table to have a primary key), but users are nevertheless *strongly* recommended to follow such a discipline in practice. We will do so throughout this book. See Chapter 12 for further discussion.

At this point the reader may be wondering why a database such as that in Fig. 1.2 is called "relational" anyway. The answer is simple: "Relation" is just a mathematical term for a table (to be precise, a table of a certain specific kind—details to follow in Chapter 5). Thus, for example, we can say that the database of Fig. 1.2 consists of three *relations*. For the most part, in fact, we will take "relation" and "table" as synonymous in this book. Relational systems have their origin in the mathematical theory of relations; of course, this does not mean that you need to be a mathematician in order to use a relational system, but it does mean that there is a respectable body of theoretical results that can be applied to practical problems of database usage, such as the problem of database design.

If it is true that a relation is just a table, then why not simply call it a table and have done with it? The answer is that we very often do (and in this book we usually will). However, it is worth taking a moment to under-

---

*This sentence does not mean that there cannot be pointers *at the physical storage level*—there certainly can, and indeed there certainly will. But all such pointers are *concealed from the user*. We are concerned here purely with the logical level of the system. See the further discussion of this point in the next section.

stand why the term "relation" was introduced in the first place. Briefly, the explanation is as follows. Relational systems are based on what is called *the relational model of data.* The relational model, in turn, is an abstract theory of data that is based in part on the mathematical theory mentioned earlier. The principles of the relational model were originally laid down in 1969–70 by one man, Dr. E. F. Codd, at that time a researcher in IBM. It was late in 1968 that Codd, a mathematician by training, first realized that the discipline of mathematics could be used to inject some solid principles and rigor into a field—database management—that, prior to that time, was all too deficient in any such qualities. Codd's ideas were first widely published in a now classic paper, "A Relational Model of Data for Large Shared Data Banks" (*Communications of the ACM 13,* No. 6, June 1970). Since that time, those ideas (by now almost universally accepted) have had a wide-ranging influence on just about every aspect of database technology, and indeed on other fields as well, such as the field of artificial intelligence and natural language processing.

Now, the relational model as originally formulated by Codd very deliberately made use of certain terms—such as the term "relation" itself—that were not familiar in data processing circles at that time, even though the concepts in some cases were. The trouble was, many of the more familiar terms were very fuzzy. They lacked the precision necessary to a formal theory of the kind that Codd was proposing. For example, consider the term "record." At different times that single term can mean either a record *instance* or a record *type;* a *COBOL-style* record (which allows repeating groups) or a *flat* record (which does not); a *logical* record or a *physical* record; a *stored* record or a *virtual* record; and so on. The formal relational model therefore does not use the term "record" at all; instead, it uses the term "tuple" (short for "*n*-tuple"), which was given a precise definition by Codd when he first introduced it. We do not give that definition here; for our purposes, it is sufficient to say that the term "tuple" corresponds approximately to the notion of a *flat record instance* (just as the term "relation" corresponds approximately to the notion of a table). If you wish to study some of the more formal literature on relational database systems, you will of course have to familiarize yourself with the formal terminology, but in this book we are not trying to be very formal, and we will stick for the most part to terms such as "record" that are reasonably familiar. One formal term we will use somewhat, however, is the term "primary key" introduced earlier in this section.

Fig. 1.3 shows the terms we will be using most heavily (table, record, row, field, column, also primary key). For interest it also gives the corresponding formal term in each case. Note that we use the terms "record" and "row" interchangeably, and the terms "field" and "column" likewise.

Formal relational term	Informal equivalents
relation	table
tuple	record, row
attribute	field, column
primary key	unique identifier

Fig. 1.3 Some terminology

Note also, therefore, that we are definitely taking "record" to mean "record instance" and "field" to mean "field type."

1.3 THE SQL LANGUAGE

As already explained, DB2—in common with numerous other products, from IBM and other vendors—supports the relational language SQL ("Structured Query Language"). This language is used to formulate relational operations (i.e., operations that define and manipulate data in relational form). In this section, we present a brief introduction to the SQL language.

First the definitional operations. Fig. 1.2 (the suppliers-and-parts database) of course represents that database as it might appear at some particular instant in time; it is a *snapshot* of the database. Fig. 1.4, by contrast, shows the *structure* of that database; it shows how the database might be defined or described, using SQL "data definition" statements.*

As you can see, the definition includes one CREATE TABLE statement for each of the three tables. The CREATE TABLE statement is, as already indicated, an example of a SQL data definition statement. Each CREATE TABLE statement specifies the name of the table to be created, the names and data types of the columns of that table, and the primary key of the table (possibly some additional information also, not illustrated in Fig. 1.4; see Chapters 5 and 12).

It is not our purpose at this juncture to describe the CREATE TABLE statement in detail; that detailed description appears later, in Chapter 5. One point that does need to be stressed right at the outset, however, is that CREATE TABLE is an *executable statement*. (In fact, every statement in the SQL language is executable, except for a few that are used in embedded

---

*Throughout this book we show SQL statements, commands, etc., in upper case, for clarity. In practice it is usually more convenient to enter such statements and commands in lower case. DB2 will accept both.

```
CREATE TABLE S
   ( S#        CHAR(5) NOT NULL,
     SNAME     CHAR(20),
     STATUS    SMALLINT,
     CITY      CHAR(15),
     PRIMARY KEY ( S# ) ) ;

CREATE TABLE P
   ( P#        CHAR(6) NOT NULL,
     PNAME     CHAR(20),
     COLOR     CHAR(6),
     WEIGHT    SMALLINT,
     CITY      CHAR(15),
     PRIMARY KEY ( P# ) ) ;

CREATE TABLE SP
   ( S#        CHAR(5) NOT NULL,
     P#        CHAR(6) NOT NULL,
     QTY       INTEGER,
     PRIMARY KEY ( S#, P# ) ) ;
```

Fig. 1.4 The suppliers-and-parts database (data definition)

SQL only—see Chapters 13 and 15.) If the three CREATE TABLEs in Fig. 1.4 were to be entered at a terminal, exactly as shown, the system would actually build the three tables, then and there. Initially, of course, those tables would be empty—that is, they would each contain just the row of column headings, no data rows as yet. However, we could subsequently go on to insert such data rows—possibly via the SQL INSERT statement, to be discussed in Chapter 8*—and, in just a few minutes' work, we could have a (probably small, but still useful and usable) database at our disposal, and could start doing some useful things with it. So this simple example illustrates right away one of the advantages of relational systems in general, and DB2 in particular: They are very easy to use (ease of "getting on the air" is of course just one aspect of ease of use in general). As a result, they can make users very productive. We shall see many other advantages later.

Note: Although it really has nothing to do with the subject of this section (namely, the SQL language), it is worth mentioning in passing that DB2 is specifically designed to be easy to install as a *system*—by which we mean that, not only is it easy (as indicated above) to "install" or create a new DB2 database at any time, but it is also easy to install the overall DB2 system in the first place. In other words, the process of building the neces-

---

*In the interests of accuracy, it should be mentioned that no rows could actually be inserted into any of the tables until an index has been created on that table's primary key. See Chapter 12 for further discussion.

sary library data sets, specifying the required system parameters, defining certain system defaults, etc., is deliberately made as simple as possible. Sample programs are provided to verify that system installation has been performed correctly. The overall procedure should typically take from one to two working days.

To continue with the example: Having created our three tables, and loaded some records into them, we can now start doing useful work with them, using SQL *data manipulation* statements. One of the things we can do is *data retrieval,* which is specified in SQL by the SELECT statement. Fig. 1.5 illustrates the use of that statement.

A particularly significant feature of most relational systems, including in particular DB2 (and SQL/DS, incidentally), is that the same relational language (here SQL) is available at *two different interfaces,* namely an interactive interface (DB2I—"DB2 Interactive"—in the case of DB2) and an application programming interface. The two interfaces are both illustrated in Fig. 1.5:

(a) Fig. 1.5(a) shows an example of the interactive interface, DB2I. Here the user has typed the SELECT statement at a terminal, and DB2 has responded—through its DB2I component—by displaying the result ("London") directly at that terminal.

(b) Fig. 1.5(b) shows essentially the same SELECT statement embedded in an application program (a PL/I program, in the example). In this second case the statement will be executed when the program is executed, and the result "London" will be returned, not to a terminal, but to the program variable XCITY (by virtue of the INTO clause in the SELECT; XCITY is just an input area within the program).

Thus, SQL is both an *interactive query language* and a *database programming language.* Furthermore, this remark applies to the entire SQL

(a) Interactive (DB2I):

```
SELECT CITY                          Result:  CITY
FROM    S                                     ------
WHERE   S# = 'S4' ;                           London
```

(b) Embedded in PL/I (could be COBOL, FORTRAN, etc.):

```
EXEC SQL SELECT CITY                 Result:  XCITY
         INTO   :XCITY                        ------
         FROM    S                            London
         WHERE   S# = 'S4' ;
```

Fig. 1.5 A retrieval example

language; that is, any SQL statement that can be entered at a terminal can alternatively be embedded in a program. Note in particular that the remark applies even to statements such as CREATE TABLE; you can create tables from within an application program, if it makes sense in your application to do so (and if you are authorized to perform such operations). SQL statements can be used with programs written in any of the following languages: APL, BASIC, C, COBOL, FORTRAN, PL/I, and System/370 Assembler Language (see Chapters 2 and 13 for further discussion).

Note: Interactive SQL and embedded SQL do differ from each other on certain points of detail, of course. For example, each embedded SQL statement must be prefixed with EXEC SQL in order to distinguish it from the surrounding host language statements (see Fig. 1.5(b) for an illustration). Likewise, the SELECT statement of Fig. 1.5(b) needs an INTO clause to designate the input area, as we have seen, and the host language variable named in that clause has a colon prefix in order to distinguish it from a database column name. So of course it is not one hundred percent true to say that the SELECT statement is the same at both interfaces. But it is broadly true, if we overlook the minor differences of detail.

We are now in a position to understand how DB2 looks to the user. By "user" here we mean either an end-user at an online terminal or an application programmer writing in one of the DB2-supported host languages such as PL/I. (We note in passing that the term "user" will be used consistently throughout this book with either or both of these two meanings.) As already explained, each such user will be using SQL to operate on tables. See Fig. 1.6.

The first point to be made concerning the figure is that there will normally be many users, of both kinds, all operating on the same data at the same time. DB2 will automatically apply the necessary controls (basically locking—see Chapter 14) to ensure that those users are all protected from one another; i.e., DB2 will guarantee that one user's updates cannot cause another user's operations to produce an incorrect result.

Next, note that tables, like users, also come in two kinds. The two kinds of tables are called *base tables* and *views*.

- A base table is a "real" table—i.e., a table that physically exists, in the sense that there exist physically stored records, and possibly physical indexes, in one or more MVS files (actually VSAM linear data sets), that directly represent that table in storage. Tables S, P, and SP in Fig. 1.4 are all base tables.

- By contrast, a view is a "virtual" table—i.e., a table that does not directly exist in physical storage, but looks to the user as if it did. Views can be thought of as different ways of looking at the "real" tables. As

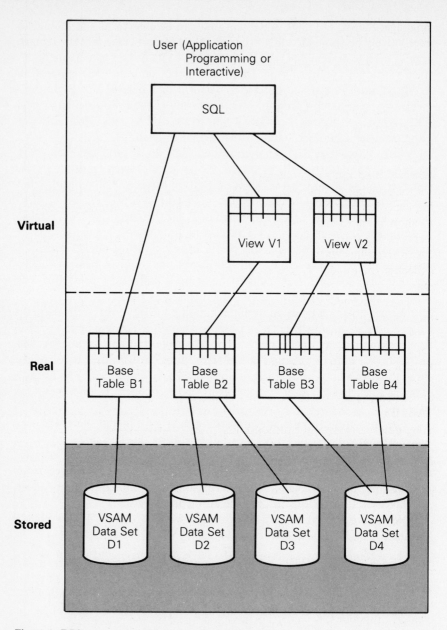

Fig. 1.6 DB2 as perceived by an individual user

a trivial example, a given user might have a view of the suppliers base table S in which only those suppliers in London are visible. Views are defined, in a manner to be explained in Chapter 10, in terms of one or more of the underlying base tables.

Note: The foregoing should not be interpreted as saying that a base table is *physically stored* as a table—i.e., as a set of physically adjacent stored records, with each stored record consisting simply of a direct copy of a row of the base table. There are numerous differences of detail between a base table and its storage representation (see Chapter 16). The point is, however, that users can always think of base tables as physically existing, without having to concern themselves with how those tables are actually implemented in storage. In fact, the whole point of a relational database is to allow users to deal with data in the form of tables per se, instead of in terms of the storage representation of such tables. To repeat from Section 1.2, a relational database is a database that is *perceived by its users* as a collection of tables. It is *not* just a database in which data is physically stored as tables.

Like base tables, views can be created at any time. The same is true of indexes. (The CREATE TABLE statement already discussed is for creating "real" or base tables. There is an analogous CREATE VIEW statement for creating views or "virtual" tables, and an analogous CREATE INDEX statement for creating indexes. All of these statements will be discussed in detail in later chapters.) Similarly, base tables, and views and indexes, can all be "dropped" (that is to say, destroyed) at any time, using DROP TABLE or DROP VIEW or DROP INDEX. With regard to indexes, however, note carefully that although the user (that is, *some* user, probably a database administrator—see Chapter 11) is responsible for creating and destroying them, users are *not* responsible for saying when those indexes should be used. Indexes are never mentioned in SQL data manipulation statements such as SELECT. The decision as to whether or not to use a particular index in responding to, say, a particular SELECT operation is made by the system, not by the user. We shall have more to say on this topic in the next chapter.

The primary user interface to DB2 is the SQL language. We have already indicated (a) that SQL can be used in both interactive and embedded environments, and (b) that it provides both data definition and data manipulation functions. (In fact, as we shall see later, it provides certain "data control" functions as well.) The major data definition functions—

```
CREATE TABLE
CREATE VIEW
CREATE INDEX
```

```
DROP TABLE
DROP VIEW
DROP INDEX
```

—have already been touched on. The major data manipulation functions (in fact, the only ones, if we temporarily disregard some embedded-only functions) are

```
SELECT
INSERT
UPDATE
DELETE
```

We give examples (Fig. 1.7) of SELECT and UPDATE to illustrate an additional point, namely the fact that SQL data manipulation statements typically operate on *entire sets of records,* instead of just on one record at a time. Given the sample data of Fig. 1.2, the SELECT statement (Fig. 1.7(a)) returns a set of four values, not just a single value; and the UPDATE statement (Fig. 1.7(b)) changes two records, not just one. In other words, SQL is a *set-level language.*

```
(a) SELECT S#                    Result: S#
    FROM   SP                            --
    WHERE  P# = 'P2' ;                   S1
                                         S2
                                         S3
                                         S4


(b) UPDATE S                     Result: Status doubled for suppliers
    SET    STATUS = 2 * STATUS           in London (i.e., S1 and S4)
    WHERE  CITY = 'London' ;
```

Fig. 1.7 SQL data manipulation examples

Set-level languages such as SQL are sometimes described as "nonprocedural," on the grounds that users specify *what,* not *how* (i.e., they say what data they want without specifying a procedure for getting it). The process of "navigating" around the physical database to locate the desired data is performed automatically by the system, not manually by the user. (For this reason, relational systems are sometimes described as "automatic navigation" systems.) However, "nonprocedural" is not really a very satisfactory term, because procedurality and nonprocedurality are not absolutes. The best that can be said is that some language *A* is either more or less procedural than some other language *B*. Perhaps a better way of putting matters is to say that a language such as SQL is at *a higher level of abstrac-*

tion than a language such as COBOL or PL/I.* With a language like SQL, in other words, the system handles more of the details than it does with a language like COBOL. Fundamentally, it is this *raising of the level of abstraction* that is responsible for the increased productivity that relational systems such as DB2 can provide.

1.4 SUMMARY

This brings us to the end of this preliminary chapter, in which we have sketched some of the most significant features of DB2, IBM's relational database management system for the MVS operating system. We have seen in outline what it means for a system to be relational; we have discussed the relational (tabular) data structure; and we have described some of the operators available in SQL for operating on data in that tabular form. In particular, we have touched on the three categories of SQL statement (data definition, data manipulation, and data control), and given examples from the first two of those categories. We remind the reader that:

(a) All SQL statements are executable;

(b) Every SQL statement that can be entered at a terminal can also be included in a program, and that program can be written in APL, BASIC, C, COBOL, FORTRAN, PL/I, or Assembler Language;

(c) SQL data manipulation statements (SELECT, UPDATE, etc.) are all set-level.

In the next two chapters we will examine the internal structure and principal components of DB2, and we will discuss the environments in which DB2 runs. We will also take a quick look at some important DB2-related products.

EXERCISES

1.1 What does it mean to say that DB2 is a relational system?

1.2 Given the sample data of Fig. 1.2, show the effect of each of the following SQL statements.

---

*Or a language such as the database languages of nonrelational systems, come to that. For example, DL/I (the user language for IMS) operates essentially one record at a time.

```
(a) SELECT  SNAME
    FROM    S
    WHERE   STATUS = 30 ;

(b) SELECT  S#, P#
    FROM    SP
    WHERE   QTY > 200 ;

(c) UPDATE  SP
    SET     QTY = QTY + 300
    WHERE   QTY < 300 ;

(d) DELETE
    FROM    SP
    WHERE   QTY = 500
    OR      QTY < 200 ;

(e) INSERT
    INTO    SP (S#, P#, QTY)
    VALUES  ('S3','P1',500) ;
```

1.3 What is DB2I?

1.4 What is a repeating group?

1.5 Define the terms *relation* and *relational database*.

1.6 (a) Give a possible CREATE TABLE statement for the CELLAR table of Fig. 1.1. (b) Write an *embedded* PL/I-SQL statement to retrieve the number of bottles of 1981 Zinfandel from that table.

1.7 Define the terms *base table* and *view*.

1.8 What do you understand by the term "automatic navigation"?

1.9 Define the term *primary key*.

ANSWERS TO SELECTED EXERCISES

1.1 A relational system such as DB2 is a system in which the data is perceived as tables (and nothing but tables), and the operators available to the user are operators that generate new tables from old.

```
1.2 (a) SNAME
        -----
        Blake
        Adams

    (b) S#  P#
        --  --
        S1  P1
        S1  P3
        S2  P1
        S2  P2
        S4  P4
        S4  P5
```

```
(c)  S#   P#   QTY
     --   --   ---
     S1   P2   500
     S1   P4   500
     S1   P5   400
     S1   P6   400
     S3   P2   500
     S4   P2   500
```

(Only altered rows shown.)

(d) Rows (S1,P5,100) and (S1,P6,100) are deleted from table SP.

(e) Row (S3,P1,500) is inserted into table SP.

1.3 DB2I—"DB2 Interactive"—is the DB2 component that (among other things) allows SQL statements to be entered and executed interactively. For more information, see Chapter 17.

1.4 A repeating group is (conceptually) a column of a table that contains multiple data values per row (different numbers of values in different rows). Repeating groups are not permitted in a relational database. *Note:* An explanation of, and justification for, this apparent restriction can be found in the book *An Introduction to Database Systems: Volume I,* by C. J. Date (Addison-Wesley, 1986).

1.5 A relation is a table (without repeating groups!). A relational database is a database that is perceived by its users as a collection of relations. *Note:* More precise definitions are given in Appendix B.

1.6 (a) CREATE TABLE CELLAR
```
           ( WINE     CHAR(16)  NOT NULL,
             YEAR     INTEGER   NOT NULL,
             BOTTLES  INTEGER,
           PRIMARY KEY ( WINE, YEAR ) ) ;
```

(b) EXEC SQL SELECT BOTTLES
```
               INTO   :XBOTT
               FROM   CELLAR
               WHERE  WINE = 'Zinfandel'
               AND    YEAR = 81 ;
```

1.7 A base table is a "real" table; it has some direct storage representation. A view is a "virtual" table; it does not have any direct storage representation of its own. A view is like a window on to one or more underlying base tables, through which the data (or some subset of the data) in those underlying tables can be observed, possibly in some rearranged structure.

1.8 "Automatic navigation" means that the system assumes the responsibility of searching through the physical database to locate the data the user has requested. Users specify what they want, not how to get to what they want.

1.9 Informally, a primary key is just a unique identifier for a table. For example, the primary key for the parts table P is the field P#; given a P# value *p*, that value *p* can be used to identify an individual part record and to distinguish that record from all others appearing in the P table.

A more formal definition of the term is given in Chapter 12.

CHAPTER
◆ 2 ◆

System Structure

2.1 MAJOR COMPONENTS

The internal structure of DB2 is quite complex, as is only to be expected of a state-of-the-art system that provides all of the functions normally found in a modern DBMS. The product thus contains a very large number of internal components. From a high-level point of view, however, DB2 can be regarded as having just three *major* components, each of which divides up into numerous subcomponents. The three major components are as follows (refer to Fig. 2.1).

1. The *system services* component, which supports system operation, operator communication, logging, and similar functions;

2. The *locking services* component, which provides the necessary controls for managing concurrent access to data;

3. The *database services* component, which supports the definition, retrieval, and update of user and system data.

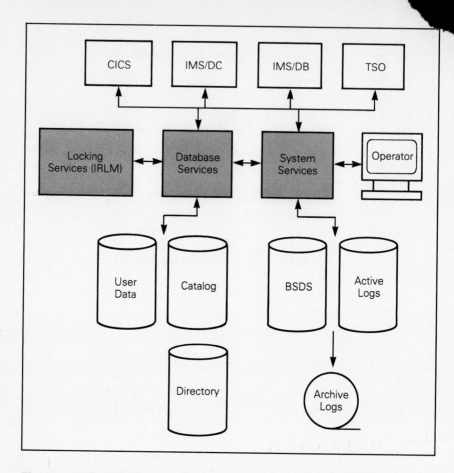

Fig. 2.1 DB2 structure

Of these three components, only the last is directly relevant to the user (whether end-user or application programmer); the first two, although of course crucial to the overall functioning of the system, are for the most part "transparent to the user." In this chapter, therefore, we will just give a quick overview of the system services and locking services components; we will then go on to discuss the database services component in more detail.*

---

*A couple of additional comments: First, each of the three major components runs in a separate MVS address space. This fact notwithstanding, the entire DB2 system can be started or stopped by a single operator command. Second, DB2 Version 2 Release 2 adds a fourth major component, the *Distributed Data Facility* (DDF),

2.2   SYSTEM SERVICES

The system services component handles all system-wide tasks, including:

- Controlling connexions to other MVS subsystems (CICS, IMS/DC, IMS/DB, and TSO). See Chapter 3 for more information on using DB2 in conjunction with each of these subsystems.

- Handling system startup, shutdown, and operator communication.

- Managing the system log. The system log is a set of predefined disk data sets that are used to record information for recovering system and database data in the event of a failure. As each active log data set becomes full, DB2 switches to a new one and copies the old one to an *archive* log data set on disk or tape. When all the active log data sets are full, they are recycled (i.e., DB2 starts using the first one again). Dual copies of both the active and the archive log can be maintained to allow DB2 to recover data if an error occurs on (one copy of) the log itself. All log data set information is recorded in a duplexed system data set known as the *Boot Strap Data Set (BSDS)*. Utilities are provided for maintaining and listing the BSDS.

- Gathering system-wide statistics, performance, auditing, and accounting information. This information is collected by the DB2 *Instrumentation Facility* and written to either a Systems Management Facility (SMF) or Generalized Trace Facility (GTF) data set. A separate product, the DB2 Performance Monitor (DB2PM), is provided for producing batch reports and interactive graphics from this data set.

2.3   LOCKING SERVICES

Locking services are provided by an MVS subsystem called the IMS Resource Lock Manager (IRLM). Despite the appearance of the term "IMS" in the name, the IRLM does not really have anything to do with IMS per se; rather, it is a general-purpose lock manager. It is used by DB2 to control concurrent access to data, regardless of whether IMS is present in the system or not. The DB2 locking scheme is described in more detail in Chapter 14.

2.4   DATABASE SERVICES

The primary purpose of the database services component is to support the definition, retrieval, and update of database data—in other words, to im-

---

which runs in an address space of its own. We defer discussion of DDF to Chapter 26.

plement the functions of the SQL language. The necessary support is provided by a series of five subcomponents, which we refer to as follows:

> Precompiler
>
> Bind
>
> Runtime Supervisor*
>
> Data Manager
>
> Buffer Manager

Together, these components allow (a) the preparation of application programs for execution and (b) the subsequent execution of those programs. The functions of the individual components (in outline) are as follows.

- Precompiler

  The Precompiler is a preprocessor for the host programming languages (PL/I, COBOL, etc.). Its function is to analyze a host language source module, stripping out all the SQL statements it finds and replacing them by host language CALL statements. (At run time those CALLs will pass control— indirectly—to the Runtime Supervisor.) From the SQL statements it encounters, the Precompiler constructs a *Database Request Module* (DBRM), which becomes input to the Bind component (discussed in the next paragraph).

- Bind

  The function of the Bind component is to compile one or more DBRMs to produce an *application plan*. The application plan contains a set of internal control structures, representing the compiled form of the original SQL statements from which the DBRMs were built. In particular, it includes calls on the Data Manager component (see below).

  Observe that the foregoing paragraph amounts to saying that DB2 is a *compiling system:* Bind performs a compiling function for SQL statements, much as the host language compiler provides a compiling function for the host language statements in which those SQL statements are embedded. We shall return to this point in Section 2.5.

  Note: The first release of DB2 genuinely did compile SQL statements into actual machine code. As indicated above, however, the current version of DB2 compiles such statements into a set of internal con-

---

*The IBM manuals do not use the term "Runtime Supervisor"; instead, they refer to something called the *Relational Data System* (RDS). However, the scope of the RDS includes the functions of the Precompiler and Bind in addition to the functions that we ascribe to the Runtime Supervisor. We therefore prefer our term.

trol structures (in effect a higher-level intermediate language), not into machine code per se. Those control structures are then used to drive a set of generalized I/O routines within the Data Manager. (One advantage of this change is that application plans are more compact than they used to be.) For simplicity, however, we will continue to regard Bind as compiling SQL statements into "code," even though that code is no longer true machine code per se.

- Runtime Supervisor

  The Runtime Supervisor is resident in main storage when the application program is executing. Its job is to oversee that execution. When the application program requests some database operation to be performed (i.e., when it wishes to execute a SQL statement, loosely speaking), control goes first to the Runtime Supervisor, which uses the control information in the plan to request the appropriate operations on the part of the Data Manager.

- Data Manager

  You can think of the Data Manager as a *very sophisticated access method*. It performs all of the normal access method functions— search, retrieval, update, index maintenance, and so on. Broadly speaking, the Data Manager is the component that manages the physical database(s). It invokes other system components as necessary to perform detailed functions such as locking, logging, physical I/O operations, etc., during the performance of its basic task.

- Buffer Manager

  The Buffer Manager is the component responsible for physically transferring data between the external medium and (virtual) storage; in effect, it performs the actual I/O operations. It employs sophisticated buffering techniques, such as read-ahead buffering ("sequential prefetch") and look-aside buffering, to get the best performance out of the buffer pools under its care and to minimize the amount of physical I/O actually performed.

Fig. 2.2 summarizes the foregoing in the form of a control flow diagram. In the next section we will take a more detailed look at the principal steps in this overall process. First, however, to conclude the present section, we briefly mention a couple of additional functions of the database services component:

- *System tables:* The database services component also manages a set of system data tables. Those tables contain certain control and descriptor

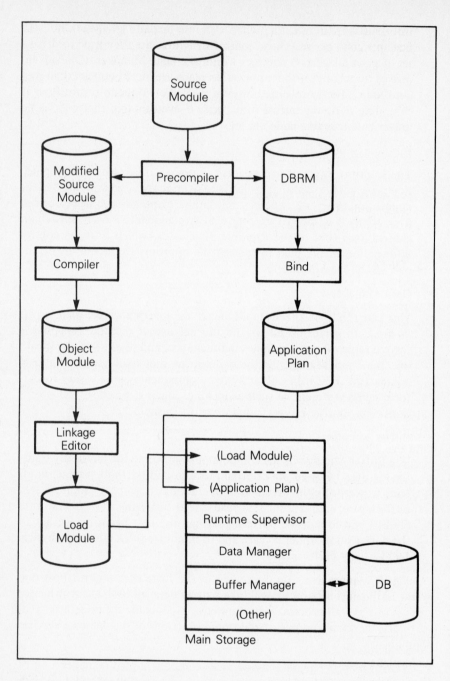

Fig. 2.2 DB2 application program preparation and execution (overview)

information regarding (e.g.) user data tables and their columns, database backup operations, database indexes, and so forth. Collectively, the system tables fall into two groups, known as the *catalog* and the *directory,* respectively. From the user's point of view, the difference between the two is as follows: The catalog is accessible by means of SQL data retrieval statements, which can be used (e.g.) to produce reports for use by database administrators (see Chapter 9 for more information on the catalog); the directory cannot be accessed via SQL and is intended purely for DB2's own internal use.

- *Utilities:* The database services component also includes a set of utilities for performing such functions as database loading and database reorganization. A list of such utilities and a sketch of the functions they perform is given in Chapter 17.

2.5 DETAILED CONTROL FLOW

In this section we consider in detail what is involved in preparing and executing a DB2 application program. First, we consider an example of a PL/I program P (more accurately, PL/I source module P) that includes one or more SQL statements.*† Before P can be compiled by the PL/I compiler, it must be *precompiled* by the DB2 Precompiler (Fig. 2.3).

As explained in the previous section, the DB2 Precompiler removes all SQL statements it finds in P and replaces them by PL/I CALL statements.‡ (Those CALLs are directed to the DB2 Language Interface module—see below.) It uses the SQL statements to build a *Database Request Module* (DBRM) for P, which it stores away as a member of an MVS partitioned data set. The DBRM contains a copy of the original SQL statements, together with certain additional information. The Precompiler also produces a source listing, showing the original source code, diagnostics, cross-reference information, etc.

---

*We take PL/I for definiteness. The overall process is of course essentially the same for the other host languages—at least for the compiled languages (C, COBOL, FORTRAN, Assembler Language). It is a little different for the interpreted languages (APL, BASIC). Details of the differences are beyond the scope of this chapter.

†If P also includes any CICS statements (of the form EXEC CICS ... ;), then it must also be processed by the CICS Preprocessor. The DB2 Precompiler and the CICS Preprocessor can be run in either order, but it is usually better in practice to run the DB2 Precompiler first.

‡It leaves a copy of each SQL statement in the modified source module in the form of a comment.

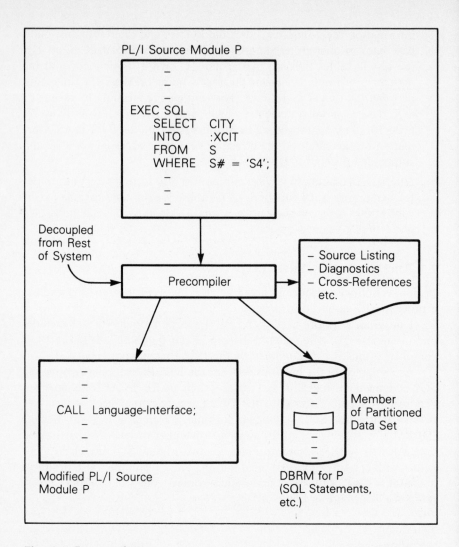

Fig. 2.3 Precompilation

Next, the modified PL/I source module is compiled and link-edited in the normal way (except that the DB2 Language Interface module, which is supplied as part of the DB2 product, must be part of the input to the Linkage Editor; the purpose of that module is basically to make PL/I, COBOL, etc., all look the same to DB2). Let us agree to refer to the output of this step as "PL/I load module *P.*"

Now we come to the Bind step (Fig. 2.4).

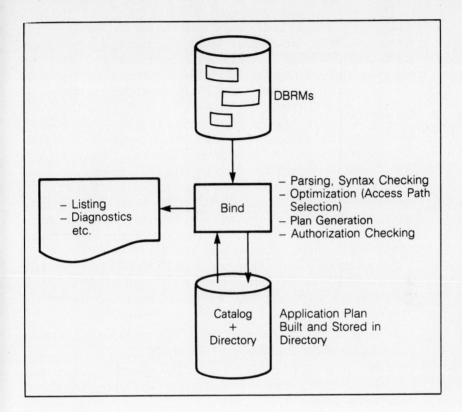

Fig. 2.4 Bind

Bind is really an *optimizing compiler:* Its function is to convert high-level database requests (in effect, SQL statements) into optimized internal form. The input to Bind is a set of one or more DBRMs (there will be more than one if the original PL/I program consists of more than one external procedure—i.e., more than one source module). The output from Bind (i.e., the compiled form of those DBRMs) is called an *application plan,* and is stored away in the DB2 directory (refer to the previous section for a brief description of the directory). The major functions of Bind, then, are as follows.

- Syntax Checking

Bind examines the SQL statements in the input DBRM(s), parses them, and reports on any syntax errors it finds. Such checks are necessary, even though the Precompiler has already performed similar checks, because the Precompiler is decoupled from the rest of DB2: It can run even when DB2 is not available—it can even run on a different machine—and its output is not automatically protected. Thus, Bind cannot assume that its input is valid Precompiler output—the user might have constructed an invalid "DBRM" via some other mechanism.

- Optimization

Bind includes an *optimizer* as an important subcomponent. The function of the optimizer is to choose, for each SQL manipulative statement it processes, an optimal access strategy for implementing that statement. Remember that data manipulation statements such as SELECT specify only what data the user wants, not how to get to that data; the *access path* for getting to that data will be chosen by the optimizer. Programs are thus independent of such access paths (for further discussion of this important point, see later in this section).

As an example of the foregoing, consider the SELECT statement shown in the PL/I source module *P* in Fig. 2.3. Even in that very simple case, there are probably at least two ways of performing the required retrieval:

1. By doing a physical sequential scan of (the stored version of) table S until the record for supplier S4 is found;

2. If there is an index on the S# column of that table—which there probably will be*—then by using that index and hence going directly to the S4 record.

The optimizer will choose which of these two strategies to adopt. In general, the optimizer will make its choice on the basis of such considerations as the following:

- Which tables are referenced in the SQL statement (there may be more than one)

- How big those tables are

- What indexes exist

- How selective those indexes are

- How the data is physically clustered on the disk

- The form of the WHERE clause in the request

and so on. Bind will then generate code that is *tightly bound* to (i.e., highly dependent on) the optimizer's choice of strategy. For example,

---

*Recall that field S# is the primary key for table S. The primary key of a table must always be supported by a UNIQUE index in DB2. For details, see Chapters 5 and 12.

if the optimizer decides to make use of an index called X, then there will be code in the application plan that refers explicitly to index X.

- Plan Generation

  This is the process of actually building the application plan.

- Authorization Checking

  Bind will also check authorization; that is, it will check that the user doing the binding (i.e., the user who invoked Bind—see Chapter 17) is allowed to perform the operations requested in the DBRM(s) to be bound. We shall examine authorization in detail in Chapter 11.

Finally we get to execution time. Since the original program has now effectively been broken into two pieces (load module and application plan), those two pieces must somehow be brought back together again at execution time. This is how it works (see Fig. 2.5). First, the PL/I load module P is loaded into main storage; it starts to execute in the usual way. Sooner or later it reaches the first call to the DB2 Language Interface module. That module gets control and passes control in turn to the Runtime Supervisor. The Runtime Supervisor then retrieves the application plan from the DB2 directory, loads it into main storage, and passes control to it. The application plan in turn invokes the Data Manager, which performs the necessary operations on the actual stored data and passes results back (as appropriate) to the PL/I program.

Note: The foregoing explanation is slightly oversimplified. DB2 application plans are actually *segmented* (one segment for each SQL statement in the original program), and the Runtime Supervisor actually retrieves *segments,* not entire plans, on an "as needed" basis. The purpose of this refinement is to economize on memory utilization; if a given program contains 50 SQL statements, but only 10 of them are actually executed on a given run, then only 20 percent of that plan actually needs to be fetched into memory on that particular run (loosely speaking).

Our discussions so far have glossed over one extremely important point, which we now explain. First, as already indicated, DB2 is a compiling system; database statements are *compiled* (at Bind time) into internal form. By contrast, most older database systems—certainly all nonrelational systems, to this writer's knowledge—are *interpretive* in nature. Now, compilation is certainly advantageous from the point of view of performance; it will nearly always yield better runtime performance than will interpretation.*

---

*This claim is (obviously) especially true for repetitive transactions, i.e., transactions that are executed over and over again in a production environment. What is perhaps not so obvious is that compiling can provide a significant performance

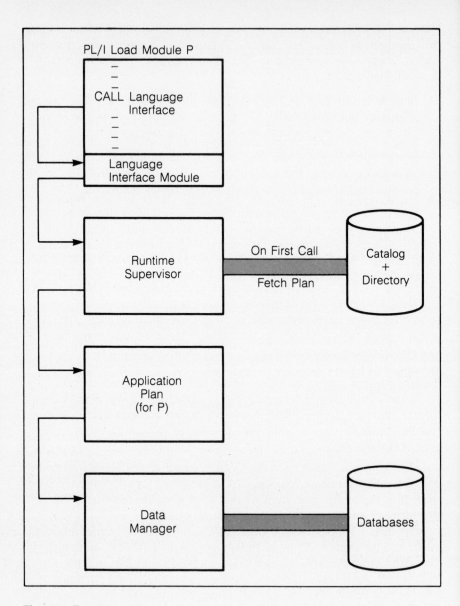

Fig. 2.5 Execution time

However, it suffers from the following significant drawback: *It is possible that decisions made by the "compiler"* (actually Bind) *at compilation time are no longer valid at execution time.* The following simple example will serve to illustrate the problem:

1. Suppose program *P* is compiled (bound) on Monday, and Bind decides to use an index—say index *X*—in its strategy for *P.* Then the application plan for *P* will include explicit references to *X,* as explained earlier.

2. On Tuesday, some (authorized) user issues the statement

   ```
   DROP INDEX X ;
   ```

3. On Wednesday, some user tries to execute the program *P.* What happens?

What does happen is the following. When an index is dropped, DB2 examines the catalog to see which application plans (if any) are dependent on that index. Any such plans it finds it marks "invalid." When the Runtime Supervisor retrieves such a plan for execution, it sees the "invalid" marker, *and therefore invokes Bind to produce a new plan*—i.e., to choose some different access strategy and then to recompile the original SQL statements (which have been kept in the catalog) in accordance with that new strategy. Provided the recompilation is successful, the new plan replaces the old one, and the Runtime Supervisor continues with that new plan. Thus the entire rebind process (or "automatic bind" as it is called) is "transparent to the user"; the only effect that might be observed is a slight delay in the execution of the first SQL statement in the program (possibly some change in overall program performance also, of course; the point is, however, that there should be no effect on program *logic*).

Note carefully that the automatic recompilation we are talking about here is a *SQL* recompilation, not a *PL/I* recompilation. It is not the PL/I program that is invalidated by the dropping of the index, only the application plan.

We can now see how it is possible for programs to be independent of physical access paths—more specifically, how it is possible to create and drop such paths without at the same time having to rewrite programs. As stated earlier, SQL data manipulation statements such as SELECT and UPDATE never include any explicit mention of such paths. Instead, they simply indicate what data the user is interested in; and it is the system's responsibility (actually Bind's responsibility) to choose a path for getting to

---

advantage in the ad hoc query environment also. For further discussion of this point, see later in this section.

that data, and to change to another path if the old one no longer exists. We say that systems like DB2 provide a high degree of *physical data independence:* Users and user programs are not dependent on the physical structure of the stored database. The advantage of such a system—a highly significant advantage—is that it is possible to make changes in the physical database (e.g., for performance reasons) *without having to make any corresponding changes in application programs.* In a system without such independence, application programmers have to devote some significant portion of their time—a figure of 50 percent is quite typical—to making changes to existing programs that are necessitated merely by changes to the physical database. In a system like DB2, by contrast, those programmers can concentrate exclusively on "real work"—i.e., on the production of new applications.

One further point concerning the foregoing: Our example was in terms of a dropped *index,* and perhaps that is the commonest case in practice. However, a similar sequence of events occurs when any object (not just an index) is dropped—likewise when an authorization is revoked (see Chapter 11). Thus, for example, dropping a table will cause all plans that refer to that table to be flagged as invalid. Of course, the automatic rebind will only work in this case if another table has been created with the same name as the old one by the time the rebind is done (and maybe not even then, if there are significant differences between the old table and the new one).

Given the fact that DB2 performs automatic rebinds if an existing object (say an index) is dropped, the reader may be wondering whether it will also do automatic rebinds if a new object is created. The answer is no, it will not. The reason for this state of affairs is that there can be no guarantee in this case that rebinding will actually be profitable; automatic rebind might simply mean a lot of unnecessary work (existing plans might already be using an optimum strategy). The situation is different with DROP—a plan will simply not work if it relies on a nonexistent object, so rebind is mandatory in this case. Hence, if you create a new index, and you have some existing plan that you suspect could now profitably be replaced, then it is your responsibility to request an explicit rebind for that plan. Explicit rebind is discussed in Chapter 17.

We conclude this chapter by noting that SQL is *always* compiled in DB2, never interpreted, even when the statements in question are submitted interactively (e.g., via DB2I). In other words, if you enter (say) a SELECT statement at the terminal, then that statement will be compiled and an application plan generated for it; that plan will then be executed; and finally, after execution has completed, that plan will be discarded. Performance tests have indicated that, even in the interactive case, compilation almost always results in better overall performance than interpretation. The advantage of compilation is that the process of physically accessing the required data is done by compiled code—that is, by code that is tightly tailored to the specific request, not by generalized, interpretive code. The disadvantage is of course that there is a cost in doing the compilation, i.e., in producing that tightly tailored code. But the advantage almost always outweighs the disadvantage, sometimes dramatically so. It is only when the query is extremely simple that the cost of doing the compilation might be greater than the potential savings. An example of such a simple query might be, "Retrieve the supplier record for supplier S1"—that is, a request for a single, specific record, given a value for a field that identifies that record uniquely. Notice that this query does not really exploit the set-level facilities of SQL at all.

EXERCISES

2.1 Name the major components of DB2.

2.2 Draw a diagram showing the overall process of program preparation and program execution in DB2.

2.3 List the principal functions of Bind.

2.4 Define *physical data independence.* Explain how DB2 provides such independence. Why is physical data independence desirable?

ANSWERS TO SELECTED EXERCISES

2.1 The major DB2 components are the system services, locking services, and database services components (though in fact it is not really accurate to think of the locking services subsystem—the IRLM—as a component of DB2 per se). The database services component, in turn, divides into the Precompiler, Bind, Runtime Supervisor, Data Manager, and Buffer Manager components.

Note: A fourth major component has been added in DB2 Version 2 Release 2, the Distributed Data Facility (DDF). See Chapter 26.

2.2 See Fig. 2.2 in Section 2.5.

2.3 The four principal functions of Bind are syntax checking, optimization, plan generation, and authorization checking. We amplify the optimization function slightly here, since it is so critical. Optimization is the process of deciding a strategy for implementing relational requests (i.e., SQL statements). The optimizer's choice of strategy is based on information contained in the catalog regarding physical storage structure, availability of indexes, data value distributions, etc.

2.4 Physical data independence means that users and user programs do not depend on the physical structure of the database. User requests (i.e., SQL statements) are formulated purely in terms of the logical structure (i.e., in terms of tables and fields); the choice of physical access paths to implement those requests is made by the system (actually by the optimizer), not by the user. As a result, the physical structure of the database can be changed—e.g., for performance reasons—without requiring any user programs to be rewritten.

◆ 3 ◆

Operating Environments
and Related Products

3.1 OPERATING ENVIRONMENTS

DB2 applications fall into a number of different categories:

1. IMS batch
2. IMS/DC
3. CICS
4. TSO online
5. TSO batch
6. Pure batch

(refer to Fig. 3.1). We explain the differences among these various categories as follows.

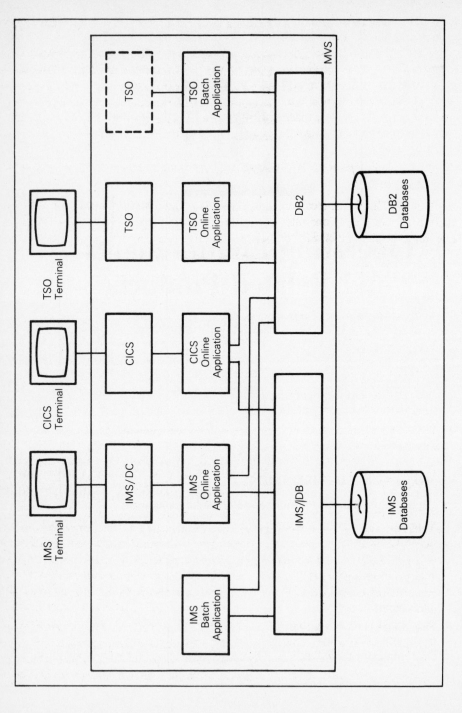

Fig. 3.1 DB2 operating environments

1. A DB2 application running under IMS batch is a conventional IMS batch application that accesses DB2 data (via SQL statements) as well as IMS data (via DL/I database calls). IMS serves as the necessary *transaction manager* in such an environment. *Note:* The reader is warned that the term "transaction" has different interpretations in different systems. See Chapter 14 for an explanation of the interpretation used in this book. For readers who may already be familiar with IMS, we should perhaps stress the point that we are *not* using the normal IMS interpretation.

2. A DB2 application running under IMS/DC is an online application that is invoked from an IMS/DC terminal and uses the data communications (DC) facilities of IMS/DC (i.e., DL/I DC calls) to exchange messages with that terminal. Like an IMS batch DB2 application, an IMS/DC DB2 application can access both DB2 data and IMS data. (Unlike other DB2 applications, it can also access IMS Fast Path data.) The combination of DB2 with IMS/DC acts as a *full-function database/data communications* (DB/DC) *system,* with IMS acting as the transaction manager (again, see Chapter 14).

3. A DB2 application running under CICS is an online application that is invoked from a CICS terminal and uses the facilities of CICS to exchange messages with that terminal. Like an IMS batch or IMS/DC DB2 application, a CICS DB2 application can access both DB2 data and IMS data (also VSAM data). The combination of DB2 with CICS also acts as a full-function DB/DC system, with CICS acting as the transaction manager (once again, see Chapter 14).

4. TSO is an MVS component that enables programs to be invoked and executed interactively from a TSO terminal. In particular, it allows DB2 to be invoked from such a terminal. If DB2 is invoked in this manner, and if DB2 in turn invokes a user application, then that application is said to be a "TSO online" DB2 application. Such an application can operate on DB2 data but not on IMS data. DB2 itself serves as the transaction manager in this case. *Note:* The application can use ISPF, GDDM, and TSO screen management facilities to communicate with the terminal.

5. TSO (or more precisely the TSO Terminal Monitor Program, TMP) can also execute as a batch job. If it does, and if it then invokes DB2, and if DB2 in turn then invokes a user application, then that application is said to be a "TSO batch" DB2 application (refer to Section 17.2 in Chapter 17 for more details regarding this possibility). A TSO batch DB2 application, like a TSO online DB2 application, can operate on

DB2 data but not on IMS data. Again DB2 itself serves as the transaction manager in this case.

6. It is also possible—though somewhat unusual—for a "pure" MVS batch application (i.e., a batch application running directly under MVS instead of under IMS or TSO) to operate on DB2 data, thanks to a somewhat esoteric set of features known as the DB2 Call Attach Facility, CAF (not shown in Fig 3.1). CAF is intended for users who need more direct control of the environment for some reason than the cases discussed above can provide. Generalized applications provided by third-party software vendors might well use the facilities of CAF. (As a matter of fact, the IBM-provided "generalized application" QMF—discussed in Part III of this book—is implemented via CAF.) The details of CAF are beyond the scope of this book.

7. Finally, all DB2 application types—IMS batch, IMS/DC, CICS, TSO online, TSO batch, and pure batch—can execute concurrently. They can even share the same DB2 databases (and the same IMS databases, where applicable, and where permitted by IMS itself and/or MVS).

For the reader who may be unfamiliar with MVS and/or IMS and/or CICS and/or TSO, we offer the following words of encouragement: It is not necessary to be familiar with these products in order to understand the capabilities of DB2. All that is necessary is to understand that an application that uses the facilities of DB2 must operate either

(a) "stand alone" as a pure MVS batch application using the Call Attach Facility (not the normal case, however), or

(b) under the control of exactly one of IMS (batch or IMS/DC), CICS, or (via TSO) DB2 itself.

It is also important to realize that the various categories are not interchangeable. That is, a DB2 application that is designed to run under (e.g.) IMS/DC cannot be moved to (e.g.) the CICS environment without some coding changes. The changes in question have to do with the portions of the application that interact with the transaction manager, however, not the portions that perform database operations; the database operations are the same in all cases.

3.2 RELATED PRODUCTS

The IBM "Relational Productivity Family" (mentioned in the Preface and discussed in some detail in Part III of this book) includes a large number of companion products in addition to DB2 (mostly only rather loosely integrated with the base DB2 system, however). Of those companion products, the principal ones are as follows:

- SQL/DS (Structured Query Language/Data System)

  As mentioned in Chapter 1, SQL/DS is a relational DBMS for the VM and VSE environments. It supports a dialect of SQL that is very similar to that of DB2. To be more precise, data manipulation operations and "logical" data definition operations are basically the same in the two products (though there are some interesting discrepancies); stored data formats are not the same, however, and hence "physical" data definition operations are not the same either.* But it is fairly easy to move data from one product to the other, using IBM's "Data Extract" product DXT (see below).

- QMF (Query Management Facility)

  QMF is an ad hoc query and report-writing product for both DB2 and SQL/DS. It supports (among other things) ad hoc SQL access to DB2 and SQL/DS data; the QMF dialect of SQL is essentially identical to the dialect supported by DB2 and SQL/DS. QMF is described in detail in Chapter 19 and Appendix G.

- AS (Application System)

  AS is an end-user application development facility for both DB2 and SQL/DS (as well as for other IBM products). It provides a very wide range of facilities, including query, report-writing, business graphics, statistics, financial planning, and others. AS is discussed in Chapter 20.

- CSP (Cross System Product)

  CSP is an application development system for DP professionals. Like AS, it supports both DB2 and SQL/DS as well as other IBM products.

---

*It is not just in the stored data format that the two products differ, of course; numerous other distinctions can be drawn, most of them having to do with the fact that DB2 was specifically designed for the large-system (MVS) environment and SQL/DS was not. For example, the amount of data that can be stored online in a DB2 system is constrained in practice only by the amount of online storage available, whereas SQL/DS is limited to a single online database of 64 billion bytes (theoretical maximum; the practical maximum is somewhat less). Likewise, the DB2 security mechanism is considerably more elaborate than that of SQL/DS, reflecting the fact that there are probably many more users, and many more categories of user, in a DB2 installation than in a SQL/DS installation. But it is not the purpose of this book to spell out all such differences in detail.

CSP-generated DB2 applications can execute under either CICS or TSO. CSP is described in Chapter 21.

■   ADF (Application Development Facility)

ADF—or, to give it its full name, IMS Application Development Facility II (IMSADF II)—is also a DP professional application generator. It supports DB2 but not SQL/DS. ADF-generated DB2 applications can execute under either IMS/DC or CICS. ADF is described in Chapter 22.

■   DXT (Data Extract)

DXT is a generalized data copying program. It allows IMS, VSAM, SAM, SQL/DS, DB2 or other data to be copied to a SQL/DS or DB2 database. DXT can be used to download data from a production system to a query system (e.g., from a centralized DB2 system to a departmental SQL/DS system); it might also be used to help in migration from an older system to DB2 (or SQL/DS). DXT is discussed in depth in Chapter 23.

■   ECF (Enhanced Connectivity Facilities)
    HDBV (Host Data Base View)

ECF is a set of IBM products with the overall objective of allowing a PC user to access data on a connected mainframe. The data on the mainframe can be managed by a variety of MVS or VM products, including in particular DB2 and SQL/DS; it can be copied down to the PC, where it can be accessed via any of several familiar PC products, such as Lotus 1-2-3 or dBase III. HDBV is a specific example of a product that can use ECF. ECF and HDBV are described in Chapter 24.

■   DBRAD (Data Base Relational Application Directory)

DBRAD is a directory product for DB2 and SQL/DS. It stores information regarding application programs, application data objects, etc., together with their interrelationships, in a set of DB2 or SQL/DS tables. DBRAD is intended to help in the development and maintenance of database applications (especially CSP applications). It can also be used to assist with data and system administration. DBRAD is described in depth in Chapter 25.

In addition to the products listed above, all of which (except SQL/DS) are considered in more detail later in this book, there are a number of others that should at least receive a brief mention here:

- DBEDIT (Data Base Edit Facility)

   DBEDIT provides a "fill-in-the-blanks" interface for the creation and execution of simple forms-based query, maintenance, and data entry applications. It supports both DB2 and SQL/DS.

- IBM Expert System Environment

   This product is an expert system shell that assists in the development of knowledge-based applications. It provides interfaces to DB2 and SQL/DS that allow such applications to access relational data.

- Knowledgetool

   The purpose of this tool, like that of the IBM Expert System Environment product, is to support the construction of knowledge-based applications; it differs from that other product in that it provides a PL/I-like interface for specifying the knowledge base. Applications built via Knowledgetool can access DB2 and SQL/DS data.

- DB2/VSAM Transparency

   DB2/VSAM Transparency allows VSAM data to be moved into a DB2 database and then permits old VSAM applications to run unchanged against the migrated data.

- OS/2 Database Manager

   The Extended Edition of IBM's PS/2 operating system OS/2 includes a Database Manager that is broadly compatible with SQL/DS and DB2.

- OS/400 Database Manager

   The operating system for IBM's Application System/400, namely OS/400, also includes a SQL-based DBMS, variously referred to as the OS/400 Database Manager or as SQL/400.

   And the list goes on. It can be seen that the problem is not lack of products—rather, it is a problem of choice (how to select the right product set for a given set of needs?). The solution to that problem, of course, is highly dependent on the user's own environment and so is beyond the scope of this book. However, we do present (in Part III of the book) a thorough treatment of the major products in the list, together with a general discussion of requirements, functions, and product categories at a survey level. Part III also provides a brief overview of some of the other IBM products and also of selected nonIBM products that cooperate in some manner with DB2.

PART

II

THE DB2 DATABASE
MANAGEMENT SYSTEM

CHAPTER

◆ 4 ◆

Basic Objects and Operators

4.1 INTRODUCTION

In this chapter we describe the basic scalar (i.e., elementary) objects and operators supported by DB2. The basic data object is the *scalar value;* for example, the object appearing at the intersection of a given row and a given column of a given table is a scalar value. Each scalar value is of some particular scalar data type. For each such data type, there is also an associated format for writing literal values (i.e., constants) of that type. Scalar data types and constants are discussed in Sections 4.2 and 4.3, respectively.

Scalar objects can be operated upon by means of certain scalar operators. For example, two numeric values can be added together by means of the scalar arithmetic operator " + ", and can be tested for equality by means of the scalar comparison operator " = ". In addition, DB2 provides certain scalar functions (e.g., the substring function SUBSTR), which can also be regarded as scalar operators. Scalar objects and operators can be combined to form scalar expressions. The operators available for each data type, and the corresponding scalar expressions, are discussed in Section 4.4. Section 4.5 then discusses the general operations of assignment and comparison. Finally, Section 4.6 considers the problem of missing values or missing information.

Note: "Scalar value," "scalar operator," and "scalar expression" are not official DB2 terms. We use them because they are more descriptive and more precise than the official terms, which are simply "value," "operator," and "expression," respectively. On the other hand, "scalar function" is an official DB2 term; it is used in order to distinguish such functions from the "aggregate" (or column) functions to be described in Chapter 7.

4.2 DATA TYPES

DB2 supports the following scalar data types.

Numeric Data

INTEGER	Fullword binary integer, 31 bits and sign
SMALLINT	Halfword binary integer, 15 bits and sign
DECIMAL(p,q)	Packed decimal number, p digits and sign $(0 < p < 16)$, with assumed decimal point q digits from the right $(0 <= q <= p)$
FLOAT(p)	Floating point number n, say, represented by a binary fraction f of p binary digits precision $(-1 < f < +1, 0 < p < 54)$ and a binary integer exponent e $(-65 < e < +64)$, such that $n = f * (16 ** e)$

Notes:

1. The symbol "**" stands for exponentiation. The approximate range of magnitudes for n is 5.4E–79 to 7.2E+75 (see the explanation of float constants in Section 4.3 for an explanation of this notation).

2. Although we use the symbol "**" in our explanations, note that DB2 does not in fact support any such operator (see Section 4.4).

3. If $p < 22$ the number n is single precision and occupies a fullword, otherwise it is double precision and occupies a doubleword.

String Data

CHARACTER(*n*)	Fixed length string of exactly *n* 8-bit characters (0 < *n* < 255)
VARCHAR(*n*)	Varying length string of up to *n* 8-bit characters (0 < *n;* maximum value of *n* depends on a number of factors, but in general must be less than the pagesize for the tablespace containing the table—see Chapter 16)
GRAPHIC(*n*)	Fixed length string of exactly *n* 16-bit characters (0 < *n* < 128)
VARGRAPHIC(*n*)	Varying length string of up to *n* 16-bit characters (0 < *n;* maximum value of *n* depends on a number of factors, but in general must be less than half the pagesize for the tablespace containing the table—see Chapter 16)

Date/Time Data

DATE	Date, represented as a sequence of eight unsigned packed decimal digits (*yyyymmdd*), occupying four bytes; permitted values are legal dates in the range January 1st, 1 A.D., to December 31st, 9999 A.D.
TIME	Time, represented as a sequence of six unsigned packed decimal digits (*hhmmss*), occupying three bytes; permitted values are legal times in the range midnight to midnight, i.e., 000000 to 240000
TIMESTAMP	"Timestamp" (combination of date and time, accurate to the nearest microsecond), represented as a sequence of 20 unsigned packed decimal digits (*yyyymmddhhmmssnnnnnn*), occupying ten bytes; permitted values are legal timestamps in the range 00010101000000000000 to 99991231240000000000

Notes:

1. The following abbreviations and alternative spellings are permitted:

INT	for	INTEGER
DECIMAL(*p*)	for	DECIMAL(*p*,0)

DECIMAL	for	DECIMAL(5)
DEC	for	DECIMAL
FLOAT	for	FLOAT(53)
REAL	for	FLOAT(21)
DOUBLE PRECISION	for	FLOAT(53)
CHARACTER	for	CHARACTER(1)
CHAR	for	CHARACTER
LONG VARCHAR	for	VARCHAR(n), where n is the maximum that DB2 will allow
GRAPHIC	for	GRAPHIC(1)
LONG VARGRAPHIC	for	VARGRAPHIC(n), where n is the maximum that DB2 will allow

2. The GRAPHIC and VARGRAPHIC data types are intended for dealing with double-byte character sets—i.e., character sets with more than 256 distinct characters (e.g., Kanji), in which each character is represented by a 16-bit encoding. It is in fact possible to mix 8- and 16-bit characters within the same string, but the details are beyond the scope of this book.

3. If the length n is greater than 254 for VARCHAR or 127 for VARGRAPHIC (or if LONG VARCHAR or LONG VARGRAPHIC is specified explicitly), the value is a "long string" and is subject to severe restrictions. Long strings are intended for the handling of free-format data such as text, rather than simple formatted data such as a part number or a supplier city. Long string values can be used in assignment operations, either to the database (INSERT or UPDATE) or from the database (SELECT); however, they cannot be used in any operation that would involve a long string comparison. Thus, for example, long strings cannot be indexed, nor can they be referenced in a WHERE clause (except with LIKE) or a GROUP BY clause or an ORDER BY clause, and so on. (See Chapters 6 and 7 for an explanation of these last two clauses.) For completeness, we list the restrictions here. A long string cannot appear in any of the following contexts:

- PRIMARY KEY
- FOREIGN KEY
- CREATE INDEX
- any function (except SUBSTR and LENGTH)
- DISTINCT
- WHERE (except in a LIKE predicate)
- GROUP BY
- HAVING (except in a LIKE predicate)

- ORDER BY
- UNION (unless ALL is specified)

4. From this point on, we will reserve the term "character string" to mean data of type CHAR or VARCHAR, the term "graphic string" to mean data of type GRAPHIC or VARGRAPHIC, and the unqualified term "string" to mean data of both string types generically.

5. The character string data types CHAR and VARCHAR (and LONG VARCHAR) can optionally include the additional specification FOR BIT DATA—for example:

```
READING  CHAR(32)  FOR BIT DATA
```

The meaning of this specification is that the character string in question (READING in the example) will contain "bit data," i.e., it is to be considered as an uninterpreted byte string (indeed, it might have been clearer to introduce a new BYTE(*n*) data type). In particular, if the string is included as part of a message transmitted between the DB2 system—which uses the standard IBM EBCDIC character code—and some other system, say a PC, that uses some different character code—say ASCII—then character code conversion is *not* to be performed on that string value.

4.3 CONSTANTS

In this section we summarize the various kinds of literal value or constant supported in DB2:

integer   Written as a signed or unsigned decimal integer, with no decimal point

      Examples: 4   -95   +364   0

decimal   Written as a signed or unsigned decimal number, with a decimal point

      Examples: 4.   -95.7   +364.05 0.007

float   Written as a decimal or integer constant, followed by the letter E, followed by an integer constant

      Examples: 4E3 -95.7E46 +364E-5 0.7E1

      Note: The expression xEy represents the value $x * (10^{**} y)$

character string	Written *either* as a string of characters enclosed in single quotes* *or* as a string of pairs of hexadecimal digits (representing the EBCDIC encodings of the characters concerned) enclosed in single quotes and preceded by the letter X

Examples: `'123 Main St.'`
`'PIG'`
`X'F1F2F340D481899540E2A34B'`
`X'D7C9C7'`

(the 1st and 3rd of these examples represent the same value, as do the 2nd and 4th)

graphic string	Written as a string of double-byte characters preceded by the "shift out" character $X'OE'$ and followed by the "shift in" character $X'OF'$, the whole enclosed in single quotes and preceded by the letter G†

Example: `G'<string>'`

(the shift out and shift in characters have been shown as "<" and ">", respectively; "string" represents the required string of graphic characters)

date	Written as a character string constant of the form *mm/dd/yyyy,* enclosed in single quotes (but see "Notes on Date/Times" below)

Examples: `'1/18/1941'`
`'12/25/1989'`

time	Written as a character string constant of the form *hh:mm* AM or *hh:mm* PM, enclosed in single quotes (but see "Notes on Date/Times" below)

Examples: `'10:00 AM'`
`'9:30 PM'`

---

*As usual, a single quote must be represented as two consecutive single quotes within a character string constant.

†This is the normal format. The format in PL/I contexts is slightly different. See the IBM manuals for details.

timestamp   Written as a character string constant of the form *yyyy-mm-dd-hh.mm.ss.nnnnnn,* enclosed in single quotes (but see "Notes on Date/Times" below)

Examples: `'1990-4-28-12.00.00.000000'`
                      `'1944-10-17-18.30.45'`

Notes on Date/Times:

1. Strictly speaking there is no such thing as a date constant. Instead, there are *character string representations of date values.* If a character string value—in particular, a character string constant—appears in a context that requires a date value, then that character string will be interpreted as a date value, provided of course that it is of the appropriate form (a conversion error will occur if it is not). We will use the term "date string" to refer to a character string that represents a valid date.

2. The remarks of the previous paragraph apply to times and timestamps also, mutatis mutandis. We will use the terms "time string" and "timestamp string" to refer to character strings that represent valid time and timestamp values.

3. Several different character string representations of dates and times are supported: US style, European style, etc. A variety of methods (installation options, Precompiler options, etc.) are available for specifying the style to be used in any particular context. The examples above all use US style. See Appendix C for further discussion.

4. We remark that a peculiarity of US-style time strings in DB2 is that they do not include a seconds component, as can be seen from the discussion of "time constants" above. Nevertheless, the internal representation of a time value always does include such a component.

5. Leading zeros can be omitted from the month and day portions of a date or timestamp string and from the hours portion of a time or timestamp string. The seconds portion (including the preceding colon or period) can be omitted entirely from a time string (in fact, it must be so omitted from a US-style time string); an implicit specification of zero is assumed. Trailing zeros can be omitted from the microseconds portion of a timestamp string; the microseconds portion (including the preceding period) can also be omitted entirely, in which case an implicit specification of zero is assumed.

6. The full DB2 support for dates and times is quite complex. For this reason we defer a detailed account of that support to an appendix (Appendix C).

Data Types of Constants

Constant data types are as indicated below:

integer	INTEGER
decimal	DECIMAL(p,q), where p and q are the actual precision and scale specified
float	FLOAT(53)
character string	VARCHAR(n), where n is the actual length specified
graphic string	VARGRAPHIC(n), where n is the actual length specified

Note in particular that string constants are always taken to be varying length. Also, all constants are assumed to have the NOT NULL property (see Section 4.6).

4.4 SCALAR OPERATORS AND FUNCTIONS

DB2 provides a number of builtin scalar operators and functions that can be used in the construction of scalar expressions. We summarize those operators and functions below, for purposes of reference. *Note:* For a discussion of the builtin *aggregate* functions, see Chapter 7. For more details on the functions having to do with dates and times, see Appendix C.

- Numeric operators

  DB2 supports the usual numeric operators $+$, $-$, $*$, and $/$, all with the obvious meanings. *Note:* The $+$ and $-$ operators can be used with dates, times, and timestamps as well as with numbers (again, see Appendix C for details).

- Concatenation

  The concatenation operator $\|$ can be used to concatenate two character strings or two graphic strings. It is written as an infix operation; e.g., the expression INITIALS $\|$ LASTNAME can be used to concatenate the values of INITIALS and LASTNAME.

- CHAR

  Converts a date, time, or timestamp to its character string representation.

- DATE

  Converts a scalar value to a date.

- DAY

  Extracts the day portion of a date or timestamp (or "date duration"—see Appendix C).

- DAYS

  Converts a date or timestamp to a number of days.

- DECIMAL

  Converts a number to decimal representation (with specified precision).

- DIGITS

  Converts a number (decimal or integer) to character string representation. (Strangely, there is no converse function to convert a character string representation of a number into the corresponding numeric value.)

- FLOAT

  Converts a number to floating point representation.

- HEX

  Converts a scalar value to a character string representing the internal hexadecimal encoding of the value.

- HOUR

  Extracts the hours portion of a time or timestamp (or "time duration"—see Appendix C).

- INTEGER

  Converts a number to integer representation.

- LENGTH

  Computes the length of a scalar value in bytes (or double-bytes, for graphic data).

- MICROSECOND

  Extracts the microseconds portion of a timestamp.

- MINUTE

  Extracts the minutes portion of a time or timestamp (or "time duration"—see Appendix C).

- MONTH

  Extracts the month portion of a date or timestamp (or "date duration"—see Appendix C).

- SECOND

  Extracts the seconds portion of a time or timestamp (or "time duration"—see Appendix C).

- SUBSTR

  Extracts a substring of a string. For example, the expression SUBSTR (SNAME,1,3) extracts the first three characters of the specified supplier name.

- TIME

  Converts a scalar value to a time.

- TIMESTAMP

  Converts either a single scalar value or a pair of scalar values, representing a date and time respectively, to a timestamp.

- VALUE

  Converts a null into a nonnull value (see Section 4.6).

- VARGRAPHIC

  Converts a character string into a graphic string.

- YEAR

  Extracts the year portion of a date or timestamp (or "date duration"—see Appendix C).

Special Registers

DB2 also supports a number of "special registers" (this term is taken from COBOL; "zero-argument builtin scalar functions" would perhaps be more accurate, or at least more descriptive). The special registers currently defined are USER, CURRENT SQLID, CURRENT DATE, CURRENT TIME, CURRENT TIMESTAMP, and CURRENT TIMEZONE. A reference to a special register returns a scalar value, as follows:

- USER

  Returns the "primary authorization ID." See Chapter 11 for an illustration of the use of USER.

- CURRENT SQLID

  Returns the "current authorization ID." Again, see Chapter 11 for further discussion.

- CURRENT DATE

  Returns the current date, i.e., the date "today."

- CURRENT TIME

  Returns the current time, i.e., the time "now."

- CURRENT TIMESTAMP

  Returns the current timestamp, i.e., the date "today" concatenated with the time "now."

- CURRENT TIMEZONE

  Returns a "time duration" (see Appendix C) representing (typically) the displacement of the local time zone from Greenwich Mean Time. Note that the value returned by each of CURRENT DATE, CURRENT TIME, and CURRENT TIMESTAMP is based on a reading of the local clock, incremented in each case by the value of CURRENT TIMEZONE.

  For examples of the use of the various date/time special registers, see Appendix C once again.

Scalar Expressions

As indicated at the beginning of this section, the scalar operators and functions can be used (in conjunction with scalar operands and arguments) to construct scalar expressions. A scalar expression is an expression whose operands are simple scalar values and whose value in turn is another such scalar value.* Generally speaking, such expressions can appear wherever a *constant* of the appropriate type is permitted—for example, as operands in SELECT, WHERE, and HAVING clauses (see Chapters 6–8)—though, regrettably, there are many exceptions to this simple general rule. Such exceptions are noted later at appropriate points in the book.

There are six types of scalar expression, characterized according to the data type of the value they represent: numeric, character string, graphic string, date, time, and timestamp expressions. We give examples here of the

---

*For details regarding the data type, precision, etc., of the result of a scalar expression, the reader is referred to the IBM manuals.

first two types only; graphic string expressions are syntactically similar to character string expressions, and date, time, and timestamp expressions are discussed in Appendix C. Note that (as several of the examples below suggest) parentheses can always be used in an expression to force a desired order of evaluation. Note too that the aggregate functions discussed in Chapter 7 can also be used within certain scalar expressions, since they each return a scalar value.

Numeric expressions:

```
STATUS
WEIGHT * 454
SALARY + COMMISSION + BONUS
( QTY + 1500 ) / 75.2
( LENGTH ( SNAME ) - 1 ) * 2
50 - ( AVG ( QTY ) / 100 )
```

Character string expressions:

```
PNAME
INITIALS || LASTNAME
SUBSTR ( SNAME, 1, 3 )
'NNNN' || SUBSTR ( DIGITS ( QTY ), 8, 2 )
MIN ( COLOR )
USER
```

4.5 ASSIGNMENTS AND COMPARISONS

Assignments

Assignment operations are performed when values are retrieved from the database (e.g., via SELECT) or stored into the database (e.g., via UPDATE). In general, an assignment involves assigning the value of some scalar expression (the *source*) to some scalar object (the *target*). The data type of the source and the data type of the target must be *compatible*. Compatibility is defined as follows:

1. All numbers are compatible with one another.
2. All character strings are compatible with one another.
3. All graphic strings are compatible with one another.
4. All dates are compatible with one another. Dates and character strings are also compatible with one another.
5. All times are compatible with one another. Times and character strings are also compatible with one another.
6. All timestamps are compatible with one another. Timestamps and character strings are also compatible with one another.

7. In Cases 4, 5, and 6 above, the character string in question must be a valid date string or time string or timestamp string (as applicable), unless it is being assigned to, in which case its value is irrelevant. See Appendix C for further discussion.

8. There are no other instances of compatibility.

Note 1: The target of an assignment in an INSERT or UPDATE operation must be represented by an unqualified name. See Chapters 5 and 6 for a discussion of qualified and unqualified names.

Note 2: In a string assignment, the source can be a substring of a given string (specified by means of the SUBSTR function), but the target cannot. Likewise, in a date/time assignment, the source can be—for example—the days component of a given date/time (specified by means of the DAY function), but the target cannot.

Comparisons

Comparisons are performed under many circumstances—for example, when DB2 is eliminating duplicate values (see the discussion of DISTINCT in Chapter 6). A comparison is also one kind of *predicate* (though not the only kind); predicates are used in WHERE and HAVING clauses (see Chapters 6–8). Comparisons can be regarded as a special kind of scalar expression, but a scalar expression that evaluates to a truth value instead of to one of the DB2-supported data types. The general form of a comparison is

    comparand   operator   comparand

where:

(a) The two comparands must be compatible, as that term is defined under "Assignments" above. In other words, the comparands must be scalar expressions of the same type—i.e., both numeric or both character string or ... (etc.). The data types of the two expressions are not required to be absolutely identical, but for performance reasons it is usually a good idea if they are.

(b) The operator is any of the following: $=$, $\sim =$ (not equals), $<$, $\sim <$, $< =$, $>$, $\sim >$, $> =$.*

---

*For typographic reasons we use the tilde ($\sim$) to represent "not" in "not equals," "not less than," etc. DB2 actually uses the PL/I-style "not" symbol. DB2 also allows "not equals" to be written as $< >$ (for reasons of compatibility with the SQL standard).

Comparisons are evaluated as follows:

- Numbers compare algebraically (negative values are considered to be smaller than positive values, regardless of their absolute magnitude).

- Strings (character or graphic) compare in accordance with their internal byte encoding. If two strings of different lengths are to be compared, the shorter is conceptually padded at the right with blanks to make it the same length as the other before the comparison is done.

- Dates and times and timestamps compare in accordance with the obvious chronologic ordering. See Appendix C for further discussion.

Examples:

```
WEIGHT * 454 > 1000
SUBSTR (PNAME,1,1) = 'C'
REVIEW_DATE < CURRENT DATE
SUM (QTY) > 500
```

The last of these examples makes use of an aggregate function (SUM). See Chapter 7 for a discussion of aggregate functions.

4.6 MISSING INFORMATION

To complete this chapter on basic objects and operators, it is necessary to say something regarding missing information. The problem of missing information is one that is frequently encountered in the real world. For example, historical records sometimes include such entries as "Date of birth unknown"; meeting agendas often show a speaker as "To be announced"; and police records may include the entry "Present whereabouts unknown." Hence it is desirable to have some way of dealing with such situations in our formal database systems.

SQL systems such as DB2 represent such missing information by means of special markers called *nulls** (or by nonnull default values; we ignore this latter possibility until further notice). If a given record has a null in a given field position, it means that the value of that field is unknown (or perhaps does not apply) in the record in question. For example, a shipment record might contain a null QTY (we know that the shipment exists but we do not know the quantity shipped); or a part record might contain a null COLOR (perhaps COLOR is irrelevant for some kinds of part). Note carefully that null is not the same as (e.g.) blank or zero; in fact, it is not really

---

*Also known as *null values*. However, this usage is deprecated, since (as explained subsequently) the whole point of null is precisely that it is not a value.

a data value at all in the usual sense of that term, which is why we referred to nulls as "markers" above.

In general, any field can contain nulls *unless* the definition of that field explicitly specifies NOT NULL (see Chapter 5). If a given field is allowed to contain nulls, and a record is inserted into the table and no value is provided for that field, DB2 will automatically place a null in that position.

- Suppose, for example, that NOT NULL is specified for field S# in table S. The effect of this specification is to guarantee that every record in table S will always contain a genuine (i.e., nonnull) S# value; in other words, a value must always be provided for field S# when a record is inserted into the S table, and updating an existing S# value to null will not be allowed.*

- Suppose also, by contrast, that NOT NULL is *not* specified for field STATUS in that same table. Then field STATUS might be null in some S record; in other words, it is possible to insert an S record without providing a STATUS value, and updating an existing STATUS value to null will be allowed.

Aside: In DB2, a column that can accept nulls is physically represented in the stored database by two columns, the data column itself and a hidden indicator column, one byte wide, that is stored as a prefix to the actual data column. An indicator column value of binary ones indicates that the corresponding data column value is to be ignored (i.e., taken as null); an indicator column value of binary zeros indicates that the corresponding data column value is to be taken as genuine. But the indicator column is always (of course) "transparent to the user."

The specification NOT NULL in a field definition can optionally be extended to include the additional specification WITH DEFAULT. NOT NULL WITH DEFAULT means that the field in question cannot contain nulls, but that it is nevertheless still legal to omit a value for the field on INSERT. If a record is inserted and no value is provided for some field to which NOT NULL WITH DEFAULT applies, DB2 automatically places one of the following nonnull default values in that position:

- Zero for numeric fields
- Blanks for fixed length string fields
- Empty (zero-length string) for varying length string fields
- The value of CURRENT DATE or CURRENT TIME or CURRENT

---

*In fact, NOT NULL *must* be specified for field S#, because it is the primary key for table S. See Chapters 5 and 12.

TIMESTAMP, as appropriate, for date, time, or timestamp fields (except as explained in Appendix C)

Nonnull default values (unlike nulls) are genuine, legal data values.

To return to nulls per se: Let us consider the effect of nulls on scalar expressions. Consider, for example, the numeric expression

```
WEIGHT * 454
```

where WEIGHT represents the weight of some part, Px say. What if the weight of part Px happens to be null?—what then is the value of the expression? The answer is that it also is considered to be null. In general, in fact, *any* scalar numeric expression is considered to evaluate to null if any of the operands of that expression is itself null. Thus, e.g., if WEIGHT happens to be null, then all of the following expressions also evaluate to null:

```
WEIGHT + 454      454 + WEIGHT      + WEIGHT
WEIGHT - 454      454 - WEIGHT      - WEIGHT
WEIGHT * 454      454 * WEIGHT
WEIGHT / 454      454 / WEIGHT
```

Analogous considerations apply to string expressions and to date, time, and timestamp expressions. *Note:* The effect of nulls on aggregate functions such as SUM is discussed in Chapter 7.

Comparisons are also affected by the presence of nulls. Let A and B be two expressions that are compatible for comparison purposes (see Section 4.5). If A evaluates to null or B evaluates to null *or both,* then (in the context of a WHERE or HAVING clause) each of the comparisons

```
A = B      A ~= B
A < B      A ~< B      A >= B
A > B      A ~> B      A <= B
```

evaluates, not to *true* or *false,* but to the *unknown* truth value. The *unknown* truth value is defined by the following truth tables (where T = *true,* F = *false,* and ? = *unknown*):

```
AND | T ? F        OR  | T ? F        NOT|
----+------        ----+------        ---+---
 T  | T ? F         T  | T T T         T | F
 ?  | ? ? F         ?  | T ? ?         ? | ?
 F  | F F F         F  | T ? F         F | T
```

Note in particular, therefore, that (in the context of a WHERE or HAVING clause) two nulls are not considered to be equal to one another. Despite this fact, however, two nulls *are* considered to be equal (equivalently, to be duplicates of each other) for purposes of indexing (UNIQUE—see Chapter 5) and duplicate elimination (DISTINCT—see Chapter 6) and ordering (ORDER BY—see Chapter 6) and grouping (GROUP BY—see Chapter 7).

The question of the effect of nulls on comparisons is discussed further in Chapter 6.

The scalar function VALUE (mentioned briefly in Section 4.4) can be useful in dealing with nulls. Suppose for the sake of the example that nulls are permitted for the COLOR field in table P. Then the query

```
SELECT P#, VALUE ( COLOR, 'Color irrelevant' )
FROM   P ;
```

will return the character string "Color irrelevant" for any part for which the color is given as null in the database. In general, VALUE takes a sequence of arguments of compatible data types, and returns either the value of the first nonnull argument in the sequence, or null if the arguments are all null.

One final point: In certain contexts—but *not* in general scalar expressions, and not in a SELECT clause—the special zero-argument function NULL can be used to represent null.* For instance:

```
UPDATE S
SET    STATUS = NULL
WHERE  CITY = 'Paris' ;
```

Author's note: It is this writer's opinion that nulls, at least as currently defined and implemented in SQL, are far more trouble than they are worth and should be avoided; they display very strange and inconsistent behavior and can be a rich source of error and confusion. (Please note that these comments and criticisms apply to any system that supports SQL-style nulls, not just to DB2 specifically. An extensive discussion of the problems that can be caused by SQL-style nulls can be found in the book *Relational Database: Selected Writings,* by C. J. Date, Addison-Wesley, 1986.) In this book, therefore, we will generally specify either NOT NULL or NOT NULL WITH DEFAULT for all fields, unless we are trying to illustrate some specific point involving nulls.

---

*DB2 does not actually consider NULL to be a "zero-argument function" (nor is it a constant or "special register"), because it cannot appear in all contexts in which such objects can appear. Exactly what DB2 does consider it to be is not at all clear.

CHAPTER

◆ 5 ◆

Data Definition

5.1 INTRODUCTION

In this chapter we examine the SQL data definition statements of DB2 in some detail. It is convenient to divide those statements into two broad classes, which we may very loosely characterize as *logical* and *physical*— "logical" having to do with objects that are genuinely of interest to users, such as base tables and views, and "physical" having to do with objects that are primarily of interest to the system, such as disk volumes. Needless to say, matters are not really as clearcut as this simple classification would suggest—some "logical" statements include parameters that are really "physical" in nature, and vice versa, and some statements do not fit neatly into either category. But the classification is convenient as an aid to understanding, and we will stay with it for now. The present chapter is concerned only with "logical" data definition.

The principal logical data definition statements are listed below:

```
CREATE TABLE        CREATE VIEW        CREATE INDEX
ALTER TABLE
DROP TABLE          DROP VIEW          DROP INDEX
```

(*Note:* There is also an ALTER INDEX statement, but it falls totally into the "physical" category. There is no ALTER VIEW statement.) We defer discussion of CREATE and DROP VIEW to Chapter 10; the remaining statements above are the subject of the present chapter.

5.2   BASE TABLES

A base table is an (important) special case of the more general concept "table." Let us therefore begin by making that more general concept a little more precise.

Definition

A *table* in a relational system consists of a row of *column headings,* together with zero or more rows of *data values* (different numbers of data rows at different times). For a given table:

(a) The column heading row specifies one or more columns (giving, among other things, a data type for each);

(b) Each data row contains exactly one scalar value for each of the columns specified in the column heading row. Furthermore, all the values in a given column are of the same data type, namely the data type specified in the column heading row for that column.

Two points arise in connexion with the foregoing definition.

1. Note that there is no mention of *row ordering*. Strictly speaking, the rows of a relational table are considered to be unordered. (The rows of a relation constitute a mathematical *set,* and sets in mathematics do not have any ordering.) It is possible, as we shall see in Chapter 6, to *impose* an order on those rows when they are retrieved in response to a query, but such an ordering should be regarded as nothing more than a convenience for the user—it is not intrinsic to the notion of a table per se.

2. In contrast to the first point, the columns of a table *are* considered to be ordered, left to right. (At least, they are considered to be so ordered in most systems, including in particular DB2.) For example, in the suppliers table S (see Fig. 1.2 in Chapter 1), column S# is the first column, column SNAME is the second column, and so on. In practice, however, there are very few situations in which that left-to-right ordering is sig-

nificant, and even those can be avoided with a little discipline. Such avoidance is to be recommended, as we shall explain later.

Aside: Of course, rows and columns do have a physical ordering in the stored version of the table on the disk; what is more, those physical orderings can and do have a very definite effect on system performance. The point is, however, that those physical orderings are (in most situations, and ideally in all situations) *transparent to the user.*

To turn now to base tables specifically: A base table is an *autonomous, named* table. By "autonomous," we mean that the table exists in its own right—unlike (e.g.) a view, which does not exist in its own right but is derived from one or more base tables (it is merely an alternative way of looking at those base tables). By "named," we mean that the table is explicitly given a name via an appropriate CREATE statement—unlike (e.g.) a table that is merely constructed as the result of a query, which does not have any explicit name of its own and has only ephemeral existence (for examples of such unnamed tables, see the two result tables in Fig. 1.1 in Chapter 1).

CREATE TABLE: Format 1

We are now in a position to discuss the CREATE TABLE statement in detail. The statement comes in two formats. Format 1 (the more fundamental of the two) takes the general form:

```
CREATE TABLE base-table
  ( column-definition [, column-definition ] ...
[, primary-key-definition ]
[, foreign-key-definition [, foreign-key-definition ] ... ] )
[ other parameters ] ;
```

where a "column-definition", in turn, takes the form:

```
column data-type [ NOT NULL [ WITH DEFAULT ] ]
```

The optional specification "NOT NULL [WITH DEFAULT]" has already been explained in Chapter 4 (Section 4.6). We defer detailed discussion of "primary-key-definition" and "foreign-key- definition" to Chapter 12; note, however, that although the primary key definition is in fact optional, we will always include such a definition in our examples in this book. The optional "other parameters" have primarily to do with physical storage matters and are discussed (very briefly) in Chapter 16.

Note: Square brackets are used in syntactic definitions throughout this book to indicate that the material enclosed in those brackets is optional (i.e., may be omitted). An ellipsis (...) indicates that the immediately preceding syntactic unit may optionally be repeated one or more times. Material in capitals must be written exactly as shown; material in lower case must be replaced by specific values chosen by the user.

Here is an example (the CREATE TABLE statement for table S, now shown complete):

```
CREATE TABLE S
     ( S#       CHAR(5)  NOT NULL,
       SNAME    CHAR(20) NOT NULL WITH DEFAULT,
       STATUS   SMALLINT,
       CITY     CHAR(15) NOT NULL WITH DEFAULT,
     PRIMARY KEY ( S# ) ) ;
```

The effect of this statement is to create a new, empty base table called *xyz*.S, where *xyz* is the name by which the user issuing the CREATE TABLE statement is known to the system (see Chapter 11). Entries describing the table are made in the DB2 catalog. User *xyz* can refer to the table by its full name *xyz*.S or by the abbreviated name S; other users must refer to it by its full name. The table has four columns, called *xyz*.S.S#, *xyz*.S.SNAME, *xyz*.S.STATUS, and *xyz*.S.CITY, and having the indicated data types; column *xyz*.S.S# is the primary key (note that the primary key must be explicitly declared to be NOT NULL). User *xyz* can refer to the columns of the table by their full names or by the abbreviated names S.S#, S.SNAME, S.STATUS, and S.CITY; other users must always use the *xyz* qualifier. For user *xyz* (only), the "S." portion can be omitted also if no ambiguity results. In general, the rules concerning names are as follows: User names, such as *xyz,* must be unique across the entire DB2 system; (unqualified) table names must be unique within user; and (unqualified) column names must be unique within table.* "Table" here refers to both base tables and views; that is, a view cannot have the same name as a base table.

Once the table has been created, data can be entered into it via the INSERT statement of SQL (see Chapter 8) or via the DB2 load utility (see Chapter 17).

CREATE TABLE: Format 2

Format 2 of CREATE TABLE allows the user to create a base table ("base-table-2") that is "the same shape as" some existing base table ("base-table-1"):

```
CREATE TABLE base-table-2 LIKE base-table-1 ;
```

_____

*In addition, SQL keywords (CREATE, TABLE, SELECT, etc.) cannot be used as names. The first character of any name must be "alphabetic" (A–Z or one of the special characters #, $, @), the remainder if any must be "alphabetic," numeric (0–9), or the underscore character. Table and column names are limited to a maximum of 18 characters, user names to a maximum of 8 characters.

(plus optional "other parameters" exactly as in Format 1). Here is an example:

```
CREATE TABLE SCOPY LIKE S ;
```

Table "base-table-2" inherits its column definitions—but nothing else—from "base-table-1." In the example, therefore, it is as if table SCOPY were defined as follows:

```
CREATE TABLE SCOPY
     ( S#      CHAR(5)  NOT NULL,
       SNAME   CHAR(20) NOT NULL WITH DEFAULT,
       STATUS  SMALLINT,
       CITY    CHAR(15) NOT NULL WITH DEFAULT ) ;
```

Note in particular that "base-table-2" does *not* inherit any primary or foreign key definitions from "base-table-1."

ALTER TABLE

Just as a new base table can be created at any time, via CREATE TABLE, so an existing base table can be *altered* at any time by the addition of a new column at the right, via ALTER TABLE:

```
ALTER TABLE base-table
          ADD column data-type [ NOT NULL WITH DEFAULT ] ;
```

For example:

```
ALTER TABLE S
          ADD DISCOUNT SMALLINT ;
```

This statement adds a DISCOUNT column to the S table. All existing S records are extended from four field values to five; the value of the new fifth field is null in every case (it would have been zero if NOT NULL WITH DEFAULT had been specified; note that the unqualified specification NOT NULL—i.e., with the further specification WITH DEFAULT omitted—is not allowed in ALTER TABLE). Note also, incidentally, that the expansion of existing records just described is not physically performed at the time the ALTER TABLE is executed; all that happens at that time is that the description of those records in the catalog changes. Thereafter, for a given record in the ALTERed table:

1. The next time it is read from the disk, DB2 appends the additional null or nonnull default value before passing it to the user;
2. The next time it is written to the disk, DB2 writes the physically expanded version (unless the additional value is still null or the nonnull default value, in which case the expansion still does not occur).

But from the user's perspective, it is as if the records *were* all physically expanded at ALTER TABLE time. There is no way to tell the difference.

ALTER TABLE also allows primary and foreign key specifications to be added to or removed from a given table (see Chapter 12). *Note:* Other types of alteration are possible also, but they are not nearly so important as the ones we have mentioned; we leave the details to the IBM manuals. Note in particular that ALTER TABLE does *not* support any kind of change to the width or data type of an existing column, and neither does it support the removal of an existing column.

DROP TABLE

An existing base table can be destroyed at any time by means of the SQL DROP statement:

```
DROP TABLE base-table ;
```

The specified base table is removed from the system (more precisely, the description of that table is removed from the catalog). All indexes and views defined on that base table are automatically dropped also. (All foreign key specifications that refer to that base table are also automatically dropped. See Chapter 12.)

5.3 INDEXES

Like base tables, indexes are created and dropped using SQL data definition statements. However, CREATE INDEX and DROP INDEX (also ALTER INDEX and certain data control statements) are the *only* statements in the SQL language that refer to indexes at all; other statements—in particular, data manipulation statements such as SELECT—deliberately do not include any such references. The decision as to whether or not to use some particular index in responding to a particular SQL request is made not by the user but by DB2 (actually by the optimizer subcomponent of Bind), as explained in Chapter 2.

CREATE INDEX takes the general form:

```
CREATE [ UNIQUE ] INDEX index
   ON base-table ( column [ order ]
                 [, column [ order ] ] ... )
      [ other parameters ] ;
```

The optional "other parameters" have to do with physical storage matters, as in CREATE TABLE. Each "order" specification is either ASC (ascending) or DESC (descending); if neither ASC nor DESC is specified, then ASC is assumed by default. The left-to-right sequence of naming columns

in the CREATE INDEX statement corresponds to major-to-minor ordering
in the usual way. For example, the statement

```
CREATE INDEX X ON T ( P, Q DESC, R ) ;
```

creates an index called X on (base) table T in which entries are ordered by
ascending R-value within descending Q-value within ascending P-value. The
columns P, Q, and R need not be contiguous, nor need they all be of the
same data type, nor need they be all fixed length or all varying length.

Once created, an index is automatically maintained by the Data Manager to reflect updates on the table, until such time as the index is dropped.

The UNIQUE option in CREATE INDEX specifies that no two records
in the indexed base table will be allowed to take on the same value for
the indexed field or field combination at the same time. In the case of the
suppliers-and-parts database, for example, we would have to specify the
following UNIQUE indexes in order to enforce uniqueness for the primary
keys (see Chapter 12 for further discussion):

```
CREATE UNIQUE INDEX XS  ON S  ( S# ) ;
CREATE UNIQUE INDEX XP  ON P  ( P# ) ;
CREATE UNIQUE INDEX XSP ON SP ( S#, P# ) ;
```

Now DB2 will reject any attempt to introduce a duplicate value (via an
INSERT or UPDATE operation) into field S.S# or field P.P# or (composite)
field SP.(S#,P#).

Indexes, like base tables, can be created and dropped at any time. Note,
however, that an attempt to create a UNIQUE index on a nonempty table
that already violates the uniqueness constraint will fail. Note also that (as
mentioned in Section 4.6) two nulls are considered to be equal to each other
for UNIQUE indexing purposes.

Any number of indexes can be built on a single base table. Here is
another index for table S:

```
CREATE INDEX XSC ON S ( CITY ) ;
```

UNIQUE has not been specified in this case, because multiple suppliers can
be located in the same city.

The statement to drop an index is

```
DROP INDEX index ;
```

The index is destroyed (i.e., its description is removed from the catalog). If
an existing application plan depends on that dropped index, then, as explained in Chapter 2, that plan will automatically be rebound the next time
it is invoked. Refer back to Chapter 2 if you need to refresh your memory
regarding this process.

5.4 DISCUSSION

The fact that data definition statements can be executed at any time makes DB2 a very flexible system. In older (nonrelational) systems, the addition of a new type of object, such as a new record type or a new index or a new field, is an operation not to be undertaken lightly: Typically it involves bringing the entire system to a halt,* unloading the database, revising and recompiling the database definition, and finally reloading the database in accordance with that revised definition. In such a system, it becomes highly desirable to get the database definition (and therefore, much more significantly, the database *design*) *complete* and *correct* once and for all, before starting to load and use the data—which means that

(a) the job of getting the system installed and operational can quite literally take months or even years of highly specialized people's time, and

(b) once the system is running, it can be difficult and costly, perhaps prohibitively so, to remedy early design errors.

In DB2, by contrast, it is possible to create and load just a few base tables and then to start using those tables immediately. Later, new base tables and new fields can be added in a piecemeal fashion, without having any effect on existing users of the database. It is also possible to experiment with the effects of having or not having particular indexes, again without affecting existing users at all (other than in performance, of course). Moreover, as we shall see in Chapter 10, it is even possible under certain circumstances to rearrange the structure of the database—e.g., to move a field from one table to another—and still not affect the logic of existing programs. In a nutshell, it is not necessary to go through the total database design process before any useful work can be done with the system, nor is it necessary to get everything right the first time. The system is *forgiving*.

Caveat: The foregoing should *not* be taken to mean that database design is unnecessary in a system like DB2. Of course database design is still needed. However:

- It doesn't all have to be done at once.
- It doesn't have to be perfect first time.
- Logical and physical design can be tackled separately.
- If requirements change, then the design can change too, in a comparatively painless manner.

---

*We remark in passing that many modern installations simply cannot afford to bring the system to a halt—they require nonstop (24-hour-a-day) operation. For such an installation, the comparative inflexibility of nonrelational systems is a major drawback, possibly a complete showstopper.

- Many new applications—typically small-scale applications, involving, for example, personal or departmental databases—become feasible in a system like DB2 that would simply never have been considered under an older (nonrelational) system, because those older systems were just too complicated to make such applications economically worthwhile (in particular, the upfront costs in those systems were prohibitive).

EXERCISES

5.1 Fig. 5.1 shows some sample data values for a database containing information concerning suppliers (S), parts (P), and projects (J). Suppliers, parts, and projects are uniquely identified by supplier number (S#), part number (P#), and project number (J#), respectively. The significance of an SPJ (shipment) record is that the specified supplier supplies the specified part to the specified project in the specified quantity (and the combination S#-P#-J# uniquely identifies such a record). Write a suitable set of CREATE TABLE statements for this database. *Note:* This database will be used in numerous exercises in subsequent chapters.

S	S#	SNAME	STATUS	CITY		SPJ	S#	P#	J#	QTY
	S1	Smith	20	London			S1	P1	J1	200
	S2	Jones	10	Paris			S1	P1	J4	700
	S3	Blake	30	Paris			S2	P3	J1	400
	S4	Clark	20	London			S2	P3	J2	200
	S5	Adams	30	Athens			S2	P3	J3	200
							S2	P3	J4	500
							S2	P3	J5	600
P	P#	PNAME	COLOR	WEIGHT	CITY		S2	P3	J6	400
	P1	Nut	Red	12	London		S2	P3	J7	800
	P2	Bolt	Green	17	Paris		S2	P5	J2	100
	P3	Screw	Blue	17	Rome		S3	P3	J1	200
	P4	Screw	Red	14	London		S3	P4	J2	500
	P5	Cam	Blue	12	Paris		S4	P6	J3	300
	P6	Cog	Red	19	London		S4	P6	J7	300
							S5	P2	J2	200
J	J#	JNAME	CITY				S5	P2	J4	100
	J1	Sorter	Paris				S5	P5	J5	500
	J2	Punch	Rome				S5	P5	J7	100
	J3	Reader	Athens				S5	P6	J2	200
	J4	Console	Athens				S5	P1	J4	100
	J5	Collator	London				S5	P3	J4	200
	J6	Terminal	Oslo				S5	P4	J4	800
	J7	Tape	London				S5	P5	J4	400
							S5	P6	J4	500

Fig. 5.1 The suppliers-parts-projects database

5.2 Write a set of CREATE INDEX statements for the database of Exercise 5.1 to enforce the required primary key constraints.

5.3 What are the main advantages of indexes? What are the main disadvantages?

5.4 "Uniqueness" of a field or field combination is a logical property, but it is enforced in DB2 by means of an index, which is a physical construct. Discuss.

ANSWERS TO SELECTED EXERCISES

5.1
```
CREATE TABLE S
    ( S#       CHAR(5)   NOT NULL,
      SNAME    CHAR(20)  NOT NULL WITH DEFAULT,
      STATUS   SMALLINT  NOT NULL WITH DEFAULT,
      CITY     CHAR(15)  NOT NULL WITH DEFAULT,
      PRIMARY KEY ( S# ) ) ;

CREATE TABLE P
    ( P#       CHAR(6)   NOT NULL,
      PNAME    CHAR(20)  NOT NULL WITH DEFAULT,
      COLOR    CHAR(6)   NOT NULL WITH DEFAULT,
      WEIGHT   SMALLINT  NOT NULL WITH DEFAULT,
      CITY     CHAR(15)  NOT NULL WITH DEFAULT,
      PRIMARY KEY ( P# ) ) ;

CREATE TABLE J
    ( J#       CHAR(4)   NOT NULL,
      JNAME    CHAR(10)  NOT NULL WITH DEFAULT,
      CITY     CHAR(15)  NOT NULL WITH DEFAULT,
      PRIMARY KEY ( J# ) ) ;

CREATE TABLE SPJ
    ( S#       CHAR(5)   NOT NULL,
      P#       CHAR(6)   NOT NULL,
      J#       CHAR(4)   NOT NULL,
      QTY      INTEGER,
      PRIMARY KEY ( S#, P#, J# ) ) ;
```

Note: We allow field SPJ.QTY to accept nulls purely because it is required to do so by a later exercise—not for any really good reason.

5.2
```
CREATE UNIQUE INDEX SX   ON S   ( S# ) ;
CREATE UNIQUE INDEX PX   ON P   ( P# ) ;
CREATE UNIQUE INDEX JX   ON J   ( J# ) ;
CREATE UNIQUE INDEX SPJX ON SPJ ( S#, P#, J# ) ;
```

5.3 The advantages of indexes are as follows:

(a) They can speed up direct access based on a given value for the indexed field or field combination. Without the index, a sequential scan would be required.

(b) They can speed up sequential access based on the indexed field or field combination. Without the index, a sort would be required.

(c) In DB2 in particular, UNIQUE indexes serve to enforce uniqueness constraints (especially primary key uniqueness constraints).

The disadvantages are as follows:

(a) They take up space in the database. The space taken up by indexes can easily exceed that taken up by the data itself in a heavily indexed database.

(b) While an index may well speed up retrieval operations, it will at the same time slow down update operations. Any INSERT or DELETE on the indexed table or UPDATE on the indexed field or field combination will require an accompanying update on the index.

5.4 An unfortunate state of affairs. DB2 is not quite as data independent as it ought to be.

◆ 6 ◆

Data Manipulation I:
Retrieval Operations

6.1 INTRODUCTION

SQL provides four data manipulation statements: SELECT, INSERT, UPDATE, and DELETE. This chapter and the next are concerned with the SELECT statement; Chapter 8 is concerned with the other three statements. The aim in all three chapters is to be reasonably comprehensive but *not* to replace the relevant IBM manuals. As usual, all examples are based on the suppliers-and-parts database. Also, we assume until further notice that all statements are entered interactively. The special considerations that apply to embedded SQL are ignored until Chapter 13.

Note: Many of our examples, especially those in the next chapter, are quite complex. The reader should not infer that it is SQL itself that is complex. Rather, the point is that common operations are so simple in SQL (and indeed in most relational languages) that examples of such operations tend to be rather uninteresting, and do not illustrate the full power of the language. Of course, we do show some simple examples first (Section 6.2). Section 6.3 is concerned with a slightly more complicated—but extremely important—facility known as *join*.

6.2 SIMPLE QUERIES

We start with a simple example—the query "Get supplier numbers and status for suppliers in Paris," which can be expressed in SQL as follows:

```
SELECT S#, STATUS
FROM   S
WHERE  CITY = 'Paris' ;
```

Result:
```
      S#   STATUS
      --   ------
      S2      10
      S3      30
```

The example illustrates the commonest form of the SQL SELECT statement—"*SELECT* specified fields *FROM* a specified table *WHERE* some specified condition is true." Notice that the result of the query is another table—a table that is derived in some way from the given tables in the database. In other words, the user in a relational system like DB2 is always operating in the simple tabular framework, a very attractive feature of such systems.*

Incidentally, we could equally well have formulated the query using *qualified field names* throughout:

```
SELECT S.S#, S.STATUS
FROM   S
WHERE  S.CITY = 'Paris' ;
```

The use of qualified names is often clearer (and sometimes essential, as we shall see in Section 6.3 and elsewhere).

---

*Because of this fact, we say that relational tables form a *closed system* under the retrieval operators of a language like SQL. In general, a closed system is a collection (possibly infinite) of all objects of a certain type, say OBJS, and a corresponding collection of operators, say OPS, such that:

(a) The operators in OPS apply to the objects in OBJS, and

(b) The result of applying any such operator to any such object(s) is another object in OBJS.

The practical significance of this point (in the case of relations specifically) is as follows: Since the result of one SELECT operation is another relation, it is possible, at least in principle, to apply another SELECT operation to that result, provided of course that that result has been saved somewhere. It also means, again in principle, that SELECT operations can be nested. See Sections 7.2 and 8.2 and Chapter 10 for illustrations of these points.

For reference, we show below the general form of the SELECT statement (ignoring the possibility of UNION, which is discussed in the next chapter).

```
SELECT [ ALL | DISTINCT ] item(s)
FROM    table(s)
[ WHERE   predicate ]
[ GROUP  BY field(s) ]
[ HAVING predicate ]
[ ORDER  BY field(s) ] ;
```

We now proceed to illustrate the major features of this statement by means of a rather lengthy series of examples. *Note:* The GROUP BY and HAVING clauses are discussed in Chapter 7. All of the remaining clauses are at least introduced in this chapter, though the more complex aspects of those clauses are also deferred to Chapter 7.

6.2.1 Simple Retrieval. Get part numbers for all parts supplied.

```
SELECT P#
FROM    SP ;
```

Result:
```
        P#
        --
        P1
        P2
        P3
        P4
        P5
        P6
        P1
        P2
        P2
        P2
        P4
        P5
```

Notice the duplication of part numbers in this result. DB2 does not eliminate duplicate rows from the result of a SELECT statement unless the user explicitly requests it to do so via the keyword DISTINCT, as in the next example.

6.2.2 Retrieval with Duplicate Elimination. Get part numbers for all parts supplied, with redundant duplicates eliminated.

```
SELECT DISTINCT P#
FROM    SP ;
```

Result:
```
        P#
        --
        P1
        P2
        P3
        P4
        P5
        P6
```

Note: It just so happens in this particular example that each row contains a single scalar value; the effect of the DISTINCT specification is therefore to eliminate duplicate scalar values. In general, however, DISTINCT means "eliminate duplicate *rows.*" See Example 6.3.5 in the next section for an example of the use of DISTINCT with rows containing more than one scalar value.

The alternative to DISTINCT is ALL. ALL is assumed if neither DISTINCT nor ALL is specified explicitly.

6.2.3 Retrieval of Computed Values.
For all parts, get the part number and the weight of the part in grams (part weights are given in table P in pounds).

```
SELECT P#, 'Weight in grams =', WEIGHT * 454
FROM   P ;
```

Result:
```
       P#
       --  ------------------  ----
       P1  Weight in grams =   5448
       P2  Weight in grams =   7718
       P3  Weight in grams =   7718
       P4  Weight in grams =   6356
       P5  Weight in grams =   5448
       P6  Weight in grams =   8626
```

The SELECT clause (also the WHERE and HAVING clauses, q.v.) can include general scalar expressions, involving, e.g., scalar operators such as plus and minus and scalar functions such as SUBSTR, instead of or as well as simple field names.

6.2.4 Simple Retrieval ("SELECT *").
Get full details of all suppliers.

```
SELECT *
FROM   S ;
```

Result: A copy of the entire S table.

The star or asterisk is shorthand for a list of all field names in the table(s) named in the FROM clause, in the order in which those fields are defined in the relevant CREATE (and possibly ALTER) TABLE statement(s). The SELECT statement shown is thus equivalent to:

```
SELECT S#, SNAME, STATUS, CITY
FROM   S ;
```

The star notation is convenient for interactive queries, since it saves keystrokes. However, it is potentially dangerous in embedded SQL (i.e., SQL within an application program), because the meaning of "*" may change if the program is rebound and some definitional change has occurred in the interim. In this book we will use "SELECT *" only in contexts where it is safe to do so (basically ad hoc queries only), and we recommend that actual users of DB2 do likewise.

Incidentally, it is possible to qualify the "*" by the name of the relevant table. For example, the following is legal:

```
SELECT S.*
FROM   S ;
```

6.2.5 Qualified Retrieval. Get supplier numbers for suppliers in Paris with status > 20.

```
SELECT S#
FROM   S
WHERE  CITY = 'Paris'
AND    STATUS > 20 ;
```

Result:
```
S#
--
S3
```

The condition or *predicate* following WHERE can consist of a simple *comparison* (see Chapter 4 for a definition of this term), or it can consist of multiple comparisons and/or other kinds of predicate all combined together using the Boolean operators AND, OR, and NOT, and parentheses if required to indicate a desired order of evaluation. Other kinds of predicate are discussed in numerous subsequent examples.*

6.2.6 Retrieval with Ordering. Get supplier numbers and status for suppliers in Paris, in descending order of status.

```
SELECT S#, STATUS
FROM   S
WHERE  CITY = 'Paris'
ORDER  BY STATUS DESC ;
```

Result:
```
S#  STATUS
--  ------
S3    30
S2    10
```

In general, the result table is not guaranteed to be in any particular order. Here, however, the user has specified that the result is to be arranged in a particular sequence before being displayed. Ordering may be specified in the same manner as in CREATE INDEX (see Section 5.3)—that is, as

```
column [ order ] [, column [ order ] ] ...
```

---

*We follow conventional database usage here in referring to conditions as "predicates." Strictly speaking, however, this usage is incorrect. A more accurate term would be "conditional expression" or "truth-valued expression."

where, as before, "order" is either ASC or DESC, and ASC is the default. Each "column" must identify a column of the *result table*. Thus, for example, the following is *** ILLEGAL *** :

```
SELECT  S#
FROM    S
ORDER   BY CITY ;
```

It is also possible to identify columns in the ORDER BY clause by column *number* instead of column name—i.e., by the ordinal (left-to-right) position of the column in question within the result table. This feature makes it possible to order a result on the basis of a "computed column" that does not have a name. For example, to order the result of Example 6.2.3 by ascending part number within ascending gram weight:

```
SELECT  P#, 'Weight in grams =', WEIGHT * 454
FROM    P
ORDER   BY 3, P# ;
```

The "3" refers to the third column of the result table. Result:

```
P#
--  ------------------  ----
P1  Weight in grams =   5448
P5  Weight in grams =   5448
P4  Weight in grams =   6356
P2  Weight in grams =   7718
P3  Weight in grams =   7718
P6  Weight in grams =   8626
```

6.2.7 Retrieval Using BETWEEN. Get parts whose weight is in the range 16 to 19 inclusive.

```
SELECT  P#, PNAME, COLOR, WEIGHT, CITY
FROM    P
WHERE   WEIGHT BETWEEN 16 AND 19 ;
```

Result:
```
P#  PNAME  COLOR  WEIGHT  CITY
--  -----  -----  ------  ------
P2  Bolt   Green      17  Paris
P3  Screw  Blue       17  Rome
P6  Cog    Red        19  London
```

The BETWEEN predicate is really just shorthand for a predicate involving two individual comparisons "ANDed" together. The foregoing SELECT statement is equivalent to the following:

```
SELECT  P#, PNAME, COLOR, WEIGHT, CITY
FROM    P
WHERE   WEIGHT >= 16
AND     WEIGHT <= 19 ;
```

NOT BETWEEN can also be specified—for example,

```
SELECT   P#, PNAME, COLOR, WEIGHT, CITY
FROM     P
WHERE    WEIGHT NOT BETWEEN 16 AND 19 ;
```

Result:
```
         P#   PNAME   COLOR   WEIGHT   CITY
         --   -----   -----   ------   ------
         P1   Nut     Red         12   London
         P4   Screw   Red         14   London
         P5   Cam     Blue        12   Paris
```

Like the BETWEEN predicate, the NOT BETWEEN predicate can be regarded merely as shorthand for another predicate that does not use NOT BETWEEN. Exercise: Show the "expanded form" of the foregoing example.

6.2.8 Retrieval Using IN.   Get parts whose weight is any one of the following: 12, 16, 17.

```
SELECT   P#, PNAME, COLOR, WEIGHT, CITY
FROM     P
WHERE    WEIGHT IN ( 12, 16, 17 ) ;
```

Result:
```
         P#   PNAME   COLOR   WEIGHT   CITY
         --   -----   -----   ------   ------
         P1   Nut     Red         12   London
         P2   Bolt    Green       17   Paris
         P3   Screw   Blue        17   Rome
         P5   Cam     Blue        12   Paris
```

IN, like BETWEEN, is really just shorthand. An IN predicate is logically equivalent to a predicate involving a sequence of individual comparisons all "ORed" together. For example, the foregoing SELECT statement is equivalent to the following:

```
SELECT   P#, PNAME, COLOR, WEIGHT, CITY
FROM     P
WHERE    WEIGHT = 12
OR       WEIGHT = 16
OR       WEIGHT = 17 ;
```

NOT IN is also available:

```
SELECT   P#, PNAME, COLOR, WEIGHT, CITY
FROM     P
WHERE    WEIGHT NOT IN ( 12, 16, 17 ) ;
```

Result:
```
         P#   PNAME   COLOR   WEIGHT   CITY
         --   -----   -----   ------   ------
         P4   Screw   Red         14   London
         P6   Cog     Red         19   London
```

Like IN, NOT IN is really just shorthand. Exercise: Show the "expanded form" of the foregoing example.

6.2.9 Retrieval Using LIKE.   Get all parts whose names begin with the letter C.

```
SELECT  P#, PNAME, COLOR, WEIGHT, CITY
FROM    P
WHERE   PNAME LIKE 'C%' ;
```

Result:

P#	PNAME	COLOR	WEIGHT	CITY
P5	Cam	Blue	12	Paris
P6	Cog	Red	19	London

Note, incidentally, that the following SELECT would have produced the same result:

```
SELECT  P#, PNAME, COLOR, WEIGHT, CITY
FROM    P
WHERE   SUBSTR ( PNAME, 1, 1 ) = 'C' ;
```

However, not all LIKE predicates can be reformulated in terms of SUBSTR in this manner. In general, a LIKE predicate takes the form

```
column LIKE constant
```

where "column" must designate a column of type string (CHAR, VARCHAR, GRAPHIC, or VARGRAPHIC), and "constant" must be of a compatible data type. For a given record, the predicate evaluates to *true* if the value within the designated column conforms to the pattern specified by "constant." Characters within "constant" are interpreted as follows:

- The_character (break or underscore) stands for *any single character.*
- The % character (percent) stands for *any sequence of n characters* (where *n* may be zero).
- All other characters simply stand for themselves.

In the example, therefore, the SELECT statement will retrieve records from table P for which the PNAME value begins with the letter C and has any sequence of zero or more characters following that C.

Here are some more examples of LIKE:

`ADDRESS LIKE '%Berkeley%'`	— will evaluate to *true* if ADDRESS contains the string 'Berkeley' anywhere inside it
`S# LIKE 'S__'`	— will evaluate to *true* if S# is exactly 3 characters long and the 1st is an S
`PNAME LIKE '%c___'`	— will evaluate to *true* if PNAME is 4 characters long or more and the last but three is a c

NOT LIKE is also available. For example:

```
CITY NOT LIKE '%E%'
```
—   will evaluate to *true* if CITY does not contain an E

6.2.10 Retrieval Involving NULL.
Suppose for the sake of the example that supplier S5 has a status of null, rather than 30. Get supplier numbers for suppliers with status greater than 25.

```
SELECT  S#
FROM    S
WHERE   STATUS > 25 ;
```

Result: S#
            --
            S3

Supplier S5 does not qualify. As explained in Chapter 4, whenever one of the operands of a comparison is null, then, regardless of the comparison operator involved, the result of the comparison is *never* considered to be *true*—even if the other operand is also null. In other words, if STATUS happens to be null, then none of the following comparisons evaluates to *true*:*

```
STATUS > 25
STATUS <= 25
STATUS = 25
STATUS ¬= 25
STATUS = NULL       [This is illegal syntax. See below.]
STATUS ¬= NULL      [So is this.]
STATUS > NULL       [So is this.]
STATUS <= NULL      [So is this.]
```

Thus, if we issue the query

```
SELECT  S#
FROM    S
WHERE   STATUS <= 25 ;
```

and compare the result with that of the previous query, supplier S5 will not appear in either of them. The result is:

```
S#
--
S1
S2
S4
```

---

*As explained in Chapter 4, they all evaluate to the *unknown* truth value. The SELECT statement retrieves records for which the WHERE predicate evaluates to *true*, not to *false* and not to *unknown*.

A special predicate of the form

```
column IS [ NOT ] NULL
```

is provided for testing for the presence [or absence] of null values. For example:

```
SELECT  S#
FROM    S
WHERE   STATUS IS NULL ;
```

Result: S#
            --
            S5

The syntax "STATUS = NULL" is illegal, because *nothing*—not even null itself—is considered to be equal to null (in the context of a WHERE or HAVING clause).

We note in conclusion that it is not possible to SELECT NULL; that is, the symbol NULL is not allowed in a SELECT clause. For example, the following is illegal:

```
SELECT  P#, 'Weight =', NULL
FROM    P
WHERE   WEIGHT IS NULL ;
```

6.3 JOIN QUERIES

The ability to "join" two or more tables is one of the most powerful features of relational systems. In fact, it is the availability of the join operation, almost more than anything else, that distinguishes relational from nonrelational systems (see Appendix B). So what is a join? Loosely speaking, it is *a query in which data is retrieved from more than one table.* Here is a simple example.

6.3.1 Simple Equijoin.   Get all combinations of supplier and part information such that the supplier and part in question are located in the same city (i.e., are "colocated," to coin an ugly but convenient term).

```
SELECT  S.*, P.*
FROM    S, P
WHERE   S.CITY = P.CITY ;
```

Notice that the field references in the WHERE clause here *must* be qualified by the names of the containing tables (for otherwise they would be ambiguous). Result:

S#	SNAME	STATUS	S.CITY	P#	PNAME	COLOR	WEIGHT	P.CITY
S1	Smith	20	London	P1	Nut	Red	12	London
S1	Smith	20	London	P4	Screw	Red	14	London
S1	Smith	20	London	P6	Cog	Red	19	London
S2	Jones	10	Paris	P2	Bolt	Green	17	Paris
S2	Jones	10	Paris	P5	Cam	Blue	12	Paris
S3	Blake	30	Paris	P2	Bolt	Green	17	Paris
S3	Blake	30	Paris	P5	Cam	Blue	12	Paris
S4	Clark	20	London	P1	Nut	Red	12	London
S4	Clark	20	London	P4	Screw	Red	14	London
S4	Clark	20	London	P6	Cog	Red	19	London

We have shown the two CITY columns in this result explicitly as S.CITY and P.CITY, to avoid ambiguity.

Explanation: It is clear from the English language statement of the problem that the required data comes from two tables, namely S and P. In the SQL formulation of the query, therefore, we first name both those tables in the FROM clause, and we then express the connexion between them (i.e., the fact that the CITY values must be equal) in the WHERE clause. To understand how this works, imagine yourself looking at two rows, one row from each of the two tables—say the two rows shown here:

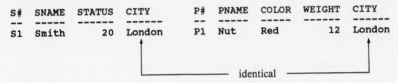

From these two rows you can see that supplier S1 and part P1 are indeed "colocated." These two rows will generate the result row

S#	SNAME	STATUS	S.CITY	P#	PNAME	COLOR	WEIGHT	P.CITY
S1	Smith	20	London	P1	Nut	Red	12	London

because they satisfy the predicate in the WHERE clause (i.e., S.CITY = P.CITY). Similarly for all other pairs of rows having matching CITY values. Notice that supplier S5 (located in Athens) does not appear in the result, because there are no parts stored in Athens; likewise, part P3 (stored in Rome) also does not appear in the result, because there are no suppliers located in Rome.

The result of this query is said to be a *join* of tables S and P over matching CITY values. The term "join" is also used to refer to the operation of constructing such a result. The condition S.CITY = P.CITY is said to be a *join condition* or *join predicate*.

A number of further points arise in connexion with this example, some major, some minor.

- There is no requirement that the fields in a join predicate be identically named, though they very often will be.

- There is no requirement that the comparison operator in a join predicate be equality, though it very often will be. Examples of where it is not are given below (Example 6.3.2 and latter part of Example 6.3.6). If it is equality, then the join is called an *equijoin*.

- The WHERE clause in a join-SELECT can include other conditions in addition to the join predicate itself. Example 6.3.3 below illustrates this possibility.

- It is of course possible to SELECT just specified fields from a join, instead of necessarily having to SELECT all of them. Examples 6.3.4– 6.3.6 below illustrate this possibility.

- The expression

```
SELECT S.*, P.*
FROM   S, P
   .....   ;
```

can be further abbreviated to simply

```
SELECT *
FROM   S, P
   .....   ;
```

Alternatively, of course, it can be expanded to

```
SELECT S#, SNAME, STATUS, S.CITY,
       P#, PNAME, COLOR, WEIGHT, P.CITY
FROM   S, P
   .....   ;
```

In this formulation, S.CITY and P.CITY in the SELECT clause *must* be referred to by their qualified names, as shown, because the unqualified name CITY would be ambiguous.

- The equijoin by definition must produce a result containing two identical columns. If one of those two columns is eliminated, what is left is called the *natural* join. To construct the natural join of S and P over cities in SQL, we could write:

```
SELECT S#, SNAME, STATUS, S.CITY,
       P#, PNAME, COLOR, WEIGHT
FROM   S, P
WHERE  S.CITY = P.CITY ;
```

Natural join is probably the single most useful form of join—so much so, that we often use the unqualified term "join" to refer to this case specifically.

- It is also possible to form a join of three, four, ..., or any number of tables. Example 6.3.5 below shows a join involving three tables.

■ The following is an alternative (and helpful) way to think about how joins may conceptually be constructed. First, form the *Cartesian product* of the tables listed in the FROM clause. The Cartesian product of a set of *n* tables is the table consisting of all possible rows *r,* such that *r* is the concatenation of a row from the first table, a row from the second table, ..., and a row from the *n*th table. For example, the Cartesian product of table S and table P (in that order) is the following table (let us call it CP):

CP	S#	SNAME	STATUS	S.CITY	P#	PNAME	COLOR	WEIGHT	P.CITY
	S1	Smith	20	London	P1	Nut	Red	12	London
	S1	Smith	20	London	P2	Bolt	Green	17	Paris
	S1	Smith	20	London	P3	Screw	Blue	17	Rome
	S1	Smith	20	London	P4	Screw	Red	14	London
	S1	Smith	20	London	P5	Cam	Blue	12	Paris
	S1	Smith	20	London	P6	Cog	Red	19	London
	S2	Jones	10	Paris	P1	Nut	Red	12	London
	.	.	.	.	.	.	.	.	.
	.	.	.	.	.	.	.	.	.
	.	.	.	.	.	.	.	.	.
	S5	Adams	30	Athens	P6	Cog	Red	19	London

The complete table contains 5 * 6 = 30 rows.

Now eliminate from this Cartesian product all those rows that do not satisfy the join predicate. What is left is the required join. In the case at hand, we eliminate from CP all those rows in which S.CITY is not equal to P.CITY; and what is left is exactly the join shown earlier.

By the way, it is perfectly possible (though perhaps unusual) to formulate a SQL query whose result is a Cartesian product. For example:

```
SELECT S.*, P.*
FROM   S, P ;
```

Result: Table CP as shown above.

6.3.2 Greater-Than Join.

Get all combinations of supplier and part information such that the supplier city follows the part city in alphabetical order.

```
SELECT S.*, P.*
FROM   S, P
WHERE  S.CITY > P.CITY ;
```

Result:

S#	SNAME	STATUS	S.CITY	P#	PNAME	COLOR	WEIGHT	P.CITY
S2	Jones	10	Paris	P1	Nut	Red	12	London
S2	Jones	10	Paris	P4	Screw	Red	14	London
S2	Jones	10	Paris	P6	Cog	Red	19	London
S3	Blake	30	Paris	P1	Nut	Red	12	London
S3	Blake	30	Paris	P4	Screw	Red	14	London
S3	Blake	30	Paris	P6	Cog	Red	19	London

6.3.3 *Join Query with an Additional Condition.* Get all combinations of supplier information and part information where the supplier and part concerned are colocated, but omitting suppliers with status 20.

```
SELECT  S.*, P.*
FROM    S, P
WHERE   S.CITY = P.CITY
AND     S.STATUS ~= 20 ;
```

Result:

S#	SNAME	STATUS	S.CITY	P#	PNAME	COLOR	WEIGHT	P.CITY
S2	Jones	10	Paris	P2	Bolt	Green	17	Paris
S2	Jones	10	Paris	P5	Cam	Blue	12	Paris
S3	Blake	30	Paris	P2	Bolt	Green	17	Paris
S3	Blake	30	Paris	P5	Cam	Blue	12	Paris

6.3.4 *Retrieving Specified Fields from a Join.* Get all supplier-number / part-number combinations such that the supplier and part in question are colocated.

```
SELECT  S.S#, P.P#
FROM    S, P
WHERE   S.CITY = P.CITY ;
```

Result:

S#	P#
S1	P1
S1	P4
S1	P6
S2	P2
S2	P5
S3	P2
S3	P5
S4	P1
S4	P4
S4	P6

6.3.5 *Join of Three Tables.* Get all pairs of city names such that a supplier located in the first city supplies a part stored in the second city. For example, supplier S1 supplies part P1; supplier S1 is located in London, and part P1 is stored in London; so (London,London) is a pair of cities in the result.

```
SELECT  DISTINCT S.CITY, P.CITY
FROM    S, SP, P
WHERE   S.S# = SP.S#
AND     SP.P# = P.P# ;
```

Result:

S.CITY	P.CITY
London	London
London	Paris
London	Rome
Paris	London
Paris	Paris

As an exercise, the reader should decide which particular supplier/part combinations give rise to which particular result rows in this example.

6.3.6 *Joining a Table with Itself.* Get all pairs of supplier numbers such that the two suppliers concerned are colocated.

```
SELECT FIRST.S#, SECOND.S#
FROM    S FIRST, S SECOND
WHERE   FIRST.CITY = SECOND.CITY ;
```

This query involves a join of table S with itself (over matching cities), as we now explain. Suppose for a moment that we had two separate copies of table S, the "first" copy and the "second" copy. Then the logic of the query is as follows: We need to be able to examine all possible pairs of supplier rows, one from the first copy of S and one from the second, and to retrieve the two supplier numbers from such a pair of rows when the city values are equal. We therefore need to be able to reference two supplier rows at the same time. In order to distinguish between the two references, we introduce two *range variables* FIRST and SECOND, each of which "ranges over" table S. At any particular time, FIRST represents some row from the "first" copy of table S, and SECOND represents some row from the "second" copy.* The result of the query is found by examining all possible pairs of FIRST/SECOND values and checking the WHERE predicate in every case:

```
S#   S#
--   --
S1   S1
S1   S4
S2   S2
S2   S3
S3   S2
S3   S3
S4   S1
S4   S4
S5   S5
```

We can tidy up this result by extending the WHERE clause as follows:

```
SELECT FIRST.S#, SECOND.S#
FROM    S FIRST, S SECOND
WHERE   FIRST.CITY = SECOND.CITY
AND     FIRST.S# < SECOND.S# ;
```

---

*Of course, DB2 does not really construct two physical copies of the table. Our explanation is purely conceptual in nature. Note also that the IBM manuals use the term "correlation name" in place of the more orthodox (and more descriptive) term "range variable."

The effect of the condition FIRST.S# $<$ SECOND.S# is twofold: (a) It eliminates pairs of supplier numbers of the form (x,x); (b) it guarantees that the pairs (x,y) and (y,x) will not both appear. Result:

```
S#  S#
--  --
S1  S4
S2  S3
```

This is the first example we have seen in which the explicit use of range variables has been necessary. However, it is never wrong to introduce range variables, even when they are not explicitly required, and sometimes they can help to make the statement clearer. (They can also save writing, if table names are on the lengthy side.) In general, a range variable is a variable that ranges over some specified table—i.e., a variable whose only permitted values are the rows of that table. In other words, if range variable R ranges over table T, then, at any given time, R represents some row or record r of T. For example, the query "Get supplier number and status for suppliers in Paris" (the example from the beginning of Section 6.2) could be expressed as follows:

```
SELECT SX.S#, SX.STATUS
FROM   S SX
WHERE  SX.CITY = 'Paris' ;
```

The range variable here is SX, and it ranges over table S. The SELECT statement can be paraphrased:

"For each possible value of the range variable SX, retrieve the S# and STATUS components of that value, if and only if the CITY component has the value Paris."

As a matter of fact, SQL *always* requires queries to be formulated in terms of range variables. If no such variables are specified explicitly, then SQL assumes the existence of *implicit* variables with the same name(s) as the corresponding table(s). For example, the query

```
SELECT *
FROM   S ;
```

is treated by SQL as if it had been expressed as follows:

```
SELECT S.*
FROM   S S ;
```

This latter formulation arguably makes it a little clearer that the symbol "S" in the expression "S.*" really means *range variable* S, not *table* S.

6.4 SUMMARY

We have now come to the end of the first of our two chapters on the SELECT statement. We have illustrated:

- The SELECT clause itself, including the use of general scalar expressions and "SELECT *"
- The use of DISTINCT to eliminate duplicate rows, including the use of DISTINCT with a join
- The FROM clause (with one or more tables), including the use of range variables
- The use of ORDER BY to order the result
- The WHERE clause, including:
  - simple comparisons
  - Boolean operators AND, OR, NOT
  - special operators [NOT] BETWEEN, [NOT] IN, [NOT] LIKE
  - special comparison "field IS [NOT] NULL"
  - join predicates

In the next chapter we will consider some more complex features of the SELECT statement—to be specific, the subquery feature, the existential quantifier, the use of aggregate functions, and the UNION operator.

EXERCISES

All of the following exercises are based on the suppliers-parts-projects database (see the exercises in Chapter 5). In each one, you are asked to write a SELECT statement for the indicated query. For convenience we repeat the structure of the database below:

```
S     ( S#, SNAME, STATUS, CITY )
      PRIMARY KEY ( S# )
P     ( P#, PNAME, COLOR, WEIGHT, CITY )
      PRIMARY KEY ( P# )
J     ( J#, JNAME, CITY )
      PRIMARY KEY ( J# )
SPJ   ( S#, P#, J#, QTY )
      PRIMARY KEY ( S#, P#, J# )
```

Simple Queries

6.1 Get full details of all projects.

6.2 Get full details of all projects in London.

6.3 Get supplier numbers for suppliers who supply project J1, in supplier number order.

6.4 Get all shipments where the quantity is in the range 300 to 750 inclusive.

6.5 Get a list of all part-color/part-city combinations, with duplicate color/city pairs eliminated.

6.6 Get all shipments where the quantity is nonnull.

6.7 Get project numbers and cities where the city has an "o" as the second letter of its name.

Joins

6.8 Get all supplier-number/part-number/project-number triples such that the indicated supplier, part, and project are all colocated.

6.9 Get all supplier-number/part-number/project-number triples such that the indicated supplier, part, and project are not colocated.

6.10 Get all supplier-number/part-number/project-number triples such that no two of the indicated supplier, part, and project are located in the same city.

6.11 Get part numbers for parts supplied by a supplier in London.

6.12 Get part numbers for parts supplied by a supplier in London to a project in London.

6.13 Get all pairs of city names such that a supplier in the first city supplies a project in the second city.

6.14 Get part numbers for parts supplied to any project by a supplier in the same city as that project.

6.15 Get project numbers for projects supplied by at least one supplier not in the same city.

6.16 Get all pairs of part numbers such that some supplier supplies both the indicated parts.

ANSWERS TO SELECTED EXERCISES

The following answers are not necessarily the only ones possible.

```
6.1 SELECT J#, JNAME, CITY
    FROM   J ;

Or: SELECT *
    FROM   J ;

6.2 SELECT J#, JNAME, CITY
    FROM   J
    WHERE  CITY = 'London' ;

Or: SELECT *
    FROM   J
    WHERE  CITY = 'London' ;
```

6.3 `SELECT DISTINCT S#`
    `FROM    SPJ`
    `WHERE   J# = 'J1'`
    `ORDER   BY S# ;`

6.4 `SELECT S#, P#, J#, QTY`
    `FROM    SPJ`
    `WHERE   QTY >= 300`
    `AND     QTY <= 750 ;`

Or: `SELECT S#, P#, J#, QTY`
    `FROM    SPJ`
    `WHERE   QTY BETWEEN 300 AND 750 ;`

6.5 `SELECT DISTINCT COLOR, CITY`
    `FROM    P ;`

6.6 `SELECT S#, P#, J#, QTY`
    `FROM    SPJ`
    `WHERE   QTY IS NOT NULL ;`

The foregoing is the "official" answer. However, the following will also work:

    `SELECT S#, P#, J#, QTY`
    `FROM    SPJ`
    `WHERE   QTY = QTY ;`

6.7 `SELECT J#, CITY`
    `FROM    J`
    `WHERE   CITY LIKE '_o%' ;`

Or: `SELECT J#, CITY`
    `FROM    J`
    `WHERE   SUBSTR ( CITY, 2, 1 ) = 'o' ;`

6.8 `SELECT S#, P#, J#`
    `FROM    S, P, J`
    `WHERE   S.CITY = P.CITY`
    `AND     P.CITY = J.CITY ;`

6.9 `SELECT S#, P#, J#`
    `FROM    S, P, J`
    `WHERE   NOT`
    `        ( S.CITY = P.CITY AND P.CITY = J.CITY ) ;`

Or: `SELECT S#, P#, J#`
    `FROM    S, P, J`
    `WHERE   S.CITY ¬= P.CITY`
    `OR      P.CITY ¬= J.CITY ;`

6.10 `SELECT S#, P#, J#`
    `FROM    S, P, J`
    `WHERE   S.CITY ¬= P.CITY`
    `AND     P.CITY ¬= J.CITY`
    `AND     J.CITY ¬= S.CITY ;`

6.11 `SELECT DISTINCT P#`
    `FROM    SPJ, S`
    `WHERE   SPJ.S# = S.S#`
    `AND     CITY = 'London' ;`

```
6.12 SELECT  DISTINCT P#
     FROM    SPJ, S, J
     WHERE   SPJ.S# = S.S#
     AND     SPJ.J# = J.J#
     AND     S.CITY = 'London'
     AND     J.CITY = 'London' ;

6.13 SELECT  DISTINCT S.CITY, J.CITY
     FROM    S, SPJ, J
     WHERE   S.S# = SPJ.S#
     AND     SPJ.J# = J.J# ;

6.14 SELECT  DISTINCT P#
     FROM    SPJ, S, J
     WHERE   SPJ.S# = S.S#
     AND     SPJ.J# = J.J#
     AND     S.CITY = J.CITY ;

6.15 SELECT  DISTINCT J.J#
     FROM    SPJ, S, J
     WHERE   SPJ.S# = S.S#
     AND     SPJ.J# = J.J#
     AND     S.CITY ~= J.CITY ;

6.16 SELECT  SPJX.P#, SPJY.P#
     FROM    SPJ SPJX, SPJ SPJY
     WHERE   SPJX.S# = SPJY.S#
     AND     SPJX.P# > SPJY.P# ;
```

CHAPTER

◆ 7 ◆

Data Manipulation II:
Retrieval Operations
(continued)

7.1 INTRODUCTION

In this chapter we complete our treatment of the SQL SELECT statement. The plan of the chapter is as follows:

- Section 7.2 introduces the concept of *subqueries* or *nested SELECTs*. As a matter of historical interest, we remark that it was the fact that one SELECT could be nested inside another that was the original justification for the "Structured" in the name "Structured Query Language"; however, later additions to the language have made nested SELECTs per se very much less important than they used to be.

- Section 7.3 is concerned with the *existential quantifier* EXISTS, a feature that (in this writer's opinion) ranks with join as one of the most important and fundamental features of the entire SQL language—though not perhaps the most easy to use.

- Section 7.4 discusses the *aggregate functions* COUNT, SUM, AVG, etc.; in particular, it describes the use of the GROUP BY and HAVING

clauses in connexion with those functions. *Note:* The official DB2 term
for "aggregate function" is "column function."

- Section 7.5 discusses the UNION operator.

- Finally, in an attempt to tie together a number of the ideas introduced
  in this and the previous chapter, Section 7.6 presents an example of a
  very complex SELECT and shows in principle how that SELECT might
  be processed by DB2.

As you can see, the chapter is rather long, and you may wish to omit
some of the more complicated portions on a first reading. However, you
should read at least the first part of each section on your first pass through.
One of the reasons for the length of the chapter is that SQL is a very redundant language, in the sense that it frequently provides several different ways
of formulating the same query. Since we are trying to be reasonably comprehensive in our coverage of that language, the chapter necessarily contains a certain amount of redundancy also.

One final introductory remark (which may not be very intelligible until
you have read the body of the chapter): Despite our general objective of
comprehensiveness, we deliberately do not include any detailed description
of the ANY and ALL versions of the comparison operators ($>$ANY,
$=$ALL, etc.). The reader who requires such a detailed description is referred to the IBM manuals. Our reasons for excluding those operators from
this book are that they are entirely superfluous—there is no query that can
be formulated with them that cannot equally well (in fact, better) be formulated using EXISTS*—and furthermore they are confusing and (in this writer's opinion) dangerously error-prone. For example, the (valid) SELECT
statement

```
SELECT  S.S#
FROM    S
WHERE   S.CITY ~=ANY ( SELECT P.CITY
                       FROM    P      ) ;
```

does *not* select supplier numbers for suppliers whose city is "not equal to
any" part city. The corresponding EXISTS formulation makes the correct
interpretation clear:

```
SELECT  S.S#
FROM    S
WHERE   EXISTS ( SELECT P.CITY
                 FROM    P
                 WHERE   P.CITY ~= S.CITY ) ;
```

---

*At least, this statement is true provided the set returned by the subquery on the
right-hand side of the comparison does not contain any nulls; otherwise it is not
true. Unfortunately, the SQL EXISTS function does not handle such cases correctly.
See the footnote on page 103.

("select supplier numbers for suppliers such that there exists some part city that is different from the supplier city"). The natural intuitive interpretation of ~= ANY as "not equal to any" is both incorrect and very misleading. Analogous criticisms apply to all of the ANY and ALL operators.

Note: For reasons of compatibility with the SQL standard, DB2 allows SOME as an alternative spelling for ANY. Needless to say, however, the foregoing criticisms apply to the SOME versions of the operators also.

7.2 SUBQUERIES

In this section we discuss *subqueries* or *nested SELECTs*. Loosely speaking, a subquery is a SELECT–FROM–WHERE expression that is nested inside another such expression.* Subqueries are typically used to represent the set of values to be searched via an IN predicate, as the following example illustrates.

7.2.1 Simple Subquery. Get supplier names for suppliers who supply part P2.

```
SELECT  SNAME
FROM    S
WHERE   S# IN
      ( SELECT S#
        FROM    SP
        WHERE   P# = 'P2' ) ;
```

Result: SNAME

           Smith
           Jones
           Blake
           Clark

Explanation: The system evaluates the overall query (conceptually, at any rate) by evaluating the nested subquery first. That subquery returns the set of supplier *numbers* for suppliers who supply part P2, namely the set (S1,S2,S3,S4). The original query is thus equivalent to the following simpler query:

```
SELECT  SNAME
FROM    S
WHERE   S# IN
      ( 'S1', 'S2', 'S3', 'S4' ) ;
```

Hence the result is as shown earlier.

The implicit name qualification in this example merits some additional discussion. Observe in particular that the "S#" to the left of the IN is im-

---

*A subquery can also include GROUP BY and HAVING clauses. ORDER BY and UNION are illegal, however.

plicitly qualified by "S", whereas the "S#" in the subquery is implicitly qualified by "SP". The general rule is as follows: An unqualified field name is assumed to be qualified by a table name (or range variable name—see Examples 7.2.3–7.2.5 below) that appears in the (unique) FROM clause that is most immediately part of the same query or subquery. In the case of the S# to the left of the IN, that clause is "FROM S"; in the case of the S# in the subquery, it is the clause "FROM SP". By way of clarification, we repeat the original query with all assumed qualifications shown explicitly:

```
SELECT  S.SNAME
FROM    S
WHERE   S.S# IN
     ( SELECT SP.S#
       FROM    SP
       WHERE   SP.P# = 'P2' ) ;
```

It is always possible to override the implicit assumptions with explicit qualifications (see Examples 7.2.3–7.2.5 below). In fact, many people feel that explicit qualification should *always* be used, even when it is strictly unnecessary, simply as a matter of good discipline. A good rule of thumb is: When in doubt, qualify.

There is one more (important) point to make before we move on to our next subquery example: The original problem—"Get supplier names for suppliers who supply part P2"—can equally well be expressed as a *join* query, as follows:

```
SELECT  S.SNAME
FROM    S, SP
WHERE   S.S# = SP.S#
AND     SP.P# = 'P2' ;
```

Explanation: The join of S and SP over supplier numbers consists of a table of 12 rows (one for each row in SP), in which each row consists of the corresponding row from SP extended with SNAME, STATUS, and CITY values for the supplier identified by the S# value in that row. Of these twelve rows, four are for part P2; the final result is thus obtained by extracting the SNAME values from those four rows.

The two formulations of the original query—one using a subquery, one using a join—are equally correct. It is purely a matter of taste as to which formulation a given user might prefer. At least, this statement is true in principle; unfortunately, there is no guarantee that the two formulations will *perform* equally well. In fact, the IBM manuals seem to indicate that the subquery formulation will never perform better than the join formulation and may very well perform worse, and hence that subqueries should generally be avoided. This fact is somewhat ironic, given that subqueries were the principal justification for the SQL language in the first place.

7.2.2 Subquery with Multiple Levels of Nesting. Get supplier names for suppliers who supply at least one red part.

```
SELECT  SNAME
FROM    S
WHERE   S# IN
      ( SELECT  S#
        FROM    SP
        WHERE   P# IN
              ( SELECT  P#
                FROM    P
                WHERE   COLOR = 'Red' ) ) ;
```

Result:
```
SNAME
-----
Smith
Jones
Clark
```

Explanation: The innermost subquery evaluates to the set (P1,P4,P6). The next outermost subquery evaluates in turn to the set (S1,S2,S4). Last, the outermost SELECT evaluates to the final result shown. In general, subqueries can be nested to any depth.

To make sure you understand this example, try the following exercises:

(a) Rewrite the query with all name qualifications shown explicitly.

(b) Write an equivalent join formulation of the same query.

7.2.3 Correlated Subquery. Get supplier names for suppliers who supply part P2 (same as Example 7.2.1).

We show another solution to this problem in order to illustrate another point.

```
SELECT  SNAME
FROM    S
WHERE   'P2' IN
      ( SELECT  P#
        FROM    SP
        WHERE   S# = S.S# ) ;
```

Explanation: In the last line here, the unqualified reference to S# is implicitly qualified by SP; the other reference is *explicitly* qualified by S. This example differs from the preceding ones in that the inner subquery cannot be evaluated once and for all before the outer query is evaluated, because that inner subquery depends on a *variable,* namely S.S#, whose value changes as the system examines different rows of table S. Conceptually, therefore, evaluation proceeds as follows:

(a) The system examines some row of table S; let us suppose this is the row for S1. The variable S.S# thus currently has the value S1, so the system evaluates the inner subquery

```
( SELECT  P#
  FROM    SP
  WHERE   S# = 'S1' )
```

to obtain the set (P1,P2,P3,P4,P5,P6). Now it can complete its processing for S1; it will select the SNAME value for S1, namely Smith, if and only if P2 is in this set (which of course it is).

(b) Next the system moves on to repeat this kind of processing for another row of table S, and so on, until all such rows have been dealt with.

A subquery such as the one in this example is said to be a *correlated* subquery. A correlated subquery is one whose value depends upon some variable that receives its value in some outer query; such a subquery therefore has to be evaluated repeatedly (once for each value of the variable in question), instead of once and for all. We show another example of a correlated subquery below (Example 7.2.5); several further examples are given in Sections 7.3 and 7.4.

Some people like to use explicit range variables in conjunction with correlated subqueries, in order to make the correlation clearer (see Example 6.3.6 in Chapter 6 if you need to refresh your memory concerning range variables). For example:

```
SELECT  SX.SNAME
FROM    S SX
WHERE   'P2' IN
      ( SELECT  P#
        FROM    SP
        WHERE   S# = SX.S# ) ;
```

The range variable in this example is SX, introduced in the FROM clause and then used as an explicit qualifier in the WHERE clause in the subquery (and in the outer SELECT clause). The operation of the overall statement can now be more clearly (and more accurately) explained as follows:

- SX is a variable that ranges over the records of table S (i.e., a variable that, at any given time, represents some record of table S).

- For each possible value of SX in turn, do the following:
  - evaluate the subquery to obtain a set, *p* say, of part numbers;
  - add the current value of SX.SNAME to the result set, if and only if P2 is in the set *p*.

In the previous version of this query, the symbol "S" was really performing two different functions: It stood for the suppliers base table itself (of course), and also for a variable that ranged over the records of that base table. As already stated, many people find it clearer to use two different symbols to distinguish between the two different functions.

It is never wrong to introduce a range variable, and sometimes it is essential (see Example 7.2.5 below).

7.2.4 Subquery and Outer Query Referring to Same Table. Get supplier numbers for suppliers who supply at least one part supplied by supplier S2.

```
SELECT DISTINCT S#
FROM    SP
WHERE   P# IN
      ( SELECT P#
        FROM    SP
        WHERE   S# = 'S2' ) ;
```

Result:
```
S#
--
S1
S2
S3
S4
```

Notice here that references to SP in the subquery do not mean the same thing as references to SP in the outer query. The two SP's are really *different variables*. Explicit range variables can be used to make this fact explicit:

```
SELECT DISTINCT SPX.S#
FROM    SP SPX
WHERE   SPX.P# IN
      ( SELECT SPY.P#
        FROM    SP SPY
        WHERE   SPY.S# = 'S2' ) ;
```

Equivalent join query:

```
SELECT DISTINCT SPX.S#
FROM    SP SPX, SP SPY
WHERE   SPX.P# = SPY.P#
AND     SPY.S# = 'S2' ;
```

Notice that at least one explicit range variable *must* be introduced in this latter formulation (why?).

7.2.5 Correlated Subquery and Outer Query Referring to Same Table. Get part numbers for all parts supplied by more than one supplier. (Another solution to this problem is given later as Example 7.4.9.)

```
SELECT DISTINCT SPX.P#
FROM    SP SPX
WHERE   SPX.P# IN
      ( SELECT SPY.P#
        FROM    SP SPY
        WHERE   SPY.S# ~= SPX.S# ) ;
```

Result:
```
P#
--
P1
P2
P4
P5
```

The operation of this query can be explained as follows: "For each row in turn, say SPX, of table SP, extract the P# value, if and only if that P# value appears in some row, say SPY, of table SP whose S# value is *not* equal to the S# value in row SPX." Note again that at least one explicit range variable *must* be used in this query.

7.2.6   Subquery with Comparison Operator Other Than IN.   Get supplier numbers for suppliers who are located in the same city as supplier S1.

```
SELECT  S#
FROM    S
WHERE   CITY =
        ( SELECT  CITY
          FROM    S
          WHERE   S# = 'S1' ) ;
```

Result: S#
            --
            S1
            S4

Sometimes the user may know that a given subquery should return exactly one value, as in this example. In such a case a simple scalar comparison operator (such as =, >, etc.) can be used in place of the more usual IN. However, an error will occur if the subquery in fact returns more than one value and IN has not been used. An error will *not* occur if the subquery returns no values at all; instead, the comparison is treated exactly as if the subquery had returned a null. In other words, if x is a scalar variable, then the comparison

```
x  simple-comparison-operator ( subquery )
```

(where "subquery" returns an empty set) evaluates, not to *true* or *false,* but to the *unknown* truth value. See Chapter 6, Example 6.2.10, and Chapter 4 for more discussion of the unknown truth value.

Note, incidentally, that the comparison in the foregoing example must be written as shown, with the subquery following the comparison operator. In other words, the following is *** ILLEGAL ***:

```
SELECT  S#
FROM    S
WHERE  (SELECT  CITY
        FROM    S
        WHERE   S# = 'S1') = CITY ;
```

Note also that, although subqueries in general can include GROUP BY and HAVING clauses (see Section 7.4), those clauses are not permitted when the subquery appears in conjunction with a simple scalar comparison operator such as =, >, etc.

7.3   THE EXISTENTIAL QUANTIFIER

7.3.1   Query Using EXISTS.   Get supplier names for suppliers who supply part P2 (same as Examples 7.2.1 and 7.2.3).

```
SELECT  SNAME
FROM    S
WHERE   EXISTS
      ( SELECT *
        FROM    SP
        WHERE   S# = S.S#
        AND     P# = 'P2' ) ;
```

Explanation: EXISTS here represents the *existential quantifier,* a notion borrowed from formal logic. Let the symbol "*x*" designate some arbitrary variable. In logic, then, the *existentially quantified predicate*

```
EXISTS x ( predicate-involving-x )
```

evaluates to *true* if and only if "predicate-involving-*x*" is *true* for some value of the variable *x*. For example, suppose the variable *x* stands for any integer in the range 1 to 10 (i.e., *x* ranges over the set of integers from 1 to 10). Then the predicate

```
EXISTS x ( x < 5 )
```

evaluates to *true*. By contrast, the predicate

```
EXISTS x ( x < 0 )
```

evaluates to *false*.

In SQL, an existentially quantified predicate is represented by an expression of the form "EXISTS (SELECT * FROM ...)". Such an expression evaluates to *true* if and only if the result of evaluating the subquery represented by the "SELECT * FROM ..." is not empty*—in other words, if and only if there exists a record in the FROM table of the subquery satisfying the WHERE condition of that subquery. (In practice, that subquery will almost certainly be of the correlated variety.)

To see how this works out in the example at hand, consider each SNAME value in turn and see whether it causes the existence test to evaluate to *true*. Suppose the first SNAME value is Smith, so that the corresponding S# value is S1. Is the set of SP records having S# equal to S1 and P# equal

---

*It evaluates to *false* otherwise; i.e., EXISTS in DB2 never returns the *unknown* truth value. As a consequence, it is possible to derive contradictory results from a DB2 database! The details are beyond the scope of this book.

to P2 empty? If the answer is no, then there exists an SP record with S# equal to S1 and P# equal to P2, and so Smith should be one of the values retrieved. Similarly for each of the other SNAME values.

Although this first example merely shows another way of formulating a query for a problem that we already know how to handle in SQL (using either join or IN), in general EXISTS is one of the most important features of the entire SQL language. In fact, any query that can be expressed using IN can alternatively be formulated using EXISTS; however, the converse is not true (see Example 7.3.3 below for an illustration).

7.3.2   *Query Using NOT EXISTS.*   Get supplier names for suppliers who do not supply part P2 (inverse of Example 7.3.1).

```
SELECT SNAME
FROM   S
WHERE  NOT EXISTS
     ( SELECT *
       FROM    SP
       WHERE   S# = S.S#
       AND     P# = 'P2' ) ;
```

Result:
```
SNAME
-----
Adams
```

The query may be paraphrased: "Select supplier names for suppliers such that there does not exist a shipment relating them to part P2." Notice how easy it is to convert the solution to the previous problem (Example 7.3.1) into this solution.

Incidentally, the parenthesized subquery in an EXISTS expression does not necessarily have to involve the "SELECT *" form of SELECT; it may, for example, be of the form "SELECT field ...". In practice, however, it almost always will be of the "SELECT *" form, as our examples have already suggested.

7.3.3   *Query Using NOT EXISTS.*   Get supplier names for suppliers who supply all parts.

There are two quantifiers commonly encountered in logic, EXISTS and *FORALL*. FORALL is the *universal* quantifier. In logic, the *universally quantified predicate*

```
FORALL x ( predicate-involving-x )
```

evaluates to *true* if and only if "predicate-involving-x" *is true* for all values of the variable x. For example, if (again) the variable x stands for any integer in the range 1 to 10, then the predicate

```
FORALL x ( x < 100 )
```

evaluates to *true,* whereas the predicate

```
FORALL x ( x < 5 )
```

evaluates to *false.*

FORALL is fundamentally what is needed to express the query at hand; what we would like to say is something like "Select supplier names where, FORALL parts, there EXISTS an SP record saying that the supplier supplies the part." Unfortunately, SQL does not directly support FORALL. However, any predicate involving FORALL can always be converted into an equivalent predicate involving EXISTS instead, by virtue of the following identity:

```
FORALL x ( p ) ≡ NOT ( EXISTS x ( NOT ( p ) ) )
```

Here p is any predicate involving the variable x. For example, suppose once again that x stands for any integer in the range 1 to 10. Then the predicate

```
FORALL x ( x < 100 )
```

(which of course evaluates to *true*) is equivalent to the predicate

```
NOT ( EXISTS x ( NOT ( x < 100 ) ) )
```

("there does not exist an x such that it is not the case that x is less than 100"—i.e., "there is no x such that x is greater than or equal to 100"). Likewise, the predicate

```
FORALL x ( x < 5 )
```

(which is *false*) is equivalent to the predicate

```
NOT ( EXISTS x ( NOT ( x < 5 ) ) )
```

("there does not exist an x such that it is not the case that x is less than 5"—i.e., "there is no x such that x is greater than or equal to 5").

As another example, suppose the variables x and y represent real numbers. Then the predicate

```
FORALL x ( EXISTS y ( y > x ) )
```

(which is *true*) is equivalent to

```
NOT ( EXISTS x ( NOT ( EXISTS y ( y > x ) ) ) )
```

("there is no real number x such that there is no real number y such that y is greater than x").*

Turning now to the problem at hand, we can convert the expression "Supplier names where, FORALL parts, there EXISTS an SP record saying that the supplier supplies the part" into the equivalent expression "Supplier names where NOT EXISTS a part such that NOT EXISTS an SP record saying that the supplier supplies the part." Hence the SQL formulation is:

```
SELECT SNAME
FROM   S
WHERE  NOT EXISTS
     ( SELECT *
       FROM   P
       WHERE  NOT EXISTS
            ( SELECT *
              FROM   SP
              WHERE  S# = S.S#
              AND    P# = P.P# ) ) ;
```

Result: SNAME

          Smith

The query may be paraphrased: "Select supplier names for suppliers such that there does not exist a part that they do not supply." In general, the easiest way to tackle complicated queries such as this one is probably to write them in a "pseudoSQL" form with FORALL quantifiers first, and then convert them, more or less mechanically, into real SQL involving NOT EXISTS instead.

7.3.4   Query Using NOT EXISTS.
Get supplier names for suppliers who supply at least all those parts supplied by supplier S2.

One way to tackle this rather complex problem is to break it down into a set of simpler problems and deal with them one at a time. Thus we can first discover the set of part numbers for parts supplied by supplier S2:

```
SELECT P#
FROM   SP
WHERE  S# = 'S2' ;
```

Result: P#
          --
          P1
          P2

---

*Incidentally, this example illustrates the important point that if the predicate involves both FORALL and EXISTS, then the order of quantifiers matters. The expression FORALL x (EXISTS y ($y > x$)) is *true*. However, the expression EXISTS y (FORALL x ($y > x$)) ("there is a real number y such that, for all real numbers x, y is greater than x"—i.e., "there exists a number greater than all other numbers"), which is obtained from the first expression by simply inverting the order of the quantifiers, is *false*.

Using CREATE TABLE and INSERT (to be discussed in Chapter 8), it is possible to save this result in a table in the database, say table TEMP. Then we can go on to discover the set of supplier names for suppliers who supply all parts listed in TEMP (very much as in Example 7.3.3):

```
SELECT SNAME
FROM    S
WHERE   NOT EXISTS
      ( SELECT *
        FROM    TEMP
        WHERE   NOT EXISTS
              ( SELECT *
                FROM    SP
                WHERE   SP.S# = S.S#
                AND     SP.P# = TEMP.P# ) ) ;
```

Result:
```
S#
--
S1
S2
```

Table TEMP can now be dropped.

It is often a good idea to handle complex queries in this step-at-a-time manner, for ease of understanding. However, it is also possible to express the entire query as a single SELECT, eliminating the need for TEMP entirely:

```
SELECT SNAME
FROM    S
WHERE   NOT EXISTS
      ( SELECT *
        FROM    SP SPY
        WHERE   S# = 'S2'
        AND     NOT EXISTS
              ( SELECT *
                FROM    SP SPZ
                WHERE   SPZ.S# = S.S#
                AND     SPZ.P# = SPY.P# ) ) ;
```

7.3.5 Query Using Implication.   Get supplier names for suppliers who supply at least all those parts supplied by supplier S2 (same as previous example).

We use this example again to illustrate another very useful concept, that of *logical implication*. The original problem can be rephrased as follows: "Get supplier names for suppliers Sx (say) such that, FORALL parts Py, *IF* supplier S2 supplies part Py, *THEN* supplier Sx supplies part Py also." The expression

```
IF p THEN q
```

(where p and q are predicates) is a *logical implication predicate.* It is defined to be equivalent to the predicate

```
NOT ( p )  OR  q
```

In other words, the implication "IF *p* THEN *q*" (also read as "*p* IMPLIES *q*") is *false* if and only if *q* is *false* and *p* is *true,* and the truth table below indicates:

```
 p  |  q  |  IF p THEN q
----+-----+--------------
 T  |  T  |      T
 T  |  F  |      F
 F  |  T  |      T
 F  |  F  |      T
```

Note: The value of "IF *p* THEN *q*" if *p* or *q* is *unknown* is left as an exercise for the reader.

Many problems are very naturally expressed in English in terms of logical implication (see the exercises at the end of this chapter for several examples). SQL does not support implication directly, but the foregoing definition shows how any predicate involving implication can easily be converted into another that does not. For example, let *p* be the predicate "Supplier S2 supplies part P*y*," and let *q* be the predicate "Supplier S*x* supplies part P*y*." Then the predicate

```
IF p THEN q
```

is equivalent to the predicate

```
NOT ( supplier S2 supplies part Py )
OR  ( supplier Sx supplies part Py )
```

or, in SQL terms,

```
NOT EXISTS
  ( SELECT *
    FROM    SP SPY
    WHERE   SPY.S# = 'S2' )
OR  EXISTS
  ( SELECT *
    FROM    SP SPZ
    WHERE   SPZ.S# = Sx
    AND     SPZ.P# = SPY.P# )
```

Hence the predicate

```
FORALL Py ( IF p THEN q )    ,
```

which is equivalent to

```
NOT EXISTS Py ( NOT ( IF p THEN q ) )    ,
```

that is, to

```
NOT EXISTS Py ( NOT ( NOT ( p )  OR  q ) )    ,
```

becomes

```
NOT EXISTS Py ( p  AND  NOT  ( q ) )    ,
```

or, in SQL terms,

```
NOT EXISTS
  ( SELECT *
    FROM    SP SPY
    WHERE   SPY.S# = 'S2'
    AND     NOT EXISTS
          ( SELECT *
            FROM    SP SPZ
            WHERE   SPZ.S# = Sx
            AND     SPZ.P# = SPY.P# ) )
```

Hence the overall query becomes

```
SELECT SNAME
FROM    S
WHERE   NOT EXISTS
      ( SELECT *
        FROM    SP SPY
        WHERE   SPY.S# = 'S2'
        AND     NOT EXISTS
              ( SELECT *
                FROM    SP SPZ
                WHERE   SPZ.S# = S.S#
                AND     SPZ.P# = SPY.P# ) ) ;
```

which is as shown before, under Example 7.3.4. Thus the notion of implication provides the basis for a systematic approach to a certain class of (rather complicated) queries and their conversion into an equivalent SQL form. Exercises 7.12–7.18 at the end of the chapter provide practice in that approach.

7.4 AGGREGATE FUNCTIONS

Although quite powerful in many ways, the SELECT statement as so far described is still inadequate for many practical problems. For example, even a query as simple as "How many suppliers are there?" cannot be expressed using only the constructs introduced up till now. SQL therefore provides a number of special *aggregate* (or *column*) *functions* to enhance its basic retrieval power. The aggregate functions currently available are COUNT, SUM, AVG, MAX, and MIN.* Apart from the special case of

---

*EXISTS is also considered as an aggregate function, but it differs from the functions discussed in the present section in that it returns a truth value (*true* or *false*), not a value of one of the recognized DB2 data types—i.e., it is not a *computational* function (so far as SQL is concerned). EXISTS also differs from the other aggregate functions in that it uses a different syntactic style (actually a more logical style).

"COUNT(*)" (see below), each of these functions operates on the collection of scalar values in one column of some table—possibly (in fact, probably) a *derived* table, i.e., a table constructed in some way from the given base tables—and produces a single scalar value, defined as follows, as its result:

COUNT — number of values in the column

SUM — sum of the values in the column

AVG — average of the values in the column

MAX — largest value in the column

MIN — smallest value in the column

For SUM and AVG, the argument must be numeric. In general, the argument may optionally be preceded by the keyword DISTINCT, to indicate that redundant duplicate values are to be eliminated before the function is applied (the alternative to DISTINCT is ALL; ALL is assumed if neither DISTINCT nor ALL is specified explicitly). For MAX and MIN, however, DISTINCT is irrelevant and should be omitted.

Aggregate functions are unfortunately subject to numerous rules and restrictions, most of them apparently arbitrary:

1. For COUNT, DISTINCT *must* be specified; the special function COUNT(*)—DISTINCT not allowed—is provided to count all rows in a table without any duplicate elimination.

2. If DISTINCT is specified, the argument must be specified as a simple column name such as WEIGHT; if DISTINCT is not specified, the argument may consist of a general scalar expression such as WEIGHT * 454. In the latter case, that expression cannot in turn involve any aggregate functions.

3. If and only if DISTINCT is not specified, the function reference can itself be an operand in a scalar expression; e.g., AVG (WEIGHT) * 2 is legal, but AVG (DISTINCT WEIGHT) * 2 is not.

4. Within any given query or subquery, DISTINCT can appear at most once at a given level of nesting (i.e., excluding any subqueries that may appear nested within the given query or subquery). For example, the following is *** ILLEGAL ***:

```
SELECT SUM ( DISTINCT QTY ), AVG ( DISTINCT QTY )
FROM    SP
   .....  ;
```

and so is this:

```
SELECT DISTINCT ...
FROM    ...
GROUP   BY ...
HAVING SUM ( DISTINCT ... ) ... ;
```

However, the following is legal:

```
SELECT DISTINCT ...
FROM    ...
WHERE   ... IN
        ( SELECT DISTINCT ...
          .....   ) ;
```

5. Any nulls in the argument column are always eliminated before the function is applied, regardless of whether DISTINCT is specified, *except* for the case of COUNT(*), where nulls are handled just like nonnull values. *Note:* The scalar function VALUE (see Section 4.6) can be used to convert nulls into nonnull values, if desired, before the aggregate function is applied.

6. If the argument happens to be an empty set, COUNT returns a value of zero; the other functions all return null. Again, the VALUE function can be used to convert such a null into some nonnull value.

Now for some specific examples of the use of aggregate functions.

7.4.1 Aggregate Function in the SELECT Clause.   Get the total number of suppliers.

```
SELECT COUNT(*)
FROM    S ;
```

Result: -
            5

Note that the result is still a table, but a table with just one column and one row.

7.4.2 Aggregate Function in the SELECT Clause, with DISTINCT.   Get the total number of suppliers currently supplying parts.

```
SELECT COUNT (DISTINCT S#)
FROM    SP ;
```

Result: -
            4

7.4.3 Aggregate Function in the SELECT Clause, with a Predicate.   Get the number of shipments for part P2.

```
SELECT COUNT(*)
FROM   SP
WHERE  P# = 'P2' ;
```

Result: -
             4

7.4.4 *Aggregate Function in the SELECT Clause, with a Predicate.* Get the total quantity of part P2 supplied.

```
SELECT SUM (QTY)
FROM   SP
WHERE  P# = 'P2' ;
```

Result: ----
             1000

Note: Unless the query includes a GROUP BY or HAVING clause (at the same level of nesting), a SELECT clause that includes any aggregate function references must consist *entirely* of such references. Thus, for example, the following is *** ILLEGAL ***:

```
SELECT P#, SUM (QTY)
FROM   SP
WHERE  P# = 'P2' ;
```

See Examples 7.4.7–7.4.9 below for an explanation of the GROUP BY and HAVING clauses.

7.4.5 *Aggregate Function in a Subquery.* Get supplier numbers for suppliers with status value less than the current maximum status value in the S table.

```
SELECT S#
FROM   S
WHERE  STATUS <
     ( SELECT MAX (STATUS)
       FROM   S ) ;
```

Result: S#
             --
             S1
             S2
             S4

7.4.6 *Aggregate Function in Correlated Subquery.* Get supplier number, status, and city for all suppliers whose status is greater than or equal to the average for their particular city.

```
SELECT S#, STATUS, CITY
FROM   S SX
WHERE  STATUS >=
     ( SELECT AVG (STATUS)
       FROM   S SY
       WHERE  SY.CITY = SX.CITY ) ;
```

```
Result:    S#   STATUS   CITY
           --   ------   ------
           S1      20    London
           S3      30    Paris
           S4      20    London
           S5      30    Athens
```

It is not possible to include the average status for each city in this result (why not?).

7.4.7 Use of GROUP BY.   Example 7.4.6 showed how it is possible to compute the total quantity supplied for some specific part. Suppose, by contrast, that it is desired to compute the total quantity supplied for *each* part: i.e., for each part supplied, get the part number and the total shipment quantity for that part.

```
       SELECT  P#, SUM (QTY)
       FROM    SP
       GROUP   BY P# ;
```

```
Result:    P#
           --   ----
           P1    600
           P2   1000
           P3    400
           P4    500
           P5    500
           P6    100
```

Explanation: The GROUP BY operator causes the table represented by the FROM clause to be rearranged into partitions or *groups,* such that within any one group all rows have the same value for the GROUP BY field.* In the example, table SP is grouped so that one group contains all the rows for part P1, another contains all the rows for part P2, and so on. The SELECT clause is then applied to each group of the partitioned table (rather than to each row of the original table). Each expression in the SELECT clause must be *single-valued per group;* e.g., it can be (one of) the field(s) named in the GROUP BY clause, or a constant, or an aggregate function such as SUM that operates on all values of a given field within a group and reduces those values to a single value.

Note that GROUP BY does not imply ORDER BY; to guarantee that the result in the foregoing example appears in P# order, the clause ORDER BY P# must be specified as well (after the GROUP BY clause).

A table can be grouped by any combination of its fields. See Section 7.6 for an illustration of grouping over more than one field.

---

*Of course, this does not mean that the table is physically rearranged in the database. Our explanation is purely conceptual in nature.

7.4.8 Use of WHERE with GROUP BY. For each part supplied, get the part number and the total and maximum quantity supplied of that part, excluding shipments from supplier S1.

```
SELECT  P#, SUM (QTY), MAX (QTY)
FROM    SP
WHERE   S# ~= 'S1'
GROUP   BY P# ;
```

Result:
```
        P#
        --  ---  ---
        P1  300  300
        P2  800  400
        P4  300  300
        P5  400  400
```

Rows that do not satisfy the WHERE clause are eliminated before any grouping is done.

7.4.9 Use of HAVING. Get part numbers for all parts supplied by more than one supplier (same as Example 7.2.5).

```
SELECT  P#
FROM    SP
GROUP   BY P#
HAVING  COUNT(*) > 1 ;
```

Result:
```
        P#
        --
        P1
        P2
        P4
        P5
```

HAVING is to groups what WHERE is to rows; thus, if HAVING is specified, GROUP BY should have been specified also.* In other words, HAVING is used to eliminate groups just as WHERE is used to eliminate rows. Expressions in a HAVING clause must be single-valued per group.

We have already shown (in Example 7.2.5) that this query can be formulated without GROUP BY (and without HAVING), using a correlated subquery. However, the formulation of Example 7.2.5 is really based on a somewhat different perception of the logic involved in answering the question. It is also possible to formulate a query using essentially the *same* logic as in the GROUP-BY/HAVING version, but without making explicit use of GROUP BY and HAVING at all:

```
SELECT  DISTINCT P#
FROM    SP SPX
WHERE   1 <
        ( SELECT  COUNT(*)
          FROM    SP SPY
          WHERE   SPY.P# = SPX.P# ) ;
```

---

*Actually it is possible—though very unusual—to omit the GROUP BY, in which case the entire table is treated as a single group.

The following version (using table P in place of SPX) may perhaps be clearer:

```
SELECT  P#
FROM    P
WHERE   1 <
        ( SELECT  COUNT (S#)
          FROM    SP
          WHERE   P# = P.P# ) ;
```

Yet another formulation uses EXISTS, as follows:

```
SELECT  P#
FROM    P
WHERE   EXISTS
        ( SELECT  *
          FROM    SP SPX
          WHERE   SPX.P# = P.P#
          AND     EXISTS
                  ( SELECT  *
                    FROM    SP SPY
                    WHERE   SPY.P# = P.P#
                    AND     SPY.S# ~= SPX.S# ) ) ;
```

All of these alternative versions are in some respects preferable to the GROUP-BY/HAVING version, in that they are at least logically cleaner, and they specifically do not require those additional language constructs. It is certainly not clear from the original statement of the problem—"Get part numbers for all parts supplied by more than one supplier"—that grouping per se is what is needed to answer the question (and indeed it is not needed). Nor is it immediately obvious that a HAVING condition is required rather than a WHERE condition. The GROUP-BY/HAVING version begins to look more like a procedural prescription for *solving* the problem, instead of just a straightforward logical statement of what the problem *is*. On the other hand, there is no denying that the GROUP-BY/HAVING version is the most succinct. Then again, there are some problems of this same general nature for which GROUP BY and HAVING are simply not adequate, so that one of the alternative approaches *must* be used; see Exercise 7.24 for an example of such a problem. And note too that GROUP BY suffers from the severe restriction that it works only to one level; it is not possible to break a table into groups, then to break each of those groups into lower-level groups, and so on, and then to apply some aggregate function, say SUM or AVG, at each level of grouping.*

7.5 UNION

The union of two sets is the set of all elements belonging to either or both of the original sets. Since a relation is a set (a set of rows), it is possible to

---

*This effect ("groups within groups," etc.) can be achieved through various front-end subsystems such as QMF, however. See Part III of this book.

construct the union of two relations; the result will be a set consisting of all rows appearing in either or both of the original relations. However, if that result is itself to be another relation and not just a heterogeneous mixture of rows, the two original relations must be *union-compatible;* that is, the rows in the two relations must be "the same shape" (loosely speaking). In DB2 terms, two tables are union-compatible, and the UNION operator can be applied to them, if and only if:

(a) They have the same number of columns, m say;

(b) For all i $(i = 1,2,...,m)$, the ith column of the first table and the ith column of the second table are compatible in the sense of Section 4.5.

Here is an example.

7.5.1   Query Involving UNION.   Get part numbers for parts that either weigh more than 16 pounds or are supplied by supplier S2 (or both).

```
SELECT  P#
FROM    P
WHERE   WEIGHT > 16

UNION

SELECT  P#
FROM    SP
WHERE   S# = 'S2' ;
```

Result: --
           P1
           P2
           P3
           P6

Several points arise from this simple example.

- Redundant duplicates are always eliminated from the result of a UNION unless the UNION operator explicitly includes the ALL qualifier (see below). Thus, in the example, part P2 is selected by both of the two constituent SELECTs, but it appears only once in the final result. By contrast, the statement

```
SELECT  P#
FROM    P
WHERE   WEIGHT > 16

UNION   ALL

SELECT  P#
FROM    SP
WHERE   S# = 'S2' ;
```

will return part numbers P1, P2, P2 (again), P3, and P6.

- The primary reason for including UNION ALL in the language is that there are many situations in which a union is required and the user *knows* that there will not be any duplicates in the result. In such a case, any attempt by the system to eliminate duplicates will simply impose an undesirable (and unnecessary) performance penalty. Examples illustrating this point appear below.*

- Any number of SELECTs can be UNIONed together. We might extend the original example (version with ALL omitted) to include part numbers for red parts by inserting

```
UNION

SELECT  P#
FROM    P
WHERE   COLOR = 'Red'
```

before the final semicolon. *Note:* The same effect could also be achieved by adding the clause

```
OR      COLOR = 'Red'
```

to the first of the original SELECTs.

- Parentheses can be used if desired to force a particular order of evaluation if multiple UNIONs are involved. Note that, for example, the expressions x UNION ALL (y UNION z) and (x UNION ALL y) UNION z are not equivalent (in general). Parentheses are unnecessary, however, if either all of the UNIONs specify ALL or none of them does.

- Any ORDER BY clause in the query must appear as part of the final SELECT only, and must identify ordering columns by their ordinal position (i.e., by number), not by name.

- The ability to include constants in a SELECT clause is frequently useful in connexion with UNION. For example, to indicate which of the two WHERE conditions each individual part in the result happens to satisfy:

```
SELECT  P#, 'weight > 16 lb'
FROM    P
WHERE   WEIGHT > 16

UNION   ALL
```

---

*Note that with UNION (in contrast to the SELECT clause and the aggregate functions) there is no explicit DISTINCT option as an alternative to ALL. Note too that if there were such an alternative the default would have to be DISTINCT, not ALL, for compatibility with earlier DB2 releases.

```
SELECT  P#, 'supplied by S2'
FROM    SP
WHERE   S# = 'S2'

ORDER   BY 2, 1 ;
```

Result: --   ---------------
             P1   supplied by S2
             P2   supplied by S2
             P2   weight > 16 lb
             P3   weight > 16 lb
             P6   weight > 16 lb

We have specified UNION ALL in this version of the problem because it is obvious now that there will be no duplicates to eliminate. (Of course, it would be nice if the optimizer could deduce this fact for itself.)

- The reader may be wondering whether DB2 also supports any analogs of the INTERSECTION and DIFFERENCE operators (since union, intersection, and difference are commonly treated together in discussions of set theory). The intersection of two sets is the set of all elements belonging to both of the original sets; the difference of two sets is the set of all elements belonging to the first of the original sets and not to the second. DB2 does not support these two operators directly, but each of them can be simulated by means of the EXISTS function. For details, the reader is referred to Appendix B.

One important use for UNION (more precisely, UNION ALL) is in the construction of what is called an *outer join*. As explained in Chapter 6, the ordinary (natural) join of two tables does not include a result row for any row in either of the two original tables that has no matching row in the other. For example, the ordinary join of tables S and P over cities does not include any result row for supplier S5 or for part P3, because no parts are stored in Athens and no suppliers are located in Rome (see Example 6.3.1). In a sense, therefore (a very imprecise sense, we hasten to add), the ordinary join may be considered to *lose information* for such unmatched rows. Sometimes, however, it may be desirable to be able to preserve that information. Consider the following example.

7.5.2   Using UNION ALL to Construct an Outer Join.   For each supplier, get the supplier number, name, status, and city, together with part numbers for all parts supplied by that supplier. If a given supplier supplies no parts at all, then show the information for that supplier in the result concatenated with a blank part number.

```
SELECT  S.*, SP.P#
FROM    S, SP
WHERE   S.S# = SP.S#
```

```
UNION  ALL

SELECT S.*, 'bb'
FROM   S
WHERE  NOT EXISTS
     ( SELECT *
       FROM   SP
       WHERE  SP.S# = S.S# ) ;
```

Result:

S#	SNAME	STATUS	CITY	P#
S1	Smith	20	London	P1
S1	Smith	20	London	P2
S1	Smith	20	London	P3
S1	Smith	20	London	P4
S1	Smith	20	London	P5
S1	Smith	20	London	P6
S2	Jones	10	Paris	P1
S2	Jones	10	Paris	P2
S3	Blake	30	Paris	P2
S4	Clark	20	London	P2
S4	Clark	20	London	P4
S4	Clark	20	London	P5
S5	Adams	30	Athens	bb

(We are using bb to represent a string of blanks.)

Explanation: The first twelve result rows as shown correspond to the first of the two SELECTs, and represent the ordinary natural join of S and SP over supplier numbers (except that the QTY column is not included). The final result row corresponds to the second of the two SELECTs, and preserves information for supplier S5, who does not supply any parts. The overall result is the *outer* natural join of S and SP over S#—again, ignoring QTY. (The ordinary join, by contrast, is sometimes referred to as an *inner* join.)

Note that UNION ALL can always be used (instead of UNION, unqualified) in constructing an outer join; it will be more efficient than the ordinary UNION, since there cannot possibly be any duplicates to eliminate.

One final comment on this example: Outer join is extremely important in practice, and it is a pity that systems do not provide direct support for it (this is a criticism of relational products in general, not just of DB2). It should not be necessary to have to indulge in circumlocutions of the kind illustrated in the example.

7.6 CONCLUSION

We have now covered all of the features of the SQL SELECT statement that we intend to illustrate in this book. To conclude the chapter, we present a very contrived example that shows how many (by no means all) of those features can be used together in a single query. We also give a conceptual algorithm for the evaluation of SQL queries in general.

7.6.1   A Comprehensive Example.   For all red and blue parts such that the total quantity supplied is greater than 350 (excluding from the total all shipments for which the quantity is less than or equal to 200), get the part number, the weight in grams, the color, and the maximum quantity supplied of that part; and order the result by descending part number within ascending values of that maximum quantity.

```
SELECT P.P#, 'Weight in grams =', P.WEIGHT * 454, P.COLOR,
       'Max shipped quantity =', MAX (SP.QTY)
FROM   P, SP
WHERE  P.P# = SP.P#
AND    P.COLOR IN ('Red','Blue')
AND    SP.QTY > 200
GROUP  BY P.P#, P.WEIGHT, P.COLOR
HAVING SUM (SP.QTY) > 350
ORDER  BY 6, P.P# DESC ;
```

Result:

```
P#                            COLOR
-- ------------------- ----  -----  ----------------------- ---
P1 Weight in grams =   5448  Red    Max shipped quantity =  300
P5 Weight in grams =   5448  Blue   Max shipped quantity =  400
P3 Weight in grams =   7718  Blue   Max shipped quantity =  400
```

Explanation: The clauses of a SELECT statement are executed in the order suggested by that in which they must be written*—with the exception of the SELECT clause itself, which is applied between the HAVING clause (if any) and the ORDER BY clause (if any). In the example, therefore, we can imagine the result being constructed as follows.

1. *FROM.* The FROM clause is evaluated to yield a new table that is the Cartesian product of tables P and SP.

2. *WHERE.* The result of Step 1 is reduced by the elimination of all rows

---

*Please note that (once again) our explanation is purely conceptual in nature. DB2 does *not* actually execute queries in the manner described (which would be intolerably inefficient in practice). Instead, it chooses some other more efficient method— a method that is, however, guaranteed to produce the same final result as the conceptual method described. Indeed, choosing such a "more efficient method" is precisely one of the functions of the optimizer (see Chapter 2).

Note also that if the query involves any UNIONs, the individual SELECT – FROM – WHERE (etc.) blocks representing the UNION operands are evaluated first in accordance with the conceptual method described (excluding the ORDER BY if any), the results are then UNIONed together, and finally the ORDER BY is applied.

that do not satisfy the WHERE clause. In the example, rows not satisfying the predicate

```
P.P# = SP.P# AND P.COLOR IN ('Red','Blue') AND SP.QTY > 200
```

are eliminated.

3. *GROUP BY.* The result of Step 2 is grouped by values of the field(s) named in the GROUP BY clause. In the example, those fields are P.P#, P.WEIGHT, and P.COLOR. *Note:* In theory P.P# alone would be sufficient as the grouping field, since P.WEIGHT and P.COLOR are themselves single-valued per part number. However, DB2 is not aware of this latter fact, and will raise an error condition if P.WEIGHT and P.COLOR are omitted from the GROUP BY clause, because they *are* included in the SELECT clause.

4. *HAVING.* Groups not satisfying the condition

```
SUM (SP.QTY) > 350
```

are eliminated from the result of Step 3.

5. *SELECT.* Each group in the result of Step 4 generates a single result row, as follows. First, the part number, weight, color, and maximum quantity are extracted from the group. Second, the weight is converted to grams. Third, the two character string constants "Weight in grams =" and "Max shipped quantity =" are inserted at the appropriate points in the row.

6. *ORDER BY.* The result of Step 5 is ordered in accordance with the specifications of the ORDER BY clause to yield the final result.

It is of course true that the query shown above is quite complex—but think how much work it is doing. A conventional program to do the same job in a language such as COBOL could easily be nine pages long instead of just nine lines as above, and the work involved in getting that program operational would be significantly greater than that needed to construct the SQL version shown. In practice, of course, most queries will be much simpler than this one anyway.

EXERCISES

As in the previous chapter, all of the following exercises are based on the suppliers-part-projects database (see the exercises in Chapter 5). In each one, you are asked to write a SELECT statement for the indicated query (except for numbers 7.15–18 and 7.26, q.v.). For convenience we repeat the structure of the database below:

```
S     ( S#, SNAME, STATUS, CITY )
      PRIMARY KEY ( S# )
P     ( P#, PNAME, COLOR, WEIGHT, CITY )
      PRIMARY KEY ( P# )
J     ( J#, JNAME, CITY )
      PRIMARY KEY ( J# )
SPJ   ( S#, P#, J#, QTY )
      PRIMARY KEY ( S#, P#, J# )
```

Within each section, the exercises are arranged in approximate order of increasing difficulty. You should try at least some of the easy ones in each group. Numbers 7.12–7.18 are quite difficult.

Subqueries

7.1 Get project names for projects supplied by supplier S1.

7.2 Get colors of parts supplied by supplier S1.

7.3 Get part numbers for parts supplied to any project in London.

7.4 Get project numbers for projects using at least one part available from supplier S1.

7.5 Get supplier numbers for suppliers supplying at least one part supplied by at least one supplier who supplies at least one red part.

7.6 Get supplier numbers for suppliers with a status lower than that of supplier S1.

7.7 Get supplier numbers for suppliers supplying some project with part P1 in a quantity greater than the average shipment quantity of part P1 for that project. (*Note:* This exercise requires the AVG function.)

EXISTS

7.8 Repeat Exercise 7.3 to use EXISTS in your solution.

7.9 Repeat Exercise 7.4 to use EXISTS in your solution.

7.10 Get project numbers for projects not supplied with any red part by any London supplier.

7.11 Get project numbers for projects supplied entirely by supplier S1.

7.12 Get part numbers for parts supplied to all projects in London.

7.13 Get supplier numbers for suppliers who supply the same part to all projects.

7.14 Get project numbers for projects supplied with at least all parts available from supplier S1.

For the next four exercises (7.15–7.18), convert the SQL SELECT statement shown back into an English equivalent.

7.15
```
SELECT DISTINCT J#
FROM   SPJ SPJX
WHERE  NOT EXISTS
```

```
              ( SELECT *
        FROM    SPJ SPJY
        WHERE   SPJY.J# = SPJX.J#
        AND     NOT EXISTS
              ( SELECT *
                FROM    SPJ SPJZ
                WHERE   SPJZ.P# = SPJY.P#
                AND     SPJZ.S# = 'S1' ) ) ;


7.16  SELECT DISTINCT J#
      FROM    SPJ SPJX
      WHERE   NOT EXISTS
            ( SELECT *
              FROM    SPJ SPJY
              WHERE   EXISTS
                    ( SELECT *
                      FROM    SPJ SPJA
                      WHERE   SPJA.S# = 'S1'
                      AND     SPJA.P# = SPJY.P# )
              AND     NOT EXISTS
                    ( SELECT *
                      FROM    SPJ SPJB
                      WHERE   SPJB.S# = 'S1'
                      AND     SPJB.P# = SPJY.P#
                      AND     SPJB.J# = SPJX.J# ) ) ;


7.17  SELECT DISTINCT J#
      FROM    SPJ SPJX
      WHERE   NOT EXISTS
            ( SELECT *
              FROM    SPJ SPJY
              WHERE   EXISTS
                    ( SELECT *
                      FROM    SPJ SPJA
                      WHERE   SPJA.P# = SPJY.P#
                      AND     SPJA.J# = SPJX.J# )
              AND     NOT EXISTS
                    ( SELECT *
                      FROM    SPJ SPJB
                      WHERE   SPJB.S# = 'S1'
                      AND     SPJB.P# = SPJY.P#
                      AND     SPJB.J# = SPJX.J# ) ) ;


7.18  SELECT DISTINCT J#
      FROM    SPJ SPJX
      WHERE   NOT EXISTS
            ( SELECT *
              FROM    SPJ SPJY
              WHERE   EXISTS
                    ( SELECT *
                      FROM    SPJ SPJA
                      WHERE   SPJA.S# = SPJY.S#
                      AND     SPJA.P# IN
                          ( SELECT P#
                            FROM    P
                            WHERE   COLOR = 'Red' )
                      AND     NOT EXISTS
                          ( SELECT *
                            FROM    SPJ SPJB
                            WHERE   SPJB.S# = SPJY.S#
                            AND     SPJB.J# = SPJX.J# ) ) ) ;
```

Aggregate Functions

7.19 Get the total number of projects supplied by supplier S1.

7.20 Get the total quantity of part P1 supplied by supplier S1.

7.21 For each part being supplied to a project, get the part number, the project number, and the corresponding total quantity.

7.22 Get project numbers for projects whose city is first in the alphabetic list of such cities.

7.23 Get project numbers for projects supplied with part P1 in an average quantity greater than the greatest quantity in which any part is supplied to project J1.

7.24 Get supplier numbers for suppliers supplying every project with part P1 in a quantity greater than the average quantity in which part P1 is supplied to that project.

Union

7.25 Construct an ordered list of all cities in which at least one supplier, part, or project is located.

7.26 Show the result of the following SELECT:

```
SELECT  P.COLOR
FROM    P
UNION
SELECT  P.COLOR
FROM    P ;
```

7.27 Construct the outer natural join of projects and shipments over project numbers.

7.28 Construct the outer natural join of parts and projects over cities.

7.29 Construct a table showing complete supplier, part, and project information (together with shipment quantity) for each shipment, together with "preserved" information for every supplier, part, and project that does not appear in the shipment table.

ANSWERS TO SELECTED EXERCISES

The following answers are not necessarily the only ones possible.

```
7.1   SELECT DISTINCT JNAME
      FROM    J
      WHERE   J# IN
            ( SELECT J#
              FROM    SPJ
              WHERE   S# = 'S1' ) ;

7.2   SELECT DISTINCT COLOR
      FROM    P
      WHERE   P# IN
```

```
              ( SELECT P#
                FROM    SPJ
                WHERE   S# = 'S1' ) ;

7.3   SELECT  DISTINCT P#
      FROM    SPJ
      WHERE   J# IN
              ( SELECT J#
                FROM    J
                WHERE   CITY = 'London' ) ;

7.4   SELECT  DISTINCT J#
      FROM    SPJ
      WHERE   P# IN
              ( SELECT P#
                FROM    SPJ
                WHERE   S# = 'S1' ) ;

7.5   SELECT  DISTINCT S#
      FROM    SPJ
      WHERE   P# IN
              ( SELECT P#
                FROM    SPJ
                WHERE   S# IN
                      ( SELECT S#
                        FROM    SPJ
                        WHERE   P# IN
                              ( SELECT P#
                                FROM    P
                                WHERE   COLOR = 'Red' ) ) ) ;

7.6   SELECT  S#
      FROM    S
      WHERE   STATUS <
              ( SELECT STATUS
                FROM    S
                WHERE   S# = 'S1' ) ;

7.7   SELECT  DISTINCT S#
      FROM    SPJ SPJX
      WHERE   P# = 'P1'
      AND     QTY >
              ( SELECT AVG(QTY)
                FROM    SPJ SPJY
                WHERE   P# = 'P1'
                AND     SPJY.J# = SPJX.J# ) ;

7.8   SELECT  DISTINCT P#
      FROM    SPJ
      WHERE   EXISTS
              ( SELECT *
                FROM    J
                WHERE   J# = SPJ.J#
                AND     CITY = 'London' ) ;

7.9   SELECT  DISTINCT SPJX.J#
      FROM    SPJ SPJX
      WHERE   EXISTS
              ( SELECT *
                FROM    SPJ SPJY
                WHERE   SPJY.P# = SPJX.P#
                AND     SPJY.S# = 'S1' ) ;
```

```
7.10  SELECT  J#
      FROM    J
      WHERE   NOT EXISTS
            ( SELECT *
              FROM    SPJ
              WHERE   J# = J.J#
              AND     P# IN
                    ( SELECT P#
                      FROM    P
                      WHERE   COLOR = 'Red' )
              AND     S# IN
                    ( SELECT S#
                      FROM    S
                      WHERE   CITY = 'London' ) ) ;

7.11  SELECT  DISTINCT J#
      FROM    SPJ SPJX
      WHERE   NOT EXISTS
            ( SELECT *
              FROM    SPJ SPJY
              WHERE   SPJY.J# = SPJX.J#
              AND     SPJY.S# ~= 'S1' ) ;

7.12  SELECT  DISTINCT P#
      FROM    SPJ SPJX
      WHERE   NOT EXISTS
            ( SELECT *
              FROM    J
              WHERE   CITY = 'London'
              AND     NOT EXISTS
                    ( SELECT *
                      FROM    SPJ SPJY
                      WHERE   SPJY.P# = SPJX.P#
                      AND     SPJY.J# = J.J# ) ) ;

7.13  SELECT  DISTINCT S#
      FROM    SPJ SPJX
      WHERE   EXISTS
            ( SELECT P#
              FROM    SPJ SPJY
              WHERE   NOT EXISTS
                    ( SELECT J#
                      FROM    J
                      WHERE   NOT EXISTS
                            ( SELECT *
                              FROM    SPJ SPJZ
                              WHERE   SPJZ.S# = SPJX.S#
                              AND     SPJZ.P# = SPJY.P#
                              AND     SPJZ.J# = J.J# ) ) ) ;
```

This rather complex SELECT statement may be paraphrased: "Get all suppliers (SPJX.S#) such that there exists a part (SPJY.P#) such that there does not exist any project (J.J#) such that the supplier does not supply the part to the project"—in other words, suppliers such that there exists some part that they supply to all projects. Note the use of "SELECT P# FROM . . ." and "SELECT J# FROM . . ." in two of the EXISTS references; "SELECT *" would not be incorrect, but "SELECT P#" (for instance) seems a fraction closer to the intuitive formulation— there must exist a *part* (identified by a part number), not just a row in the shipments table.

7.14
```
SELECT  DISTINCT J#
FROM    SPJ SPJX
WHERE   NOT EXISTS
        ( SELECT P#
          FROM    SPJ SPJY
          WHERE   SPJY.S# = 'S1'
          AND     NOT EXISTS
                  ( SELECT *
                    FROM    SPJ SPJZ
                    WHERE   SPJZ.P# = SPJY.P#
                    AND     SPJZ.J# = SPJX.J# ) ) ;
```

7.15 Get project numbers for projects that use only parts that are available from supplier S1.

7.16 Get project numbers for projects that are supplied by supplier S1 with some of every part that supplier S1 supplies.

7.17 Get project numbers for projects such that at least some of every part they use is supplied to them by supplier S1.

7.18 Get project numbers for projects that are supplied by every supplier who supplies some red part.

7.19
```
SELECT  COUNT (DISTINCT J#)
FROM    SPJ
WHERE   S# = 'S1' ;
```

7.20
```
SELECT  SUM (QTY)
FROM    SPJ
WHERE   P# = 'P1'
AND     S# = 'S1' ;
```

7.21
```
SELECT  P#, J#, SUM(QTY)
FROM    SPJ
GROUP   BY P#, J# ;
```

7.22
```
SELECT  J#
FROM    J
WHERE   CITY =
        ( SELECT MIN(CITY)
          FROM    J ) ;
```

7.23
```
SELECT  J#
FROM    SPJ
WHERE   P# = 'P1'
GROUP   BY J#
HAVING  AVG(QTY) >
        ( SELECT MAX(QTY)
          FROM    SPJ
          WHERE   J# = 'J1' ) ;
```

7.24
```
SELECT  DISTINCT S#
FROM    SPJ SPJX
WHERE   NOT EXISTS
        ( SELECT *
          FROM    J
          WHERE   NOT EXISTS
                  ( SELECT *
                    FROM    SPJ SPJY
                    WHERE   SPJY.S# = SPJX.S#
                    AND     SPJY.P# = 'P1'
```

```
                       AND     SPJY.J# = J.J#
                       AND     SPJY.QTY >
                             ( SELECT AVG (QTY)
                               FROM    SPJ SPJZ
                               WHERE   SPJZ.J# = J.J#
                               AND     SPJZ.P# = 'P1' ) ) ) ;

7.25  SELECT CITY FROM S
      UNION
      SELECT CITY FROM P
      UNION
      SELECT CITY FROM J
      ORDER  BY 1 ;


7.26  -----
      Red
      Green
      Blue

7.27  SELECT J.*, SPJ.S#, SPJ.P#, SPJ.QTY
      FROM    J, SPJ
      WHERE   J.J# = SPJ.J#
      UNION   ALL
      SELECT J.*, 'bb', 'bb', 0
      FROM    J
      WHERE   NOT EXISTS
             ( SELECT *
               FROM    SPJ
               WHERE   SPJ.J# = J.J# ) ;

7.28  SELECT P.*, J#, JNAME
      FROM    P, J
      WHERE   P.CITY = J.CITY
      UNION   ALL
      SELECT P.*, 'bb', 'bb'
      FROM    P
      WHERE   NOT EXISTS
             ( SELECT *
               FROM    J
               WHERE   J.CITY = P.CITY )
      UNION   ALL
      SELECT 'bb', 'bb', 'bb', 0, J.CITY, J.J#, J.JNAME
      FROM    J
      WHERE   NOT EXISTS
             ( SELECT *
               FROM    P
               WHERE   P.CITY = J.CITY ) ;

7.29  SELECT S.*, P.*, J.*, SPJ.QTY
      FROM    S, P, J, SPJ
      WHERE   S.S# = SPJ.S#
      AND     P.P# = SPJ.P#
      AND     J.J# = SPJ.J#
      UNION   ALL
      SELECT S.*,'bb','bb','bb', 0,'bb','bb','bb','bb', 0
      FROM    S
      WHERE   NOT EXISTS
             ( SELECT *
               FROM    SPJ
               WHERE   SPJ.S# = S.S# )
      UNION   ALL
      SELECT 'bb','bb', 0,'bb', P.*,'bb','bb','bb', 0
      FROM    P
```

```
WHERE   NOT EXISTS
      ( SELECT *
        FROM    SPJ
        WHERE   P.P# = SPJ.P# )
UNION   ALL
SELECT 'bb','bb', 0,'bb','bb','bb','bb', 0,'bb', J.*, 0
FROM    J
WHERE   NOT EXISTS
      ( SELECT *
        FROM    SPJ
        WHERE   SPJ.J# = J.J# ) ;
```

CHAPTER

◆ 8 ◆

Data Manipulation III: Update Operations

8.1 INTRODUCTION

In the last two chapters we considered the SQL retrieval statement (SELECT) in considerable detail. Now we turn our attention to the update statements INSERT, UPDATE, and DELETE. *Note:* The term "update" unfortunately has two distinct meanings in SQL—it is used generically to refer to all three operations as a class, and also specifically to refer to the UPDATE operation per se. We will distinguish between the two meanings in this book by always using lower case when the generic meaning is intended and upper case when the specific meaning is intended.

Like the SELECT statement, the three update statements operate on both base tables and views. However, for reasons that are beyond the scope of this chapter, *not all views are updatable.* If the user attempts to perform an update operation on a nonupdatable view, DB2 will simply reject the operation, with some appropriate message to the user. For the purposes of the present chapter, therefore, let us assume that all tables to be updated are base tables, and defer the question of views (and of updating views, in particular) to Chapter 10.

The next three sections discuss the three update operations in detail. The syntax of those operations follows the same general pattern as that already shown for the SELECT operation; for convenience, an outline of that general syntax for the operation in question is given at the beginning of the relevant section.

8.2 INSERT

The INSERT statement has the general form

```
INSERT
INTO    table [ ( field [, field ] ... ) ]
VALUES ( constant [, constant ] ... ) ;
```

or

```
INSERT
INTO    table [ ( field [, field ] ... ) ]
subquery ;
```

In the first format, a row is INSERTed into "table" having the specified values for the specified fields; the *i*th constant in the list of constants corresponds to the *i*th field in the list of fields.* In the second format, "subquery" is evaluated and a copy of the result (multiple rows, in general) is INSERTed into "table"; the *i*th column of that result corresponds to the *i*th field in the list of fields. In both cases, omitting the list of fields is equivalent to specifying a list of all fields in the table (see Example 8.2.2 below).

8.2.1 Single-Record INSERT.   Add part P7 (city Athens, weight 24, name and color at present unknown) to table P.

```
INSERT
INTO    P ( P#, CITY, WEIGHT )
VALUES ( 'P7', 'Athens', 24 ) ;
```

A new part record is created with the specified part number, city, and weight, and with blank values for the name and color fields (since no other value has been explicitly specified, and we assume that NOT NULL WITH DEFAULT applies to those fields). In general, the effect of omitting a value

---

*NULL is considered to be a legal constant in this context.

for some field in INSERT depends on the way that field was defined in the CREATE (or ALTER) TABLE statement:

- NOT NULL WITH DEFAULT: The field is set to the appropriate non-null default value (see Chapter 4).
- NOT NULL: The INSERT fails (the database remains unchanged).
- Otherwise: The field is set to null.

Note that the left-to-right order in which fields are named in the INSERT statement does not have to be the same as the left-to-right order in which they were specified in the CREATE (or ALTER) TABLE statement(s).

8.2.2 Single-Record INSERT, with Field Names Omitted. Add part P8 (a sprocket, color pink, weight 14, city Nice) to table P.

```
INSERT
INTO    P
VALUES ('P8', 'Sprocket', 'Pink', 14, 'Nice' ) ;
```

Omitting the list of fields is equivalent to specifying a list of all fields in the table, in the left-to-right order in which they were defined in the CREATE or ALTER TABLE statement(s). As with "SELECT *", this shorthand may be convenient for interactive SQL; however, it is potentially dangerous in embedded SQL (i.e., SQL within an application program), because the assumed list of fields may change if the program is rebound and the definition of the table has changed in the interim. In practice, we recommend always specifying the list of fields explicitly in an embedded SQL context.

8.2.3 Single-Record INSERT. Insert a new shipment with supplier number S20, part number P20, and quantity 1000.

```
INSERT
INTO    SP ( S#, P#, QTY )
VALUES ('S20', 'P20', 1000 ) ;
```

Since by definition the three update operations change the state of the database, there is always the possibility that they may change it in some incorrect way and thereby violate the integrity of the data. The example illustrates this point: The database would clearly be incorrect if the INSERT were executed, because it would now include a shipment for a nonexistent supplier and a nonexistent part. In fact, the example illustrates a very specific kind of integrity violation, namely a *referential* integrity violation. Referential integrity is discussed in detail in Chapter 12.

8.2.4   INSERT ... SELECT.   For each part supplied, get the part number and the total quantity supplied of that part (as in Example 7.4.7), and save the result in the database.

```
CREATE TABLE TEMP
      ( P#        CHAR(6) NOT NULL,
        TOTQTY   INTEGER,
        PRIMARY KEY ( P# ) ) ;

CREATE UNIQUE INDEX XTEMP ON TEMP ( P# ) ;

INSERT
INTO    TEMP ( P#, TOTQTY )
        SELECT P#, SUM(QTY)
        FROM    SP
        GROUP  BY P# ;
```

The SELECT is executed, just like an ordinary SELECT, but the result, instead of being returned to the user, is inserted into table TEMP. Now the user can do anything he or she pleases with that result—query it further, print it, even update it; none of those operations will have any effect whatsoever on the original data. Eventually, when it is no longer required, table TEMP can be dropped:

```
DROP TABLE TEMP ;
```

The foregoing example illustrates very nicely why the closure property of relational systems (discussed in Section 6.2) is so important: The overall procedure works precisely because the result of a SELECT is another table. It would *not* work if the result was something other than a table.

It is not necessary for the target table to be initially empty for an INSERT ... SELECT operation, incidentally, though for the foregoing example it is. If it is not, the new records are simply added to those already present.

8.3   UPDATE

The UPDATE statement has the general form

```
UPDATE table
SET     field = scalar-expression
      [, field = scalar-expression ] ...
[ WHERE  predicate ] ;
```

All records in "table" that satisfy "predicate" are UPDATEd in accordance with the assignments ("field = scalar-expression") in the SET clause. The "scalar-expression"'s are (at their most complex) simple scalar expressions involving fields of "table" and/or scalar functions and/or constants (no aggregate functions allowed).* For each record to be UPDATEd (i.e., each record that satisfies "predicate," or all records if the WHERE clause is omitted), references in the "scalar-expression"'s to fields within that record stand for the values of those fields before any of the assignments have been executed.

8.3.1 Single-Record UPDATE. Change the color of part P2 to yellow, increase its weight by 5, and set its city to "unknown" (i.e., NULL; we assume for the sake of the example that field P.CITY is allowed to accept nulls).

```
UPDATE P
SET     COLOR = 'Yellow',
        WEIGHT = WEIGHT + 5,
        CITY = NULL
WHERE   P# = 'P2' ;
```

8.3.2 Multiple-Record UPDATE. Double the status of all suppliers in London.

```
UPDATE S
SET     STATUS = 2 * STATUS
WHERE   CITY = 'London' ;
```

8.3.3 UPDATE with a Subquery. Set the shipment quantity to zero for all suppliers in London.

```
UPDATE SP
SET     QTY = 0
WHERE   'London' =
      ( SELECT CITY
        FROM    S
        WHERE   S.S# = SP.S# ) ;
```

8.4 DELETE

The DELETE statement has the general form

```
DELETE
FROM    table
[ WHERE   predicate ] ;
```

All records in "table" that satisfy "predicate" (or all records, if the WHERE clause is omitted) are DELETEd.

8.4.1 Single-Record DELETE. Delete supplier S5.

---

*NULL is considered to be a legal scalar expression in this context.

```
DELETE
FROM    S
WHERE   S# = 'S5' ;
```

8.4.2 *Multiple-Record DELETE.* Delete all shipments with quantity greater than 300.

```
DELETE
FROM    SP
WHERE   QTY > 300 ;
```

8.4.3 *Multiple-Record DELETE.* Delete all shipments.

```
DELETE
FROM    SP ;
```

SP is still a known table ("DELETE all records" is not a DROP), but it is now empty.

8.4.4 *DELETE with a Subquery.* Delete all shipments for suppliers in London.

```
DELETE
FROM    SP
WHERE   'London' =
       ( SELECT CITY
         FROM    S
         WHERE   S.S# = SP.S# ) ;
```

8.5 CONCLUSION

This brings us to the end of our detailed discussion of the four data manipulation statements of SQL, namely SELECT, INSERT, UPDATE, and DELETE. Most of the complexity of those statements (what complexity there is) resides in the SELECT statement; once you have a reasonable understanding of SELECT, the other statements are fairly straightforward, as you can see. In practice, of course, the SELECT statement is usually pretty straightforward as well.

Despite the foregoing, however, the update operations do suffer from one minor problem that is worth calling out explicitly, namely as follows: If the WHERE clause in UPDATE or DELETE includes a subquery, then the FROM clause in that subquery must not refer to the table that is the target of that UPDATE or DELETE. Likewise, in the subquery form of INSERT (INSERT ... SELECT), the FROM clause in that subquery must not refer to the table that is the target of that INSERT. So, for example, to delete all suppliers whose status is lower than the average, the following will *not* work:

```
DELETE
FROM    S
WHERE   STATUS <
        ( SELECT AVG (STATUS)
          FROM    S ) ;
```

Instead, it is necessary to proceed one step at a time, as follows:

```
SELECT AVG (STATUS)
FROM    S ;
```

Result: ------
                22

Hence:

```
DELETE
FROM    S
WHERE   STATUS < 22 ;
```

The reasons for the foregoing restrictions are not inherent but are merely a consequence of the way the operators are implemented in DB2.

Aside: In DB2 Version 2 there are additional restrictions that apply to the update operations in certain circumstances. See Chapter 12 for further discussion.

In conclusion, we point out that the fact that there are only four data manipulation operations in SQL is one of the reasons for the ease of use of that language (less to learn, less to remember, etc.). And the fact that there *are* only four such operations is a consequence of the simplicity of the relational data structure. As we pointed out in Chapter 1, all data in a relational database is represented in exactly the same way, namely as values in column positions within rows of tables. Since there is only one way to represent anything, we need only one operator for each of the four basic functions (retrieve, change, insert, delete). By contrast, systems based on a more complex data structure fundamentally require $4n$ operations, where n is the number of ways that data can be represented in that system. In CODASYL-based systems, for example, where data can be represented either as records or as "links" between records, we typically find a STORE operation to create a record and a CONNECT operation to create a link; an ERASE operation to destroy a record and a DISCONNECT operation to destroy a link; a MODIFY operation to change a record and a RECONNECT operation to change a link; and so on. (Actually, CODASYL systems usually provide more than two ways of representing data [and hence more than two sets of operations], but records and links are the two most important.)

EXERCISES

As usual, all of the following exercises are based on the suppliers-parts-projects database:

```
S     ( S#, SNAME, STATUS, CITY )
      PRIMARY KEY ( S# )
P     ( P#, PNAME, COLOR, WEIGHT, CITY )
      PRIMARY KEY ( P# )
J     ( J#, JNAME, CITY )
      PRIMARY KEY ( J# )
SPJ   ( S#, P#, J#, QTY )
      PRIMARY KEY ( S#, P#, J# )
```

Write INSERT, DELETE, or UPDATE statements (as appropriate) for each of the following problems.

8.1 Change the color of all red parts to orange.

8.2 Delete all projects for which there are no shipments.

8.3 Increase the shipment quantity by 10 percent for all shipments by suppliers that supply a red part.

8.4 Insert a new supplier (S10) into table S. The name and city are Smith and New York, respectively; the status is not yet known.

8.5 Construct a table containing a list of part numbers for parts that are supplied either by a London supplier or to a London project.

8.6 Construct a table containing a list of project numbers for projects that are either located in London or are supplied by a London supplier.

8.7 Add 10 to the status of all suppliers whose status is currently less than that of supplier S4.

ANSWERS TO SELECTED EXERCISES

As usual the following solutions are not necessarily unique. Also, note that some of the solutions involve the creation of a temporary result table. We have specified a primary key for each such table as a matter of good discipline; but it should be pointed out that the integrity checking implied by those primary keys will certainly lead to some performance overhead (see Chapter 12). As a consequence, an installation might decide that it is acceptable *not* to specify a primary key for such comparatively short-lived tables.

8.1
```
UPDATE P
SET    COLOR = 'Orange'
WHERE  COLOR = 'Red' ;
```

8.2
```
DELETE
FROM   J
WHERE  J# NOT IN
       ( SELECT J#
         FROM   SPJ ) ;
```

8.3
```
CREATE TABLE REDS
      ( S#   CHAR(5) NOT NULL,
        PRIMARY KEY ( S# ) ) ;

CREATE UNIQUE INDEX X3 ON REDS ( S# ) ;

INSERT INTO REDS ( S# )
        SELECT DISTINCT S#
        FROM    SPJ, P
        WHERE   SPJ.P# = P.P#
        AND     COLOR = 'Red' ;

UPDATE SPJ
SET     QTY = QTY * 1.1
WHERE   S# IN
      ( SELECT S#
        FROM    REDS ) ;

DROP TABLE REDS ;
```

Note that the following single-statement "solution" is illegal (why?).

```
UPDATE SPJ
SET     QTY = QTY * 1.1
WHERE   S# IN
      ( SELECT DISTINCT S#
        FROM    SPJ, P
        WHERE   SPJ.P# = P.P#
        AND     P.COLOR = 'Red' ) ;
```

8.4
```
INSERT
INTO   S ( S#, SNAME, CITY )
VALUES ('S10', 'Smith', 'New York' ) ;
```

8.5
```
CREATE TABLE LP
      ( P# CHAR(6) NOT NULL,
        PRIMARY KEY ( P# ) ) ;

CREATE UNIQUE INDEX X5 ON LP ( P# ) ) ;

INSERT INTO LP ( P# )
        SELECT DISTINCT P#
        FROM    SPJ
        WHERE   S# IN
              ( SELECT S#
                FROM    S
                WHERE   CITY = 'London' )
        OR      J# IN
              ( SELECT J#
                FROM    J
                WHERE   CITY = 'London' ) ;
```

8.6
```
CREATE TABLE LJ
      ( J#   CHAR(4) NOT NULL,
        PRIMARY KEY ( J# ) ) ;

CREATE UNIQUE INDEX X6 ON LJ ( J# ) ) ;

INSERT INTO LJ ( J# )
        SELECT J#
        FROM    J
        WHERE   CITY = 'London'
```

```
OR      J# IN
      ( SELECT DISTINCT J#
        FROM    SPJ
        WHERE   S# IN
              ( SELECT S#
                FROM    S
                WHERE   CITY = 'London' ) ) ;
```

Note: The following is illegal:

```
INSERT INTO LJ ( J# )
       SELECT J#
       FROM   J
       WHERE  CITY = 'London'
       UNION
       SELECT DISTINCT J#
       FROM   SPJ
       WHERE  'London' =
             ( SELECT CITY
               FROM . S
               WHERE  S.S# = SPJ.S# ) ;
```

UNION is never allowed in a subquery (in any context).

8.7
```
SELECT STATUS
FROM   S
WHERE  S# = 'S4' ;
```

Result:
```
STATUS
------
   20
```

Hence:

```
UPDATE S
SET    STATUS = STATUS + 10
WHERE  STATUS < 20 ;
```

CHAPTER
◆ 9 ◆

The Catalog

9.1 INTRODUCTION

We have mentioned the catalog several times in this book already (especially in Chapter 2). The catalog in DB2 is a system database that contains information (*descriptors*) concerning various objects that are of interest to the system itself. Examples of such objects are base tables, views, indexes, databases, application plans, access privileges, and so on. Descriptor information is essential if the system is to be able to do its job properly. For example, the optimizer component of Bind uses catalog information about indexes (as well as other information) to choose an access strategy, as explained in Chapter 2. Likewise, the authorization subsystem (see Chapter 11) uses catalog information about access privileges to grant or deny specific user requests.

A significant advantage of a relational system like DB2 is that *the catalog in such a system itself consists of relations* (or tables—*system* tables, so called to distinguish them from ordinary user tables). As a result, users can interrogate the catalog using the standard facilities of their normal query language (SQL, in the case of DB2)—a very nice feature of such systems.

In DB2 specifically, the catalog consists of some 30 or so system tables.* It is not our purpose here to give an exhaustive description of the catalog; rather, we wish merely to give a basic—and deliberately somewhat simplified—introduction to its structure and content, and to give some idea as to how the information in the catalog can be helpful to the user as well as to the system. The only catalog tables we mention at this point are the following:

- SYSTABLES

  This catalog table contains a row for every table (base table or view) in the entire system. For each such table, it gives the table name (NAME), the name of the user who created the table (CREATEDBY), the name of the user who owns the table (CREATOR), the number of columns in the table (COLCOUNT), and many other items of information. *Note:* It is possible, as we shall see in Chapter 11, for the "creator" and the "owner" of a table to be different; this is why SYSTABLES gives both. The terminology is rather confusing, however—the CREATOR column shows the table *owner,* the CREATEDBY column shows the actual *creator.*

- SYSCOLUMNS

  This catalog table contains a row for every column of every table in the entire system. For each such column, it gives the column name (NAME), the name of the table of which that column is a part (TBNAME), the name of the owner of that table (TBCREATOR), the data type of the column (COLTYPE), and many other things besides.

- SYSINDEXES

  This catalog table contains a row for every index in the system. For each such index, it gives the index name (NAME), the name of the user who created the index (CREATEDBY), the name of the owner of the index (CREATOR), the name of the indexed table (TBNAME), the name of the owner of that table (TBCREATOR), and so on.

---

*The catalog is *not* the same across different SQL implementations, because the catalog for a particular system necessarily contains a great deal of information that is specific to that system. Note in particular that the DB2 and SQL/DS catalogs are different. Appendix E contains a brief summary of the DB2 catalog tables as of Version 2 Release 1.

For example, the catalog structure for the suppliers-and-parts database might be as indicated in Fig. 9.1 (in outline; of course, almost all the details have been omitted).

SYSTABLES	NAME	CREATEDBY	CREATOR	COLCOUNT	...
	S	CJDATE	CJDATE	4	...
	P	CJDATE	CJDATE	5	...
	SP	CJDATE	CJDATE	3	...

SYSCOLUMNS	NAME	TBNAME	TBCREATOR	COLTYPE	...
	S#	S	CJDATE	CHAR	...
	SNAME	S	CJDATE	CHAR	...
	STATUS	S	CJDATE	SMALLINT	...
	CITY	S	CJDATE	CHAR	...
	P#	P	CJDATE	CHAR	...
	PNAME	P	CJDATE	CHAR	...
	COLOR	P	CJDATE	CHAR	...
	WEIGHT	P	CJDATE	SMALLINT	...
	CITY	P	CJDATE	CHAR	...
	S#	SP	CJDATE	CHAR	...
	P#	SP	CJDATE	CHAR	...
	QTY	SP	CJDATE	INTEGER	...

SYSINDEXES	NAME	CREATEDBY	CREATOR	TBNAME	TBCREATOR	...
	XS	CJDATE	CJDATE	S	CJDATE	...
	XP	CJDATE	CJDATE	P	CJDATE	...
	XSP	CJDATE	CJDATE	SP	CJDATE	...
	XSC	CJDATE	CJDATE	S	CJDATE	...

Fig. 9.1 Catalog structure for the suppliers-and-parts database (outline)

9.2 QUERYING THE CATALOG

As indicated in Section 9.1, a nice feature of the catalog in a relational system like DB2 is that it can be queried by means of ordinary SQL retrieval operations (SELECT statements), just as ordinary tables can. For example, to find out what tables contain an S# column:

```
SELECT TBNAME, TBCREATOR
FROM   SYSIBM.SYSCOLUMNS
WHERE  NAME = 'S#' ;
```

Result:

TBNAME	TBCREATOR
S	CJDATE
SP	CJDATE

The owner (CREATOR) for the catalog tables is considered to be SYSIBM. Thus, to refer to a catalog table such as SYSCOLUMNS, you will need to use SYSIBM as a prefix for the table name (as in the FROM clause in this example); otherwise, DB2 will assume that you are referring to a table of your own (i.e., the default prefix is your own system-known name, as explained in Chapter 5).

Another example: What columns does the suppliers table have?

```
SELECT  NAME
FROM    SYSIBM.SYSCOLUMNS
WHERE   TBNAME = 'S'
AND     TBCREATOR = 'CJDATE' ;
```

Result:
```
NAME
------
S#
SNAME
STATUS
CITY
```

And one more example: How many tables has user CJDATE created?

```
SELECT  COUNT(*)
FROM    SYSIBM.SYSTABLES
WHERE   CREATEDBY = 'CJDATE' ;
```

A user who is not familiar with the structure of the database can use queries such as these to discover that structure. For example, a user who wishes to query the suppliers-and-parts database (say), but does not have any detailed knowledge as to exactly what tables exist in that database and exactly what columns they contain, can use catalog queries to obtain that knowledge first before going on to formulate the data queries per se. In a traditional (nonrelational) system, those initial queries would typically have to be directed to the system *dictionary* instead of to the database. Indeed, the DB2 catalog can be regarded as a rudimentary dictionary (rudimentary, in that it contains only information that is directly needed by DB2, whereas a full-scale dictionary typically contains much additional information, such as report definitions, graph definitions, terminal descriptions, etc.). The important difference—and a significant ease-of-use benefit for DB2—is that in DB2 the catalog and the database are queried through *the same interface,* namely SQL; in traditional systems, by contrast, the dictionary and the database have always been distinct and have been accessed through different interfaces. It is interesting to speculate as to whether the DB2 catalog will ever be extended to provide a full-fledged dictionary function.

Note: After the foregoing was first written, IBM did announce an auxiliary product for DB2 (and SQL/DS) called the Data Base Relational Application Directory (DBRAD). We mentioned this product briefly in Section 3.2. DBRAD is still not a full dictionary product, but it might be considered a step in the right direction. It is described in detail in Chapter 25. In addition, there are strong indications at the time of writing that IBM will soon announce a "repository" product for DB2 (and other IBM system software products) that will provide additional dictionary capabilities.

9.3 UPDATING THE CATALOG

We have seen how the catalog can be queried by means of the SQL SELECT statement. However, the catalog *cannot* be updated using the SQL INSERT, UPDATE, and DELETE statements, and DB2 will reject any attempt to do so.* The reason is, of course, that allowing such operations would potentially be very dangerous: It would be far too easy to destroy information (inadvertently or otherwise) in the catalog so that DB2 would no longer be able to function correctly. Suppose, for example, that the following were allowed:

```
DELETE
FROM    SYSIBM.SYSCOLUMNS
WHERE   NAME = 'S#'
AND     TBNAME = 'S'
AND     TBCREATOR = 'CJDATE' ;
```

Its effect would be to remove the row

```
( S#, S, CJDATE, CHAR, ... )
```

from the SYSCOLUMNS table. *As far as DB2 is concerned, the S# column in the S table would now no longer exist*—i.e., DB2 would no longer have any knowledge of that column. Thus, attempts to access data on the basis of values of that column—e.g.,

```
SELECT CITY
FROM    S
WHERE   S# = 'S4' ;
```

—would fail (the system would produce some error message, such as "undefined column"). Perhaps worse, attempts to update supplier records could go disastrously wrong—for example, inserting a new record might conceivably cause the supplier number to be taken as the supplier name, the supplier name as the status, and so on.

For reasons such as these, INSERT, UPDATE, and DELETE operations are (as already stated) not permitted against tables in the catalog. Instead, it is the *data definition* statements (CREATE TABLE, CREATE

---

*This statement is not quite 100 percent true under DB2 Version 2. In Version 2, suitably authorized users *are* allowed to use the SQL UPDATE statement to update certain "statistics" columns in the catalog, for reasons that are beyond the scope of this chapter. See Chapter 17 for more information. We will ignore this special case for the remainder of this chapter.

INDEX, etc.) that perform such updates. For example, the CREATE TABLE statement for table S causes (a) an entry to be made for S in the SYSTABLES table and (b) a set of four entries, one for each of the four columns of the S table, to be made in the SYSCOLUMNS table. (It also causes a number of other things to happen too, which are however of no concern to us here.) Thus CREATE is in some ways the analog of INSERT for the catalog. Likewise, DROP is the analog of DELETE, and ALTER is the analog of UPDATE.

Aside: The catalog also includes entries for the catalog tables themselves, of course. However, those entries are not created by explicit CREATE TABLE operations. Instead, they are created automatically by DB2 itself as part of the system installation procedure. In effect, they are "hard-wired" into the system.

Although (as we have just seen) the regular SQL updating statements cannot normally be used to update the catalog, there are two SQL statements, namely COMMENT and LABEL, that do perform a kind of limited catalog updating function. We discuss each in turn.

COMMENT

The catalog tables SYSTABLES and SYSCOLUMNS each include a column—not shown in Fig. 9.1—called REMARKS, which can be used (in any particular row) to contain a text string that describes the object identified by the rest of that row. The COMMENT statement is used to enter such descriptions into the REMARKS column in these two tables. The following examples illustrate the two basic formats of that statement.

```
COMMENT ON TABLE S IS
       'Each row represents one supplier' ;
```

The specified string is stored in the REMARKS field in the row for table S in the SYSTABLES table, replacing any value previously stored at that position. The table being COMMENTed on can be either a base table or a view.

```
COMMENT ON COLUMN P.CITY IS
       'Location of (unique) warehouse storing this part' ;
```

The specified string is stored in the REMARKS field in the row for column P.CITY in the SYSCOLUMNS table, replacing any value previously stored at that position. The column being COMMENTed on can be a column of either a base table or a view.

Comments can be retrieved via the regular SQL SELECT statement.

LABEL

The tables SYSTABLES and SYSCOLUMNS each also include a column—again not shown in Fig. 9.1—called LABEL, which can be used (in any particular row) to contain a text string that is to be used in reports involving the object identified by the rest of that row. The LABEL statement is used to enter such strings into the LABEL column in these two tables. The following examples illustrate the two basic formats of that statement.

```
LABEL ON TABLE S IS 'Supplier' ;

LABEL ON COLUMN P.CITY IS 'Warehouse location' ;
```

One reason for introducing such labels is that they can be longer than regular DB2 names (maximum 30 characters instead of 18). Labels, like comments, can be applied to both base tables and views (or to columns thereof). They can be retrieved via the regular SQL SELECT statement (also via DESCRIBE—see Chapter 15).

9.4 SYNONYMS

It is convenient to close this chapter with a brief discussion of *synonyms,* although the topic does not really have much to do with the catalog as such (except inasmuch as synonyms are recorded in the catalog, like most other objects). Briefly, a synonym is an alternative name for a table (base table or view). In particular, you can define a synonym for a table that was created by some other user and for which you would otherwise have to use a fully qualified name. For example:

User ALPHA issues:

```
CREATE TABLE SAMPLE ... ;
```

User BETA can refer to this table as ALPHA.SAMPLE—for instance,

```
SELECT *
FROM    ALPHA.SAMPLE ;
```

Alternatively, user BETA can issue:

```
CREATE SYNONYM ZTEST FOR ALPHA.SAMPLE ;
```

and can now refer to the table as simply ZTEST—for instance,

```
SELECT *
FROM    ZTEST ;
```

The name ZTEST is completely private and local to user BETA. Another user GAMMA can also have a private and local name ZTEST, distinct from user BETA's.

Another example:

```
CREATE SYNONYM TABLES FOR SYSIBM.SYSTABLES ;
```

There is also a DROP SYNONYM statement—syntax:

```
DROP SYNONYM synonym ;
```

For example:

```
DROP SYNONYM TABLES ;
```

Dropping a table (base table or view) causes all synonyms for that table to be dropped automatically.

EXERCISES

9.1 Sketch the details of the catalog for the suppliers-parts-projects database.

Now write SELECT statements for the following queries (numbers 9.2–9.8).

9.2 Which tables include a CITY column?

9.3 How many columns are there in the shipments table?

9.4 List the names of all catalog tables.

9.5 List the names of all users that have created a table with a CITY column, together with the names of the tables concerned.

9.6 List the names of all users that have created at least one table, together with the number of tables created in each case.

9.7 Which tables have at least one index?

9.8 Which tables have more than one index?

9.9 Write statements to do the following:

(a) Create an appropriate comment on the SPJ table.

(b) Change that comment to "Ignore previous comment".

(c) Create an appropriate comment on the P# column of the SPJ table.

(d) Create an appropriate comment on the XS index.

(e) Create an appropriate label for the P# column of the SPJ table.

(f) Create an appropriate synonym for the SYSCOLUMNS table.

(g) Drop that synonym.

ANSWERS TO SELECTED EXERCISES

As usual the following solutions are not necessarily unique.

9.2
```
SELECT  TBNAME, TBCREATOR
FROM    SYSIBM.SYSCOLUMNS
WHERE   NAME = 'CITY' ;
```

9.3
```
SELECT  COLCOUNT
FROM    SYSIBM.SYSTABLES
WHERE   NAME = 'SPJ'
AND     CREATEDBY = ... ;
```

9.4
```
SELECT  NAME
FROM    SYSIBM.SYSTABLES
WHERE   CREATOR = 'SYSIBM' ;
```

9.5
```
SELECT  CREATEDBY, NAME
FROM    SYSIBM.SYSTABLES
WHERE   NAME IN
      ( SELECT  TBNAME
        FROM    SYSIBM.SYSCOLUMNS
        WHERE   NAME = 'CITY' ) ;
```

9.6
```
SELECT  CREATEDBY, COUNT(*)
FROM    SYSIBM.SYSTABLES
GROUP   BY CREATEDBY ;
```

9.7
```
SELECT  TBNAME, TBCREATOR
FROM    SYSIBM.SYSINDEXES ;
```

9.8
```
SELECT  TBNAME, TBCREATOR
FROM    SYSIBM.SYSINDEXES
GROUP   BY TBNAME, TBCREATOR
HAVING  COUNT (*) > 1 ;
```

9.9

(a) `COMMENT ON TABLE SPJ IS 'Appropriate comment' ;`

(b) `COMMENT ON TABLE SPJ IS 'Ignore previous comment' ;`

(c) `COMMENT ON COLUMN SPJ.P# IS 'Appropriate comment' ;`

(d) Trick question! It is not possible to COMMENT ON an index.

(e) `LABEL ON COLUMN SPJ.P# IS 'Part shipped' ;`

(f) `CREATE SYNONYM COLS FOR SYSIBM.SYSCOLUMNS ;`

(g) `DROP SYNONYM COLS ;`

CHAPTER
·10·

Views

10.1 INTRODUCTION

Recall from Chapter 1 that a view is a *virtual table*—that is, a table that does not exist in its own right but looks to the user as if it did. (By contrast, a base table is a *real* table, in the sense that, for each row of such a table, there really is some stored counterpart of that row in physical storage. See Chapter 16.) Views are not supported by their own, physically separate, distinguishable stored data. Instead, their *definition* in terms of other tables is stored in the catalog (actually in a catalog table called SYSVIEWS). Here is an example:

```
CREATE VIEW GOOD_SUPPLIERS
     AS SELECT S#, STATUS, CITY
        FROM   S
        WHERE  STATUS > 15 ;
```

When this CREATE VIEW is executed, the subquery following the AS (which is in fact the definition of the view) is *not* executed; instead, it is simply saved in the catalog, under the specified view name (GOOD_ SUPPLIERS). To the user, however, it is now as if there really were a table in the database called GOOD_SUPPLIERS, with rows and columns as shown in the unshaded portions (only) of Fig. 10.1 below.

```
GOOD_SUPPLIERS     S#    SNAME    STATUS    CITY
                   --    -----    ------    ------
                   S1    Smith      20      London
                   S2    Jones      10      Paris
                   S3    Blake      30      Paris
                   S4    Clark      20      London
                   S5    Adams      30      Athens
```

Fig. 10.1. GOOD_SUPPLIERS as a view of base table S (unshaded portions)

GOOD_SUPPLIERS is in effect a "window" into the real table S. Furthermore, that window is *dynamic:* Changes to S will be automatically and instantaneously visible through that window (provided, of course, that those changes lie within the unshaded portion of S); likewise, changes to GOOD_SUPPLIERS will automatically and instantaneously be applied to the real table S (see Section 10.4, later), and hence of course be visible through the window.

Now, depending on the user's level of sophistication (and perhaps also on the application concerned), the user may or may not realize that GOOD_SUPPLIERS really is a view; some users may be aware of that fact (and of the fact that there is a real table S underneath), others may genuinely believe that GOOD_SUPPLIERS is a "real" table in its own right. Either way, it makes little difference: The point is, users can operate on GOOD_SUPPLIERS just as if it were a real table (with certain exceptions, to be discussed later). For instance, here is an example of a retrieval operation (SELECT statement) against GOOD_SUPPLIERS:

```
SELECT *
FROM    GOOD_SUPPLIERS
WHERE   CITY ~= 'London' ;
```

As you can see, this SELECT certainly looks just like a normal SELECT on a conventional base table. The system (actually Bind) handles such an operation by converting it into an equivalent operation on the underlying base table (or base tables, plural—see Section 10.2). In the example, the equivalent operation is

```
SELECT S#, STATUS, CITY
FROM    S
WHERE   CITY ~= 'London'
AND     STATUS > 15 ;
```

This new statement can now be compiled—i.e., bound—and executed in the usual way. The conversion is done by (in effect) *merging* the SELECT issued by the user with the SELECT that was saved in the catalog when the view was defined. From the catalog, the system knows that "FROM GOOD_SUPPLIERS" really means "FROM S"; it also knows that any selection from GOOD_SUPPLIERS must be further qualified by the WHERE condition "STATUS > 15"; and it also knows that "SELECT *" (from GOOD_SUPPLIERS) really means "SELECT S#, STATUS, CITY" (from S). Hence it is able to translate the original SELECT on the virtual table GOOD_SUPPLIERS into an equivalent SELECT on the real table S—equivalent, in the sense that the effect of executing that SELECT on the real table S is as if there really were a base table called GOOD_SUPPLIERS and the original SELECT were executed on that.

Update operations are treated in a similar manner. For example, the operation

```
UPDATE  GOOD_SUPPLIERS
SET     STATUS = STATUS + 10
WHERE   CITY = 'Paris' ;
```

will be converted by Bind into

```
UPDATE  S
SET     STATUS = STATUS + 10
WHERE   CITY = 'Paris'
AND     STATUS > 15 ;
```

INSERT and DELETE operations are handled analogously.

10.2 VIEW DEFINITION

The general syntax of CREATE VIEW is

```
CREATE VIEW view [ ( column [, column ] ... ) ]
    AS subquery
  [ WITH CHECK OPTION ] ;
```

As usual, the subquery cannot include either UNION or ORDER BY;* apart from these restrictions, however, any SELECT that can appear as a standalone statement can also appear in a CREATE VIEW statement. Here are some examples.

---

*UNION and ORDER BY can be used in retrieval operations involving the view, of course.

```
1. CREATE VIEW REDPARTS ( P#, PNAME, WT, CITY )
       AS SELECT P#, PNAME, WEIGHT, CITY
          FROM   P
          WHERE  COLOR = 'Red' ;
```

The effect of this statement is to create a new view called *xyz*.
REDPARTS, where *xyz* is the system-known name for the user issuing the
CREATE VIEW statement. User *xyz* can refer to the view as simply
REDPARTS; other users can refer to it as *xyz*.REDPARTS (alternatively,
of course, they can introduce a synonym for it, as discussed in Chapter 9).
The view has four columns, called P#, PNAME, WT, and CITY, corresponding respectively to the four columns P#, PNAME, WEIGHT, and
CITY of the underlying base table P. If column names are not specified
explicitly in the CREATE VIEW, then the view inherits column names from
the source of the view in the obvious way (in the example, the inherited
names would be P#, PNAME, WEIGHT, and CITY). Column names *must*
be specified explicitly (for all columns of the view) if

(a) any column of the view is derived from a function, an operational ex-
    pression, or a constant (and so has no name that can be inherited), or
    if

(b) two or more columns of the view would otherwise have the same name.

See the next two examples for illustrations of each of these two cases.

```
2. CREATE VIEW PQ ( P#, TOTQTY )
       AS SELECT P#, SUM (QTY)
          FROM   SP
          GROUP  BY P# ;
```

In this example, there is no name that can be inherited for the second
column, since that column is derived from a builtin aggregate function;
hence column names *must* be specified explicitly, as shown. Notice that this
view is not just a simple row-and-column subset of the underlying base table
(unlike the views REDPARTS and GOOD_SUPPLIERS shown earlier). It
might be regarded instead as a kind of statistical summary or compression
of that underlying table.

```
3. CREATE VIEW CITY_PAIRS ( SCITY, PCITY )
       AS SELECT DISTINCT S.CITY, P.CITY
          FROM   S, SP, P
          WHERE  S.S# = SP.S#
          AND    SP.P# = P.P# ;
```

The meaning of this particular view is that a pair of city names (x,y)
will appear in the view if and only if a supplier located in city x supplies a
part stored in city y. For example, supplier S1 supplies part P1; supplier
S1 is located in London and part P1 is stored in London; and so the pair

(London,London) appears in the view. Notice that the definition of this
view involves a join, so that this is an example of a view that is derived
from multiple underlying tables.

```
4. CREATE VIEW LONDON_REDPARTS
       AS SELECT P#, WT
          FROM    REDPARTS
          WHERE   CITY = 'London' ;
```

Since the definition of a view can be any valid subquery, and since a
subquery can select data from views as well as from base tables, it is perfectly possible to define a view in terms of other views, as in this example.

```
5. CREATE VIEW GOOD_SUPPLIERS
       AS SELECT S#, STATUS, CITY
          FROM    S
          WHERE   STATUS > 15
          WITH CHECK OPTION ;
```

The clause "WITH CHECK OPTION" indicates that UPDATE and
INSERT operations against the view are to be checked to ensure that the
UPDATEd or INSERTed row satisfies the view-defining predicate
(STATUS > 15, in the example). The CHECK option is described in more
detail in Section 10.4.

The syntax of DROP VIEW is

```
DROP VIEW view ;
```

The specified view is dropped (i.e., its definition is removed from the
catalog). Any views defined in terms of that view are automatically dropped
too. Here is an example:

```
DROP VIEW REDPARTS ;
```

If a base table is dropped, all views defined on that base table (or on
views of that base table, etc.) are automatically dropped too.

There is no ALTER VIEW statement. Altering a base table (via ALTER
TABLE) has no effect on any existing views.

10.3 RETRIEVAL OPERATIONS

We have already explained in outline (in Section 10.1) how retrieval operations on a view are converted into equivalent operations on the underlying
base table(s). Usually that conversion process is quite straightforward and
works perfectly well, without any surprises for the user. Occasionally, however, such surprises can occur. In particular, problems can arise if the user
tries to treat a view field as a conventional field and that view field is derived

from something other than a simple field of the underlying base table—for example, if it is derived from a function. Consider the following example.
   View definition:

```
CREATE VIEW PQ ( P#, TOTQTY )
     AS SELECT P#, SUM (QTY)
        FROM   SP
        GROUP  BY P# ;
```

(this is the "statistical summary" view, Example 2 from Section 10.2).
   Attempted query:

```
SELECT *
FROM   PQ
WHERE  TOTQTY > 500 ;
```

If we apply the simple merging process described in Section 10.1 to combine this query with the view definition stored in the catalog, we obtain something like the following:

```
SELECT P#, SUM (QTY)
FROM   SP
WHERE  SUM (QTY) > 500
GROUP  BY P# ;
```

And this is not a valid SELECT statement. Predicates in a WHERE clause are not allowed to refer to aggregate functions such as SUM. What the original query should be converted to is something more along the following lines:

```
SELECT P#, SUM (QTY)
FROM   SP
GROUP  BY P#
HAVING SUM (QTY) > 500 ;
```

However, DB2 is not capable of performing such a conversion.
   Note: The first two releases of DB2 were particularly weak in this area; retrievals against a view could fail in numerous surprising ways (for example, if the retrieval involved a GROUP BY and the view definition did also). Matters have improved somewhat since that time, as follows: In some cases—but unfortunately not all—DB2 now recognizes when the merging process would yield an invalid SELECT statement, and instead materializes the view and applies the requested retrieval to that materialized version. But it is still not easy to characterize precisely the cases that fail and those that do not. SQL really does not do a very good job on views.

10.4   UPDATE OPERATIONS

We have already stated (in Chapter 8) that *not all views are updatable.* We are now in a position to be able to amplify that statement. *Note:* Before going any further, we should stress the point that DB2—like most other systems at the time of writing—does not in fact handle the updating of views in a very systematic manner. In what follows, therefore, we first consider the question of view updating from a somewhat theoretical standpoint, then go on to discuss the more directly practical question of how DB2 actually behaves. The whole subject of view updating in general is discussed in much more detail (but rather formally) in the book *Relational Database: Selected Writings,* by C. J. Date (Addison-Wesley, 1986).

First, consider the two views GOOD_SUPPLIERS and CITY_PAIRS defined earlier in this chapter. For convenience, we repeat their definitions below:

```
CREATE VIEW GOOD_SUPPLIERS
     AS SELECT S#, STATUS, CITY
        FROM   S
        WHERE  STATUS > 15 ;

CREATE VIEW CITY_PAIRS ( SCITY, PCITY )
     AS SELECT DISTINCT S.CITY, P.CITY
        FROM   S, SP, P
        WHERE  S.S# = SP.S#
        AND    SP.P# = P.P# ;
```

Of these two views, GOOD_SUPPLIERS is logically updatable, while CITY_PAIRS is logically not. It is instructive to examine why this is so. In the case of GOOD_SUPPLIERS:

(a) We can INSERT a new row into the view—say the row (S6,40,Rome)—by actually inserting the corresponding row (S6,bbbb,40,Rome) into the underlying base table. *Note:* As usual, we are using bbbb to represent a string of blanks.

(b) We can DELETE an existing row from the view—say the row (S1,20,London)—by actually deleting the corresponding row (S1,Smith,20,London) from the underlying base table.

(c) We can UPDATE an existing field in the view—say to change the city for supplier S1 from London to Rome—by actually making that same change in the corresponding field in the underlying base table.

We will refer to a view such as GOOD_SUPPLIERS, which is derived from a single base table by simply eliminating certain rows and certain columns of that table, *while preserving that table's primary key,* as a *key-preserving-subset* view. (Remember from Chapter 1 that the primary key is basically just a unique identifier.) Such views are inherently updatable, as the foregoing discussion shows by example.

Now consider the view CITY_PAIRS (which is certainly not a key-preserving-subset view). As explained earlier, one of the rows in that view is the row (London,London). Suppose it were possible to DELETE that row. What would such a DELETE signify?—i.e., what updates (DELETEs or otherwise) on the underlying data would such a DELETE correspond to? The only possible answer has to be "We don't know"; there is simply no way (in general) that we can go down to the underlying base tables and make an appropriate set of updates there. In fact, such an "appropriate set of updates" does not even exist; there is no set of updates (in general) that could be applied to the underlying data that would have *precisely* the effect of removing the row (London,London) from the view while leaving everything else in the view unchanged. In other words, *the original DELETE is an inherently unsupportable operation.* Similar arguments can be made to show that INSERT and UPDATE operations are also inherently not supportable on this view.

Thus we see that some views are inherently updatable, whereas others are inherently not. *Note the word "inherently" here.* It is not just a question of some systems being able to support certain updates while others cannot. *No* system can consistently support updates on a view such as CITY_PAIRS unaided (by "unaided" we mean "without help from some human user"). As a consequence of this fact, it is possible to classify views as indicated by the Venn diagram shown in Fig. 10.2.

Note carefully from the figure that although key-preserving-subset views (such as GOOD_SUPPLIERS) are always theoretically updatable, *not all theoretically updatable views are key-preserving-subset views.* In other words, there are some views that *are* theoretically updatable that are *not* key-preserving-subset views. The trouble is, although we know that such views exist, we do not know precisely which ones they are; it is still (in part) a research problem to pin down precisely what it is that characterizes such views.

Now, although it is true that DB2 does support the concept of a primary key, it is unfortunately the case that that support was added only recently—it was not included in Version 1 of the product at all. As a result, DB2's view-updating mechanism does not operate in terms of key-preserving-subset views. Instead, it operates in terms of what we will call *row-and-column-subset* views. A row-and-column-subset view is a view that is derived from a single base table by simply eliminating certain rows and certain columns of that table. A row-and-column-subset view may or may not be a key-preserving-subset view. (More precisely, all key-preserving-subset views are row-and-column-subset views, but the converse is not true.) For the purposes of this book, therefore, the important point is the following:

In DB2, only row-and-column-subset views can be updated.

(Actually even this statement is still not 100 percent accurate. We will make it more precise in a moment.) DB2 is not alone in this regard, by the way;

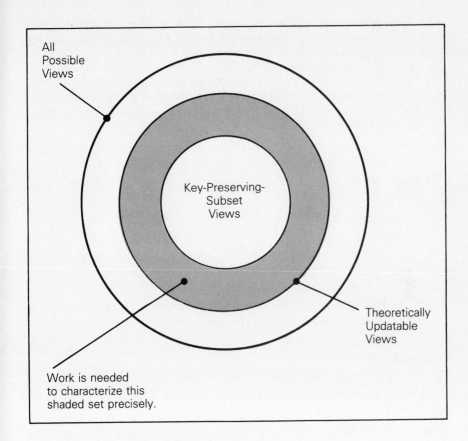

Fig. 10.2. Classification of views

very few products currently support update operations on views that are not row-and-column-subsets, and *no* product currently supports update operations on all views that are theoretically updatable.

The fact that not all views are updatable is frequently expressed as "You cannot update a join." That statement is *not* an accurate characterization of the situation, nor indeed of the problem: There are some views that are not joins that are not updatable, and there are some views that are joins that are (theoretically) updatable—although not updatable in DB2. But it is true that joins represent the "interesting case," in the sense that it would be very convenient to be able to update a view whose definition involved a join. Now, it may well be the case that such views will indeed be updatable in some future DB2 release; but we are concerned here only with what DB2 will currently allow. Let us now make it clear exactly what that is. In DB2, a view that is to accept updates must be derived from a single base table. Moreover:

(a) If a field of the view is derived from an expression involving a scalar operator or a scalar function or a constant, then INSERT operations are not allowed, and UPDATE operations are not allowed on that field. However, DELETE operations are allowed.

(b) If a field of the view is derived from an aggregate function, then the view is not updatable.

(c) If the definition of the view involves GROUP BY or HAVING, then the view is not updatable.

(d) If the definition of the view involves DISTINCT, then the view is not updatable.

(e) If the definition of the view includes a nested subquery and the FROM clause in that subquery refers to the base table on which the view is defined, then the view is not updatable.

(f) If the FROM clause in the view definition involves multiple (explicit or implicit) range variables, then the view is not updatable.

Finally, of course, a view defined over a nonupdatable view is itself not updatable.

Let us examine the reasonableness of these restrictions. We consider each of the cases (a)–(f) in turn. For each case, we begin by considering an example of a view that illustrates the restriction.

Case (a): View field derived from an expression involving a scalar operator (or a scalar function or a constant)

```
CREATE VIEW P_IN_GRAMS ( P#, GMWT )
    AS SELECT P#, WEIGHT * 454
       FROM   P ;
```

Assuming that table P is as given in Fig. 1.2 (Chapter 1), the set of rows visible through this view is as follows:

```
P_IN_GRAMS     P#    GMWT
               --    ----
               P1    5448
               P2    7718
               P3    7718
               P4    6356
               P5    5448
               P6    8626
```

It should be clear that P_IN_GRAMS cannot support INSERT operations, nor UPDATE operations on the field GMWT. (Each of those operations would require the system to be able to convert a gram weight back into pounds, without any knowledge as to how to perform such a conversion.) On the other hand, DELETE operations can be supported (e.g., deleting the row for part P1 from the view can be handled by deleting the row for part P1 from the underlying base table), and so can UPDATE operations on field P# (such UPDATEs simply require a corresponding UPDATE on field P# of that base table).

Similar considerations apply to a view that includes a field that is derived from a scalar function or a constant instead of an operational expression.

Case (b): View field derived from an aggregate function

```
CREATE VIEW TQ ( TOTQTY )
    AS SELECT SUM (QTY)
       FROM     SP ;
```

Sample value:

```
TQ    TOTQTY
      ------
       3100
```

It should be obvious that none of INSERT, UPDATE, DELETE makes any sense on this view.

Case (c): View defined with GROUP BY (and/or HAVING)

```
CREATE VIEW PQ ( P#, TOTQTY )
    AS SELECT P#, SUM (QTY)
       FROM     SP
       GROUP  BY P# ;
```

Sample values:

```
PQ    P#    TOTQTY
      --    ------
      P1      600
      P2     1000
      P3      400
      P4      500
      P5      500
      P6      100
```

It is obvious that view PQ cannot support INSERT operations, nor UPDATE operations against field TOTQTY. DELETE operations, and UPDATE operations against field P#, theoretically *could* be defined to DELETE or UPDATE all corresponding rows in table SP—for example, the operation

```
DELETE
FROM    PQ
WHERE   P# = 'P1' ;
```

could be defined to translate into

```
DELETE
FROM    SP
WHERE   P# = 'P1' ;
```

—but such operations could equally well be expressed directly in terms of table SP anyway. And it is at least arguable that a user who is issuing such operations should have to know exactly which real records are affected by those operations.

Case (d): View defined with DISTINCT

```
CREATE VIEW CC
    AS SELECT DISTINCT COLOR, CITY
       FROM   P ;
```

Sample values (with corresponding part number(s)):

```
CC    COLOR  CITY
      -----  ------
      Red    London    (from P1,P4,P6)
      Green  Paris     (from P2)
      Blue   Rome      (from P3)
      Blue   Paris     (from P5)
```

Again, it should be clear that view CC cannot support INSERT operations (INSERTs on the underlying table P require the user to specify a P# value, because part numbers are defined to be NOT NULL). As in case (c), DELETE and UPDATE operations *could* theoretically be defined (to DELETE or UPDATE all corresponding rows in P), but the remarks on this possibility under case (c) apply again here, with perhaps even more force.

Here is another example of case (d):

```
CREATE VIEW PC
    AS SELECT DISTINCT P#, COLOR
       FROM   P ;
```

Sample values:

```
PC    P#     COLOR
      --     -----
      P1     Red
      P2     Green
      P3     Blue
      P4     Red
      P5     Blue
      P6     Red
```

This is an example of a view that is obviously updatable in theory—all possible INSERT, UPDATE, and DELETE operations against the view are clearly well-defined. In fact, the view is really a row-and-column-subset view (actually, it is a key-preserving-subset view); but *DB2 is not aware of that fact.* To put it another way, DB2 is not aware of the fact that the DISTINCT specification is actually superfluous here; instead, it simply assumes that the presence of DISTINCT means that any given row of the view *might* be derived from multiple rows of the base table, as in the previous example, and so does not consider the view to be updatable.

Case (e): View involving subquery over same table

```
CREATE VIEW S_UNDER_AVG
    AS SELECT S#, SNAME, STATUS, CITY
        FROM   S
        WHERE  STATUS <
            ( SELECT AVG (STATUS)
              FROM   S ) ;
```

UPDATE and DELETE operations against S_UNDER_AVG are illegal because they would violate the restriction on such operations mentioned at the end of Chapter 8 (Section 8.5). INSERT operations are illegal also, for essentially similar reasons.

Case (f): View involving multiple (explicit or implicit) range variables

```
CREATE VIEW CITY_PAIRS ( SCITY, PCITY )
        AS SELECT DISTINCT S.CITY, P.CITY
            FROM   S, P
            WHERE  S.S# = SP.S#
            AND    SP.P# = P.P# ;
```

This view is not updatable, for reasons that have been adequately discussed already. However, consider this next example:

```
CREATE VIEW P2_SUPPLIERS
    AS SELECT S#, SNAME, STATUS, CITY
        FROM   S, SP
        WHERE  S.S# = SP.S#
        AND    SP.P# = 'P2' ;
```

This view is also not updatable in DB2, even though (once again) it is in fact a key-preserving-subset view; once again, DB2 is not capable of recognizing that fact. What makes this example interesting is that in this case a semantically equivalent view can be defined that *is* updatable, viz:

```
CREATE VIEW P2_SUPPLIERS
    AS SELECT S#, SNAME, STATUS, CITY
        FROM   S
        WHERE  S# IN
            ( SELECT S#
              FROM   SP
              WHERE  P# = 'P2' ) ;
```

This version does not violate the "multiple tables in the FROM clause" rule.

Finally, we return to the GOOD_SUPPLIERS view once again, in order to discuss a number of remaining issues. The definition of that view (to repeat) is:

```
CREATE VIEW GOOD_SUPPLIERS
    AS SELECT S#, STATUS, CITY
       FROM   S
       WHERE  STATUS > 15 ;
```

This view is a row-and-column-subset view and is therefore updatable. But note the following:

(a) A successful INSERT against GOOD_SUPPLIERS will have to generate an appropriate default value (or null) for the missing field SNAME. Of course, field SNAME must have been defined either with the specification NOT NULL WITH DEFAULT, or with the NOT NULL specification omitted entirely, if the INSERT is to succeed.

(b) With the data values given in Fig. 1.2, supplier S2 will not be visible through the GOOD_SUPPLIERS view. But that does not mean that the user can INSERT a record into that view with supplier number value S2, or UPDATE one of the other records so that its supplier number value becomes S2. Such an operation must be rejected, just as if it had been applied directly to table S.

(c) Last, consider the following UPDATE:

```
UPDATE GOOD_SUPPLIERS
SET    STATUS = 0
WHERE  S# = 'S1' ;
```

Should this UPDATE be accepted? If it is, it will have the effect of removing supplier S1 from the view, since the S1 record will no longer satisfy the view-defining predicate. Likewise, the INSERT operation

```
INSERT
INTO   GOOD_SUPPLIERS ( S#, STATUS, CITY )
VALUES ( 'S8', 7, 'Stockholm' ) ;
```

(if accepted) will create a new supplier record, but that record will instantly vanish from the view. The CHECK option (mentioned in Section 10.2) is designed to deal with such situations. If the clause

```
WITH CHECK OPTION
```

is included in the definition of a view, then all INSERTs and UPDATEs against that view will be checked to ensure that the newly INSERTed or UPDATEd record does indeed satisfy the view-defining predicate. If it does not, then the operation will be rejected.

The CHECK option can be specified only if the view is updatable *and* its definition does not include a nested subquery. If the view is such that UPDATEs are legal on certain fields only (and INSERTs are not allowed at all), then the CHECK option applies only to those UPDATE operations.

Note finally that if V is a view for which the CHECK option has been specified, and if W is a view defined on top of V, then the CHECK option for V is automatically inherited by W; that is, updates to V via W will be checked against the defining predicate for V. (This rule of inheritance was added to DB2 in Version 1 Release 3; it did not apply to the first two releases.)

10.5 LOGICAL DATA INDEPENDENCE

We have not yet really explained what views are for. One of the things they are for is the provision of what is called *logical data independence*. The notion of *physical* data independence was introduced in Chapter 2: A system like DB2 is said to provide physical data independence because users and user programs are independent of the physical structure of the stored database. A system provides *logical* data independence if users and user programs are also independent of the *logical* structure of the database. There are two aspects to such independence, namely *growth* and *restructuring*.

Growth

As the database grows to incorporate new kinds of information, so the definition of the database must also grow accordingly. (*Note:* We discuss the question of growth in the database here only for completeness; it is important, but it has nothing to do with views as such.) There are two possible types of growth that can occur:

1. The expansion of an existing base table to include a new field (corresponding to the addition of new information concerning some existing type of object—for example, the addition of a COST field to the parts base table);
2. The inclusion of a new base table (corresponding to the addition of a new type of object—for example, the addition of a projects table to the suppliers-and-parts database).

Neither of these two kinds of change should have any effect on existing users at all (unless those users have been using "SELECT *" or INSERT with the list of field names omitted; as mentioned earlier in this book, the meanings of such statements may change if they happen to be rebound and the definition of the table concerned has changed in the interim).

Restructuring

Occasionally it may become necessary to restructure the database in such a way that, although the overall information content remains the same, the placement of information within that database changes—i.e., the allocation of fields to tables is altered in some way. Before proceeding further, we make the point that such restructuring is generally undesirable; however, it is sometimes unavoidable. For example, it may be necessary to split a table "vertically," so that commonly required columns can be stored on a faster device and less frequently required columns on a slower device. Let us consider this case in some detail. Suppose for the sake of the example that it becomes necessary (for some reason—the precise reason is not important here) to replace base table S by the following two base tables:

```
SX  ( S#, SNAME, CITY )
SY  ( S#, STATUS )
```

Aside: This replacement operation is not entirely trivial, by the way. One way it might be handled is by means of the following sequence of SQL operations:

```
CREATE TABLE SX
    ( S#      CHAR(5)  NOT NULL,
      SNAME   CHAR(20) NOT NULL WITH DEFAULT,
      CITY    CHAR(15) NOT NULL WITH DEFAULT,
    PRIMARY KEY ( S# ) ) ;

CREATE UNIQUE INDEX XSX ON SX ( S# )  ;

CREATE TABLE SY
    ( S#      CHAR(5)  NOT NULL,
      STATUS  SMALLINT,
    PRIMARY KEY ( S# ) ) ;

CREATE UNIQUE INDEX XSY ON SY ( S# )  ;


INSERT INTO SX ( S#, SNAME, CITY )
    SELECT S#, SNAME, CITY
    FROM   S ;

INSERT INTO SY ( S#, STATUS )
    SELECT S#, STATUS
    FROM   S ;

DROP TABLE S ;
```

It should also be mentioned in passing that splitting a table "vertically" into two new tables, as in this example, has numerous additional implications—implications, that is, over and above the question of logical data independence that is the principal subject of the present section. For example, DB2 makes it rather difficult to maintain the two tables SX and SY "in synch" with one another once they have been created, for reasons discussed (briefly) in Chapter 12. However, now we are straying too far from the main topic of discussion. To return to that topic:

The crucial point to observe in the example is that *the old table S is the (natural) join of the two new tables SX and SY* (over supplier numbers). For example, in table S we had the row (S1,Smith,20,London); in SX we now have the row (S1,Smith,London) and in SY the row (S1,20); join them together and we get the row (S1,Smith,20,London), as before. So we create a *view* that is exactly that join, and we name it S:

```
CREATE VIEW S ( S#, SNAME, STATUS, CITY )
    AS SELECT SX.S#, SX.SNAME, SY.STATUS, SX.CITY
       FROM   SX, SY
       WHERE  SX.S# = SY.S# ;
```

Any program that previously referred to base table S will now refer to view S instead. SELECT operations will continue to work exactly as before (though they will require additional analysis during the bind process and will incur additional execution-time overhead). However, update operations will no longer work, because (as explained in Section 10.4) DB2 will not allow updates against a view that is defined as a join. In other words, a user performing update operations is not immune to this type of change, but instead must make some manual alterations to the update statements concerned (and then re-precompile and rebind them).

Thus we have shown that DB2 does *not* provide complete protection against changes in the logical structure of the database (which is why such changes are not a good idea in the first place). But things may not be as bad as they seem, even if manual program alterations are necessary. First, it is easy to discover which programs have to be altered in the light of any such changes; that information can be obtained from the catalog. Second, it is easy to find the statements that need to be changed in those programs; quite apart from anything else, they all start with the prefix EXEC SQL. Third (and most significant), SQL is a very high-level language. The number of statements that have to be changed is therefore usually small, and the meaning of those statements is usually readily apparent; as a result, the necessary changes are usually easy to make. It is *not* like having to change statements in a comparatively low-level language such as COBOL or DL/I (the database language of IMS), where the meaning of a given statement is likely to be highly dependent on the dynamic flow of control through the program to the statement in question. So, even though it is true that manual corrections must be made, the amount of work involved may not be all that great in practice.

To return to the SX-SY example for a moment: Actually, the view S (defined as the join of SX and SY) is a good example of a join view that *is* theoretically updatable. If we assume that the tables SX and SY are kept "in synch" at all times (so that any supplier appearing in SX also appears in SY, and vice versa), then the effect of all possible update operations on view S is clearly defined in terms of SX and SY. (Exercise: Do you agree with this statement?) Thus the example illustrates, not only why the ability to update join views would be a useful system feature, but also a case where such updating appears to be a feasible proposition.

10.6 ADVANTAGES OF VIEWS

We conclude this chapter with a brief summary of the advantages of views.

- They provide a certain amount of logical data independence in the face of restructuring in the database, as explained in the previous section.

- They allow the same data to be seen by different users in different ways (possibly even at the same time).

    This consideration is obviously important when there are many different categories of user all interacting with a single integrated database.

- The user's perception is simplified.

    It is obvious that the view mechanism allows users to focus on just the data that is of concern to them and to ignore the rest. What is perhaps not so obvious is that, for retrieval at least, that mechanism can also considerably simplify users' data manipulation operations. In particular, because the user can be provided with a view in which all underlying tables are joined together, the need for explicit operations to step from table to table can be greatly reduced. As an example, consider the view CITY_PAIRS, and contrast (a) the SELECT needed to find cities storing parts that are available from London using that view with (b) the SELECT needed to obtain the same result directly from the underlying base tables. In effect, the complex selection process has been moved out of the realm of data manipulation and into that of data definition (in fact, the distinction between the two realms is far from clearcut in relational languages such as SQL).

- Automatic security is provided for hidden data.

    "Hidden data" refers to data not visible through some given view. Such data is clearly secure from access through that particular view. Thus, forcing users to access the database via views is a simple but effective mechanism for authorization control. We will discuss this aspect of views in greater detail in the next chapter.

EXERCISES

10.1 Define relation SP of the suppliers-and-parts database as a view of relation SPJ of the suppliers-parts-projects database.

10.2 Create a view from the suppliers-parts-projects database consisting of all projects (project number and city fields only) that are supplied by supplier S1 or use part P1.

10.3 (a) Is your solution to Exercise 10.2 an updatable view?

(b) If it is, can the CHECK option be specified for it?

(c) If it is not, give an updatable version, and repeat part (b) of this exercise.

10.4 Create a view consisting of supplier numbers and part numbers for suppliers and parts that are not "colocated."

10.5 Create a view consisting of supplier records for suppliers that are located in London (only).

10.6 Given the view definition:

```
CREATE VIEW SUMMARY ( S#, P#, MAXQ, MINQ, AVGQ )
     AS SELECT S#, P#, MAX (QTY), MIN (QTY), AVG (QTY)
        FROM    SPJ
        GROUP  BY S#, P#
        HAVING SUM (QTY) > 50 ;
```

state which of the following operations are legal and, for those that are, give the translated equivalents. *Warning:* You will need to refer to the IBM manuals in order to be able to give a definitive set of answers to this exercise; the body of this chapter does not include quite enough information. Nevertheless, we recommend that you try the exercise anyway, because it will give you some insight into the problems of view processing. The answers we provide are accurate as of the time of writing.

```
(a) SELECT *
    FROM    SUMMARY ;

(b) SELECT *
    FROM    SUMMARY
    ORDER  BY MAXQ ;

(c) SELECT *
    FROM    SUMMARY
    WHERE   S# ~= 'S1' ;

(d) SELECT *
    FROM    SUMMARY
    WHERE   MAXQ > 250 ;

(e) SELECT MAXQ - MINQ, S#, P#
    FROM    SUMMARY
    WHERE   S# = 'S1'
    AND     P# = 'P1' ;

(f) SELECT S#
    FROM    SUMMARY
    GROUP  BY S# ;
```

```
(g)   SELECT  S#, MAXQ
      FROM    SUMMARY
      GROUP   BY S#, MAXQ ;

(h)   SELECT  S.S#, SUMMARY.AVGQ
      FROM    S, SUMMARY
      WHERE   S.S# = SUMMARY.S# ;

(i)   UPDATE SUMMARY
      SET     S# = 'S2'
      WHERE   S# = 'S1' ;

(j)   UPDATE SUMMARY
      SET     MAXQ = 1000
      WHERE   S# = 'S1' ;

(k)   DELETE
      FROM    SUMMARY
      WHERE   S# = 'S1' ;
```

10.7 State the rules concerning the updatability of views in DB2.

10.8 State the rules concerning the CHECK option.

10.9 Suppose the database is restructured in such a way that tables *A* and *B* are replaced by their natural join *C*. To what extent can the view mechanism conceal that restructuring from existing users?

10.10 Create a view consisting of names of all cities that appear either in the suppliers table or in the parts table.

ANSWERS TO SELECTED EXERCISES

10.1 The problem here is: How should the field SP.QTY be defined? The sensible answer seems to be that, for a given (S#,P#) pair, SP.QTY should be the *sum* of all SPJ.QTY values, taken over all J#'s for that (S#,P#) pair:

```
CREATE VIEW SP ( S#, P#, QTY )
     AS SELECT S#, P#, SUM (QTY)
        FROM    SPJ
        GROUP   BY S#, P# ;
```

10.2
```
CREATE VIEW JC ( J#, CITY )
     AS SELECT DISTINCT J.J#, J.CITY
        FROM    J, SPJ
        WHERE   J.J# = SPJ.J#
        AND   ( SPJ.S# = 'S1' OR
                SPJ.P# = 'P1' ) ;
```

10.3 The view defined in the answer to Exercise 10.2 above is not updatable, because it includes multiple range variables in the FROM clause. Here is an updatable version:

```
CREATE VIEW JC ( J#, CITY )
     AS SELECT J.J#, J.CITY
        FROM    J
        WHERE   J.J# IN
                ( SELECT J#
```

```
              FROM     SPJ
              WHERE    S# = 'S1' )
      OR      J.J# IN
            ( SELECT J#
              FROM     SPJ
              WHERE    P# = 'P1' ) ;
```

It is not possible to specify the CHECK option for this view, becauses its definition includes a nested subquery.

10.4 CREATE VIEW NON_COLOCATED
```
      AS SELECT S#, P#
         FROM    S, P
         WHERE   S.CITY ~= P.CITY ;
```

10.5 CREATE VIEW LONDON_SUPPLIERS
```
      AS SELECT S#, SNAME, STATUS
         FROM    S
         WHERE   CITY = 'London' ;
```

We have omitted the CITY column from the view, since we know its value must be London for every row visible through the view. Note, however, that this omission means that any record INSERTed through the view will instantly vanish from the view, since its CITY field will be set to blanks (or null).

10.6 The following (only) are illegal: (d), (i), (j), (k). Note, however, that (f), (g), and (h) were illegal also in the first two releases of DB2.

10.10 Cannot be done; SQL does not permit UNION to appear in a view definition (for no particularly good reason).

CHAPTER

·11·

Security and Authorization

11.1 INTRODUCTION

The term "security" is used in database contexts to mean the protection of the data in the database against unauthorized disclosure, alteration, or destruction. DB2, like most other relational systems, goes far beyond most nonrelational systems in the degree of security it provides. The unit of data that can be individually protected ranges all the way from an entire table to a specific data value at a specific row-and-column position within such a table. (For certain operations, in fact, the unit can even be greater than one table. For example, the unit for the console operator START and STOP commands is an entire database.) A given user can have different access privileges on different objects (e.g., SELECT privilege only on one table, SELECT and UPDATE privileges on another, and so on). Also, of course, different users can have different privileges on the same object; e.g., user *A* could have the SELECT privilege (only) on a given table, while another

173

user *B* could simultaneously have both SELECT and UPDATE privileges on that same table.

There are two more or less independent features of the system that are involved in the provision of security in DB2:

1. The view mechanism, which (as mentioned at the end of the previous chapter) can be used to hide sensitive data from unauthorized users, and

2. The authorization subsystem, which allows users having specific privileges selectively and dynamically to grant those privileges to other users, and subsequently to revoke those privileges if desired.

We examine the view mechanism in Section 11.3 and the authorization subsystem (specifically, the GRANT and REVOKE statements) in Section 11.4.

Of course, all decisions as to which specific privileges should be granted to which specific users are policy decisions, not technical ones. As such, they are clearly outside the jurisdiction of DB2 per se. All that DB2 can do is *enforce* those decisions once they are made. In order that DB2 should be able to perform this function properly:

(a) The results of those decisions must be made known to the system (this is done by means of the GRANT and REVOKE statements) and must be remembered by the system (this is done by saving them in the catalog, in the form of *authorization constraints*).

(b) There must be a means of checking a given access request against the applicable authorization constraints. (By "access request" here we mean the combination of requested operation plus target object plus requesting user.) Most such checking is done by Bind at the time the original request is bound (but see the discussion of the BIND command in Chapter 17, Section 17.2).

(c) In order that it may be able to decide which constraints are applicable to a given request, the system must be able to recognize the source of that request—that is, it must be able to recognize which particular user a particular request is coming from. Before getting into a discussion of the view mechanism and the authorization subsystem as such, then, we must first say something about user identification.

11.2 USER IDENTIFICATION

Users are known to DB2 by an "authorization identifier" (authorization ID for short). The authorization ID is what we have been referring to in earlier chapters as the user's "system-known name." If you are a legitimate user of the system, some responsible person in your organization (probably the system administrator—see Section 11.4, later) will have assigned an ID for your particular use. It is your responsibility to identify yourself by supplying that ID when you sign on to the system. Note that you do not sign on directly to DB2 itself; instead, you sign on to (e.g.) the IMS/DC or CICS data communications subsystem (see Chapter 3). That subsystem will then pass your ID on to DB2 when it passes control to DB2. Hence any validation or authentication of your ID (e.g., password checking) is done by the relevant subsystem, not by DB2. DB2 simply assumes that any request that purports to come from authorization ID *xyz* (say) does in fact come from *xyz*.

Note: DB2 Version 2 added a refinement to the foregoing in order to simplify certain operational problems that existed in Version 1. The basic point is that installations would typically like to deal with *user functional areas* rather than with individual users per se; for example, they would like to be able to grant some specific authority to "everyone in the accounting department," say, and to be able to add users to, and remove users from, the accounting department as a separate operation. With Version 2, therefore, the installation typically operates as follows:

1. Each individual user is assigned an authorization ID as described above. That ID is used to sign on to the system, and serves as the *primary* ID for the user in question. Tables and other objects that are purely private to that user will typically be created under the control of, and hence be owned by, that primary ID.

2. Each functional area (e.g., each department) in the organization is also assigned an authorization ID. However, that ID is typically *not* given sign-on authority; users sign on to the system under their primary ID, as explained in the previous paragraph. Once signed on, users can operate under their primary ID, or—using a new SQL statement, SET CURRENT SQLID—they can switch to a *secondary* ID (i.e., one of the functional area IDs). An external subsystem such as IBM's RACF (Resource Access Control Facility) keeps track of the secondary ID(s) that can legitimately be used by a given primary ID. Observe that a given primary ID can have any number of secondary IDs, also that the same secondary ID can be used by any number of primary IDs. *Note:* "CURRENT SQLID" is a special register, like CURRENT DATE, CURRENT TIME, etc. (see Chapter 4). Its value is an authorization ID.

3. The SET CURRENT SQLID statement has the format:

```
SET CURRENT SQLID = sqlid
```

where "sqlid" can be a character string constant, a host variable (if the SET statement is embedded in a host program—see Chapter 13), or USER. USER has the effect of restoring the primary ID as the current ID. (USER, like CURRENT SQLID, is a special register whose value is an authorization ID.)

Under the foregoing scheme, for example, user Joe can create a table that belongs to the accounting department *and that continues to do so even if Joe leaves that department and is removed from the system.* Any user that can use the accounting department ID as a secondary ID can access that table using that ID. The catalog shows the table as having the accounting department as its owner (confusingly called the CREATOR in the catalog table SYSTABLES) and as having been CREATED BY user Joe (CREATEDBY is another column in SYSTABLES, as explained in Chapter 9).

One final remark: Despite the foregoing, it still seems more intuitive to talk in terms of users rather than authorization IDs, and we will continue to do so for the remainder of this chapter. But the reader should clearly understand that when we say (for example) "User JUDY," we really mean "Any user operating under the (primary or secondary) authorization ID JUDY."

11.3 VIEWS AND SECURITY

To illustrate the use of views for security purposes, we present a series of examples, based once again (for the most part) on the suppliers-and-parts database. *Note:* The creator of a view must have at least the SELECT privilege on every table referenced in the view definition. See the discussion of access privileges in the next section.

1. For a user permitted access to complete supplier records, but only for suppliers located in Paris:

```
CREATE VIEW PARIS_SUPPLIERS
    AS SELECT S#, SNAME, STATUS, CITY
       FROM   S
       WHERE  CITY = 'Paris' ;
```

Users of this view see a "horizontal subset"—or (better) a row subset or *value-dependent* subset—of base table S.

2. For a user permitted access to all supplier records, but not to supplier ratings (STATUS values):

```
CREATE VIEW S#_NAME_CITY
    AS SELECT S#, SNAME, CITY
       FROM   S ;
```

Users of this view see a "vertical subset"—or (better) a column subset or *value-independent* subset—of base table S.

3. For a user permitted access to supplier records for suppliers in Paris (only), but not to supplier ratings:

```
CREATE VIEW PARIS_S#_NAME_CITY
    AS SELECT S#, SNAME, CITY
        FROM    S
        WHERE   CITY = 'Paris' ;
```

Users of this view see a row-and-column subset of base table S.

4. For a user permitted access to catalog rows (i.e., SYSTABLES entries) for tables created by that user only:

```
CREATE VIEW MY_TABLES
    AS SELECT *
        FROM    SYSIBM.SYSTABLES
        WHERE   CREATEDBY = USER ;
```

As explained in Section 11.2, USER is a "special register"—i.e., a builtin zero-argument scalar function (see Chapter 4)—whose value is an authorization ID. It can appear wherever a character string constant can appear. The authorization ID in question is the primary ID for the user issuing the *manipulative* statement that causes the USER reference to be evaluated. In the case at hand, for instance, it does not represent the ID of the user who creates the view, but rather the ID of the user who *uses* the view. For example, if user Joe issues the statement

```
SELECT *
FROM    MY_TABLES ;
```

then DB2 (actually Bind) will effectively convert that statement into

```
SELECT *
FROM    SYSIBM.SYSTABLES
WHERE   CREATEDBY = 'JOE' ;
```

Like the view in the first example above, this view represents a "horizontal subset" of the underlying base table. In the present example, however, different users see different subsets (in fact, no two users' subsets overlap). Such views are sometimes described as *context-dependent,* because their precise value depends on the context in which they are used.

5. For a user permitted access to average shipment quantities per supplier, but not to any individual quantities:

```
CREATE VIEW AVQ ( S#, AVGQTY )
    AS SELECT S#, AVG(QTY)
        FROM    SP
        GROUP   BY S# ;
```

Users of this view see a *statistical summary* of the underlying base table SP.

As the foregoing examples illustrate, the view mechanism of DB2 provides a very important measure of security "for free" ("for free" because the view mechanism is included in the system for other purposes anyway, as explained in Chapter 10). What is more, many authorization checks—even value-dependent checks—can be applied at compile time (i.e., bind time) instead of at execution time, a significant performance benefit. However, the view-based approach to security does suffer from some slight awkwardness on occasion—in particular, if some user needs different privileges over different subsets of the same table at the same time. Consider the following example. Suppose a given user is allowed to SELECT ratings (i.e., status values) for all suppliers but is allowed to UPDATE them only for suppliers in Paris. Then two views will be needed:

```
CREATE VIEW ALL_RATINGS
     AS SELECT S#, STATUS
        FROM   S ;

CREATE VIEW PARIS_RATINGS
     AS SELECT S#, STATUS
        FROM   S
        WHERE  CITY = 'Paris' ;
```

SELECT operations can be directed at ALL _ RATINGS but UPDATE operations must be directed at PARIS _ RATINGS instead. This fact can lead to rather obscure programming. Consider, for example, the structure of a program that scans and prints all supplier ratings and also updates some of them (those for suppliers in Paris) as it goes.

Another drawback has to do with the fact that, when a record is INSERTed or UPDATEd through a view, DB2 does not require that the new or updated record satisfy the view-defining predicate. It is possible to impose such a requirement via the CHECK option, but (as explained in Chapter 10) the CHECK option cannot always be used, and in any case it *is* an option—it does not have to be specified. Thus, for example, view PARIS_SUPPLIERS above can prevent the user from seeing suppliers who are not in Paris, but in the absence of the CHECK option it cannot prevent the user from inserting such a supplier or from moving an existing Paris supplier to some other city. Of course, any such operation will cause the new or updated record to vanish from the view, but it will still appear in the underlying base table.

11.4 GRANT AND REVOKE

The view mechanism discussed in Section 11.3 allows the database to be conceptually divided up into subsets (possibly overlapping subsets) in various ways so that sensitive information can be hidden from unauthorized users. However, it does not allow for the specification of the operations that *authorized* users may execute against those subsets. That function is performed by the SQL statements GRANT and REVOKE, which we now discuss.

First, in order to be able to perform any operation at all on any object at all, the user must hold the appropriate *privilege* (or authority) for the operation and object in question; otherwise, the operation will be rejected with an appropriate error message or exception code. For example, even to execute such a simple statement as

```
SELECT *
FROM    S ;
```

successfully, the user must hold the SELECT privilege on table S.

DB2 recognizes a wide range of privileges. Broadly speaking, however, every privilege falls into one of the following classes:

(a) *Table* privileges, which have to do with operations such as SELECT that apply to tables (both base tables and views);

(b) *Plan* privileges, which are concerned with such things as the authority to execute a given application plan;

(c) *Database* privileges, which apply to such operations as the creation of a table within a particular database;

(d) *Use* privileges, which have to do with the use of certain storage objects, namely storage groups, tablespaces, and buffer pools (see Chapter 16); and finally

(e) *System* privileges, which apply to certain system-wide operations, such as the operation of creating a new database.

There are also certain "bundled" privileges, which serve in effect as shorthand for collections of other privileges (not always from just one of the foregoing five classes). In particular, the *system administration* privilege (SYSADM) is shorthand for the collection of all other privileges in the system. Thus a user holding the SYSADM privilege can perform any operation in the entire system, providing it is legal. (An example of an operation that would not be "legal" in this sense would be an attempt to drop one of the catalog tables. Even a user with SYSADM authority cannot do that.)

We now present a description (slightly simplified) of how the overall security mechanism works. When DB2 is first installed, part of the installation process involves the designation of a specially privileged user as the *system administrator* for that DB2 system. (The system administrator is identified to DB2 by an authorization ID, of course, just like everyone else.) That user, who is automatically given the SYSADM privilege, will be responsible for overall control of the system throughout the system's lifetime; for example, monitoring DB2 execution and collecting performance statistics are part of the system administrator's job. But here we are concerned only with security considerations. To return to the main thread of the discussion, therefore: Initially, then, there is one user who can do everything—in particular, he or she can grant privileges to other users—and nobody else can do anything at all.

Note, incidentally, that although the system administrator is of course a holder of the SYSADM privilege, not all holders of the SYSADM privilege are the system administrator; other users can subsequently be granted the SYSADM privilege also, *but that privilege can subsequently be revoked again.* The SYSADM privilege can never be revoked from the system administrator.*

Next, a user who creates an object—say a base table—is automatically given full privileges on that object, including in particular the privilege of granting such privileges to another user. Of course, "full privileges" here does not include privileges that do not make sense. For example, if user U has the SELECT privilege (only) on base table T, and if U creates some view V that is based on T, then U certainly does not receive any update privileges on V. Likewise, if U creates a view V that is a join of tables $T1$ and $T2$, then U does not receive any update privileges on V, regardless of whether U holds such privileges on $T1$ and $T2$, because DB2 does not permit *any* update operations against a join view.

GRANT

Granting privileges is done by means of the GRANT statement. The general format of that statement is:

```
GRANT privileges [ ON [ type ] objects ] TO users ;
```

---

*Of course, this remark should not be construed to mean that there really is a single person who is the system administrator for all time (even if, e.g., that person leaves the company). Rather, there is a single *authorization ID* that is considered by the system to identify the system administrator. Anyone who can sign on to the system under that ID (and can supply the necessary password) will be treated as the system administrator so long as he or she remains signed on. The password *can* of course be changed from time to time, and probably should be.

where "privileges" is a list of one or more privileges, separated by commas, or the phrase ALL PRIVILEGES;* "users" is either a list of one or more authorization IDs, separated by commas, or the special keyword PUBLIC (meaning all users); "objects" is a list of names of one or more objects (all of the same type), separated by commas; and "type" indicates the type of that object or those objects (if "type" is omitted, it is assumed to be TABLE—see the last example under "Table privileges" below). The ON clause does not apply when the privileges being granted are system privileges. Here are some examples:

Table privileges:

```
GRANT SELECT ON TABLE S TO CHARLEY ;

GRANT SELECT, UPDATE (STATUS,CITY) ON TABLE S
               TO JUDY, JACK, JOHN ;

GRANT ALL PRIVILEGES ON TABLE S, P, SP TO PHIL, TED ;

GRANT SELECT ON TABLE P TO PUBLIC ;

GRANT DELETE ON S TO PHIL ;
```

Plan privileges:

```
GRANT EXECUTE ON PLAN PLANB TO JUDY ;
```

Database privileges:

```
GRANT CREATETAB ON DATABASE DBX TO SHARON ;
```

User SHARON is permitted to create tables in database DBX. See Chapter 16 for a discussion of databases.

Use privileges:

```
GRANT USE OF TABLESPACE DBX.TS76 TO TOM ;
```

User TOM is permitted to use tablespace TS76 in database DBX to store any tables he may create. Again, see Chapter 16 for further discussion.

System privileges:

```
GRANT CREATEDBC TO JACQUES, MARYANN ;
```

---

*ALL PRIVILEGES does not literally mean all privileges, but rather all privileges for which the user issuing the GRANT has grant authority. See the discussion of the GRANT option, later. The keyword PRIVILEGES in ALL PRIVILEGES is just noise and can be omitted.

Users JACQUES and MARYANN are permitted to create new databases. If they do so, they will automatically be given the DBCTRL privilege over those databases (see the end of this section).

It is not our purpose here to give a complete and exhaustive treatment of all of the numerous privileges that DB2 recognizes. We will, however, give a complete treatment of table privileges, since those are probably the ones of widest interest. The privileges that apply to tables (both base tables and views) are as follows:

```
SELECT
UPDATE    (can be column-specific)
DELETE
INSERT
```

The remaining two apply to base tables only:

```
ALTER    (privilege to execute ALTER TABLE on the table)
INDEX    (privilege to execute CREATE INDEX on the table)
```

To *create* a base table, as already mentioned, requires CREATETAB authority for the database to which the table is to belong.* To create a view requires SELECT authority on every table referenced in the definition of that view, as mentioned in Section 11.3. Note that SELECT authority, unlike UPDATE authority, is not column-specific. The reason for this fact is that the effect of a column-specific SELECT authority can always be obtained by granting (non-column-specific) SELECT authority on a *view* consisting of just the relevant columns.

REVOKE

If user *U1* grants some privilege to some other user *U2,* user *U1* can subsequently *revoke* that privilege from user *U2*. Revoking privileges is done by means of the REVOKE statement, whose general format is very similar to that of the GRANT statement:

```
REVOKE privileges [ ON [ type ] objects ] FROM users ;
```

Revoking a given privilege from a given user causes all application plans dependent on that privilege to be flagged as invalid, and hence causes an automatic rebind on the next invocation of each such plan. The process is

---

*There is no specific "DROP" privilege for dropping a base table, nor for dropping a view. Instead, a table (base table or view) can be dropped only by its owner or by a user holding appropriate administrative authority (e.g., SYSADM; see the subsection on "Bundled Privileges" at the end of this section).

essentially analogous to what happens when an object such as an index is dropped.

Here are some examples of the REVOKE statement:

```
REVOKE SELECT ON TABLE S FROM CHARLEY ;

REVOKE UPDATE ON TABLE S FROM JOHN ;

REVOKE CREATETAB ON DATABASE DBX FROM NANCY, JACK ;

REVOKE SYSADM FROM SAM ;
```

It is not possible to be column-specific when revoking an UPDATE privilege.

The GRANT Option

If user *U1* has the authority to grant a privilege *P* to another user *U2,* then user *U1* also has the authority to grant that privilege *P* to user *U2* "with the GRANT option" (by specifying WITH GRANT OPTION in the GRANT statement). Passing the GRANT option along from *U1* to *U2* in this manner means that *U2* in turn now has the authority to grant the privilege *P* to some third user *U3*. And therefore, of course, *U2* also has the authority to pass the GRANT option for *P* along to *U3* as well, etc., etc. For example:

User *U1:*

```
GRANT SELECT ON TABLE S TO U2 WITH GRANT OPTION ;
```

User *U2:*

```
GRANT SELECT ON TABLE S TO U3 WITH GRANT OPTION ;
```

User *U3:*

```
GRANT SELECT ON TABLE S TO U4 WITH GRANT OPTION ;
```

And so on. If user *U1* now issues

```
REVOKE SELECT ON TABLE S FROM U2 ;
```

then the revocation will *cascade* (that is, *U2*'s GRANT to *U3* and *U3*'s GRANT to *U4* will also be revoked automatically). Note, however, that it does *not* follow that *U2* and *U3* and *U4* no longer have SELECT authority on table S—they may additionally have obtained that authority from some other user *U5*. When *U1* REVOKEs, it is only authorities that are derived from *U1* that are in fact canceled. For example, consider the following sequence of events:

User *U1* at time *t1:*

```
GRANT SELECT ON TABLE S TO U2 WITH GRANT OPTION ;
```

User *U5* at time *t2:*

GRANT SELECT ON TABLE S TO U2 WITH GRANT OPTION ;

User *U2* at time *t3:*

GRANT SELECT ON TABLE S TO U3 ;

User *U1* at time *t4:*

REVOKE SELECT ON TABLE S FROM U2 ;

(*t1* < *t2* < *t3* < *t4*). User *U1's* REVOKE at time *t4* will not in fact remove the SELECT privilege on table S from user *U2*, because user *U2* has also received that privilege from *U5* at time *t2*. Furthermore, since user *U2's* GRANT to user *U3* was at time *t3* and *t3* > *t2*, it is possible that that GRANT was of the privilege that was received from user *U5* rather than from *U1*, so user *U3* does not lose the privilege either. And if the REVOKE at time *t4* is from user *U5* instead of user *U1*, users *U2* and *U3* would *still* keep the privilege; *U2* keeps the privilege received from *U1*, and *U2's* GRANT *could* have been of the privilege received from *U1* instead of *U5*, and so *U3* again does not lose the privilege either. However, suppose by contrast that the sequence of events had been as follows:

User *U1* at time *t1:*

GRANT SELECT ON TABLE S TO U2 WITH GRANT OPTION ;

User *U2* at time *t2:*

GRANT SELECT ON TABLE S TO U3 WITH GRANT OPTION ;

User *U5* at time *t3:*

GRANT SELECT ON TABLE S TO U2 WITH GRANT OPTION ;

User *U1* at time *t4:*

REVOKE SELECT ON TABLE S FROM U2 ;

User *U1's* REVOKE at time *t4* will not remove the SELECT privilege on table S from user *U2*, because user *U2* has also received that privilege from *U5* at time *t3*. In contrast with the previous example, however, it *will* remove the privilege from user *U3* at this time, because user *U2's* GRANT at time *t2* *must* have been of the privilege received from user *U1*.

It is not possible to revoke the GRANT option without at the same time revoking the privilege to which that option applies.

Bundled (Administrative) Privileges

We conclude this section with a brief sketch of the five "bundled" privileges, namely SYSADM, DBADM, DBCTRL, DBMAINT, and SYSOPR.

- SYSADM

  SYSADM ("system administrator") authority allows the holder to execute any operation that the system supports.

- DBADM

  DBADM ("database administration") authority on a specific database allows the holder to execute any operation that the system supports on that database.

- DBCTRL

  DBCTRL ("database control") authority on a specific database allows the holder to execute any operation that the system supports on that database, *except* for operations that access the data content of that database (e.g., utility operations such as "recover database" are allowed, but SQL data manipulation operations are not).

- DBMAINT

  DBMAINT ("database maintenance") authority on a specific database allows the holder to execute read-only maintenance functions (such as the utility operation "image copy") on that database.

- SYSOPR

  SYSOPR ("system operator") authority allows the holder to carry out console operator functions on the system (such as starting and stopping system trace activities).

For a particular database, DBADM subsumes DBCTRL, and DBCTRL subsumes DBMAINT. SYSADM, of course, subsumes everything.

11.5 CONCLUSION

By this point the reader may be feeling a little overwhelmed by the extent of the security facilities available with DB2. We therefore summarize below the authorization requirements that are most directly relevant to ordinary *users* (as we have defined that term—i.e., end-users or application programmers).

1. First, an application programmer needs no particular authority at all to precompile a source module (and hence to create a database request module or DBRM).

2. Binding one or more DBRMs to produce a new application plan requires the BINDADD privilege (which is a system privilege, incidentally, not a plan privilege).

3. Replacement of an existing application plan by an updated version, which may have to be done several times during the application development process, requires the BIND privilege (which is a plan privilege).

4. A user issuing the BIND command should normally have the appropriate privileges for all SQL statements in the DBRM(s) to be bound (but see the discussion of the BIND command in Chapter 17, Section 17.2).

5. Execution of a program that invokes an application plan requires the EXECUTE privilege (a plan privilege) for that plan. Table privileges (etc.) are *not* required.

6. Execution of a SQL statement (or indeed any other kind of operation) through the interactive interface DB2I (or through QMF, etc.) requires the privilege(s) appropriate to that particular statement or operation.

We conclude with the following observations.

1. First, the entire DB2 security mechanism is optional. It can be disabled if desired at DB2 start-up time. If it is, then of course anyone can do anything (anything that makes sense, that is; for example, it is still not possible to drop a catalog table). We have ignored this possibility (for obvious reasons) throughout the bulk of this chapter.

2. There is no point in a DBMS providing an extensive set of security controls if it is possible to bypass those controls. DB2's security mechanism would be almost useless if (for example) it were possible to access DB2 data from a conventional MVS program via conventional VSAM calls (remember from Chapter 1 that DB2 data is stored in VSAM linear data sets). For this reason, DB2 works in harmony with all the other software components in its environment—MVS, TSO, VSAM, IMS, CICS, etc.—to guarantee that the total system is secure. In particular, DB2's VSAM data sets can be protected by any or all of the following: MVS passwords, VSAM passwords, RACF (Resource Access Control Facility), and/or third-party security products. In addition, the security facilities of IMS and CICS can be used to provide all of the standard IMS and CICS controls—for example, to restrict the set of terminals from which specific applications or commands can be invoked.

3. Finally, DB2 also provides an *audit facility* by which an audit trail can be created showing attempted security violations (among other things). The audit information is written (via the DB2 Instrumentation Facility) to SMF or GTF data sets, not to DB2 tables. (SMF—"Systems Measurement Facility"—and GTF—"Generalized Trace Facility"—are standard MVS components.) Auditing can be restricted to specific tables and/or specific operations and can be dynamically and selectively started and stopped. The following items can be audited:

- authorization failures
- GRANT and REVOKE operations
- CREATE/ALTER/DROP TABLE operations
- first SELECT (per table per transaction)
- first update (per table per transaction)
- BINDs
- utility operations

Auditing is requested for a given table by means of the AUDIT option on CREATE and ALTER TABLE. AUDIT NONE (default) means no auditing; AUDIT CHANGES means audit INSERT/UPDATE/DELETE operations; AUDIT ALL means audit SELECT operations as well. Changing the AUDIT option (via ALTER TABLE) invalidates all application plans that use the table in question; as usual, such plans will automatically be rebound the next time they are invoked.

EXERCISES

Exercises 11.1 and 11.2 refer to a base table called STATS, defined as follows:

```
CREATE TABLE STATS
     ( USERID      CHAR(8)   NOT NULL,
       SEX         CHAR(1),
       DEPENDENTS  DECIMAL(2),
       OCCUPATION  CHAR(20),
       SALARY      DECIMAL(7),
       TAX         DECIMAL(7),
       AUDITS      DECIMAL(2),
     PRIMARY KEY ( USERID ) ) ;
```

11.1 Write SQL statements to give:

(a) User Ford SELECT privileges over the entire table.

(b) User Smith INSERT and DELETE privileges over the entire table.

(c) Each user SELECT privileges over that user's own record (only).

(d) User Nash SELECT privileges over the entire table and UPDATE privileges over the SALARY and TAX fields (only).

(e) User Todd SELECT privileges over the USERID, SALARY, and TAX fields (only).

(f) User Ward SELECT privileges as for Todd and UPDATE privileges over the SALARY and TAX fields (only).

(g) User Pope full privileges (SELECT, UPDATE, INSERT, DELETE) over records for preachers (only).

(h) User Jones SELECT privileges as for Todd and UPDATE privileges over the TAX and AUDITS fields (only).

(i) User King SELECT privileges for maximum and minimum salaries per occupation class, but no other privileges.

(j) User Clark DROP privileges on the table.

11.2 For each of parts (a) through (j) under Exercise 11.1, write SQL statements to remove the indicated privilege(s) from the user concerned.

11.3 Let p represent some privilege; let $U1, U2, \ldots, U8$ be a set of authorization IDs; and let $U1$ and $U5$ initially be the only holders of p. Further, assume that $U1$ and $U5$ hold the GRANT option for p. Consider the following sequence of events (note that all GRANTs include the specification WITH GRANT OPTION):

```
User U1 at time t1:    GRANT p TO U2 WITH GRANT OPTION ;
User U1 at time t2:    GRANT p TO U3 WITH GRANT OPTION ;
User U1 at time t3:    GRANT p TO U4 WITH GRANT OPTION ;
User U2 at time t4:    GRANT p TO U6 WITH GRANT OPTION ;
User U5 at time t5:    GRANT p TO U2 WITH GRANT OPTION ;
User U5 at time t6:    GRANT p TO U3 WITH GRANT OPTION ;
User U5 at time t7:    GRANT p TO U6 WITH GRANT OPTION ;
User U4 at time t8:    GRANT p TO U7 WITH GRANT OPTION ;
User U1 at time t9:    REVOKE p FROM U2 ;
User U1 at time t10:   REVOKE p FROM U4 ;
User U3 at time t11:   GRANT p TO U1 WITH GRANT OPTION ;
User U1 at time t12:   REVOKE p FROM U3 ;
User U3 at time t13:   GRANT p TO U7 WITH GRANT OPTION ;
User U5 at time t14:   REVOKE p FROM U6 ;
User U1 at time t15:   GRANT p TO U5 WITH GRANT OPTION ;
User U5 at time t16:   GRANT p TO U8 WITH GRANT OPTION ;
User U8 at time t17:   GRANT p TO U5 WITH GRANT OPTION ;
User U1 at time t18:   GRANT p TO U8 WITH GRANT OPTION ;
User U5 at time t19:   REVOKE p FROM U8 ;
User U1 at time t20:   GRANT p TO U3 WITH GRANT OPTION ;
```

At the end of this sequence, who still holds p?

ANSWERS TO SELECTED EXERCISES

11.1 (a) `GRANT SELECT ON TABLE STATS TO FORD ;`

   (b) `GRANT INSERT, DELETE ON TABLE STATS TO SMITH ;`

(c) CREATE VIEW MY_REC
         AS SELECT *
            FROM   STATS
            WHERE   USERID = USER ;

     GRANT SELECT ON TABLE MY_REC TO PUBLIC ;

(d) GRANT SELECT, UPDATE (SALARY, TAX)
            ON TABLE STATS TO NASH ;

(e) CREATE VIEW UST
         AS SELECT USERID, SALARY, TAX
            FROM   STATS ;

     GRANT SELECT ON TABLE UST TO TODD ;

(f) CREATE VIEW UST
         AS SELECT USERID, SALARY, TAX
            FROM   STATS ;

     GRANT SELECT, UPDATE (SALARY, TAX)
            ON TABLE UST TO WARD ;

(g) CREATE VIEW PREACHERS
         AS SELECT *
            FROM   STATS
            WHERE   OCCUPATION = 'Preacher' ;

     GRANT ALL PRIVILEGES ON TABLE PREACHERS TO POPE ;

"ALL PRIVILEGES" on a base table includes ALTER and INDEX privileges; on a view (like PREACHERS), it does not, since these operations do not apply to views.

(h) CREATE VIEW UST
         AS SELECT USERID, SALARY, TAX
            FROM   STATS ;

     CREATE VIEW UTA
         AS SELECT USERID, TAX, AUDITS
            FROM   STATS ;

     GRANT SELECT ON TABLE UST TO JONES ;

     GRANT UPDATE (TAX, AUDITS) ON TABLE UTA TO JONES ;

(i) CREATE VIEW SALBOUNDS (OCCUPATION, MAXSAL, MINSAL)
         AS SELECT OCCUPATION, MAX (SALARY), MIN (SALARY)
            FROM   STATS
            GROUP   BY OCCUPATION ;

     GRANT SELECT ON SALBOUNDS TO KING ;

(j) GRANT SYSADM TO CLARK ;

Dropping a table is not an explicitly grantable privilege. A table can be dropped only by its owner or by someone holding the SYSADM privilege or the DBADM privilege over the database containing the table.

11.2 (a) `REVOKE SELECT ON TABLE STATS FROM FORD ;`

(b) `REVOKE INSERT, DELETE ON TABLE STATS FROM SMITH ;`

(c) `REVOKE SELECT ON TABLE MY_REC FROM PUBLIC ;`

Or perhaps simply:

`DROP VIEW MY_REC ;`

For (d) through (j) below we generally ignore the possibility of simply dropping the view (if applicable).

(d) `REVOKE SELECT, UPDATE ON TABLE STATS FROM NASH ;`

(e) `REVOKE SELECT ON TABLE UST FROM TODD ;`

(f) `REVOKE SELECT, UPDATE ON TABLE UST FROM WARD ;`

(g) `REVOKE ALL PRIVILEGES ON PREACHERS FROM POPE ;`

"ALL PRIVILEGES" in REVOKE does not literally mean all privileges, but rather all privileges that the user issuing the REVOKE has granted.

(h) `REVOKE SELECT ON TABLE UST FROM JONES ;`

    `REVOKE UPDATE ON TABLE UTA FROM JONES ;`

(i) `REVOKE SELECT ON TABLE SALBOUNDS FROM KING ;`

(j) `REVOKE SYSADM FROM CLARK ;`

11.3 All users except *U4* and *U6* (i.e., users *U1, U2, U3, U5, U7, U8*) still hold *p*.

CHAPTER

◆ 12 ◆

Integrity

12.1 INTRODUCTION

The term "integrity" is used in database contexts to refer to the accuracy, validity, or correctness of the data in the database. Maintaining integrity is of paramount importance, for obvious reasons; and it is desirable, again for obvious reasons, that the task of maintaining integrity be handled by the system rather than by the user (to the maximum extent possible). In order that it may carry out this task, the system needs to be aware of any *integrity constraints* or *rules* that apply to the data; it then needs to monitor update operations to ensure that they do not violate any of those constraints or rules. As a trivial example,* the suppliers-and-parts database might be subject to the rule that supplier numbers must conform to a certain pattern,

---

*Trivial it may be, but it cannot readily be handled in the current version of DB2.

consisting of an "S" followed by up to four decimal digits. INSERT and UPDATE operations should therefore be monitored to ensure that they do not introduce a supplier number that fails to conform to this pattern.

The general idea, then, is that integrity constraints should be specified as part of the database definition; they will then be stored in the system catalog, and used by the system to control updates to the database. Now, any given database is likely to be subject to a very large number of constraints. For example, the following might all be constraints that apply to the suppliers-and-parts database:

- Supplier numbers must be of the form S*nnnn* (where *nnnn* stands for up to four decimal digits);
- Part numbers must be of the form P*nnnnn* (where *nnnnn* stands for up to five decimal digits);
- Supplier status values must be in the range 1–100;
- Supplier and part cities must be drawn from a certain list;
- Part colors must be drawn from a certain list;
- Part weights must be greater than zero;
- Shipment quantities must be a multiple of 100;
- All red parts must be stored in London;
- If the supplier city is London, then the status must be 20;

and so on. However, most such constraints are *specific,* in the sense that they apply to one specific database. All of the examples above are specific in this sense. The relational model, by contrast, includes two *general* integrity rules—general, in the sense that they apply, not just to some specific database such as suppliers-and-parts, but rather to *every* database (or, at least, every database that claims to conform to the model). These two general rules have to do, respectively, with *primary keys* and with what are called *foreign keys.* They are discussed in detail in Sections 12.2 (primary keys) and 12.3 (foreign keys). It is perhaps worth mentioning that DB2 does a reasonably good job on the two general integrity rules (as of Version 2, when primary and foreign key support was introduced); unfortunately, it is still rather weak on database-specific rules.

Following the discussions in Sections 12.2 and 12.3, Sections 12.4–12.6 go on to examine certain specific aspects of the DB2 support for these concepts in more depth. Specifically, Section 12.4 treats the question of referential cycles, Section 12.5 discusses some implementation restrictions, and Section 12.6 covers a number of miscellaneous integrity topics.

12.2   PRIMARY KEYS

We have referred informally to the term "primary key" several times already in this book. Informally, the primary key of a table is just a unique identifier for that table. For example, the primary keys for tables S, P, and SP of the suppliers-and-parts database are S.S#, P.P#, and SP.(S#,P#), respectively. Note that, as the last of these examples indicates, the primary key is allowed to be *composite;* in fact, it is possible, though perhaps unusual, to have a table where the only unique identifier (i.e., the primary key) is the composite column consisting of the combination of *all* the columns in the table—i.e., the table is "all key." An example would be the table that results from eliminating the QTY column from table SP.

It is also possible, though again unusual, for a table to have *more than one* unique identifier. As an example, let us suppose that every supplier always has a unique supplier number *and* a unique supplier name. (This happens to be the case with our sample data values—Fig. 1.2—but here we are supposing that it is true *for all time;* it is not just chance, i.e., it is not just a question of the values that happen to appear in the table at some specific instant.) In such a case we would say that the table has multiple *candidate* keys; we would then choose one of those candidate keys to be the *primary* key, and the remainder would then be said to be *alternate* keys.

Let us now make these ideas a little more precise.

Definition

Column CK (possibly composite) of table T is a *candidate key* for T if and only if it satisfies the following two time-independent properties:

1. *Uniqueness:*
   At any given time, no two rows of T have the same value for CK.

2. *Minimality:*
   If CK is composite, then no component of CK can be eliminated without destroying the uniqueness property.

Note that the relational model *requires* every table to have at least one candidate key, and hence *requires* every table to have a primary key, as we shall see in a moment. *Note:* This requirement is equivalent to the requirement that, at any given time, no two rows in the table are identical. DB2 unfortunately does not have such a requirement; we shall return to this point also in a moment.

Next, from the set of candidate keys for a given table, exactly one is designated as *the primary key* for that table; the remainder, if any, are called *alternate keys.* An alternate key is thus a candidate key that is not the primary key. *Note:* The rationale by which the primary key is chosen, in cases where there are several candidate keys, is outside the scope of the relational model per se. In practice the choice is usually straightforward. However, it is important to understand that, in practice, it is the *primary* key that is the really significant one; candidate and alternate keys are merely concepts that necessarily arise during the process of defining the more important concept "primary key."

So why are primary keys important? One obvious answer to this question is that primary key support is prerequisite to foreign key support, as we shall see in Section 12.3. A more fundamental answer is that primary keys provide the basic *record-level addressing mechanism* in a relational system. That is, the only system-guaranteed way of pinpointing some specific record or row is *by its primary key value.* For example, the SQL request

```
SELECT *
FROM    P
WHERE   P# = 'P3' ;
```

is guaranteed to retrieve (at most) one record. By contrast, the request

```
SELECT *
FROM    P
WHERE   CITY = 'Paris' ;
```

will retrieve an unpredictable number of records, in general. It follows that *primary keys are just as fundamental to the successful operation of a relational system as main memory addresses are to the successful operation of the underlying machine.* Tables that do not have a primary key—i.e., tables that permit duplicate rows—are bound to display strange and anomalous behavior in certain circumstances (details beyond the scope of this book). This is why we *strongly* recommend that users always conform to the primary key discipline. As indicated above, DB2 does in fact permit tables to exist that have no primary key, but we *strongly* recommend that users never exercise this option.

One further preliminary remark before we get into the details of DB2 per se: Although it is true that *all* relational tables do in fact possess a primary key, in practice it is *base* tables to which the concept is most directly applicable and for which it is most important. DB2 does permit—but unfortunately does not require—the definition of primary keys for base tables.

Primary Key Definition in DB2

Primary keys can be defined when the base table is created via CREATE TABLE, or added to an existing base table via ALTER TABLE. CREATE

TABLE is the normal case; ALTER TABLE is intended mainly to assist in migrating tables from an earlier DB2 release that did not support primary keys. A UNIQUE index is required to enforce primary key uniqueness. Also, every column participating in the primary key must be explicitly declared to be NOT NULL.

Here again is the syntax of CREATE TABLE, Format 1 (repeated from Chapter 5, but ignoring the optional "other parameters"):

```
CREATE TABLE base-table
  ( column-definition [, column-definition ] ...
  [, primary-key-definition ]
  [, foreign-key-definition [, foreign-key-definition ] ... ] ) ;
```

where "primary-key-definition" is as follows:

```
PRIMARY KEY ( column [, column ] ... )
```

(for the syntax of "foreign-key-definition," see Section 12.3). Here is an example:

```
CREATE TABLE SP
     ( S#      CHAR(5)   NOT NULL,
       P#      CHAR(6)   NOT NULL,
       QTY     INTEGER,
     PRIMARY KEY ( S#, P# ) ... ) ;
```

(The "..." represents some missing foreign key definitions. Again, see Section 12.3.)

After the base table (with its primary key) has been created, it still cannot be accessed via SQL data manipulation operations—in DB2 parlance, its definition is still "incomplete"—until an appropriate UNIQUE index has also been created. That index must be on *exactly* the columns that make up the primary key (no additional columns), in *exactly* the proper left-to-right order (no permutations).* For example:

```
CREATE UNIQUE INDEX XSP ON SP ( S#, P# ) ;
```

The index that enforces primary key uniqueness is referred to as the *primary index* for the table in question. Once the primary index has been created, the table is available for use, and DB2 will reject any attempt to violate the primary key uniqueness constraint. *Note:* If the primary index is subsequently dropped, the table will become "incomplete" again (it cannot even be used for pure retrieval operations), and it will remain so until an appropriate index has been created once again.

---

*ASC/DESC specifications and other index parameters (see Chapter 5) make no difference here, of course.

Here is the syntax for adding a primary key to an existing base table:

```
ALTER TABLE base-table primary-key-definition ;
```

A suitable UNIQUE index must already exist for this ALTER TABLE to succeed, and all columns involved must have been declared to be NOT NULL. The base table must not already possess a defined primary key.

It is also possible to remove the primary key definition from an existing base table:

```
ALTER TABLE base-table DROP PRIMARY KEY ;
```

Any foreign key definitions (see Section 12.3) that previously referred to the now dropped primary key will automatically be dropped. (The user must hold the ALTER privilege on the tables containing those foreign keys.) The primary index will *not* be dropped, but it will lose its "primary" status.

Entity Integrity

We conclude this section with a note on the first of the two general integrity rules of the relational model, namely the *entity* integrity rule, which is as follows:

- No component of the primary key of a base table is allowed to accept nulls.

The justification for this rule is basically that primary key values in base tables serve to identify entities in the real world—for example, supplier number values in table S serve to identify suppliers—and it simply does not make sense to record information in the database about an entity whose identity is unknown. For further discussion, see Appendix B.

Note carefully that, in the case of composite primary keys, the entity integrity rule says that every individual value of the primary key must be *wholly* (not just partially) nonnull. In the case of the shipments table, for example, with composite primary key SP.(S#,P#), S# and P# must *both* have "nulls not allowed"; neither S# nor P# is allowed to accept nulls.

DB2 supports the entity integrity rule, because it requires an explicit declaration of NOT NULL for all primary key components and hence enforces the "nulls not allowed" constraint.

12.3 FOREIGN KEYS

Consider the following (attempted) INSERT operation on the usual suppliers-and-parts database (a repeat of Example 8.2.3):

```
INSERT
INTO    SP ( S#, P#, QTY )
VALUES ( 'S20', 'P20', 1000 ) ;
```

It should be clear that, if this INSERT were to be accepted, there would be a loss of integrity, because the database would now include a shipment for a nonexistent supplier and a nonexistent part. In fact, the example illustrates a very specific kind of loss of integrity, namely a loss of *referential* integrity. In this section we examine the question of referential integrity in some detail. As the example suggests, the basic idea is quite simple:

- It is clear in the case of suppliers-and-parts that every value appearing in column SP.S# at any given time ought simultaneously to appear in column S.S# (the primary key of the S table)—for otherwise the database would include a shipment for a nonexistent supplier. Likewise, every value appearing in column SP.P# at any given time ought simultaneously to appear in column P.P# (the primary key of the P table), for otherwise the database would include a shipment for a nonexistent part.

- Columns such as SP.S# and SP.P# are examples of what are called *foreign keys*. We can define this concept (loosely) as follows: A foreign key is a column (possibly composite) in one table whose values are required to match values of the primary key in some other table (or possibly in the same table—see later).

  Note, incidentally, that the converse is *not* a requirement— that is, the primary key corresponding to some given foreign key might contain a value that currently does not appear as a value of that foreign key. In the case of the sample data for suppliers-and-parts in Fig. 1.2, for instance, the supplier number S5 appears in table S but not in table SP (supplier S5 does not currently supply any parts).

- A foreign key value represents a *reference* to the record containing the matching primary key value (the *referenced record* or *target record*). The problem of ensuring that the database does not contain any invalid foreign key values is therefore known as the *referential integrity* problem. The constraint that values of a given foreign key must match values of the corresponding primary key is known as a *referential constraint*. We refer to the table that contains the foreign key as the *referencing* table and the table that contains the corresponding primary key as the *referenced table* or *target table*. We can represent the situation (in the case of suppliers and parts) by means of the following diagram:

$$S \longleftarrow SP \longrightarrow P$$

(each arrow means that there is a foreign key in the table from which the arrow emerges that refers to the primary key of the table to which the arrow points).

Two asides: First, DB2 documentation (perversely) shows the arrows going the other way (i.e., from the target table to the referencing table). Our convention accords better with intuition and is consistent with relational literature. Second, DB2 uses the terms "parent table" and "dependent table" instead of "target table" and "referencing table," respectively. We prefer our own terms, for reasons too numerous to be stated here.

We now proceed to make these ideas a little more precise. We begin with a formal definition of the term "foreign key"—a definition, however, that is deliberately a trifle more restrictive than that adopted in DB2. We will return to this point in a moment.

Definition

Column FK (possibly composite) of base table T2 is a *foreign key* if and only if it satisfies the following two time-independent properties:

1. Each value of FK is either wholly null or wholly nonnull. (By "wholly null or wholly nonnull," we mean that, if FK is composite, then each value of FK either has all components null or all components nonnull, not a mixture.)

2. There exists a base table T1 (the target table) with primary key PK such that each nonnull value of FK is identical to the value of PK in some row of T1.

T1 and T2 are not necessarily distinct; that is, a table might include a foreign key whose (nonnull) values are required to match values of the primary key of that same table. As an example, consider the table

```
EMP  ( EMP#, ..., SALARY, ..., MGR_EMP#, ... )
```

in which column MGR_EMP# represents the employee number of the manager of the employee identified by EMP#. Here EMP# is the primary key and MGR_EMP# is a foreign key that refers to it. A table such as EMP in this example is known in DB2 as a *self-referencing* table. *Exercise:* Invent some sample data for this table.

Notice that foreign keys, unlike primary keys, must sometimes have "nulls allowed." (We remark, however, that nulls in a foreign key column are likely to be of "value does not exist" variety, rather than the "value unknown" variety.) As an example, consider the self-referencing table

EMP shown above. What is the value of MGR_EMP# for the president of the company?

Note: As mentioned earlier, our definition of foreign key is slightly more restrictive than the definition actually used in DB2. The fact is, there is a certain amount of disagreement in the open literature as to the most satisfactory definition of the term. For example, some authorities (and some systems, including DB2, as we shall see) do not require composite foreign key values to be wholly null or wholly nonnull, but instead allow some components to be null and others nonnull simultaneously. Likewise, some authorities allow there to be multiple target tables instead of just one. The foreign key definition given above is offered in the belief that:

(a) It is the most satisfactory in most commonly-occurring practical situations; and

(b) It is upward-compatible with a weaker definition (such as one that permits partially null composite foreign keys), should such a weakening ever prove desirable.

Let us consider some of the implications of the foreign key concept. To fix our ideas, let us concentrate on the suppliers table S and the shipments table SP, where we have a referential constraint from SP.S# in the SP table to S.S# in the S table (for simplicity, let us ignore the parts table P). It should be clear that there are basically four potential situations in which the referential constraint might be violated, namely as follows:

- *Case 1:* An INSERT on the SP table might introduce a shipment for which there is no matching supplier. For example:

```
INSERT
INTO    SP ( S#, P#, QTY )
VALUES ( 'S20', ... ) ;
```

- *Case 2:* An UPDATE on column SP.S# of the SP table might introduce a shipment supplier number for which there is no matching supplier. For example:

```
UPDATE SP
SET    S# = 'S20'
WHERE  ... ;
```

- *Case 3:* A DELETE on the S table might remove a supplier for which there exists a matching shipment. For example:

```
DELETE
FROM    S
WHERE   S# = 'S1' ;
```

- *Case 4:* An UPDATE on column S.S# of the S table might remove a supplier number for which there exists a matching shipment. For example:

```
UPDATE S
SET    S# = 'S20'
WHERE  S# = 'S1' ;
```

In order to enforce the referential constraint, therefore, the system must somehow deal with all four of these cases. Let us now turn to the question of foreign key support in DB2 specifically; in particular, let us see how DB2 deals with each of the four potential problems just outlined. We begin by explaining how foreign keys are defined in the first place.

Foreign Key Definition in DB2

Like primary keys, foreign keys can be defined when the base table is created (via CREATE TABLE) or added to an existing base table (via ALTER TABLE). CREATE TABLE is the more usual case; however, ALTER TABLE is needed if there is a constraint cycle (see Section 12.4) or if the table is being migrated from an earlier DB2 release. *Note:* There is no requirement that there be an index on a foreign key, but indexes are usually a good idea for performance reasons. For example, it is very common to perform a primary-key-to-foreign-key join, and an index on the foreign key may very well improve the performance of such a join. The performance of referential integrity enforcement can also be improved by the use of indexes.

The syntax of a foreign key definition is as follows:

```
FOREIGN KEY [ foreign-key ] ( column [, column ] ... )
        REFERENCES base-table [ ON DELETE effect ]
```

where "effect" is RESTRICT or CASCADE or SET NULL. If the ON DELETE clause is omitted, ON DELETE RESTRICT is assumed. Here is an example:

```
CREATE TABLE SP
    ( S#        CHAR(5)   NOT NULL,
      P#        CHAR(6)   NOT NULL,
      QTY       INTEGER,
    PRIMARY KEY ( S#, P# ) ,
    FOREIGN KEY SFK ( S# ) REFERENCES S
                           ON DELETE CASCADE ,
    FOREIGN KEY PFK ( P# ) REFERENCES P
                           ON DELETE RESTRICT ) ;
```

Explanation:

1. Let T2 be the table containing the foreign key, and let T1 be the target table (i.e., the table named in the REFERENCES specification), thus:

$$T2 \longrightarrow T1$$

Table T1 must have a defined primary key, and must be "complete" in the sense of Section 12.2 (i.e., the index that enforces primary key uniqueness must already exist).

2. The optional "foreign-key" is a name (a *constraint name*) that will be used by DB2 in diagnostic messages relating to this foreign key (it is also used in ALTER ... DROP statements—see later in this section). We have introduced the names SFK and PFK in our example. If the user does not supply a foreign key name, DB2 will assign one anyway, derived from the name of the first (or only) column participating in the foreign key in question. *Note:* The foreign key name is *not* considered as a column name and cannot be used in data manipulation statements such as SELECT.

3. The foreign key and the target primary key must contain the same number of columns, n say, and the ith column of the foreign key and the ith column of the target primary key must have exactly the same data type (i here is in the range 1 to n and refers to the left-to-right order in which the columns are listed in the containing foreign or primary key definition). Note, therefore, that a foreign key will be composite if and only if the primary key it matches is composite also.

4. The ON DELETE clause defines the *delete rule* for the target table with respect to this foreign key—that is, it defines what happens if an attempt is made to delete a record from the target table (i.e., a target record). As explained above, the possible specifications are RESTRICT, CASCADE, and SET NULL (and RESTRICT is assumed if nothing is specified). The meanings are as follows:

- RESTRICT: The delete is "restricted" to the case where there are no matching records in table T2 (it is rejected if any such records exist).

- CASCADE: The delete "cascades" to delete all matching records in table T2 also.
  - Note that table T2 might in turn be referenced by a foreign key in some other table T3. If it is, then if any delete on table T1 cascades to some record R2 in table T2, then the effect is exactly as if an attempt had been made to delete that record R2 directly; i.e., it depends on the delete rule specified for the foreign key from T3 to T2. And so on, recursively, to any number of levels.

- SET NULL: In this case, the foreign key must have "nulls allowed." The target record is deleted and the foreign key is set to null in all matching records in table T2.
  - If the foreign key is composite, then DB2 actually requires only that *at least one component* of the foreign key have nulls allowed, and SET NULL sets such components (only) to null in matching records and leaves other components unchanged. (A composite foreign key

value that is partly null is ALWAYS regarded as satisfying the referential constraint in DB2, *regardless of the values of the nonnull components*—a state of affairs that can lead to great complexity. For this reason among others, we strongly recommend that composite foreign keys either have nulls allowed for all components or nulls not allowed for all components, not a mixture of the two; and if they have nulls allowed, we strongly recommend that each individual value of the foreign key either has all components null or all components nonnull, not a mixture of the two.)

With the SP definition shown above, therefore, an attempt to delete a specific supplier record will cascade to delete all shipments for that supplier also; an attempt to delete a specific part record will succeed only if there are no shipments for that part.

5. There is no "ON UPDATE" clause to define an "update rule" for (the primary key of) the target table with respect to this foreign key. Instead, any attempt to update the primary key in a record of the target table is "restricted" to the case where there are no matching records in the referencing table (it is rejected if any such records exist). In effect, therefore, the only update rule supported is RESTRICT, and that rule can be stated only implicitly, not explicitly.

6. One slight oddity is that, in order to define a foreign key (via either CREATE TABLE or ALTER TABLE—see below) that refers to some target table T1, the user must possess the ALTER privilege on table T1. (Generally, the ALTER privilege is what is needed in order to execute an ALTER TABLE operation on the table in question. However, defining a foreign key referring to T1 does not involve an ALTER TABLE on T1.) By contrast, a user who deletes a record in table T1 and thereby deletes or updates one or more records in some other table T2 (thanks to a CASCADE or SET NULL delete rule) does *not* require any particular privilege—not even the SELECT privilege—on table T2.

Let us now see how these rules enable DB2 to deal with the four potential problem cases identified earlier. Once again we use the suppliers-and-parts example to fix our ideas.

- *Case 1:* An INSERT on the SP table might introduce a shipment for which there is no matching supplier.

   This situation is prevented by virtue of the fact that SP.S# is a foreign key in table SP matching the primary key S.S# of table S. Such an INSERT will simply be rejected. Of course, an INSERT that introduces a shipment for a supplier that does already exist in table S (and a part that does already exist in table P) will be accepted.

- *Case 2:* An UPDATE on column SP.S# of the SP table might introduce a shipment supplier number for which there is no matching supplier.

  This situation is also prevented by virtue of the fact that SP.S# is a foreign key in table SP matching the primary key S.S# of table S. Such an UPDATE will simply be rejected. Of course, an UPDATE that introduces an SP.S# value that does already exist in table S (and does not introduce an SP.P# value that does not already exist in table P) will be accepted.

- *Case 3:* A DELETE on the S table might remove a supplier for which there exists a matching shipment.

  This situation is handled by the delete rule (CASCADE in the sample definition shown earlier). In general, RESTRICT would mean that the delete will be accepted only if there *are* no such matching shipments; CASCADE would mean that any such matching shipments will be removed anyway; and SET NULL (not possible in the case of suppliers-and-parts, because SP.S# does not have "nulls allowed") would mean that any such matching shipments will not be removed but will be updated so that they are no longer "matching."

- *Case 4:* An UPDATE on column S.S# of the S table might remove a supplier number for which there exists a matching shipment.

  This situation is handled by the (implicit) update rule RESTRICT, which means that the update will be accepted only if no such matching shipments exist.

We now briefly discuss the use of ALTER TABLE to add and remove foreign key definitions. The syntax for adding such a definition is as follows:

```
ALTER TABLE base-table foreign-key-definition ;
```

If "base-table" is nonempty (as it might be if it is a table that is being migrated from an earlier release of DB2), adding a foreign key definition causes DB2 to set an internal "check pending" condition on the data. The data now cannot be accessed by SQL at all, not even for retrieval, until the condition has been cleared (i.e., until it has been ascertained that all referential constraints are satisfied). The DB2 CHECK utility can be used to help find and correct any referential constraint violations. *Note:* The CHECK utility and the "check pending" condition are discussed further in Chapter 17 (Section 17.4).

The syntax for removing a foreign key definition is:

```
ALTER TABLE base-table DROP FOREIGN KEY foreign-key ;
```

Here "foreign-key" is the foreign key *name* assigned when the foreign key was defined.

One final point regarding data definition: If a base table is dropped, any foreign key definitions referring to that table are dropped automatically (perhaps surprisingly, the user does *not* have to hold the ALTER privilege on the tables containing those foreign keys). The delete rules (CASCADE, etc.) for those foreign keys are *not* invoked (thus, e.g., dropping table S does not cause all records in table SP to be deleted).

Referential Integrity

For completeness, we close this section with a note on the second of the two general integrity rules of the relational model, namely the referential integrity rule. The referential integrity rule simply states that the database must not contain any unmatched foreign key values (i.e., nonnull foreign key values for which there does not exist a matching value of the corresponding primary key). DB2 obviously enforces this rule, as the discussions above demonstrate.

12.4 REFERENTIAL CYCLES

Section 12.3 explained the basic foreign key concept and described the relevant DB2 data definition statements. An understanding of the material of that section is probably sufficient to deal with most of the situations that are likely to arise in practice. However, there are a number of additional detailed points that need to be made in any reasonably comprehensive treatment of the subject. The points in question (a slightly mixed bag) are discussed in this section and in Sections 12.5–12.6, later. This section deals with referential cycles.

First we need to introduce the concept of a "referential path" (not an official DB2 term). Let tables Tn, T(n−1), ..., T2, T1 be such that there is a referential constraint from table Tn to table T(n−1), a referential constraint from table T(n−1) to table T(n−2), ..., and a referential constraint from table T2 to table T1:

$$Tn \longrightarrow T(n-1) \longrightarrow T(n-2) \longrightarrow \ldots \longrightarrow T2 \longrightarrow T1$$

Then the chain of arrows from Tn to T1 represents a referential path from Tn to T1. We can define this concept (recursively) as follows: There is a *referential path from table Tn to table T1* if and only if (a) table Tn references table T1 directly or (b) table Tn references some table T(n−1) such that there is a referential path from table T(n−1) to table T1.

Now we can define the term *referential cycle* (or constraint cycle). Briefly, we say that a referential cycle exists if there is a referential path from some table T to itself. One special case, the self-referencing table, has already been mentioned in Section 12.3; a self-referencing table constitutes a cycle involving just a single table. More generally, however, a cycle might involve any number of tables: If there is a referential constraint from table Tn to table $T(n-1)$, a referential constraint from table $T(n-1)$ to table $T(n-2)$, ..., a referential constraint from table T2 to table T1, and a referential constraint from table T1 to the original table Tn, then we have a cycle involving n tables (i.e., a cycle of length n):

$$Tn \longrightarrow T(n-1) \longrightarrow T(n-2) \longrightarrow \ldots \longrightarrow T2 \longrightarrow T1 \longrightarrow Tn$$

Here is an example of a cycle of length two:

```
EMP  ( EMP#, ..., SALARY, ..., DEPT# ... )

DEPT ( DEPT#, ..., MGR_EMP#, ..., BUDGET ... )
```

In table EMP, EMP# is the primary key and DEPT# is a foreign key referring to DEPT; in table DEPT, DEPT# is the primary key and MGR_EMP# (employee number for the department manager) is a foreign key referring to EMP.

In order to specify the referential constraints that form a cycle, it is necessary to use ALTER TABLE for at least one of those specifications, because a FOREIGN KEY clause cannot refer to a table that does not yet exist. Also (as mentioned in Section 12.3), a FOREIGN KEY clause cannot refer to a table that does not yet have an index to enforce uniqueness on its primary key. The general pattern is thus:

```
CREATE TABLE T1 ( ... PRIMARY KEY ... ) ;
CREATE UNIQUE INDEX ON T1 ( primary key ) ;

CREATE TABLE T2 ( ... PRIMARY KEY ... ,
      FOREIGN KEY ... REFERENCES T1 ... ) ;
CREATE UNIQUE INDEX ON T2 ( primary key ) ;
.........................

CREATE TABLE Tn ( ... PRIMARY KEY ... ,
      FOREIGN KEY ... REFERENCES T(n-1) ... ) ;
CREATE UNIQUE INDEX ON Tn ( primary key ) ;

ALTER TABLE T1 FOREIGN KEY ... REFERENCES Tn ... ;
```

By way of example, we give the data definition (in outline) for the EMP/DEPT cycle introduced above:

```
CREATE TABLE EMP
      ( EMP#      NOT NULL ,
        ...       ,
        SALARY    ,
        ...       ,
        DEPT#     ,
        ...       ,
      PRIMARY KEY ( EMP# ) ) ;
```

```
CREATE UNIQUE INDEX XEMP ON EMP ( EMP# ) ;

CREATE TABLE DEPT
     ( DEPT#     NOT NULL ,
         ...        ,
       MGR_EMP# ,
         ...      ,
       BUDGET   ,
         ...      ,
     PRIMARY KEY ( DEPT# ) ,
     FOREIGN KEY MFK ( MGR_EMP# ) REFERENCES EMP ) ;

CREATE UNIQUE INDEX XDEPT ON DEPT ( DEPT# ) ;

ALTER TABLE EMP FOREIGN KEY DFK ( DEPT# ) REFERENCES DEPT ;
```

Note that the foregoing pattern applies even in the self-referencing case; that is, the foreign key has to be defined via ALTER TABLE, not as part of the original CREATE TABLE.

Note: In general, it is likely in a cycle that at least one of the foreign keys will have nulls allowed. In the cycle shown above, for example, at least one of the two foreign keys EMP.DEPT# and DEPT.MGR_EMP# will probably have nulls allowed; for otherwise it would be impossible to INSERT the first record (either an EMP record or a DEPT record) into the database—*unless* the tables are populated by means of the LOAD utility with referential integrity checking disabled. See Chapter 17 (Section 17.4) for further discussion of this latter possibility.

Referential cycles are subject to certain special restrictions. See Section 12.5 immediately following.

12.5 IMPLEMENTATION RESTRICTIONS

The current release of DB2 suffers from certain implementation restrictions, which we summarize in the present section. *Note:* It might be possible to relax some of these restrictions at some future time. The basic problem in most cases is that (for performance reasons) DB2 applies the primary and foreign key integrity checks to each individual record *as it updates that record,* whereas in some cases it ought really to defer the checking to the end of the overall statement. (In fact, in some cases it ought to defer the checking to "COMMIT time," i.e., to the end of the *transaction.* See Chapter 14 for a discussion of transactions and COMMIT time.) But DB2 does not support any such deferred checking.

▪ As a trivial example, suppose we had a table T with two records, with primary key values 1 and 2 respectively. Consider the request "double every primary key value in T." The correct result is that the records should now have primary key values 2 and 4, respectively. However, DB2 will reject the request entirely, on the grounds that if it updated the record with primary key value 1 first (to yield 2), it would run into a primary key uniqueness violation.

As a consequence of such record-at-a-time integrity checking, *different record-level processing sequences might yield different results* (in general); in other words, the result of a given set-level SQL operation might be unpredictable. Most of the restrictions explained below (both in the present subsection and the next) represent attempts to outlaw situations in which such unpredictability might otherwise occur.

The restrictions are as follows.

1. Any UPDATE statement that assigns a value to a primary key must be "single-record" (i.e., there must be at most one record at execution time that satisfies the predicate in the WHERE clause). Thus, for example, the following UPDATE is definitely valid (because S# is the primary key for table S):

```
UPDATE S
SET     S# = 'S10'
WHERE   S# = 'S5' ;
```

whereas the following may or may not be valid, depending on the values in the database:

```
UPDATE S
SET     S# = 'S10'
WHERE   CITY = 'Athens' ;
```

2. No UPDATE CURRENT statement is allowed to update a primary key value. (See Chapter 13 for an explanation of UPDATE CURRENT.)

3. The following additional restrictions apply to self-referencing tables:

- The delete rule must be CASCADE.

- DELETE CURRENT is not allowed. (See Chapter 13 for an explanation of DELETE CURRENT.)

- INSERT ... SELECT is allowed only if it inserts at most one record, i.e., the SELECT selects at most one record.

Delete-Connected

To explain the remaining restrictions, we need to introduce yet another term, "delete-connected." The basic idea here is that table Tn is considered to be delete-connected to table T1 if and only if a DELETE on table T1 can either *affect* or *be affected by* the content of table Tn. More precisely, table Tn is said to be *delete-connected* to table T1 if and only if (a) table Tn references table T1 directly or (b) table Tn references table $T(n-1)$ directly and there is a referential path from table $T(n-1)$ to table T1 in which every delete rule is CASCADE:

$$\text{Tn} \xrightarrow{\;*\;} T(n-1) \xrightarrow{\;C\;} T(n-2) \xrightarrow{\;C\;} \ldots \xrightarrow{\;C\;} T2 \xrightarrow{\;C\;} T1$$

(the "C"s here represent a CASCADE delete rule, the asterisk stands for any delete rule—i.e., this particular delete rule is immaterial). Observe that—depending on the content of Tn—an attempt to delete rows from T1 can

(a) cause rows to be deleted from Tn, if the "*" delete rule is CASCADES;

(b) cause rows to be updated in Tn, if the "*" rule is NULLIFIES;

(c) fail, if the "*" rule is RESTRICTED.

In other words, a DELETE on T1 can indeed either "affect or be affected by" the content of Tn.

Note: It follows immediately from the definition that every table is delete-connected to every table it references directly. It follows also that every self-referencing table is delete-connected to itself.

Now we can state the remaining restrictions.

4. If

(a) the user issues a DELETE on table T1, and

(b) table Tn is delete-connected to table T1, and

(c) the WHERE clause in the DELETE statement includes a subquery,

then the FROM clause in that subquery must not refer to table Tn unless the delete rule from Tn to $T(n-1)$—i.e., the last delete rule in the path—is RESTRICT. For example, if the referential constraint from shipments (table SP) to suppliers (table S) has a delete rule of CASCADE, then the following attempt to delete all suppliers who supply no parts is (unfortunately, and perhaps rather surprisingly) *** ILLEGAL ***:

```
DELETE
FROM    S
WHERE   NOT EXISTS
        ( SELECT *
          FROM    SP
          WHERE   SP.S# = S.S# ) ;
```

Instead, the user should first compile a list of relevant supplier numbers, and then delete all suppliers whose number is given in that list as a separate operation.

5. If table Tn is delete-connected to table T1 via two or more distinct referential paths, then every foreign key in table Tn that is involved in any of those paths must have the same delete rule, and furthermore that rule must not be SET NULL. For an illustration of this restriction, see Exercise 12.7 at the end of the chapter.

6. In a cycle of length greater than one, no table is allowed to be delete-connected to itself. For example, consider the EMP/DEPT cycle discussed in Section 12.4.

- Suppose first that we try to specify a CASCADE delete rule for both foreign keys:

$$\text{EMP} \xrightarrow[\text{C}]{\text{C}} \text{DEPT}$$

  Then:

(a) EMP and DEPT are each delete-connected to the other (because each references the other directly);

(b) In addition, EMP is delete-connected to itself, because it references DEPT directly and there is a (rather short!) referential path from DEPT to EMP in which "every" (i.e., the only) delete rule is CASCADE. (Likewise, DEPT is also delete-connected to itself.)

The structure is thus illegal.

- Suppose, by contrast, that we try to specify a SET NULL or RESTRICT delete rule for the foreign key EMP.DEPT#, but we leave the delete rule for the foreign key DEPT.MGR_EMP# as CASCADE:

$$\text{EMP} \xrightarrow[\text{C}]{\text{N/R}} \text{DEPT}$$

  Then:

(a) EMP and DEPT are again each delete-connected to the other, as before, because each references the other directly;

(b) EMP is still delete-connected to itself, because it references DEPT directly and DEPT references EMP and the delete rule from DEPT to EMP is CASCADE.

The structure is thus still illegal. (Note, however, that DEPT is now *not* delete-connected to itself.)

- Suppose, therefore, that we specify SET NULL (or RESTRICT) for the foreign key EMP.DEPT# and SET NULL (or RESTRICT) for the foreign key DEPT.MGR_EMP#:

$$\text{EMP} \xrightarrow[\text{N} \neq \text{R}]{\text{N/R}} \text{DEPT}$$

Now no table is delete-connected to itself, and the structure is legal.

We leave it as an exercise for the reader to invent some sample data for the EMP and DEPT tables and to see exactly what can go wrong if either table is delete-connected to itself.

12.6 MISCELLANEOUS TOPICS

We conclude this chapter with a brief mention of a few miscellaneous integrity topics.

Composite Keys

As explained earlier in the chapter, the relational model does permit primary and foreign keys to be composite. However, there are good reasons, most of them beyond the scope of this book, to be very sparing in the use of composite keys. In fact, every time a composite key arises during the database design process, it is a good idea to ask yourself very carefully whether it might not be better to introduce a new, simple (noncomposite) column to act as the key instead. In the case of shipments, for example, it might be worth introducing a new SHIP# column ("shipment number") as the primary key. (The composite column SP.(S#,P#) would then be an alternate key.) For further discussion of this point, the reader is referred to the book *Relational Database: Selected Writings,* by C. J. Date (Addison-Wesley, 1986).

Even if you do decide to use composite keys, we recommend that you still treat them for the most part as *indivisible entity identifiers* (except perhaps for retrieval purposes); in other words, treat them as if they were simple, even though they are in fact composite. In order to adhere to this guideline:

1. Do not allow key values to be partly null.

2. Do not allow keys to overlap.

This is not the place to examine these recommendations in depth; they are discussed in more detail in a paper (still in preparation at the time of writing) devoted to foreign keys and related matters, by C. J. Date (see Appendix H).

Other Integrity Constraints

As explained in Section 12.1, every database will be subject to numerous additional integrity constraints, over and above the basic primary and foreign key constraints described in Sections 12.2–12.5. We give below a complete list (not a very long list!) of additional integrity features supported by DB2.

- Data type checking

  DB2 will ensure that every value introduced into a given column is of the appropriate data type. For example, it will reject an attempt to introduce the string 'XYZ' into a column defined as DECIMAL.

- NOT NULL

  See Chapter 4. Of course, it is not only primary key columns that need to be specified NOT NULL, in general.

- UNIQUE indexes

  See Chapter 5. Of course, it is not only primary keys that need to be unique, in general.

- CHECK option in view definitions

  See Chapter 10.

- Validation procedures (VALIDPROCs)

  See Chapter 16.

Utilities

Referential integrity has several implications for DB2 utility functions such as LOAD and RECOVER. See Chapter 17 for further discussion.

EXERCISES

12.1 Define the terms *primary key* and *foreign key*.

12.2 State the entity integrity rule and the referential integrity rule.

12.3 Write a suitable set of data definition statements to specify the necessary primary and foreign key integrity constraints for the suppliers-parts-projects database (Fig. 5.1).

12.4 How would your answer to Exercise 12.3 be different if the database were being migrated from an earlier release of DB2 that did not support primary and foreign keys?

12.5 Using the sample suppliers-parts-projects data values from Fig. 5.1, say what the effect of each of the following operations is:

(a) UPDATE project J7, setting CITY to New York

(b) UPDATE part P5, setting P# to P4

(c) UPDATE supplier S5, setting S# to S8

(d) DELETE supplier S3, if the relevant delete rule is CASCADE

(e) DELETE part P2, if the relevant delete rule is RESTRICT

(f) DELETE project J4, if the relevant delete rule is SET NULL

(g) UPDATE shipment S1-P1-J1, setting S# to S2

(h) UPDATE shipment S5-P5-J5, setting J# to J7

(i) UPDATE shipment S5-P5-J5, setting J# to J8

(j) INSERT shipment S5-P6-J7

(k) INSERT shipment S4-P7-J6

(l) INSERT shipment S1-P2-null

12.6 Is there any point in declaring a primary key to be NOT NULL WITH DEFAULT?

12.7 (Based on an example in *An Introduction to the Unified Database Language,* in *Relational Database: Selected Writings,* by C. J. Date, Addison-Wesley, 1986.) An education database contains information about an in-house company training scheme. For each training course, the database contains details of all prerequisite courses for that course and all offerings for that course; and for each offering it contains details of all teachers and all students for that offering. The database also contains information about employees. The relevant tables are as follows:

```
COURSE     ( COURSE#, TITLE )
PREREQ     ( SUP_COURSE#, SUB_COURSE# )
OFFERING   ( COURSE#, OFF#, OFFDATE, LOCATION )
TEACHER    ( COURSE#, OFF#, EMP# )
STUDENT    ( COURSE#, OFF#, EMP#, GRADE )
EMPLOYEE   ( EMP#, ENAME, JOB )
```

The meaning of the PREREQ table is that the superior course, represented by SUP_COURSE#, has the subordinate course, represented by SUB_COURSE#, as an immediate prerequisite; the other tables are intended to be self-explanatory. Write a suitable set of SQL data definitions for this database.

12.8 Invent a database of your own that involves a cycle of referential constraints. Invent some sample data for that database. Write an appropriate set of data definitions, with suitable PRIMARY KEY and FOREIGN KEY clauses. Consider the effects of some sample INSERTs, DELETEs, and primary and foreign key UPDATEs on your sample data.

12.9 Suppose it is required to change the supplier number of supplier Sx to Sy (where Sx and Sy are given).

(a) First, the following UPDATE will not work. Why not?

```
UPDATE S
SET    S# = Sy
WHERE  S# = Sx ;
```

(b) Second, the following sequence of UPDATEs also will not work. Again, why not?

```
UPDATE SP
SET     S# = Sy
WHERE   S# = Sx ;

UPDATE S
SET     S# = Sy
WHERE   S# = Sx ;
```

(c) In fact, it will almost certainly be necessary to write a program to handle the problem. You are therefore recommended to return to this exercise and to write such a program after reading Chapter 13 on embedded SQL.

ANSWERS TO SELECTED EXERCISES

We remind the reader that it is usually a good idea to have an index on a foreign key. However, such indexes are not included in the answers below (except in those cases where the foreign key is in fact the leading portion of the primary key of the containing table, where the primary key index provides the desired function automatically).

```
12.3  CREATE TABLE S
          ( S#      CHAR(5)   NOT NULL ,
            SNAME   CHAR(20)  NOT NULL WITH DEFAULT ,
            STATUS  SMALLINT  NOT NULL WITH DEFAULT ,
            CITY    CHAR(15)  NOT NULL WITH DEFAULT ,
          PRIMARY KEY ( S# ) ) ;

      CREATE UNIQUE INDEX XS ON S ( S# ) ;

      CREATE TABLE P
          ( P#      CHAR(6)   NOT NULL ,
            PNAME   CHAR(20)  NOT NULL WITH DEFAULT ,
            COLOR   CHAR(6)   NOT NULL WITH DEFAULT ,
            WEIGHT  SMALLINT  NOT NULL WITH DEFAULT ,
            CITY    CHAR(15)  NOT NULL WITH DEFAULT ,
          PRIMARY KEY ( P# ) ) ;

      CREATE UNIQUE INDEX XP ON P ( P# ) ;

      CREATE TABLE J
          ( J#      CHAR(4)   NOT NULL ,
            JNAME   CHAR(10)  NOT NULL WITH DEFAULT ,
            CITY    CHAR(15)  NOT NULL WITH DEFAULT ,
          PRIMARY KEY ( J# ) ) ;

      CREATE UNIQUE INDEX XJ ON J ( J# ) ;

      CREATE TABLE SPJ
          ( S#      CHAR(5)   NOT NULL ,
            P#      CHAR(6)   NOT NULL ,
            J#      CHAR(4)   NOT NULL ,
            QTY     INTEGER ,
          PRIMARY KEY ( S#, P#, J# ) ,
          FOREIGN KEY SFK ( S# ) REFERENCES S
                                 ON DELETE CASCADE ,
```

```
        FOREIGN KEY PFK ( P# ) REFERENCES P
                               ON DELETE CASCADE ,
        FOREIGN KEY JFK ( J# ) REFERENCES J
                               ON DELETE CASCADE ) ;

CREATE UNIQUE INDEX XSPJ ON SPJ ( S#, P#, J# ) ;
```

12.4 Remove the PRIMARY KEY and FOREIGN KEY clauses from the CREATE TABLE statements and replace them by the following:

```
ALTER TABLE S    PRIMARY KEY ( S# ) ;
ALTER TABLE P    PRIMARY KEY ( P# ) ;
ALTER TABLE J    PRIMARY KEY ( J# ) ;
ALTER TABLE SPJ PRIMARY KEY ( S#, P#, J# ) ;

ALTER TABLE SPJ FOREIGN KEY SFK ( S# ) REFERENCES S
                                       ON DELETE CASCADE ;
ALTER TABLE SPJ FOREIGN KEY PFK ( P# ) REFERENCES P
                                       ON DELETE CASCADE ;
ALTER TABLE SPJ FOREIGN KEY JFK ( J# ) REFERENCES J
                                       ON DELETE CASCADE ;
```

There will now be a "check pending" condition in effect and the data will not be available (not even for retrieval) until the condition has been cleared.

12.5 (a) Accepted
   (b) Rejected (violates primary key constraint on P and implicit "update rule" RESTRICT on P.P#)
   (c) Rejected (violates implicit "update rule" RESTRICT on S.S#)
   (d) Accepted (supplier S3 and all shipments for supplier S3 deleted)
   (e) Rejected (violates delete rule RESTRICT on P)
   (f) Impossible (delete rule cannot be SET NULL, because SPJ.J# must be NOT NULL—it is part of the primary key of SPJ)
   (g) Accepted
   (h) Rejected (violates primary key constraint on SPJ)
   (i) Rejected (violates foreign key constraint on SPJ.J#)
   (j) Accepted
   (k) Rejected (violates foreign key constraint on SPJ.P#)
   (l) Rejected (violates entity integrity on SPJ)

12.6 Probably not—except possibly if the primary key is of data type DATE or TIME or (perhaps most likely) TIMESTAMP. See Appendix C, Section C.4.

12.7
```
CREATE TABLE COURSE
        ( COURSE# ... NOT NULL ,
          TITLE   ... NOT NULL WITH DEFAULT ,
        PRIMARY KEY ( COURSE# ) ) ;

CREATE UNIQUE INDEX XC ON COURSE ( COURSE# ) ;

CREATE TABLE PREREQ
        ( SUP_COURSE# ... NOT NULL ,
          SUB_COURSE# ... NOT NULL ,
        PRIMARY KEY ( SUB_COURSE#, SUP_COURSE# ) ,
        FOREIGN KEY SUP ( SUP_COURSE# ) REFERENCES COURSE
                                        ON DELETE RESTRICT ,
        FOREIGN KEY SUB ( SUB_COURSE# ) REFERENCES COURSE
                                        ON DELETE RESTRICT ) ;
```

```
CREATE UNIQUE INDEX XPQ
               ON PREREQ ( SUP_COURSE#, SUB_COURSE# ) ;

CREATE TABLE OFFERING
       ( COURSE#  ... NOT NULL ,
         OFF#     ... NOT NULL ,
         OFFDATE  ... NOT NULL WITH DEFAULT ,
         LOCATION ... NOT NULL WITH DEFAULT ,
       PRIMARY KEY ( COURSE#, OFF# ) ,
       FOREIGN KEY OFK ( COURSE# ) REFERENCES COURSE
                                   ON DELETE CASCADE ) ;

CREATE UNIQUE INDEX XO ON OFFERING ( COURSE#, OFF# ) ;

CREATE TABLE EMPLOYEE
       ( EMP#   ... NOT NULL ,
         ENAME  ... NOT NULL WITH DEFAULT ,
         JOB    ... NOT NULL WITH DEFAULT ,
       PRIMARY KEY ( EMP# ) ) ;

CREATE UNIQUE INDEX XE ON EMPLOYEE ( EMP# ) ;

CREATE TABLE TEACHER
       ( COURSE# ... NOT NULL ,
         OFF#    ... NOT NULL ,
         EMP#    ... NOT NULL ,
       PRIMARY KEY ( COURSE#, OFF#, EMP# )
       FOREIGN KEY TC ( COURSE#, OFF# ) REFERENCES OFFERING
                                   ON DELETE CASCADE ,
       FOREIGN KEY TE ( EMP# )        REFERENCES EMPLOYEE
                                   ON DELETE CASCADE ) ;

CREATE UNIQUE INDEX XT ON TEACHER ( COURSE#, OFF#, EMP# ) ;

CREATE TABLE STUDENT
       ( COURSE# ... NOT NULL ,
         OFF#    ... NOT NULL ,
         EMP#    ... NOT NULL ,
         GRADE   ... NOT NULL WITH DEFAULT ,
       PRIMARY KEY ( COURSE#, OFF#, EMP# )
       FOREIGN KEY SC ( COURSE#, OFF# ) REFERENCES OFFERING
                                   ON DELETE CASCADE ,
       FOREIGN KEY SE ( EMP# )        REFERENCES EMPLOYEE
                                   ON DELETE CASCADE ) ;

CREATE UNIQUE INDEX XS ON STUDENT ( COURSE#, OFF#, EMP# ) ;
```

Note: Columns TEACHER.COURSE# and STUDENT.COURSE# could also be regarded as foreign keys, both of them referring to COURSE. However, if the referential constraints from TEACHER to OFFERING, STUDENT to OFFERING, and OFFERING to COURSE are all properly maintained, the referential constraints from TEACHER to COURSE and STUDENT to COURSE will be maintained automatically. Note, however, that if those latter constraints are explicitly declared, then the delete rules *must* be stated as CASCADE, to be consistent with the existing declarations (see the discussion of the fifth restriction in Section 12.5).

12.8 A simple example of a structure that involves a cycle might be a banking system, in which each account has one owner (a bank customer), each bank customer has one personal banker (a bank officer), and each personal banker has one account giving information about that personal banker's customers.

12.9 (a) The attempt to UPDATE the supplier record for supplier Sx will not work
(in general) because of the implicit RESTRICT rule on updating primary
keys; supplier Sx might currently have some matching shipments.

(b) The attempt to UPDATE the shipment records for supplier Sx first will
not work for two reasons: First, it would violate the foreign key constraint;
second, DB2 does not currently permit multiple-record UPDATEs on primary keys (note that SP.S# is a component of the primary key of SP, as
well as being a foreign key).

(c) Here is a possible program to perform the update:

```
UPDS#: PROC OPTIONS (MAIN) ;          /* change S# "Sx" to "Sy" */

        DCL SX                CHAR(5) ;
        DCL SY                CHAR(5) ;
        DCL SNAME             CHAR(20) ;
        DCL STATUS            FIXED BINARY(15) ;
        DCL CITY              CHAR(15) ;
        DCL P#                CHAR(6) ;
        DCL MORE_SHIPMENTS BIT(1) ;

     EXEC SQL INCLUDE SQLCA ;

     EXEC SQL DECLARE Y CURSOR FOR
             SELECT S.SNAME, S.STATUS, S.CITY
             FROM   S
             WHERE  S.S# = :SX
             FOR UPDATE OF SNAME ;

     EXEC SQL DECLARE Z CURSOR FOR
             SELECT SP.P#
             FROM   SP
             WHERE  SP.S# = :SX ;

     EXEC SQL WHENEVER NOT FOUND CONTINUE ;
     EXEC SQL WHENEVER SQLERROR CONTINUE ;
     EXEC SQL WHENEVER SQLWARNING CONTINUE ;

     ON CONDITION ( DBEXCEPTION )
     BEGIN ;
        PUT SKIP LIST ( SQLCA ) ;
        EXEC SQL ROLLBACK ;
        GO TO QUIT ;
     END ;

   GET LIST ( SX, SY ) ;
   EXEC SQL OPEN Y ;
   IF SQLCODE ~= 0
   THEN SIGNAL CONDITION ( DBEXCEPTION ) ;

   /* fetch column values for supplier Sx */
   EXEC SQL FETCH Y INTO :SNAME. :STATUS, :CITY ;
   IF SQLCODE ~= 0
   THEN SIGNAL CONDITION ( DBEXCEPTION ) ;

   /* make sure supplier Sx stays X-locked -- see Chap. 14 --  */
   /* thus preventing concurrent creation of new shipments for */
   /* supplier Sx and concurrent UPDATE/DELETE on supplier Sx  */
   EXEC SQL UPDATE S
            SET    SNAME = :SNAME       /* effectively a no-op */
            WHERE  CURRENT OF Y ;
```

```
    IF SQLCODE ~= 0
    THEN SIGNAL CONDITION ( DBEXCEPTION ) ;

    /* insert new supplier Sy record */
    EXEC SQL INSERT
              INTO    S ( S#, SNAME, STATUS, CITY )
              VALUES ( :SY, :SNAME, :STATUS, :CITY ) ;
    IF SQLCODE ~= 0
    THEN SIGNAL CONDITION ( DBEXCEPTION ) ;

    /* prepare to loop through shipments for Sx */
    EXEC SQL OPEN Z ;
    IF SQLCODE ~= 0
    THEN SIGNAL CONDITION ( DBEXCEPTION ) ;
    MORE_SHIPMENTS = '1'B ;

    /* loop through shipments for Sx */
    DO WHILE ( MORE_SHIPMENTS ) ;
       EXEC SQL FETCH Z INTO :P# ;
       SELECT ;                    /* a PL/I SELECT, not a SQL SELECT */
          WHEN ( SQLCODE = 100 )
             MORE_SHIPMENTS = '0'B ;
          WHEN ( SQLCODE ~= 100 & SQLCODE ~= 0 )
             SIGNAL CONDITION ( DBEXCEPTION ) ;
          WHEN ( SQLCODE = 0 )
             DO ;
                /* update current shipment -- */
                /* but not via cursor Z  !!! */
                EXEC SQL UPDATE SP
                            SET    S# = :SY
                            WHERE  S# = :SX
                            AND    P# = :P# ;
                IF SQLCODE ~= 0
                THEN SIGNAL CONDITION ( DBEXCEPTION ) ;
             END ;
       END ;    /* PL/I SELECT */
    END ;   /* DO WHILE */
    EXEC SQL CLOSE Z ;
    /* delete supplier Sx */
    EXEC SQL DELETE
              FROM    S
              WHERE   CURRENT OF Y ;
    IF SQLCODE ~= 0
    THEN SIGNAL CONDITION ( DBEXCEPTION ) ;
    EXEC SQL CLOSE Y ;
    EXEC SQL COMMIT ;
QUIT:
    RETURN ;
END ;   /* UPDS# */
```

The foregoing code assumes that any attempt to introduce a new shipment for supplier Sx (via an INSERT or UPDATE on table SP) will request at least a shared lock on the supplier record for Sx (see Chapter 14). We remark that this example provides additional evidence in support of the claim in Section 12.4 that it is often a good idea to avoid composite keys: If table SP had a noncomposite primary key SHIP#, the entire loop over shipments could be replaced by the single statement

```
UPDATE SP
SET     S# = Sy
WHERE   S# = Sx ;
```

Of course, if DB2 supported a CASCADE update rule (as it should), the entire program could be replaced by the single UPDATE statement shown in part (a) of the exercise:

```
UPDATE S
SET    S# = Sy
WHERE  S# = Sx ;
```

CHAPTER

◆13◆

Application Programming I: Embedded SQL

13.1 INTRODUCTION

In Chapter 1 we explained that SQL was used in DB2 both as an interactive query language and as a database programming language. Up to this point, however, we have more or less ignored the programming aspects of SQL and have tacitly assumed (where it made any difference) that the language was being used interactively. Now we turn our attention to those programming aspects specifically. In the present chapter we discuss the principal ideas behind "embedded SQL" (as it is usually called); in the next chapter we examine the concept of transaction processing; and in Chapter 15 we present an introduction (only) to a somewhat more complex subject, namely "dynamic SQL." But first things first.

The fundamental principle underlying embedded SQL, which we refer to as *the dual-mode principle,* is that *any SQL statement that can be used at the terminal can also be used in an application program.* Of course, as pointed out in Chapter 1, there are various differences of detail between a given interactive SQL statement and its corresponding embedded form, and SELECT statements in particular require significantly extended treatment in the programming environment (see Section 13.4); but the principle is nevertheless broadly true. (Its converse is not, incidentally; that is, there are a number of SQL statements that are programming statements only and cannot be used interactively, as we shall see.)

Note clearly that the dual-mode principle applies to the entire SQL language, not just to the data manipulation operations. It is true that the data manipulation operations are far and away the ones most frequently used in a programming context, but there is nothing wrong in embedding (for example) CREATE TABLE statements in a program, if it makes sense to do so for the application at hand.

The programming languages currently supported by DB2—the so-called "host languages"—are PL/I, COBOL, FORTRAN, C, APL, BASIC, and System/370 Assembler Language. In Section 13.2 we consider the mechanics of embedding SQL in these languages. Then in Sections 13.3 and 13.4 we present the major ideas behind the embedding of SQL data manipulation statements specifically. Finally, in Section 13.5, we present a comprehensive programming example.

Note: For reasons of brevity and definiteness, all of our examples are given in terms of PL/I. But of course the ideas are fairly general and translate into the other host languages with only comparatively minor differences. At least, this statement is true for the other compiled languages (COBOL, FORTRAN, C, Assembler Language); the interpreted languages (APL, BASIC) do not follow the same pattern but instead make use of the dynamic SQL facilities discussed in Chapter 15. The reader is referred to the IBM manuals for details of the differences among the different host languages.

13.2 PRELIMINARIES

Before we can get into the embedded SQL statements per se, it is necessary to cover a number of preliminary details. Most of those details are illustrated by the program fragment shown in Fig. 13.1.

Points arising:

1. Embedded SQL statements are prefixed by EXEC SQL (so that they can easily be distinguished from statements of the host language), and are terminated by a special termination symbol (a semicolon for PL/I).

2. An *executable* SQL statement (from now on we will usually drop the "embedded") can appear wherever an executable host statement can

```
DCL GIVENS# CHAR(5) ;
DCL RANK    FIXED BIN(15) ;
DCL CITY    CHAR(15) ;
DCL ALPHA   ... ;
DCL BETA    ... ;

EXEC SQL DECLARE S TABLE
              ( S#      CHAR(5)  NOT NULL,
                SNAME   CHAR(20) NOT NULL WITH DEFAULT,
                STATUS  SMALLINT,
                CITY    CHAR(15) NOT NULL WITH DEFAULT ) ;

EXEC SQL INCLUDE SQLCA ;

    ...........

IF ALPHA > BETA THEN
GETSTC:
  EXEC SQL SELECT STATUS, CITY
           INTO   :RANK, :CITY
           FROM   S
           WHERE  S# = :GIVENS# ;
    ...........

PUT SKIP LIST ( RANK, CITY ) ;
```

Fig. **13.1** Fragment of a PL/I program with embedded SQL

appear. Note the qualifier "executable" here: Unlike interactive SQL, embedded SQL includes some statements that are purely declarative, not executable. For example, DECLARE TABLE is not an executable statement, and neither is DECLARE CURSOR (see Section 13.4).

3. SQL statements can include references to host variables; such references are prefixed with a colon to distinguish them from SQL field names. Host variables can appear in SQL data manipulation statements wherever a constant is permitted. They are also used to designate a target for retrieval. In other words, they can appear in the following positions (loosely speaking):

- INTO clause in SELECT or FETCH (target to be retrieved into)
- SELECT clause (value to be retrieved)
- WHERE or HAVING clause (value to be compared)
- SET clause in UPDATE (value to be assigned)
- VALUES clause in INSERT (value to be inserted)
- element of a scalar expression in SELECT, WHERE, HAVING, or SET (not VALUES), where that expression in turn evaluates to the value to be retrieved, compared, or assigned

They can also appear in SET CURRENT SQLID (see Chapter 11) and in certain embedded-only statements (details to follow). They cannot appear in any other SQL contexts.

4. Any tables (base tables or views) used in the program can optionally be declared by means of an EXEC SQL DECLARE TABLE statement, in order to make the program more self-documenting and to enable the Precompiler to perform certain diagnostic checks on the manipulative statements. See the discussion of DCLGEN in Section 13.5.

5. After any SQL statement has been executed, feedback information is returned to the program in an area called the SQL Communication Area (SQLCA). In particular, a numeric status indicator is returned in a field of the SQLCA called SQLCODE. A SQLCODE value of zero means that the statement executed successfully; a positive value means that the statement did execute, but constitutes a warning that some exceptional condition occurred (for example, a value of $+100$ indicates that no data was found to satisfy the request); and a negative value means that an error occurred and the statement did not complete successfully.* In principle, therefore, every SQL statement in the program should be followed by a test on SQLCODE (and appropriate action taken if the value is not what was expected), but we do not show any such tests in Fig. 13.1. (In practice such explicit testing of SQLCODE values may *not* be necessary, as we show in Section 13.5.)

The SQL Communication Area is included in the program by means of the EXEC SQL INCLUDE SQLCA statement.†

6. As indicated in paragraph 3 above, the embedded SQL SELECT statement requires an INTO clause, specifying the host variables to which values retrieved from the database are to be assigned. The variables in that INTO clause can be scalar variables or structures; a structure is considered simply as a shorthand for the list of scalars that make up that structure. Structures can also be used in the VALUES clause in INSERT.

7. Host variables must have a data type compatible with the SQL data type of fields they are to be compared with or assigned to or from. Data type compatibility is defined in Chapter 4 (Section 4.5). If significant digits or characters are lost on assignment (either to or from the database) because the receiving field is too small, a warning or error indication is returned to the program in the SQLCA.

8. Host variables and database fields can have the same name. A host variable can be an element of a structure. For example:

```
DCL 1 STRUC,
    2 S#  CHAR(5),
    2 ... ;
```

---

*This description is slightly oversimplified. See Section 13.5 (description of the WHENEVER statement) for further discussion.

†The EXEC SQL INCLUDE statement can also be used to include program source text from a partitioned data set.

```
EXEC SQL SELECT ...
         FROM   S
         WHERE  S# = :STRUC.S# ;
```

Note that PL/I-style name qualification is used for host variable references, not COBOL-style (:STRUC.S#, not :S# OF STRUC), even when the host language is in fact COBOL.

So much for the preliminaries. In the rest of this chapter we concentrate on the SQL data manipulation operations SELECT, UPDATE, DELETE, and INSERT specifically. As already indicated, most of those operations can be handled in a fairly straightforward fashion (i.e., with only minor changes to their syntax). SELECT statements require special treatment, however. The problem is that executing a SELECT statement causes a *table* to be retrieved—a table that, in general, contains multiple records—and languages such as PL/I, COBOL, etc., are simply not well equipped to handle more than one record at a time. It is therefore necessary to provide some kind of bridge between the set-at-a-time level of the SQL SELECT statement and the record-at-a-time level of the host; and *cursors* provide such a bridge. A cursor is a new kind of SQL object, one that applies to embedded SQL only (because of course interactive SQL has no need of it). It consists essentially of a kind of *pointer* that can be used to run through a set of records, pointing to each of the records in the set in turn and thus providing addressability to those records one at a time. However, we defer detailed discussion of cursors to Section 13.4, and consider first (in Section 13.3) those statements that have no need of them.

13.3 OPERATIONS NOT INVOLVING CURSORS

The data manipulation statements that do not need cursors are as follows:

- "Singleton SELECT"
- UPDATE (except the CURRENT form—see Section 13.4)
- DELETE (again, except the CURRENT form—Section 13.4)
- INSERT

We give examples of each of these statements in turn.

13.3.1 Singleton SELECT.   Get status and city for the supplier whose supplier number is given by the host variable GIVENS#.

```
EXEC SQL SELECT STATUS, CITY
         INTO   :RANK, :CITY
         FROM   S
         WHERE  S# = :GIVENS# ;
```

We use the term "singleton SELECT" to mean a SELECT statement for which the retrieved table contains at most one row. In the example if there exists exactly one record in table S satisfying the WHERE condition, then the STATUS and CITY values from that record will be delivered to the host variables RANK and CITY as requested, and SQLCODE will be set to zero. If no S record satisfies the WHERE condition, SQLCODE will be set to +100; and if more than one does, the program is in error, and SQLCODE will be set to a negative value. In these last two cases, the host variables RANK and CITY will remain unchanged if SQLCODE = + 100, and will be unpredictable otherwise.

The foregoing example raises another point. What if the SELECT statement does indeed select exactly one record, but the STATUS value in that record happens to be null? (Remember from Chapter 5 that STATUS was not defined to be NOT NULL, so nulls are possible.) With the SELECT statement as shown above, an error will occur (SQLCODE will be set to a negative value). In general, if there is a chance that the source of a retrieval operation might be null, the user should include an *indicator variable* in the INTO clause in addition to the normal target variable, as illustrated in the following example.

```
EXEC SQL SELECT STATUS, CITY
         INTO    :RANK:RANKIND, :CITY
         FROM    S
         WHERE   S# = :GIVENS# ;
IF RANKIND = -1 THEN /* STATUS was null */ ... ;
```

If the field to be retrieved is null and an indicator variable has been specified, then that indicator variable will be set to the value −1* and the ordinary target variable will remain unchanged. Indicator variables are specified as shown—i.e., immediately following the corresponding ordinary target variable and separated from that target variable by a colon. They should be declared as 15-bit signed binary integers.

Note: Indicator variables should not be used in a WHERE or HAVING clause. For example, the following is illegal:

```
RANKIND = -1 ;
EXEC SQL SELECT CITY
         INTO    :CITY
         FROM    S
         WHERE   STATUS = :RANK:RANKIND ;
```

The correct way to select cities where the status is null is:

---

*It will be set to −2 if the null is not directly derived from a database field but is instead generated by DB2. DB2 will generate a null if an error (e.g., division by zero or a data type conversion error) occurs in computing the value of some expression to be retrieved.

```
EXEC SQL SELECT CITY
              INTO    :CITY
              FROM    S
              WHERE   STATUS IS NULL ;
```

13.3.2 INSERT.   Insert a new part (part number, name, and weight given by host variables PNO, PNAME, PWT, respectively; color and city unknown) into table P.

```
EXEC SQL INSERT
              INTO    P ( P#, PNAME, WEIGHT )
              VALUES ( :PNO, :PNAME, :PWT ) ;
```

We are assuming here that nulls or default values are allowed for fields P.COLOR and P.CITY.

Indicator variables can be used in the VALUES clause. For example, if PCOLOR and PCITY are two further host variables, and if COLORIND and CITYIND are corresponding indicator variables, then the sequence

```
COLORIND = -1 ;
CITYIND  = -1 ;
EXEC SQL INSERT
              INTO    P ( P#, PNAME, COLOR, WEIGHT, CITY )
              VALUES ( :PNO, :PNAME, :PCOLOR:COLORIND,
                        :PWT,    :PCITY:CITYIND ) ;
```

has the same effect as the INSERT shown previously (assuming that nulls are allowed for fields P.COLOR and P.CITY).

13.3.3 UPDATE.   Increase the status of all London suppliers by the amount given by the host variable RAISE.

```
EXEC SQL UPDATE S
              SET     STATUS = STATUS + :RAISE
              WHERE   CITY = 'London' ;
```

If no S records satisfy the WHERE condition, SQLCODE will be set to $+100$. Indicator variables can appear on the right-hand side of an assignment in the SET clause; for example, the sequence

```
RANKIND = -1 ;
EXEC SQL UPDATE S
              SET     STATUS = :RANK:RANKIND
              WHERE   CITY = 'London' ;
```

will set the status for all London suppliers to null. So also of course will the statement

```
EXEC SQL UPDATE S
              SET     STATUS = NULL
              WHERE   CITY = 'London' ;
```

13.3.4 DELETE.   Delete all shipments for suppliers whose city is given by the host variable CITY.

```
EXEC SQL DELETE
         FROM    SP
         WHERE   :CITY =
               ( SELECT  CITY
                 FROM    S
                 WHERE   S.S# = SP.S# ) ;
```

Again SQLCODE will be set to +100 if no records satisfy the WHERE condition.

For simplicity, we will ignore indicator variables and the possibility of nulls in most of what follows (both in this chapter and in the next two chapters).

13.4 OPERATIONS INVOLVING CURSORS

Now we turn to the case of a SELECT that selects a whole set of records, not necessarily just one. As explained in Section 13.2, what is needed here is a mechanism for accessing the records in the set one by one; and *cursors* provide such a mechanism. The process is illustrated in outline in the example of Fig. 13.2, which is intended to retrieve supplier details (S#, SNAME, and STATUS) for all suppliers in the city given by the host variable Y.

```
EXEC SQL DECLARE X CURSOR FOR          /* define cursor X     */
         SELECT S#, SNAME, STATUS
         FROM    S
         WHERE   CITY = :Y ;

EXEC SQL OPEN X ;                       /* execute the query   */
         DO for all S records accessible via X ;
             EXEC SQL FETCH X INTO :S#, :SNAME, :STATUS ;
                                        /* fetch next supplier */
             .........
         END ;
EXEC SQL CLOSE X ;                      /* deactivate cursor X */
```

Fig. 13.2. Retrieving multiple records

Explanation:

1. The DECLARE X CURSOR ... statement defines a cursor called X, with an associated query as specified by the SELECT that forms part of that DECLARE. The SELECT is not executed at this point; DECLARE CURSOR is a purely declarative statement.

2. The SELECT *is* (effectively) executed when the cursor is opened (in the procedural part of the program), using the current value of the host variable Y.

3. The FETCH ... INTO ... statement is then used to retrieve records of the result table one at a time. The INTO clause in that statement must spec-

ify a list of *n* host variables, where *n* is the number of expressions in the SELECT clause in the cursor declaration. (Note that the SELECT in the cursor declaration does not have an INTO clause of its own.) Each time the FETCH is executed, the current value of the *i*th expression in the SELECT clause in the cursor declaration is assigned to the *i*th variable in the INTO clause (*i* = 1 to *n*). In the example, therefore, the supplier number is assigned to the host variable S#, the supplier name to the host variable SNAME, and the status to the host variable STATUS. (For simplicity we have given each host variable the same name as the corresponding database field.)

4. Since there will be multiple records in the result table (in general), the FETCH will normally appear within a loop (DO ... END in PL/I); the loop will be repeated so long as there are more records still to come in that result table. An attempt to FETCH the next record when no records remain will set SQLCODE to +100; that condition can then be used to cause exit from the loop on the next attempt at iteration.

5. On exit from the loop, cursor X is closed (deactivated) via an appropriate CLOSE statement.

Now let us consider cursors and cursor operations in more detail. First, a cursor is declared by means of a DECLARE CURSOR statement, which takes the general form

```
EXEC SQL DECLARE cursor CURSOR
         FOR union-expression
     [ FOR UPDATE OF field(s) | ORDER BY field(s) ] ;
```

where "union-expression" is defined as follows —

```
union-term   |   union-expression UNION [ ALL ] union-term
```

—and "union-term" in turn is either a SELECT–FROM–WHERE–GROUP BY–HAVING expression or a union-expression in parentheses. *Note:* This is the general form of a cursor declaration. In practice, most such declarations do not involve UNION at all (see, e.g., Fig. 13.2).

As already stated, the DECLARE CURSOR statement is declarative, not executable; it declares a cursor with the specified name and having the specified union-expression permanently associated with it. Notice that that union-expression can include (and typically will include) host variable references. If the cursor will be used in UPDATE CURRENT statements (see later in this section), then the declaration must include a FOR UPDATE clause, specifying all fields that will be updated via this cursor; if not, and if DELETE CURRENT statements will also not be used (again, see later in this section), then it may optionally include an ORDER BY clause (possibly with ASC/DESC specifications), exactly as in a conventional SELECT statement. That ORDER BY clause will control the order in which result rows are retrieved via FETCH. Note, therefore, that it is not possible to retrieve a set of records via a cursor in some specified order *and* UPDATE (or DELETE) some of those records via that same cursor at the same time. See Exercise 13.4 at the end of this chapter.

A program can include any number of DECLARE CURSOR statements, each of which must (of course) be for a different cursor.

Three executable statements are provided specifically for operating on cursors: OPEN, FETCH, and CLOSE.

1. The statement

```
EXEC SQL OPEN cursor ;
```

opens or *activates* the specified cursor (which must not currently be open). In effect, the union-expression associated with that cursor is executed (using the current values for any host variables referenced within that expression); a set of records is thus identified and becomes the *active set* for the cursor. The cursor also identifies a *position* within that set, namely the position just before the first record in the set. (Active sets are always considered to have an ordering, so that the concept of position has meaning. The ordering is either that defined by ORDER BY, if specified, or a system-determined ordering otherwise.)

2. The statement

```
EXEC SQL FETCH cursor INTO target [, target ] ... ;
```

where each "target" is of the form

```
: host-variable [ : host-variable ]
```

(as in singleton SELECT), and where the identified cursor must be open, advances that cursor to the next record in the active set and then assigns values from that record to host variables as explained earlier. If there is no next record when FETCH is executed, then SQLCODE is set to $+100$ and no data is retrieved.

Note, incidentally, that FETCH (i.e., "fetch next") is the *only* cursor movement operation. It is not possible to move a cursor (e.g.) "forward three positions" or "backward two positions" or "directly to the ith record," etc.

3. The statement

```
EXEC SQL CLOSE cursor ;
```

closes or *deactivates* the specified cursor (which must currently be open). The cursor now has no corresponding active set. However, it can subsequently be opened again, in which case it will acquire another active set—probably not exactly the same set as before, especially if the values of host variables referenced in the cursor declaration have changed in the meantime. Note that changing the values of those host variables while the cursor is open has no effect on the active set.

Two further statements can include references to cursors. These are the CURRENT forms of UPDATE and DELETE. If a cursor, X say, is currently positioned on a particular record in the database, then it is possible to UPDATE or DELETE the "current of X," i.e., the record on which X is positioned. Syntax:

```
EXEC SQL UPDATE table
         SET    field = scalar-expression
              [, field = scalar-expression ] ...
         WHERE  CURRENT OF cursor ;

EXEC SQL DELETE
         FROM   table
         WHERE  CURRENT OF cursor ;
```

For example:

```
EXEC SQL UPDATE S
         SET    STATUS = STATUS + :RAISE
         WHERE  CURRENT OF X ;
```

UPDATE CURRENT and DELETE CURRENT are not permitted if the cursor declaration involves UNION (with or without ALL) or ORDER BY, or if the union-expression in that declaration would define a nonupdatable view if it were part of a CREATE VIEW statement (see Section 10.4 in Chapter 10). In the case of UPDATE CURRENT, as explained earlier, the cursor declaration must include a FOR UPDATE clause identifying all the fields that appear as targets of a SET clause in an UPDATE CURRENT statement for that cursor.

13.5 A COMPREHENSIVE EXAMPLE

We conclude this chapter with a somewhat contrived, but nevertheless comprehensive, example (Fig. 13.3) to illustrate a number of additional points. The program accepts four input values: a part number (GIVENP#), a city name (GIVENCIT), a status increment (GIVENINC), and a status level (GIVENLVL). The program scans all suppliers of the part identified by GIVENP#. For each such supplier, if the supplier city is GIVENCIT, then the status is increased by GIVENINC; otherwise, if the status is less than GIVENLVL, the supplier is deleted. (We assume that corresponding shipments are automatically deleted also, by virtue of a CASCADE delete rule.)

```
SQLEX: PROC OPTIONS (MAIN) ;

      DCL GIVENP#        CHAR(6) ;
      DCL GIVENCIT       CHAR(15) ;
      DCL GIVENINC       FIXED BINARY(15) ;
      DCL GIVENLVL       FIXED BINARY(15) ;
      DCL S#             CHAR(5) ;
      DCL SNAME          CHAR(20) ;
      DCL STATUS         FIXED BINARY(15) ;
      DCL CITY           CHAR(15) ;
      DCL DISP           CHAR(7) ;
      DCL MORE_SUPPLIERS BIT(1) ;

      EXEC SQL INCLUDE SQLCA ;

      EXEC SQL DECLARE S TABLE
                  ( S#       CHAR(5)   NOT NULL,
                    SNAME    CHAR(20)  NOT NULL WITH DEFAULT,
                    STATUS   SMALLINT,
                    CITY     CHAR(20)  NOT NULL WITH DEFAULT ) ;

      EXEC SQL DECLARE SP TABLE
                  ( S#       CHAR(5)   NOT NULL,
                    P#       CHAR(6)   NOT NULL,
                    QTY      INTEGER   NOT NULL WITH DEFAULT ) ;

      EXEC SQL DECLARE Z CURSOR FOR
                  SELECT S#, SNAME, STATUS, CITY
                  FROM   S
                  WHERE  EXISTS
                     ( SELECT *
                       FROM   SP
                       WHERE  SP.S# = S.S#
                       AND    SP.P# = :GIVENP# )
                  FOR UPDATE OF STATUS ;

      EXEC SQL WHENEVER NOT FOUND CONTINUE ;
      EXEC SQL WHENEVER SQLERROR CONTINUE ;
      EXEC SQL WHENEVER SQLWARNING CONTINUE ;

      ON CONDITION ( DBEXCEPTION )
      BEGIN ;
         PUT SKIP LIST ( SQLCA ) ;
         EXEC SQL ROLLBACK ;
         GO TO QUIT ;
      END ;
```

Fig. 13.3 A comprehensive example (part 1 of 2)

In all cases supplier information is listed on the printer, with an indication of how that particular supplier was handled by the program.

Points arising:

1. First, we have ignored throughout the possibility that some item to be retrieved might be null. This simplification was introduced purely to reduce the size of the example.

2. Next, note the two DECLAREs for tables S and SP. It is obvious that

```
    GET LIST ( GIVENP#, GIVENCIT, GIVENINC, GIVENLVL ) ;
    EXEC SQL OPEN Z ;
    IF SQLCODE ~= 0
    THEN SIGNAL CONDITION ( DBEXCEPTION ) ;
    MORE_SUPPLIERS = '1'B ;
    DO WHILE ( MORE_SUPPLIERS ) ;
        EXEC SQL FETCH Z INTO :S#, :SNAME, :STATUS, :CITY ;
        SELECT ;                /* a PL/I SELECT, not a SQL SELECT */
        WHEN ( SQLCODE = 100 )
            MORE_SUPPLIERS = '0'B ;
        WHEN ( SQLCODE ~= 100 & SQLCODE ~= 0 )
            SIGNAL CONDITION ( DBEXCEPTION ) ;
        WHEN ( SQLCODE = 0 )
            DO ;
                DISP = 'bbbbbbb' ;
                IF CITY = GIVENCIT
                THEN
                    DO ;
                        EXEC SQL UPDATE S
                                SET    STATUS = STATUS + :GIVENINC
                                WHERE  CURRENT OF Z ;
                        IF SQLCODE ~= 0
                        THEN SIGNAL CONDITION ( DBEXCEPTION ) ;
                        DISP = 'UPDATED' ;
                    END ;
                ELSE
                    IF STATUS < GIVENLVL
                    THEN
                        DO ;
                            EXEC SQL DELETE
                                    FROM   S
                                    WHERE  CURRENT OF Z ;
                            IF SQLCODE ~= 0
                            THEN SIGNAL CONDITION ( DBEXCEPTION ) ;
                            DISP = 'DELETED' ;
                        END ;
                PUT SKIP LIST ( S#, SNAME, STATUS, CITY, DISP ) ;
            END ;    /* WHEN ( SQLCODE = 0 ) ... */
        END ;    /* PL/I SELECT */
    END ;    /* DO WHILE */
    EXEC SQL CLOSE Z ;
    EXEC SQL COMMIT ;
QUIT:
    RETURN ;
END ;    /* SQLEX */
```

Fig. 13.3 A comprehensive example (part 2 of 2)

those declarations are nothing but slight textual variations on the corresponding CREATE TABLE statements of SQL. A special utility program, the declarations generator (DCLGEN), is provided to construct such declarations on the user's behalf. (*Note:* The name DCLGEN is usually pronounced "deckle gen," with a soft g.) Basically, DCLGEN uses the information in the DB2 catalog to build both

(a) a DECLARE TABLE statement for the table, and

(b) a corresponding PL/I or COBOL declaration for a structure the same shape as the table (to be used as a target for retrieval and/or a source for update).

DCLGEN stores its output as a member of a partitioned data set under a user-specified name. That output can then be included into a host program by means of the statement

```
EXEC SQL INCLUDE member ;
```

where "member" is the name of the member concerned.

It can be seen from the foregoing that DCLGEN (like the catalog) provides some of the functions that have traditionally been considered the responsibility of a separate dictionary product in older systems.

3. As explained in Section 13.2, every SQL statement should in principle be followed by a test of the returned SQLCODE value. The WHENEVER statement is provided to simplify this process. The WHENEVER statement has the syntax:

```
EXEC SQL WHENEVER condition action ;
```

where "condition" is one of the following:

```
NOT FOUND
SQLWARNING
SQLERROR
```

and "action" is either CONTINUE or a GO TO statement. WHENEVER is not an executable statement; rather, it is a directive to the Precompiler. "WHENEVER condition GO TO label" causes the Precompiler to insert an "IF condition GO TO label" statement after each executable SQL statement it encounters. "WHENEVER condition CONTINUE" causes the Precompiler not to insert any such statements (the implication being that the programmer will insert such statements by hand). The three "conditions" are defined as follows:

NOT FOUND	means	SQLCODE = 100
SQLWARNING	means	SQLCODE > 0 and SQLCODE ~ = 100
		or SQLWARN0 is 'W'
SQLERROR	means	SQLCODE < 0

Note: SQLWARN0 is another field in the SQLCA. It is set to W if certain nondisastrous exceptions occur—for example, if a string value from the database has to be truncated during FETCH because the target host variable is too small. For details, see the IBM manuals. We have ignored SQLWARN0 entirely in the code of Fig. 13.3.

Each WHENEVER statement the Precompiler encounters on its sequential scan through the program text (for a particular condition) overrides the previous one it found (for that condition). At the start of the program text there is an implicit WHENEVER statement for each of the three possible conditions, specifying CONTINUE in each case.

In the sample program, all exception-testing is done explicitly, for tutorial reasons. If any exception occurs, control is passed to a procedure that prints diagnostic information (the SQL Communication Area, in the example), issues a ROLLBACK (see the next paragraph below), and then branches to the final RETURN.

4. When a program updates the database in some way, that update should initially be regarded as *tentative only*—tentative in the sense that, if something subsequently goes wrong, *the update may be undone* (either by the program itself or by the system). For example, if the program encounters an unexpected error, say an overflow condition, and terminates abnormally, then the system will automatically undo all such tentative updates on the program's behalf. Updates remain tentative until one of two things happens:

(a) A COMMIT statement is executed, which makes all tentative updates firm ("committed"); or

(b) A ROLLBACK statement is executed, which undoes all tentative updates.

Once committed, an update is guaranteed never to be undone (this is the definition of "committed").

In the example, the program issues COMMIT when it reaches its normal termination, but issues ROLLBACK if any SQL exception is encountered. Actually, that explicit COMMIT is not necessary; the system will automatically issue a COMMIT on the program's behalf for any program that reaches normal termination. It will also automatically issue a ROLLBACK on the program's behalf for any program that does not reach normal termination; in the example, however, an explicit ROLLBACK *is* necessary, because the program is designed to reach its normal termination even if a SQL exception occurs.

Note: The foregoing discussion assumes a TSO environment. COMMIT and ROLLBACK are legal only in that environment. Under IMS (either IMS/DC or IMS batch) and CICS, the effects of COMMIT and ROLLBACK are obtained via corresponding IMS and CICS operations. The entire question of "committed updates" and the related notion of *transaction processing* are considered in much greater depth in the next chapter.

EXERCISES

13.1 Using the suppliers-parts-projects database, write a program with embedded SQL statements to list all supplier records, in supplier number order. Each supplier record should be immediately followed in the listing by all project records for projects supplied by that supplier, in project number order.

13.2 Why do you think the FOR UPDATE clause is required?

13.3 Revise your solution to Exercise 13.1 to do the following in addition:
  (a) Increase the status by 50 percent for any supplier who supplies more than two projects;
  (b) Delete any supplier who does not supply any projects at all.

13.4 Write a program to read and print all part records in part number order, deleting every tenth one as you go.

13.5 (Harder.) Given the tables

```
CREATE TABLE PARTS
    ( P# ... NOT NULL,
      DESCRIPTION ... ,
    PRIMARY KEY ( P# ) ) ;

CREATE TAELE PART_STRUCTURE
    ( MAJOR_P# ... NOT NULL,
      MINOR_P# ... NOT NULL,
      QTY       ... ,
    PRIMARY KEY ( MAJOR_P#, MINOR_P# ) ,
    FOREIGN KEY ( MAJOR_P# ) REFERENCES PARTS ... ,
    FOREIGN KEY ( MINOR_P# ) REFERENCES PARTS ... ) ;
```

where PART_STRUCTURE shows which parts (MAJOR_P#) contain which other parts (MINOR_P#) as first-level components, write a SQL program to list all component parts of a given part, to all levels (the "parts explosion" problem). *Note:* The following sample values may help you visualize this problem:

MAJOR_P#	MINOR_P#	QTY
P1	P2	2
P1	P4	4
P5	P3	1
P3	P6	3
P6	P1	9
P5	P6	8
P2	P4	3

13.6 Return to Exercise 12.9 in Chapter 12 if you have not already answered it.

ANSWERS TO SELECTED EXERCISES

13.1 There are basically two ways to write such a program. The first involves two cursors, CS and CJ say, defined along the following lines:

```
EXEC SQL DECLARE CS CURSOR FOR
         SELECT S#, SNAME, STATUS, CITY
         FROM   S
         ORDER  BY S# ;

EXEC SQL DECLARE CJ CURSOR FOR
         SELECT J#, JNAME, CITY
         FROM   J
         WHERE  J# IN
              ( SELECT J#
                FROM   SPJ
                WHERE  S# = :CS_S# )
         ORDER BY J# ;
```

When cursor CJ is opened, host variable CS_S# will contain a supplier number value, fetched via cursor CS. The procedural logic is essentially as follows:

```
EXEC SQL OPEN CS ;
DO for all S records accessible via CS ;
   EXEC SQL FETCH CS INTO :CS_S#, :CS_SN, :CS_ST, :CS_SC ;
   print CS_S#, CS_SN, CS_ST, CS_SC ;
   EXEC SQL OPEN CJ ;
   DO for all J records accessible via CJ ;
      EXEC SQL FETCH CJ INTO :CJ_J#, :CJ_JN, :CJ_JC ;
      print CJ_J#, CJ_JN, CJ_JC ;
   END ;
   EXEC SQL CLOSE CJ ;
END ;
EXEC SQL CLOSE CS ;
```

The trouble with this solution is that it does not exploit the set-level processing capabilities of SQL to the full. In effect, the programmer is hand-coding a join. The second approach uses a single cursor, and so does take advantage of SQL's set-level capabilities; unfortunately, however, the join required is an *outer* join, so the program must first construct that outer join, as follows. (This second solution may therefore be less efficient than the first, because it effectively requires the same data to be scanned multiple times. Direct SQL support for an outer join operator, which is desirable anyway for usability reasons, might alleviate this problem.)

```
EXEC SQL DECLARE CSJ CURSOR FOR
         SELECT S#, SNAME, STATUS, S.CITY, J#, JNAME, J.CITY
         FROM   S, SPJ, J
         WHERE  S.S# = SPJ.S# AND SPJ.J# = J.J#
         UNION  ALL
         SELECT S#, SNAME, STATUS, S.CITY, 'bb', 'bb', 'bb'
         FROM   S
         WHERE  NOT EXISTS
              ( SELECT * FROM SPJ WHERE SPJ.S# = S.S# ) ;
         ORDER  BY 1, 5 ;

EXEC SQL OPEN CSJ ;
DO for all records accessible via CSJ ;
   EXEC SQL FETCH CSJ INTO :CS_S#, :CS_SN, :CS_ST, :CS_SC,
                          :CJ_J#, :CJ_JN, :CJ_JC ;
   IF CS_S# different from previous iteration
   THEN print CS_S#, CS_SN, CS_ST, CS_SC ;
   print CJ_J#, CJ_JN, CJ_JC ;
END ;
EXEC SQL CLOSE CSJ ;
```

13.2 Suppose the program includes a DECLARE CURSOR statement of the form

```
EXEC SQL DECLARE C CURSOR FOR
           SELECT ...
           FROM   T
           ...... ;
```

The DB2 Bind component is responsible for choosing an access path corresponding to the cursor C. Suppose it chooses an index based on field F of table T. The "active set" of records accessible via C when C is activated will then be ordered according to values of F. If the program were allowed to UPDATE a value of F via the cursor C—i.e., via an UPDATE statement of the form

```
EXEC SQL UPDATE T
           SET    F = ...
           WHERE  CURRENT OF C ;
```

—then the updated record would probably have to be "moved" (logically speaking), because it would now belong in a different position with respect to the ordering of the active set. In other words, cursor C would effectively jump to a new position, with unpredictable results. To avoid such a situation, the user must warn Bind of any fields to be updated, so that access paths based on those fields will *not* be chosen.

13.3 Cursor CSJ in the second of our two solutions to Exercise 13.1 does not permit updates, because its declaration involves a UNION. For this problem, therefore, we are forced to use the first approach. Note also that cursor CS in that first solution does not permit updates either, because its declaration involves an ORDER BY. Apart from these considerations, the solution is basically straightforward. The relevant embedded statements are

```
EXEC SQL UPDATE S
           SET    STATUS = STATUS * 1.5
           WHERE  S# = :CS_S# ;

EXEC SQL DELETE
           FROM   S
           WHERE  S# = :CS_S# ;
```

13.4 Outline procedure:

```
EXEC SQL DECLARE CP CURSOR FOR
           SELECT P#, PNAME, COLOR, WEIGHT, CITY
           FROM   P
           ORDER  BY P# ;

count = 0 ;
EXEC SQL OPEN CP ;
DO for all P records accessible via CP ;
   EXEC SQL FETCH CP INTO :P#, :PNAME, :COLOR, :WEIGHT :CITY ;
   print P#, PNAME, COLOR, WEIGHT, CITY ;
   count = count + 1 ;
   IF count is a multiple of 10 THEN
   EXEC SQL DELETE FROM P WHERE P# = :P# ;
END ;
EXEC SQL CLOSE CP ;
```

Note that the "DELETE FROM P" cannot be of the DELETE CURRENT variety, because the declaration of cursor CP involves an ORDER BY clause.

13.5 This is a good example of a problem that SQL in its current form does not handle well. The basic difficulty is as follows: We need to "explode" the given part to n levels, where the value of n is unknown at the time of writing the program. If it were possible, the most straightforward way of performing such an n-level "explosion" would be by means of a recursive program, in which each recursive invocation creates a cursor, as follows (pseudocode):

```
    GET LIST ( GIVENP# ) ;
    CALL RECURSION ( GIVENP# ) ;
    RETURN ;

RECURSION: PROC ( UPPER_P# ) RECURSIVE ;
    DCL UPPER_P# ... ;
    DCL LOWER_P# ... ;
    EXEC SQL DECLARE C "reopenable" CURSOR FOR
            SELECT MINOR_P#
            FROM   PART_STRUCTURE
            WHERE  MAJOR_P# = :UPPER_P# ;

    print UPPER_P# ;
    EXEC SQL OPEN C ;
    DO for all PART_STRUCTURE records accessible via C ;
        EXEC SQL FETCH C INTO :LOWER_P# ;
        CALL RECURSION ( LOWER_P# ) ;
    END ;
    EXEC SQL CLOSE C ;
END ; /* of RECURSION */
```

We have assumed that the (fictitious) specification "reopenable" means that it is legal to issue "OPEN C" for a cursor C that is already open, and that the effect of such an OPEN is to create a new *instance* of the cursor for the specified query (using the current values of any host variables referenced in that query). We have further assumed that references to C in FETCH (etc.) are references to the "current" instance of C, and that CLOSE destroys that instance and reinstates the previous instance as "current." In other words, we have assumed that a reopenable cursor forms a *stack,* with OPEN and CLOSE serving as the "push" and "pop" operators for that stack.

Unfortunately, those assumptions are purely hypothetical today. There is no such thing as a reopenable cursor in SQL today (indeed, an attempt to issue "OPEN C" for a cursor C that is already open will fail). The foregoing code is illegal. But the example makes it clear that "reopenable cursors" would be a very desirable extension to current SQL.

Since the foregoing procedure does not work, we give a sketch of one possible (but very inefficient) procedure that does.

```
    GET LIST ( GIVENP# ) ;
    CALL RECURSION ( GIVENP# ) ;
    RETURN ;
```

```
RECURSION: PROC ( UPPER_P# ) RECURSIVE ;
   DCL UPPER_P# ... ;
   DCL LOWER_P# ... INITIAL ( 'bbbbbb' ) ;
   EXEC SQL DECLARE C CURSOR FOR
               SELECT MINOR_P#
               FROM    PART_STRUCTURE
               WHERE   MAJOR_P# = :UPPER_P#
               AND     MINOR_P# > :LOWER_P#
               ORDER   BY MINOR_P# ;

   DO forever ;
      print UPPER_P# ;
      EXEC SQL OPEN C ;
      EXEC SQL FETCH C INTO :LOWER_P# ;
      IF not found THEN RETURN ;
      IF found THEN
      DO ;
         EXEC SQL CLOSE C ;
         CALL RECURSION ( LOWER_P# ) ;
      END ;
   END ;
END ; /* of RECURSION */
```

Note in this solution that the same cursor is used on every invocation of RECURSION. (By contrast, new instances of UPPER_P# and LOWER_P# are created dynamically each time RECURSION is invoked; those instances are destroyed at completion of that invocation.) Because of this fact, we have to use a trick—

```
... AND MINOR_P# > :LOWER_P# ORDER BY MINOR_P#
```

—so that, on each invocation of RECURSION, we ignore all immediate components (LOWER_P#s) of the current UPPER_P# that have already been processed.

C H A P T E R

◆ **14** ◆

Application Programming II:
Transaction Processing

14.1 INTRODUCTION

The notion of transaction processing was touched on briefly at the end of
the previous chapter. In this chapter, we explain in more detail what exactly
a transaction is and what is meant by the term "transaction management."
In particular, we discuss the problems of recovery and concurrency control
that the transaction concept is intended to solve. Also, of course, we examine the relevant aspects of DB2 and SQL in some detail. Note, however,
that much of the chapter is very general and could apply with little change
to many other systems. The reader who is already familiar with the basic
ideas of transaction processing might like to skip the background explanations and go directly to the SQL-specific material in Sections 14.3 and 14.5–
14.7.

14.2   WHAT IS A TRANSACTION?

A transaction (as we use the term) is a *logical unit of work*. Consider the following example. Suppose for the sake of the example that table P, the parts table, includes an additional field TOTQTY representing the total shipment quantity for the part in question. In other words, the value of TOTQTY for any given part is equal to the sum of all SP.QTY values, taken over all SP records for that part. Now consider the following sequence of operations, the intent of which is to add a new shipment (S5,P1,1000) to the database:

```
EXEC SQL WHENEVER SQLERROR GO TO UNDO ;
EXEC SQL INSERT
         INTO    SP ( S#, P#, QTY )
         VALUES ('S5','P1',1000) ;
EXEC SQL UPDATE P
         SET     TOTQTY = TOTQTY + 1000
         WHERE   P# = 'P1' ;
EXEC SQL COMMIT ;
         GO TO FINISH ;
UNDO :
  EXEC SQL ROLLBACK ;
FINISH :    RETURN ;
```

The INSERT adds the new shipment to the SP table, the UPDATE updates the TOTQTY field for part P1 appropriately.

The point of this example is that what is presumably intended to be a single, atomic operation—"Create a new shipment"—in fact involves *two* updates to the database. What is more, the database is not even consistent between those two updates; it temporarily violates the requirement that the value of TOTQTY for part P1 is supposed to be equal to the sum of all SP.QTY values for part P1. Thus a logical unit of work (i.e., a transaction) is not necessarily just one SQL operation; rather, it is a *sequence* of several such operations, in general, that transforms a consistent state of the database into another consistent state, without necessarily preserving consistency at all intermediate points.

Now, it is clear that what must *not* be allowed to happen in the example is for one of the two updates to be executed and the other not (because then the database would be left in an inconsistent state). Ideally, of course, we would like a cast-iron guarantee that both updates will be executed. Unfortunately, it is impossible to provide any such guarantee: There is always a chance that things will go wrong, and go wrong moreover at the worst possible moment. For example, a system crash might occur between the two updates, or an I/O error might occur on the second of them, etc. But a system that supports *transaction processing* does provide the next best thing to such a guarantee. Specifically, it guarantees that if the transaction executes some updates and then a failure occurs (for whatever reason) before the transaction reaches its normal termination, *then those updates will be undone.* Thus the transaction *either* executes in its entirety *or* is totally canceled (i.e., made as if it never executed at all). In this way a sequence of operations that is fundamentally not atomic can be made to look as if it really were atomic from an external point of view.

The system component that provides this atomicity (or semblance of atomicity) is known as the *transaction manager,* and the COMMIT and ROLLBACK operations are the key to the way it works:

- The COMMIT operation signals *successful* end-of-transaction: It tells the transaction manager that a logical unit of work has been successfully completed, the database is (or should be) in a consistent state again,* and all of the updates made by that unit of work can now be "committed" or made permanent.

- The ROLLBACK operation, by contrast, signals *unsuccessful* end-of-transaction: It tells the transaction manager that something has gone wrong, the database might be in an inconsistent state, and all of the updates made by the logical unit of work so far must be "rolled back" or undone.

In the example, therefore, we issue a COMMIT if we get through the two updates successfully, which will commit the changes in the database and make them permanent. If anything goes wrong, however—i.e., if either UPDATE returns a negative SQLCODE value—then we issue a ROLLBACK instead, to undo any changes made so far.

Note: For the sake of the example, we show the COMMIT and ROLLBACK operations explicitly. However, as mentioned at the end of Chapter 13, under DB2 the system will automatically issue a COMMIT for any program that reaches its normal termination, and will automatically issue a ROLLBACK for any program that does not (regardless of the reason; in particular, if a program terminates abnormally because of a *system* failure, a ROLLBACK will be issued on its behalf when the system is restarted). In the example, therefore, we could have omitted the explicit COMMIT, but not the explicit ROLLBACK.

At this juncture the reader may be wondering how it is possible to undo an update. The answer is that (as mentioned in Chapter 2) the system in-

---

*For simplicity we assume throughout this chapter that the application interacts with just one database—or, equivalently, that in this context the term "database" refers to the collection of *all* data used by the application, no matter how many distinct DB2 databases that data actually spans. See Chapter 16 for an explanation of what the term "database" really means in the DB2 context.

cludes a *log,* in which details of all update operations—in particular, before and after values—are recorded. (In fact, the log entry for any given update is written to the log *before* that update is applied to the database. See the next section for an explanation of this point.) Thus, if it becomes necessary to undo some particular update, the system can use the corresponding log entry to restore the updated item to its previous value.

One final point: As explained in Chapter 1, the data manipulation statements of SQL are *set-level* and typically operate on multiple records at a time. What then if something goes wrong in the middle of such a statement? For example, is it possible that a multiple-record UPDATE could update some of its target records and then fail before updating the rest? The answer is no, it is not; DB2 guarantees that all SQL statements are individually atomic, at least so far as their effect on the database is concerned. If an error does occur in the middle of such a statement, then the database will remain totally unchanged.

14.3   COMMIT AND ROLLBACK

From the previous section, it should be clear that COMMIT and ROLLBACK are not really database operations at all, in the sense that SELECT, UPDATE, etc., are database operations. The COMMIT and ROLLBACK statements are not instructions to the DBMS. Instead, they are instructions to the *transaction manager;* and the transaction manager is certainly not part of the DBMS—on the contrary, the DBMS is subordinate to the transaction manager, in the sense that the DBMS is just one of possibly several "resource managers" that provide services to transactions running under that transaction manager. In the case of DB2 in particular, there are several such transaction managers, corresponding to the several different environments in which DB2 transactions can operate. As explained (in different terms) in Chapter 3:

- A transaction running under IMS batch can use the services of two resource managers—IMS/DB and DB2. IMS acts as the transaction manager in this case.

- A transaction running under IMS/DC can use the services of three resource managers—IMS/DC, IMS/DB, and DB2. Again, IMS acts as the transaction manager in this case.

- A transaction running under CICS can also use the services of three resource managers—CICS, IMS/DB, and DB2. Here CICS acts as the transaction manager.

- A transaction running under TSO (online or batch) can use the services of just one resource manager, namely DB2. Here DB2 itself acts as the transaction manager.

Consider a transaction that updates both an IMS database and a DB2 database. If that transaction completes successfully, then *all* of its updates, to both IMS data and DB2 data, must be committed; conversely, if it fails, then *all* of its updates must be rolled back. It must not be possible for the IMS updates to be committed and the DB2 updates rolled back (or conversely); for then the transaction would no longer be atomic (all or nothing). Thus, it obviously does not make sense for the transaction to issue, say, a COMMIT to IMS and a ROLLBACK to DB2; and even if it issued the same instruction to both, the system could still fail in between the two, with unfortunate results. Instead, therefore, the transaction issues a single *system-wide* COMMIT (or ROLLBACK) to the appropriate transaction manager, and the transaction manager in turn guarantees that all resource managers will commit or will roll back the updates they are responsible for *in unison*. (What is more, it provides that guarantee even if the system fails in the middle of the process, thanks to a protocol known as *two-phase commit*. But the details of that protocol are beyond the scope of this book.) That is why the DBMS(s) is (are) subordinate to the transaction manager; COMMIT and ROLLBACK must be global (system-wide) operations, and the transaction manager acts as the necessary central control point to ensure that this is so.

The foregoing also explains why "commit" and "rollback" functions are requested differently in different environments. Since they are not really database operations at all, but rather transaction manager operations, they must be requested in the style prescribed for the transaction manager in question. In the TSO environment, where DB2 itself serves as the transaction manager, they are requested via the explicit SQL operators COMMIT and ROLLBACK (details below). In the IMS and CICS environments, they are requested via the corresponding IMS and CICS calls, details of which can be found in the IBM manuals for those systems. In the remainder of this section, we concentrate on the TSO environment specifically.*

Before getting into details of the COMMIT and ROLLBACK statements as such, we first define the important notion of "synchronization point" (abbreviated synchpoint). A synchpoint represents a boundary point between two consecutive transactions; loosely speaking, it corresponds to the end of a logical unit of work, and thus to a point at which the database is in a state of consistency. Program initiation, COMMIT, and ROLLBACK each establish a synchpoint, and no other operation does. (Remember, however, that COMMIT and ROLLBACK may sometimes be implicit.)

---

*We also concentrate on the *application programming* environment. It is possible to enter COMMIT and ROLLBACK statements interactively, but the practice is not recommended because (as will become clear later in this chapter) it might mean that locks will be held for an undesirably long time.

COMMIT

The SQL COMMIT statement takes the form

```
COMMIT [ WORK ] ;
```

A successful end-of-transaction is signaled and a synchpoint is established. All updates made by the program since the previous synchpoint are committed. All open cursors are closed. All record locks are released; locks acquired via LOCK TABLE may or may not be released (see Sections 14.5 and 14.6).

The optional operand WORK is purely a noiseword and has no effect on the execution of the statement.

ROLLBACK

The SQL ROLLBACK statement takes the form

```
ROLLBACK [ WORK ] ;
```

An unsuccessful end-of-transaction is signaled and a synchpoint is established. All updates made by the program since the previous synchpoint are undone. All open cursors are closed. All record locks are released; locks acquired via LOCK TABLE may or may not be released (see Sections 14.5 and 14.6).

The optional operand WORK is purely a noiseword and has no effect on the execution of the statement.

A number of points arise from the foregoing definitions that are worth spelling out explicitly.

1. First, note that *every* SQL operation in DB2 is executed within the context of some transaction. This includes data definition operations such as CREATE TABLE and data control operations such as GRANT. It also includes SQL operations that are entered interactively (e.g., through DB2I). The synchpoints for operations entered through DB2I are established in a manner to be explained in Chapter 17 (Section 17.2).

2. It follows from the definitions that transactions cannot be nested inside one another, because each COMMIT (or ROLLBACK) terminates one transaction and starts another.

3. As a consequence of the previous point, we can see that a single program execution consists of a *sequence* of one or more transactions (frequently but not necessarily just one). If it is just one, it will often be possible to code the program without any explicit COMMIT or ROLLBACK statements at all.

Finally, it follows from all of the above that transactions are not only the unit of work but also the unit of *recovery*. For if a transaction successfully COMMITs, then the transaction manager must guarantee that its updates will be permanently established in the database, even if the system crashes the very next moment. It is quite possible, for instance, that the system will crash after the COMMIT has been honored but before the updates have been physically written to the database (they may still be waiting in the main storage buffer and so be lost at the time of the crash). Even if that happens, the system's restart procedure will still install those updates in the database; it is able to discover the values to be written by examining the relevant entries in the log. (It follows that the log must be physically written before COMMIT processing can complete. This rule is known as the *Write-Ahead Log Protocol.*) Thus the restart procedure will recover any units of work (transactions) that completed successfully but did not manage to get their updates physically written prior to the crash; hence, as stated earlier, the transaction can reasonably be defined as the unit of recovery.

14.4 THREE CONCURRENCY PROBLEMS

DB2 is a *shared system;* that is, it is a system that allows any number of transactions to access the same database at the same time. Any such system requires some kind of *concurrency control mechanism* to ensure that concurrent transactions do not interfere with each other's operation, and of course DB2 includes such a mechanism, namely *locking*. For the benefit of readers who may not be familiar with the problems that can occur in the absence of such a mechanism—in other words, with the problems that such a mechanism must be able to solve—this section is devoted to an outline explanation of those problems. We defer specific discussion of the DB2 facilities to Sections 14.5-14.7. Readers who are already familiar with the basic ideas of concurrency control may wish to turn straight to those sections.

There are essentially three ways in which things can go wrong—three ways, that is, in which a transaction, though correct in itself, can nevertheless produce the wrong answer because of interference on the part of some other transaction* (in the absence of suitable controls, of course). The three problems are:

1. The *lost update* problem,

---

*Note that the interfering transaction may also be correct in itself. It is the *interleaving* of operations from the two correct transactions that produces the overall incorrect result.

2. The *uncommitted dependency* problem, and

3. The *inconsistent analysis* problem.

We consider each in turn.

The Lost Update Problem

Consider the situation illustrated in Fig. 14.1. That figure is intended to be read as follows: Transaction A retrieves some record R at time $t1$; transaction B retrieves that same record R at time $t2$; transaction A updates the record (on the basis of the values seen at time $t1$) at time $t3$; and transaction B updates the same record (on the basis of the values seen at time $t2$, which are the same as those seen at time $t1$) at time $t4$. Transaction A's update is lost at time $t4$, because transaction B overwrites it without even looking at it.

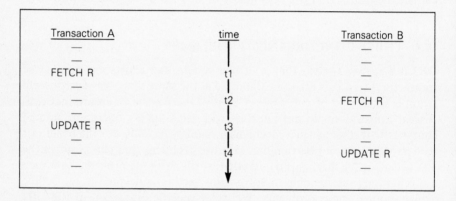

Fig. 14.1 Transaction A loses an update at time $t4$

The Uncommitted Dependency Problem

The uncommitted dependency problem arises if one transaction is allowed to retrieve (or, worse, update) a record that has been updated by another transaction and has not yet been committed by that other transaction. For if it has not yet been committed, there is always a possibility that it never will be committed but will be rolled back instead—in which case the first transaction will have seen some data that now no longer exists (and in a sense "never" existed). Consider Figs. 14.2 and 14.3.

In the first example (Fig. 14.2), transaction A sees an uncommitted update (also called an uncommitted change) at time $t2$. That update is then

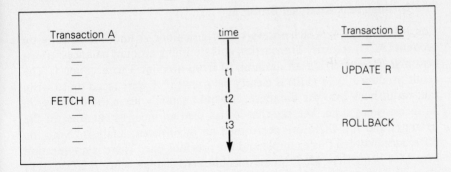

Fig. 14.2 Transaction *A* becomes dependent on an uncommitted change at time *t2*

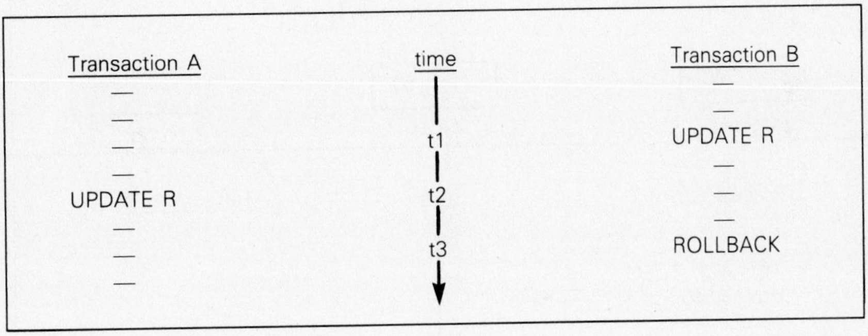

Fig. 14.3 Transaction *A* updates an uncommitted change at time *t2*, and loses that update at time *t3*

undone at time *t3*. Transaction *A* is therefore operating on a false assumption—namely, the assumption that record *R* has the value seen at time *t2*, whereas in fact it has whatever value it had prior to time *t1*. As a result, transaction *A* may well produce incorrect output. Note, incidentally, that the ROLLBACK of transaction *B* may be due to no fault of *B*'s—it could, for example, be the result of a system crash. (And transaction *A* may already have terminated by that time, in which case the crash would not cause a ROLLBACK to be issued for *A* also.)

The second example (Fig. 14.3) is even worse. Not only does transaction *A* become dependent on an uncommitted change at time *t2*, but it actually loses an update at time *t3*—because the ROLLBACK at time *t3* causes record *R* to be restored to its value prior to time *t1*. This is another version of the lost update problem.

The Inconsistent Analysis Problem

Consider Fig. 14.4, which shows two transactions *A* and *B* operating on account (ACC) records: Transaction *A* is summing account balances, transaction *B* is transferring an amount 10 from account 3 to account 1. The result produced by *A* (110) is clearly incorrect; if *A* were to go on to write that result back into the database, it would actually leave the database in an inconsistent state. We say that *A* has seen an inconsistent state of the database and has therefore performed an inconsistent analysis. Note the difference between this example and the previous one: There is no question here of *A* being dependent on an uncommitted change, since *B* COMMITs all its updates before *A* sees ACC 3.

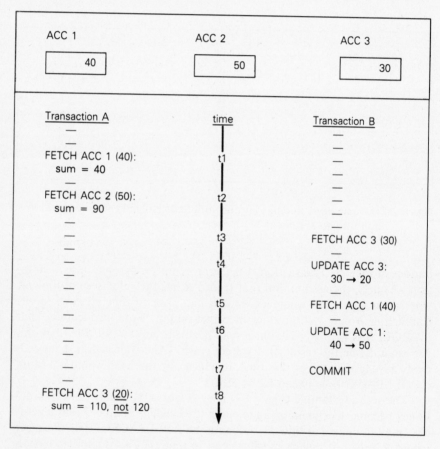

Fig. 14.4 Transaction *A* performs an inconsistent analysis

14.5 HOW DB2 SOLVES THE THREE CONCURRENCY PROBLEMS

As mentioned at the beginning of the previous section, the DB2 concurrency control mechanism—like that of most other systems commercially available—is based on a technique known as *locking*. The basic idea of locking is simple: When a transaction needs an assurance that some object that it is interested in—typically a database record—will not change in some unpredictable manner while its back is turned (as it were), it *acquires a lock* on that object. The effect of the lock is to lock other transactions out of the object, and thereby to prevent them from changing it. The first transaction is thus able to carry out its processing in the certain knowledge that the object in question will remain in a stable state for as long as that transaction wishes it to.

We now give a more detailed explanation of the way locking works in DB2 specifically. We start by making some simplifying assumptions:

1. We assume for the most part that the only kind of object that is subject to the locking mechanism is the database record, i.e., a row of a base table. However, perhaps we should point out right away that:

(a) Index entries are also subject to locking, just as database records are, and for exactly the same reasons;

(b) DB2 does not *physically* lock database records, it locks entire "pages," or entire tables, or even larger units. (A page is a unit of physical storage. See Chapter 16.)

More details are given in Section 14.6.

2. We discuss only two kinds of lock, namely shared locks (S locks) and exclusive locks (X locks). Other types of lock exist in some systems (in fact, DB2 itself supports additional types, as we will see), but S and X are the most important ones for present purposes. *Note:* S and X locks are sometimes referred to as read and write locks, respectively.

3. We consider record-level operations only (FETCH, UPDATE CURRENT, etc.). For locking purposes, set-level operations (SELECT–FROM–WHERE, etc.) can be thought of just as shorthand for an appropriate series of record-level operations.

4. We assume that if a transaction requests a lock that is not currently available, the transaction simply waits until it is. In practice, the installation can specify a maximum wait time; then, if any transaction ever reaches this threshold in waiting for a lock, it "times out" and the lock request fails (a negative SQLCODE is returned).

5. We assume that RR ("repeatable read") isolation level is in effect. See

Section 14.6 for an explanation of this assumption, also for an explanation of the effects of relaxing it.

We now proceed with our detailed explanations.

1. First, if transaction *A* holds an exclusive (X) lock on record *R,* then a request from transaction *B* for a lock of either type on *R* will cause *B* to go into a wait state. *B* will wait until *A*'s lock is released.

2. Next, if transaction *A* holds a shared (S) lock on record *R,* then:

(a) A request from transaction *B* for an X lock on *R* will cause *B* to go into a wait state (and *B* will wait until *A*'s lock is released);

(b) A request from transaction *B* for an S lock on *R* will be granted (that is, *B* will now also hold an S lock on *R*).

These first two points can conveniently be summarized by means of a *compatibility matrix* (Fig. 14.5). The matrix is interpreted as follows: Consider some record *R;* suppose transaction *A* currently holds a lock on *R* as indicated by the entries in the column headings (dash = no lock); and suppose some distinct transaction *B* requests a lock on *R* as indicated by the entries down the left-hand side (for completeness we again include the "no lock" case). An N indicates a *conflict* (*B*'s request cannot be satisfied and *B* goes into a wait state), a Y indicates compatibility (*B*'s request is satisfied). The matrix is obviously symmetric.

	X	S	—
X	N	N	Y
S	N	Y	Y
—	Y	Y	Y

Fig. 14.5 Lock type compatibility matrix (X, S)

To continue with our explanations:

3. Transaction requests for record locks are always implicit. When a transaction successfully FETCHes a record, it automatically acquires an S lock on that record. When a transaction successfully updates a record, it automatically acquires an X lock on that record (if it already holds an S lock on the record, as it will in a FETCH/update sequence, then the update "promotes" the S lock to X level).

4. All locks are held until the next synchpoint.*

Now we are in a position to see how DB2 solves the three problems described in the previous section. Again we consider them one at a time.

The Lost Update Problem

Fig. 14.6 is a modified version of Fig. 14.1, showing what would happen to the interleaved execution of that figure under the locking mechanism of DB2. As you can see, transaction A's UPDATE at time $t3$ is not accepted, because it is an implicit request for an X lock on R, and such a request conflicts with the S lock already held by transaction B; so A goes into a wait state. For analogous reasons, B goes into a wait state at time $t4$. Now both transactions are unable to proceed, so there is no question of any update being lost. DB2 thus solves the lost update problem by reducing it to another problem!—but at least it does solve the original problem. The new problem is called *deadlock*. To see how DB2 solves the deadlock problem, see Section 14.7.

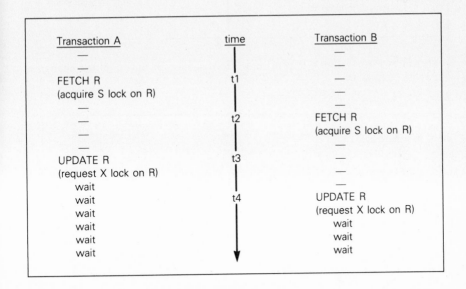

Fig. 14.6 No update is lost, but deadlock occurs at time $t4$

---

*X locks are always held until the next synchpoint. S locks are also held until that time, provided that (as we assume) RR isolation level is in effect. See Section 14.6 for further discussion.

The Uncommitted Dependency Problem

Figs. 14.7 and 14.8 are, respectively, modified versions of Figs. 14.2 and 14.3, showing what would happen to the interleaved executions of those figures under the locking mechanism of DB2. As you can see, transaction *A*'s operation at time *t2* (FETCH in Fig. 14.7, UPDATE in Fig. 14.8) is not

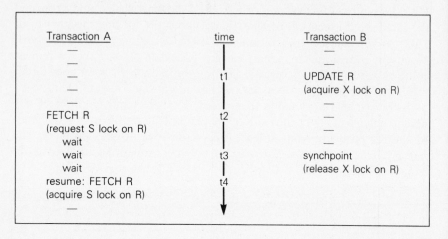

Fig. 14.7 Transaction *A* is prevented from seeing an uncommitted change at time *t2*

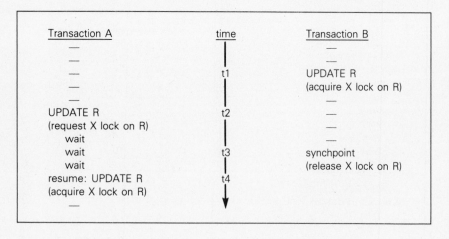

Fig. 14.8 Transaction *A* is prevented from updating an uncommitted change at time *t2*

accepted in either case, because it is an implicit request for a lock on *R*, and such a request conflicts with the X lock already held by *B;* so *A* goes into a wait state. It remains in that wait state until *B* reaches a synchpoint (either COMMIT or ROLLBACK), when *B*'s lock is released and *A* is able to proceed; and at that point *A* sees a *committed* value (either the pre-*B* value, if *B* terminates with a ROLLBACK, or the post-*B* value otherwise). Either way, *A* is no longer dependent on an uncommitted update.

The Inconsistent Analysis Problem

Fig. 14.9 is a modified version of Fig. 14.4, showing what would happen to the interleaved execution of that figure under the locking mechanism of DB2. As you can see, transaction *B*'s UPDATE at time *t6* is not accepted, because it is an implicit request for an X lock on ACC 1, and such a request

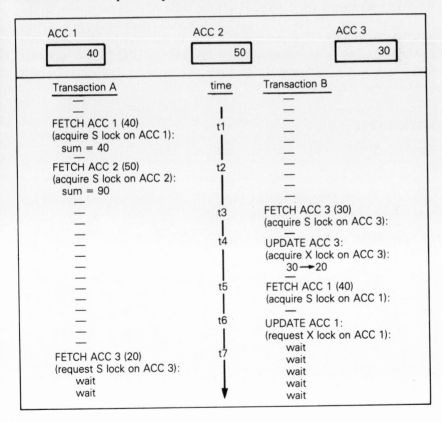

Fig. 14.9 Inconsistent analysis is prevented, but deadlock occurs at time *t7*

conflicts with the S lock already held by *A;* so *B* goes into a wait state. Likewise, transaction *A*'s FETCH at time *t7* is also not accepted, because it is an implicit request for an S lock on ACC 3, and such a request conflicts with the X lock already held by *B;* so *A* goes into a wait state also. Thus (again) DB2 solves the original problem (the inconsistent analysis problem, in this case) by forcing a deadlock. As already mentioned, deadlock is discussed in Section 14.7.

14.6 EXPLICIT LOCKING FACILITIES

In addition to the implicit locking mechanism described in the previous section, DB2 provides certain explicit facilities which the programmer should at least be aware of (though the implicit facilities will be adequate in many situations). The explicit facilities—a somewhat mixed bag—consist of (1) the SQL statement LOCK TABLE, (2) the ISOLATION parameter on the BIND command, (3) the tablespace LOCKSIZE parameter, and (4) the ACQUIRE/RELEASE parameters on the BIND command. *Note:* The BIND command is the command that invokes the DB2 Bind component and produces an application plan from one or more Database Request Modules. See Chapter 17.

LOCK TABLE

The SQL LOCK TABLE statement takes the form

```
LOCK TABLE table IN mode MODE ;
```

where "mode" is SHARE or EXCLUSIVE, and where "table" must designate a base table, not a view. For example:

```
LOCK TABLE SP IN EXCLUSIVE MODE ;
```

This LOCK TABLE acquires an X lock on the *entire SP base table* on behalf of the transaction issuing the statement. Of course, the transaction may have to wait for a while before it can acquire the lock, if some other transaction already holds a conflicting lock, either on the table itself or on some record within that table. Once the lock is acquired, no other transaction will be able to acquire any lock on the table or on any part of it—in other words, no other transaction will be able to access any part of the table in any way—until the original lock is released. When that original lock is released depends on the RELEASE parameter on BIND (see later in this section).

If SHARE is specified instead of EXCLUSIVE, then the transaction will of course acquire an S lock instead of an X lock. Again, of course, it may have to wait before it can acquire the lock. Once the lock is acquired, other transactions will not be able to acquire an X lock on the table or on any part of it until the original lock is released, but they *will* be able to acquire an S lock on the table or on some part of it before that time.

The purpose of the LOCK TABLE statement is as follows. If a transaction accesses a large number of individual records and locks them one at a time as described in the previous section, then the locking overhead for that transaction may be quite high, in terms of both space and time (space for holding the locks in main storage and time for acquiring them). Consider, for example, a program that scans and prints some large percentage of the entire SP table. For such a program, it may well be better to acquire a single table-level lock as in the example above, and thus to dispense with the need for record-level locks (for that table) entirely. Of course, concurrency will suffer, but the performance of the individual transaction will improve, possibly to such an extent that overall system throughput will improve also.

Acquiring a table-level X lock will indeed (as just suggested) dispense with the need for record-level locks entirely for the table concerned. Acquiring a table-level S lock will dispense with the need for record-level S locks, but not for record-level X locks (again, for the table concerned); that is, if the program updates any record in the table, it will still need to acquire an X lock on that particular record, in order to prevent concurrent transactions from seeing an uncommitted change.

Note: If the table in question resides in a "segmented tablespace" (see Chapter 16), LOCK TABLE does indeed lock the table per se. If the table resides in some other kind of tablespace, however, LOCK TABLE actually locks the *entire tablespace* that contains that table. In some cases, therefore, DB2 may physically lock more than the user has asked for, because some tablespaces will contain more than one table. Again, see Chapter 16 for further information regarding tablespaces.

The ISOLATION Parameter

The ISOLATION parameter on the BIND command specifies the *isolation level* for the application plan being bound. There are two possible values, RR ("repeatable read") and CS ("cursor stability"). RR is the default.

- "Cursor stability" means that if a transaction using the plan:

(a) obtains addressability to some particular record by setting a cursor to point to it, and thus

(b) acquires a lock on that record, and then

(c) relinquishes its addressability to the record without updating it, and so

(d) does not promote its existing lock to X level, then

(e) that existing lock can be released without having to wait for the next synchpoint.

- "Repeatable read" means that record-level S locks are held until the next synchpoint, like X locks.

Isolation level CS may provide more concurrency than isolation level RR, but from a theoretical standpoint, at least, it is generally not a good idea (that is why RR is the default). The problem with CS is that a transaction operating at that level may have a record changed "behind its back," as in Fig. 14.4, and so may produce a wrong answer. In fact, if a transaction operates under isolation level CS, then it is *always* theoretically possible to define a second transaction that can run interleaved with the first in such a way as to produce an overall incorrect result. By contrast, a transaction that operates under isolation level RR can behave completely as if it were executing in a single-user system.*

The explanations of Section 14.5 ("How DB2 Solves the Three Concurrency Problems") require some slight modification if isolation level CS is in effect, as follows:

- If a transaction obtains addressability to a record under CS, and if there is a possibility that the transaction may update that record (e.g., if the cursor was defined to be FOR UPDATE), then DB2 gives the transaction an "update lock" (U lock) instead of an S lock.

- U locks are compatible with S locks but not with other U locks (and of course not with X locks); that is, if transaction *A* holds a U lock on record *R,* then a request from transaction *B* for a U (or X) lock on *R* will cause *B* to go into a wait state. If transaction *A* now updates *R,* its U lock will be promoted to X level; otherwise the U lock will be released (like an S lock) when *A* relinquishes addressability to *R.*

The advantage of U locks (intuitively speaking) is that they may reduce the number of deadlocks. See Exercises 14.2 and 14.3 at the end of the chapter.

Note finally that although it is specified as part of the BIND command rather than as part of the program, the programmer does need to be aware

---

*On the other hand, RR can lead to unacceptable overhead in some situations (especially as it applies to the entire plan, not just to individual tables). In such cases, it might be better to specify CS for the plan, and then use explicit LOCK TABLE operations on individual tables to achieve the effect of RR for just those tables.

of the isolation level, because the logic of the program may depend on it (i.e., it may affect the way the program has to be coded).

The LOCKSIZE Parameter

(We mention this topic here only for completeness. The following description might not make much sense until the reader has studied Chapter 16.)

The implicit locking mechanism of DB2 is defined in terms of record-level locks, as explained in Section 14.5. However, that definition is a *logical* definition. Physically, DB2 locks data in terms of *pages* or *tables* or *tablespaces*. That is, when a given transaction logically locks some individual record, DB2 physically locks the page or the table or the tablespace that contains that record, depending on what was specified as the LOCKSIZE for the relevant tablespace in the CREATE or ALTER TABLESPACE operation. For a given tablespace, the LOCKSIZE can be specified as PAGE, TABLE, TABLESPACE, or ANY:

- TABLESPACE means that all locks acquired on data in the tablespace will be at the tablespace level.

- TABLE means that locks acquired on data in the tablespace will be at the table level. TABLE applies only to segmented tablespaces.

- PAGE means that locks acquired on data in the tablespace will be at the page level whenever possible. Our discussions in Section 14.5 tacitly assumed page-level locking. Sometimes, however, DB2 may still acquire locks at the table or tablespace level, even if page-level locking is specified (details beyond the scope of this text).

- ANY (which is the default) means that DB2 itself will decide the appropriate physical unit of locking for the tablespace *for each plan*—e.g., one plan may acquire locks at the page level, while another acquires them at the tablespace level, both on the same tablespace. Also, in some cases DB2 may acquire page-level locks initially (for some given plan and some given tablespace), but then trade all those locks in for a single table- or tablespace-level lock, if the number of page-level locks reaches some installation-specified threshold (a process known as *lock escalation*).

The ACQUIRE/RELEASE Parameters

(Again we mention this topic here primarily for completeness. For further discussion, see the IBM manuals.)

Despite the discussion of page- and table-level locking above, the fact is that DB2 *always* implicitly acquires locks of some kind—sometimes shared or exclusive locks, sometimes less restrictive "intent" locks—at the tablespace level. The ACQUIRE and RELEASE parameters on the BIND command specify when such tablespace-level locks are to be acquired and released. For ACQUIRE, the possible specifications are USE and ALLOCATE; for RELEASE, they are COMMIT and DEALLOCATE.

- ACQUIRE (USE) means that such implicit locks are acquired on first use; i.e., tablespaces are locked when they are first "touched." ACQUIRE (ALLOCATE) means that such locks are acquired when the plan is "allocated" (loosely, when the program begins execution).

- RELEASE (COMMIT) means that all tablespace-level locks are released at each synchpoint—both implicitly acquired locks and locks acquired explicitly via LOCK TABLE. RELEASE (DEALLOCATE) means that all such locks are held until the plan is "deallocated" (loosely, when the program terminates). If ACQUIRE (ALLOCATE) is specified, RELEASE (DEALLOCATE) must be specified also.

Note: Locks obtained via dynamic SQL (see Chapter 15) are always acquired on first use and released at the next synchpoint, regardless of what has been specified for the ACQUIRE and RELEASE parameters. In the case of segmented tablespaces, ACQUIRE and RELEASE affect the acquisition and release of table-level locks also.

14.7 DEADLOCK

We have seen how locking can be used to solve the three basic problems of concurrency. Unfortunately, however, we have also seen that locking introduces problems of its own, principally the problem of deadlock. Section 14.5 gave two examples of deadlock. Fig. 14.10 shows a slightly more generalized version of the problem. *Note:* The LOCK operations shown in that figure are intended to represent any operations that acquire locks, not necessarily SQL LOCK TABLE statements specifically.

Deadlock is a situation in which two or more transactions are in a simultaneous wait state, each one waiting for one of the others to release a lock before it can proceed. Fig. 14.10 shows a deadlock involving two transactions, but deadlocks involving three, four, ... transactions are also possible, at least in theory. In practice, however, deadlocks almost never involve more than two transactions.

If a deadlock occurs, the system will detect it and break it. Breaking a deadlock involves choosing one of the deadlocked transactions as the *victim* and—depending on the transaction manager concerned—either rolling it back automatically or requesting it to roll itself back (a request that cannot be refused, incidentally). Either way, the transaction will release its locks

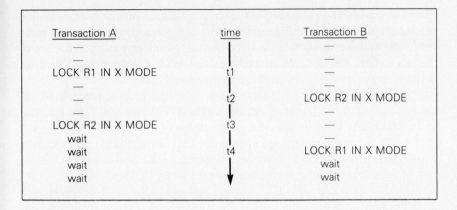

Fig. 14.10 An example of deadlock

and thus allow some other transaction to proceed. In general, therefore, *any operation that requests a lock*—which means *any executable SQL operation*—may be rejected with a negative SQLCODE indicating that the transaction has just been selected as the victim in a deadlock situation and has either been rolled back or is requested to do so. The problem of deadlock is thus a significant one so far as the application programmer is concerned, because application programs may need to include explicit code to deal with it if it arises. For example:

```
EXEC SQL ... ;
IF SQLCODE = value indicating "deadlock victim"
THEN DO ;
        EXEC SQL ROLLBACK ;
        reinitialize variables from initial input data ;
        GO TO beginning of program ;
     END ;
```

Here we are assuming that the program has saved its initial input data somewhere (not in the database!—why not?) in preparation for just such an eventuality.

14.8 SUMMARY

In this rather lengthy chapter we have discussed the question of transaction management, both in general terms and as it is addressed in DB2 specifically. A transaction is a logical unit of work—also a unit of recovery and (as can be seen from the last few sections) a unit of concurrency. Transaction management is the task of supervising the execution of transactions in such a way that each transaction can be considered as an all-or-nothing proposition, even given the possibility of arbitrary failures on the part of either individual transactions or the system itself, and given also the fact that multiple independent transactions may be executing concurrently and accessing the same data. In fact, the overall function of the system might well be defined as *the reliable execution of transactions.*

In DB2 specifically, transactions are delimited by *synchpoints,* which are established by program initiation, COMMIT (successful termination), and ROLLBACK (unsuccessful termination). (*Note:* COMMIT and ROLLBACK are the operations used in the TSO environment; other, analogous operations are used in other environments.) DB2 guarantees the atomicity of such transactions, as explained in Sections 14.2 and 14.3.

Concurrency control in DB2 is based on locking. Basically, every record a transaction accesses is locked; if the transaction goes on to update the record, then that lock will be promoted to exclusive level. Exclusive locks are held until the next synchpoint. This simple protocol solves the three basic problems of concurrency, but also introduces the possibility of deadlock; hence application programs must be prepared to deal with that eventuality. Deadlock is signaled by a negative SQLCODE value that may potentially be returned after any SQL operation that requests a lock.

EXERCISES

14.1 The following list represents the sequence of events in an interleaved execution of a set of DB2 transactions *T1, T2, ..., T12,* all operating under isolation level RR. *A, B, ..., H* are intended to be records, not cursors.

```
time t0        ..........
time t1    (T1)  :  FETCH A
time t2    (T2)  :  FETCH B
   -       (T1)  :  FETCH C
   -       (T4)  :  FETCH D
   -       (T5)  :  FETCH A
   -       (T2)  :  FETCH E
   -       (T2)  :  UPDATE E
   -       (T3)  :  FETCH F
   -       (T2)  :  FETCH F
   -       (T5)  :  UPDATE A
   -       (T1)  :  COMMIT
   -       (T6)  :  FETCH A
   -       (T5)  :  ROLLBACK
   -       (T6)  :  FETCH C
   -       (T6)  :  UPDATE C
   -       (T7)  :  FETCH G
   -       (T8)  :  FETCH H
   -       (T9)  :  FETCH G
   -       (T9)  :  UPDATE G
   -       (T8)  :  FETCH E
   -       (T7)  :  COMMIT
   -       (T9)  :  FETCH H
   -       (T3)  :  FETCH G
```

```
    -       (T10) :  FETCH A
    -       (T9)  :  UPDATE H
    -       (T6)  :  COMMIT
    -       (T11) :  FETCH C
    -       (T12) :  FETCH D
    -       (T12) :  FETCH C
    -       (T2)  :  UPDATE F
    -       (T11) :  UPDATE C
    -       (T12) :  FETCH A
    -       (T10) :  UPDATE A
    -       (T12) :  UPDATE D
    -       (T4)  :  FETCH G
time tn          ..........
```

Are there any deadlocks at time *tn*?

14.2 Draw a compatibility matrix showing the interactions among lock types X, U, and S.

14.3 Consider the concurrency problems illustrated in Figs. 14.1–14.4 once again. What would happen in each case if all transactions were executing under isolation level CS instead of RR?

14.4 The following list represents the sequence of events in an interleaved execution of a set of DB2 transactions *T1, T2, ..., T12*, all operating under isolation level CS. As in Exercise 14.1, *A, B, ..., H* are records, not cursors. All FETCHes are intended to be "FOR UPDATE."

```
time t0          ..........
time t1   (T1)  :  FETCH A
time t2   (T2)  :  FETCH B
    -     (T1)  :  FETCH C
    -     (T4)  :  FETCH D
    -     (T5)  :  FETCH A
    -     (T2)  :  FETCH E
    -     (T2)  :  UPDATE E
    -     (T3)  :  FETCH F
    -     (T2)  :  FETCH F
    -     (T1)  :  COMMIT
    -     (T5)  :  UPDATE A
    -     (T6)  :  FETCH A
    -     (T5)  :  ROLLBACK
    -     (T6)  :  FETCH C
    -     (T6)  :  UPDATE C
    -     (T7)  :  FETCH G
    -     (T8)  :  FETCH H
    -     (T9)  :  FETCH G
    -     (T8)  :  FETCH E
    -     (T7)  :  COMMIT
    -     (T9)  :  UPDATE G
    -     (T9)  :  FETCH H
    -     (T3)  :  FETCH G
    -     (T10) :  FETCH A
    -     (T6)  :  COMMIT
    -     (T11) :  FETCH C
    -     (T12) :  FETCH D
    -     (T2)  :  UPDATE B
    -     (T10) :  UPDATE A
    -     (T4)  :  FETCH G
time tn          ..........
```

Are there any deadlocks at time *tn*?

14.5 (Modified version of Exercise 12.4) Write a program to read and print all part records in part number order, deleting every tenth one as you go, and beginning a new transaction after every tenth record.

ANSWERS TO SELECTED EXERCISES

14.1 At time *tn no* transactions are doing any useful work at all! There is one deadlock, involving transactions *T2, T3, T9,* and *T8;* in addition, *T4* is waiting for *T9, T12* is waiting for *T4,* and *T10* and *T11* are both waiting for *T12.* We can represent the situation by means of a graph (the *Wait-For Graph*), in which the nodes represent transactions and a directed edge from node *Ti* to node *Tj* indicates that *Ti* is waiting for *Tj.* Edges are labeled with the name of the record and level of lock they are waiting for. Note that *T1, T6,* and *T7* have all completed successfully and *T5* has completed unsuccessfully.

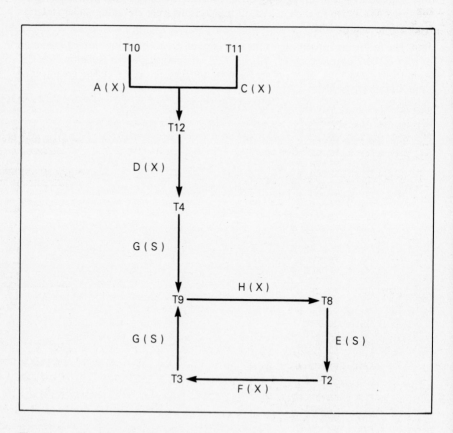

Fig. 14.11 The Wait-For Graph for Exercise 14.1

14.2 See Fig. 14.12

	X	U	S	—
X	N	N	N	Y
U	N	N	Y	Y
S	N	Y	Y	Y
—	Y	Y	Y	Y

Fig. 14.12 Lock type compatibility matrix (X, U, S)

14.3 Effects of isolation level CS:

- The lost update problem (Fig. 14.1): *B*'s FETCH at time *t2* is not accepted, because it is an implicit request for a U lock on *R,* and such a request conflicts with the U lock already held by *A. B* waits until *A* has updated *R* (thereby promoting its U lock to X level) and then reached a synchpoint (at which time *A*'s lock is released, and *B* is able to resume). *B* is thus forced to see the effect of *A*'s update.

- The uncommitted dependency problem (Figs. 14.2, 14.3): *A*'s operation at time *t2* is not accepted, because it is an implicit request for an S lock (at least) on *R,* and such a request conflicts with the X lock already held by *B. A* waits until *B* reaches a synchpoint, when *B*'s lock is released and *A* is able to proceed; and at that point *A* sees a committed value of *R* (either the pre-*B* value, if *B* terminates with ROLLBACK, or the post-*B* value otherwise). Either way, *A* is no longer dependent on an uncommitted change.

- The inconsistent analysis problem (Fig. 14.4): Isolation level CS does not solve this problem; *A* must execute under RR in order to retain its locks until the next synchpoint, for otherwise it will still produce the wrong answer. (Alternatively, of course, *A* could use LOCK TABLE to lock the entire accounts table. This solution would work under both CS and RR isolation levels.)

14.4 At time *tn* only transactions *T10* and *T11* are doing any useful work. There is one deadlock, involving transactions *T2, T3, T9,* and *T8;* in addition, *T4* is waiting for *T9,* and *T12* is waiting for *T4* (refer to Fig. 14.13). Note that *T1, T6,* and *T7* have all completed successfully and *T5* has completed unsuccessfully.

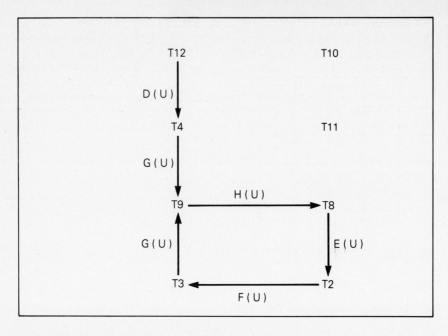

Fig. 14.13 The Wait-For Graph for Exercise 14.4

14.5 This exercise is typical of a wide class of applications, and the following represents the typical approach to implementing such applications:

```
EXEC SQL DECLARE CP CURSOR FOR
         SELECT P#, PNAME, COLOR, WEIGHT, CITY
         FROM    P
         WHERE   P# > previous_P#
         ORDER   BY P# ;

previous_P# = 'bbbbbb' ;
eof = false ;
DO WHILE (eof = false) ;
   EXEC SQL OPEN CP ;
   DO count = 1 TO 10 ;
      EXEC SQL FETCH CP INTO :P#, ... ;
      IF SQLCODE = +100 THEN
         DO ;
            EXEC SQL CLOSE CP ;
            EXEC SQL COMMIT ;
            eof = true ;
         END ;
      ELSE print P#, ... ;
   END ;
   EXEC SQL DELETE FROM P WHERE P# = :P# ;
   EXEC SQL CLOSE CP ;
   EXEC SQL COMMIT ;
   previous_P# = P# ;
END ;
```

Observe that we lose position within the parts table at the end of each transaction (even if we did not close cursor CP explicitly, the COMMIT would close it automatically anyway). The foregoing code will therefore not be particularly efficient, because each new transaction requires a search on the parts table in order to reestablish position. The inefficiency is unavoidable, however. Matters may be improved somewhat if there happens to be an index on field P.P# (as in fact there will be, since P.P# is the primary key for table P), and the optimizer chooses that index as the access path for the table.

·15·

Application Programming III:
Dynamic SQL

15.1 INTRODUCTION

"Dynamic SQL" consists of a set of embedded SQL facilities that are provided specifically to allow the construction of generalized, online (and possibly interactive) applications—where by "online application" we mean a program that is written to support access to the database from an end-user at an online terminal. (The statements of dynamic SQL cannot themselves be entered interactively—they are available only in the embedded environment.) The topic of this chapter is therefore somewhat specialized; basically, the only people who need to know the material are people directly concerned with the writing of generalized applications. Other readers may wish to ignore the chapter altogether, at least on a first reading.

Consider what a typical online application has to do. In outline, the steps it must go through are as follows.

1. Accept a command from the terminal.
2. Analyze that command.
3. Issue appropriate SQL statements to the database.
4. Return a message and/or results to the terminal.

If the set of commands the program can accept is fairly small, as in the case of (perhaps) a program handling airline reservations, then the set of possible SQL statements to be issued may also be small and can be "hardwired" into the program. In this case, Steps 2 and 3 above will consist simply of logic to examine the input command and then branch to the part of the program that issues the predefined SQL statement(s). If, on the other hand, there can be great variability in the input—in other words, if the application is reasonably generalized—then it may not be practicable to predefine and "hardwire" SQL statements for every possible command. Instead, it will probably be necessary to construct the required SQL statements dynamically, and then to bind and execute those constructed statements dynamically. The facilities of dynamic SQL are provided to assist in this process.

Incidentally, the process just described is exactly what happens when SQL statements themselves are entered interactively—for example, through DB2I. DB2I itself is a generalized online application; it is ready to accept an extremely wide variety of input, namely any valid (or invalid!) SQL statement. It uses the facilities of dynamic SQL to construct suitable SQL statements corresponding to its input, to bind and execute those constructed statements, and to return messages and results back to the terminal.

If the statement to be dynamically bound and executed is a SELECT statement, special considerations apply. (As in ordinary embedded SQL, retrieval is more complicated and involves more work on the part of the user.) Section 15.2 therefore considers the other statements first, then Section 15.3 addresses the problem of SELECT statements specifically.

15.2 HANDLING STATEMENTS OTHER THAN SELECT

The two principal statements of dynamic SQL are PREPARE and EXECUTE. Their use is illustrated by the following (accurate but unrealistically simple) PL/I example.

```
        DCL     SQLSOURCE CHAR(256) VARYING ;
 EXEC SQL DECLARE SQLOBJ STATEMENT ;

        SQLSOURCE = 'DELETE FROM SP WHERE QTY < 100' ;
 EXEC SQL PREPARE SQLOBJ FROM :SQLSOURCE ;
 EXEC SQL EXECUTE SQLOBJ ;
```

Explanation:

1. SQLSOURCE is a PL/I varying length character string variable in which the program will construct the source form (i.e., character string representation) of some SQL statement (a DELETE statement, in our particular example).

2. SQLOBJ, by contrast, is a *SQL* variable, not a PL/I variable, that will be used (conceptually) to hold the object form (i.e., application plan representation) of the SQL statement whose source form is given in SQLSOURCE. (The names SQLSOURCE and SQLOBJ are arbitrary, of course.) The name SQLOBJ is said to be a *statement name*.

3. The assignment statement "SQLSOURCE = ... ;" assigns to SQLSOURCE the source form of a SQL DELETE statement. (As suggested in Section 15.1, the process of constructing such a source statement is likely to be somewhat more complicated in practice, involving the input and analysis of some command from the terminal.)

4. The PREPARE statement then takes that source statement and compiles (binds) it to produce an executable version, which it stores in SQLOBJ.

5. Finally, the EXECUTE statement executes that SQLOBJ version and thus (in the example) causes the actual DELETE to occur. Feedback information from the DELETE will be returned in the SQLCA as usual.

Note, incidentally, that since it denotes a SQL variable, not a PL/I variable, the statement name SQLOBJ does *not* have a colon prefix in the PREPARE and EXECUTE statements.

PREPARE

The syntax of the PREPARE statement is as follows.

```
EXEC SQL PREPARE statement FROM string ;
```

Here "string" is an expression of the host language that yields the character string representation of a SQL statement, and "statement" is the name of a SQL variable that will be used to contain the PREPAREd (i.e., compiled) version of that SQL statement. The statement to be PREPAREd must be one of the following (only):

```
UPDATE   (including CURRENT form)
DELETE   (including CURRENT form)
INSERT
SELECT   (excluding INTO form)

CREATE
DROP
ALTER
```

```
COMMENT
LABEL

GRANT
REVOKE

COMMIT
ROLLBACK
LOCK

EXPLAIN
```

In other words, the following statements cannot be PREPAREd: CLOSE, DECLARE CURSOR, DECLARE STATEMENT, DECLARE TABLE, DESCRIBE, EXECUTE, FETCH, INCLUDE, OPEN, PREPARE, SELECT (INTO form), SET CURRENT SQLID, and WHENEVER. Also, the source form of a statement to be PREPAREd must not include either EXEC SQL or a statement terminator. Nor can it include any host variable references.

EXECUTE

The syntax of the EXECUTE statement is as follows.

```
EXEC SQL EXECUTE statement [ USING argument(s) ] ;
```

The PREPAREd SQL statement in the SQL variable identified by "statement" is executed. The USING clause is explained in the subsection "Arguments and Parameters" immediately following.

Arguments and Parameters

As already indicated, SQL statements that are to be PREPAREd cannot include any references to host variables. However, they can include *parameters,* denoted in the source form of the statement by question marks. Basically, parameters can appear wherever host variables can appear (with certain exceptions—details beyond the scope of this book). For example:

```
SQLSOURCE = 'DELETE
            FROM    SP
            WHERE   QTY > ?
            AND     QTY < ?' ;

EXEC SQL PREPARE SQLOBJ FROM :SQLSOURCE ;
```

Arguments to replace the parameters are specified when the statement is EXECUTEd, via the USING clause. For example:

```
EXEC SQL EXECUTE SQLOBJ USING :LOW, :HIGH ;
```

In the example, the statement actually executed is equivalent to the ordinary embedded SQL statement

```
EXEC SQL DELETE FROM SP WHERE QTY > :LOW AND QTY < :HIGH ;
```

In general, the USING clause in the EXECUTE statement takes the form

```
USING argument [ , argument ] ...
```

where each "argument" in turn takes the form

```
: host-variable [ : host-variable ]
```

just like a target reference in an INTO clause. (The optional second host variable is a null indicator variable.) The *i*th argument in the list of arguments corresponds to the *i*th parameter (i.e., *i*th question mark) in the source form of the PREPAREd statement.

15.3 HANDLING SELECT STATEMENTS

As indicated earlier, the procedure outlined in Section 15.2 is adequate for the dynamic preparation and execution of all SQL operations (all SQL operations that may legally be PREPAREd, that is), except SELECT. The reason that SELECT is different is that it returns data to the program; all the other statements return feedback information (in the SQLCA) only.

A program using SELECT needs to know something about the data values to be retrieved, since it has to specify a set of target variables to receive those values. In other words, it needs to know at least how many values there will be in each result row, and also what the data types and lengths of those values will be. If the SELECT is generated dynamically, it will usually not be possible for the program to know this information in advance; therefore, it must obtain the information dynamically, using another dynamic SQL statement called DESCRIBE. In outline, the procedure such a program must go through is as follows.

1. It builds and PREPAREs the SELECT statement *without* an INTO clause. (As indicated in Section 15.2, a SELECT statement that is to be PREPAREd must not include an INTO clause.)
2. It uses DESCRIBE to interrogate the system about the results it can expect when the SELECT is executed. The description of those results is returned in an area called the SQL Descriptor Area (SQLDA).
3. Next, it allocates storage for a set of target variables to receive those

results in accordance with what it has just learned from DESCRIBE, and places the addresses of those target variables back into the SQLDA.

4. Finally, it retrieves the result rows one at a time by means of a cursor, using the cursor statements OPEN, FETCH, and CLOSE. It can also use UPDATE CURRENT and DELETE CURRENT statements on those rows, if appropriate (however, those statements will probably have to be PREPAREd and EXECUTEd versions).

In order to make these ideas a little more concrete, we present a simple example to show what such a program might look like (in outline). The example is written in PL/I. Note that it *must* be written in a language like PL/I that provides explicit support for dynamic storage allocation. IBM OS/VS COBOL, for example, does not provide any such support; hence a generalized online application that is to perform data retrieval cannot be written in OS/VS COBOL. (An online application that is to use only the facilities described in Section 15.2 can be written in OS/VS COBOL if desired, however.)

```
            DCL SQLSOURCE CHAR(256) VARYING ;
EXEC SQL DECLARE SQLOBJ STATEMENT ;
EXEC SQL DECLARE X CURSOR FOR SQLOBJ ;

EXEC SQL INCLUDE SQLDA ;
/* Let the maximum number of expected values to be      */
/* retrieved be N.                                      */
            SQLSIZE = N ;
            ALLOCATE SQLDA ;

            SQLSOURCE = 'SELECT * FROM SP WHERE QTY > 100' ;
EXEC SQL PREPARE SQLOBJ FROM :SQLSOURCE ;

EXEC SQL DESCRIBE SQLOBJ INTO SQLDA ;

/* Now SQLDA contains the following information (among  */
/* other things):                                       */
/*  - actual number of values to be retrieved in SQLN   */
/*  - name (or label), data type, and length of ith     */
/*                            value in SQLVAR(i)         */

/* Using the information returned by DESCRIBE, the       */
/* program can now allocate a storage area for each      */
/* value to be retrieved, and place the address of the   */
/* ith such area in SQLVAR(i). Then:                     */

EXEC SQL OPEN X ;
            DO WHILE ( more-records-to-come ) ;
                EXEC SQL FETCH X
                        USING DESCRIPTOR SQLDA ;
                .....
            END ;
EXEC SQL CLOSE X ;
```

Explanation:

1. SQLSOURCE and SQLOBJ are basically as in Section 15.2; SQLSOURCE will contain the source form of a SQL statement (a SELECT statement, of course, in this example), and SQLOBJ will contain the corresponding object form. X is a cursor for that SELECT; note that it is declared by a new form of the DECLARE CURSOR statement, as follows.

```
EXEC SQL DECLARE cursor CURSOR FOR statement ;
```

2. The declaration of the SQL Descriptor Area is brought into the program by the statement

```
EXEC SQL INCLUDE SQLDA ;
```

This statement generates a declaration for a PL/I BASED structure called SQLDA, also a declaration for a numeric variable called SQLSIZE. The program must set SQLSIZE to the value N (where N is an upper bound on the number of values to be retrieved per row by the SELECT statement), then allocate storage for SQLDA (the amount of storage allocated will be a function of the value of SQLSIZE).

3. Next, the desired SELECT statement is constructed in source form in SQLSOURCE, and is then PREPAREd to yield the corresponding object form in SQLOBJ. Then the program issues a DESCRIBE against SQLOBJ to obtain a description of the values expected per row from the SELECT. That description consists of two parts:

(a) The actual number of values to be retrieved (in a field of SQLDA called SQLN);

(b) The name or label,* the data type, and the length for each of those values (in an array of entries within SQLDA called SQLVAR).

Using this description, the program can now allocate storage for each of the values described. It then places the addresses of the storage areas it allocates back into the SQLDA—actually into the SQLVAR array.

4. Finally, the program uses OPEN, FETCH, and CLOSE statements on cursor X to retrieve the actual data. Note, however, that a new form of the FETCH statement is used; instead of an INTO clause, it has a USING DESCRIPTOR clause, and the structure named in that clause (usually SQLDA) in turn identifies the target variables for the values to be retrieved.

---

*See the discussion of the LABEL statement in Chapter 9.

It is also possible to PREPARE a SELECT statement that includes parameters (identified by question marks). For example:

```
SQLSOURCE = 'SELECT *
             FROM    SP
             WHERE   QTY  >  ?
             AND     QTY  <  ?' ;

EXEC SQL PREPARE SQLOBJ FROM :SQLSOURCE ;
```

Arguments are specified in the corresponding OPEN statement. For example:

```
EXEC SQL OPEN X USING :LOW, :HIGH ;
```

(EXECUTE does not apply to SELECT. The function of EXECUTE is performed by OPEN when the statement to be executed is a SELECT.)

15.4   CONCLUSION

This brings us to the end of our discussion of the facilities of dynamic SQL, and indeed to the end of our three chapters on SQL application programming. Of those three chapters:

- Chapter 13 describes all the major principles of the embedded SQL approach. The material of that chapter is thus relevant to all SQL programming, and should be of interest to anyone who is concerned in any way with application programming in DB2.

- Chapter 14 is also concerned with principles that are relevant to all users—to be specific, it discusses the concepts of transaction management (concurrency and recovery), and it shows how those concepts are exposed in the SQL language. However, the nature of SQL is such that users need to worry explicitly about such matters only very rarely; most of the time, DB2's implicit mechanisms are entirely adequate.

- The present chapter, by contrast, has been concerned with a very specialized topic, namely that of how to write a generalized online application in SQL. Such an application requires the facilities of dynamic SQL—principally the PREPARE and EXECUTE statements, and (if it is a SELECT statement that is to be PREPAREd) also the DESCRIBE statement. *Note:* The other portions of the language are sometimes referred to as *static* SQL, to distinguish them from the dynamic facilities that we have been discussing in this chapter.

  It should be pointed out that it is of course possible to use the facilities of dynamic SQL whenever greater variability is required than is provided by the conventional static statements. In other words, it is not quite true to say that generalized online applications are the sole justification for dynamic SQL, though that statement is really not very wide of the mark. For example, the following statement:

```
EXEC SQL SELECT * FROM :TNV ;
```

(where TNV is not the name of a table but the name of a host variable whose *value* is the name of a table) is not a valid SELECT statement in conventional static SQL, but dynamic SQL can be used to achieve the desired effect.

To conclude the entire set of three chapters, we offer the following comment. The fact that DB2 uses essentially the same language (SQL) for both interactive and programmed access to the database has one very significant consequence: It means that the database portions of an application program can be tested and debugged interactively. Using the interactive interface, it is very easy for a programmer to create some test tables, load data into them, execute (interactive versions of) the programmed SQL statements against them, query the tables and/or the catalog to see the effect of those statements, and so on. In other words, the interactive interface provides a very convenient *programmer debugging facility*. Of course, it is attractive for other reasons too; for example, the data definition process is normally carried out through this interface, and so too is the process of granting and revoking authorization. Also, of course, the interface provides a rudimentary but serviceable ad hoc query facility.

CHAPTER

·16·

Storage Structure

16.1 INTRODUCTION

As explained in Chapter 5, the data definition statements of SQL can conveniently be divided into two classes, namely logical and physical—the logical statements having to do with objects that are genuinely of interest to users, such as base tables and views, and the physical statements having to do with objects that are more of interest to administrators (i.e., system administrators and database administrators). In this chapter we take a brief look at the latter class of objects. The data definition statements corresponding to those objects are somewhat complicated, however, involving (as they necessarily must) a great deal of low-level detail. For that reason, we will not describe those statements in detail here; we content ourselves with the observation that they fall into the same broad pattern as the logical statements, in the sense that, for each kind of object, there is a CREATE statement, an ALTER statement, and a DROP statement. (Even this simple remark is not 100 percent true, as a matter of fact—not all kinds of object permit all three kinds of operation. But we leave all discussion of the details to the IBM manuals.)

Fig. 16.1 is a schematic representation of the major storage objects and their interrelationships. The figure is meant to be interpreted as follows.

- The total collection of stored data is divided up into a number of disjoint databases—several user databases and several system databases, in general. One system database, the catalog database, is shown in the figure.

- Each database is divided up into a number of disjoint "spaces"—several tablespaces and several indexspaces, in general. A "space" is a dynamically extendable collection of *pages,* where a page is a block of physical storage (it is the unit of I/O, i.e., the unit transferred between primary and secondary storage in a physical I/O operation).

- Each tablespace contains one or more stored tables. A stored table is the physical representation of a base table. A given stored table must be wholly contained within a single tablespace.

- Each indexspace contains exactly one index. A given index must be wholly contained within a single indexspace. A given stored table and all its associated indexes must be wholly contained within a single database.

- As explained in Chapter 10, views are not stored objects at all. They are included in the figure just to illustrate the point that a given view can span multiple databases—that is, it can include data from multiple stored tables, and those stored tables do not necessarily all have to be from the same database.

- Each "space" (tablespace or indexspace) has an associated *storage group.** A storage group is a collection of direct access volumes, all of the same device type. When a given space needs to be extended, storage is acquired from the appropriate storage group. The spaces in a given database do not all have to have the same storage group, nor do all the spaces that share a given storage group have to come from the same database. Note, therefore, that storage groups are in a sense the most "physical" of all the various storage objects in DB2; databases, tablespaces, etc., are all still somewhat "logical."

Before we go on to amplify the foregoing ideas, we make one further introductory remark concerning *system defaults.* The basic idea behind sys-

---

*A partitioned space can have a distinct storage group for each partition. See Section 16.3.

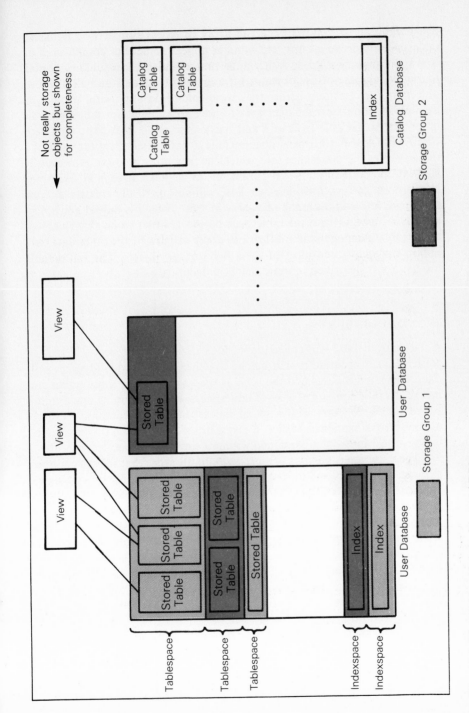

Not really storage objects but shown for completeness

Fig. 16.1 The major storage objects of DB2

279

tem defaults is as follows: The full array of storage objects—databases, tablespaces, storage groups, etc.—might appear somewhat complicated at first sight, and it would be rather unfortunate (indeed, it would be counter to the overall ease-of-use objective) if users had to understand all of those objects in their entirety before they were able to do any useful work. For example, it should not be necessary to have to know about tablespaces in order just to be able to create and use a new table. Now, the complete CREATE TABLE statement does include a parameter (''IN tablespace'') that specifies the tablespace into which the new table is to go. However, it is always possible to omit that parameter (as we have done in all examples in this book so far), in which case DB2 will automatically create a *default* tablespace and will place the new table in that. Thus it is indeed not necessary to be familiar with the tablespace notion in order to be able to create a new table. Analogous simplifications apply to most of the other data definition statements and most of the other storage objects. The full default mechanism is described in more detail in Section 16.8.

16.2 DATABASES

A database in DB2 is a collection of logically related objects— that is, a collection of stored tables that belong together in some way, together with their associated indexes and the various spaces containing those tables and indexes. It thus consists of a set of tablespaces, each containing one or more stored tables, together with a set of indexspaces, each containing exactly one index. As explained earlier, a given stored table and all its associated indexes must be wholly contained within a single database.

The database is *the unit of start/stop,* in the sense that the system operator can make a given database available or unavailable for processing via an appropriate START or STOP command. Note, therefore, that objects are grouped together into the same database primarily for operational reasons; users (in our sense of the term) need have no concern for databases at all, but can simply concentrate on the *data,* i.e., on tables (base tables and views; note that SQL data manipulation statements such as SELECT, INSERT, etc., refer only to tables, never to databases). Tables can be moved from one database to another without having any logical impact on users or user programs. Note also that (as suggested toward the end of the previous section) a database is not even a particularly ''physical'' kind of object; in particular, it is typically *not* a single disk, or single set of disks, but consists rather of portions of many disks, other portions of which might well be allocated to other databases.

16.3 TABLESPACES

A tablespace can be thought of as a *logical address space* on secondary storage that is used to hold one or more stored tables ("logical" because it is typically not just a set of physically adjacent areas). As the amount of data in those tables grows (or as their number increases), so storage will be acquired from the appropriate storage group and added to the tablespace accordingly. One tablespace can be up to approximately 64 billion bytes in size, and there is effectively no limit to the number of tablespaces in a data-base, nor to the number of databases.* The pages in a given tablespace are either all 4K bytes or all 32K bytes in size (K = 1024).

Fundamentally, the tablespace is the storage unit for recovery and reor-ganization purposes; that is, it is the unit that can be recovered via the RECOVER utility or reorganized via the REORG utility (see Chapter 17). If the tablespace is very large, however, recovery and reorganization could take a very long time. DB2 therefore provides the option to *partition* a large tablespace into smaller pieces; for a partitioned tablespace, the unit of recovery and reorganization is the individual partition, rather than the en-tire tablespace.

Tablespaces come in three varieties, *simple, partitioned,* and *seg-mented.* We discuss each in turn. *Note:* Version 1 of DB2 supported simple and partitioned tablespaces only, and "simple" at that time just meant "not partitioned." Segmented tablespaces were added in Version 2.

Simple Tablespaces

A simple tablespace can contain more than one table, though one is perhaps the normal case. One reason for having more than one is that stored records from different tables can be clustered together in such a way as to improve access times to logically related records. For example, if tables S and SP were stored in the same tablespace, then it would be possible (by loading the data in an appropriately interleaved manner) to store all the shipment records for supplier S1 close to (i.e., on the same page as) the supplier rec-ord for S1, all the shipment records for supplier S2 close to the supplier record for S2, and so on. Queries such as "Get details of supplier S1 and all corresponding shipments"—in particular, certain join queries—will then be handled more efficiently, since the number of I/O operations will be reduced. A similar remark applies to referential integrity enforcement; for

---

*As a matter of interest, 64 billion bytes (in 4K pages) is approximately equivalent to 128 volumes (i.e., 32 units) of IBM 3380D direct access storage.

example, deleting a supplier and cascading that delete to all corresponding shipments will also be more efficient if the data is appropriately clustered.

Note, however, that such cross-table clustering will not be maintained (in general) in the face of arbitrary updates; moreover, neither the optimizer nor the REORG utility has any understanding of such clustering. Furthermore, sequential access ("tablespace scan") may well be slowed down, inasmuch as the system will now have to scan not only records of the table concerned, but also records of other tables that happen to be mixed in with the first table. In most situations, one table per tablespace is probably the most satisfactory arrangement in the simple tablespace case.

Partitioned Tablespaces

As indicated earlier, partitioned tablespaces are intended for tables that are sufficiently large (hundreds of thousands or even millions of rows) that it is operationally difficult to deal with the entire table as a unit (e.g., for recovery purposes). A partitioned tablespace thus contains exactly one (normally large) table, partitioned in accordance with value ranges of a partitioning field or field combination. For example, if the shipments table SP were stored in a partitioned tablespace, then it could be partitioned by values of the P# field, such that all shipments for part P1 were stored in partition one, all shipments for part P2 were stored in partition two, and so on. A clustering index (see Section 16.6) is required for the partitioning field or field combination; furthermore, that field or field combination cannot be UPDATEd.

As already stated, individual partitions of a partitioned tablespace are independent of one another, in the sense that they can be independently recovered and reorganized. They can also be associated with different storage groups; thus, for example, it is possible to store different partitions on different devices and thereby spread the tablespace I/O load.

Segmented Tablespaces

Segmented tablespaces were added to DB2 in Version 2. Like simple tablespaces, they can contain any number of tables; unlike simple tablespaces, however, segmented tablespaces do not support any kind of cross-table clustering—that is, they do not allow records from different tables to be interleaved on a single page. Instead, they keep the tables physically separated, as follows.

- First, the space within the tablespace is divided up into *segments,* where a segment consists of a logically contiguous set of *n* pages (*n* must be a multiple of 4 in the range 4 to 64 and is the same for all segments in the tablespace).

- Second, no segment (and therefore certainly no page) is allowed to contain records from more than one table. If a particular table grows in size to fill all segments currently allocated to it, a new segment will be obtained for the table (by acquiring more space from the associated storage group, if necessary, as explained at the beginning of this section).

Thus, for example, table S might currently be stored in segments 1 and 3 and table SP in segments 2, 4, 5, and 6, all within the same segmented tablespace. If table S subsequently outgrows the capacity of its existing segments (1 and 3), a new segment (7) will be obtained for it.

The advantages of such an arrangement (compared with having multiple tables in a simple tablespace) include the following.

- Sequential access ("tablespace scan") to a particular table is more efficient, since there is no need to scan segments or pages that contain records of other tables.

- For internal reasons—the details are beyond the scope of this text— segmented tablespaces are much more efficient than simple (and partitioned) tablespaces in the way they handle variable-length records.

- Reorganizing the tablespace via the REORG utility will restore every table in the tablespace to its clustered order. ("Clustered order" here does not refer to cross-table clustering, it refers to physical ordering within one table. See Section 16.6 for further discussion.) Reorganizing a simple tablespace that contains multiple tables does not restore clustered order.

- LOCK TABLE on a table in a segmented tablespace genuinely does lock the table, not the entire tablespace (and likewise for all other operations in the system that would acquire locks at the tablespace level in the case of a simple or partitioned tablespace).

- If a table in a segmented tablespace is dropped, the space for that table can be reclaimed without the need to perform a reorganization of the tablespace.

- "Mass DELETE" (i.e., deleting all rows from a table—DELETE without a WHERE clause) is more efficient on a segmented tablespace than on other kinds of tablespace.

- All tables in the tablespace can be recovered as a unit (i.e., via a single invocation of the RECOVER utility). This capability is particularly useful in connexion with "referential structures" (i.e., sets of tables that are logically related by referential constraints). See Chapter 17 for further discussion. *Note:* Actually, this advantage applies to the simple tablespace case also.

16.4 STORED TABLES

A stored table is the stored representation of a base table. It consists of a set of stored records, one for each data row in the base table in question. Each stored record will be wholly contained within a single page; however, one stored table can be spread over multiple pages, and (in a simple tablespace) one page can contain stored records from multiple stored tables.

A stored record is *not* identical to the corresponding record of the base table. Instead, it consists of a byte string, made up as follows:

- A stored record prefix, containing control information such as the internal system identifier for the stored table of which this stored record is a part; followed by

- Up to *N* stored fields, where *N* is the number of columns in the base table. There will be fewer than *N* stored fields if the stored record is varying length (i.e., if it includes any varying length fields) and one or more fields at the right-hand end are set to null or the nonnull default value for the field in question; nulls and default values at the right-hand end of a varying length record are not physically stored.

Each stored field, in turn, consists of:

- A length prefix (if the field is varying length), giving the length of the actual data, including the null indicator prefix if there is one (see below);

- A null indicator prefix (if nulls are allowed), indicating whether the value in the data part of the field is to be (a) taken as a genuine data value or (b) ignored (i.e., interpreted as null);

- An encoded form of the actual data value. Stored data is encoded in such a manner that the System/370 "compare logical" instruction (CLC) will always yield the appropriate response when applied to two values of the same SQL data type. For example, INTEGER values are stored with their sign bit reversed. Thus all stored data fields are considered simply as byte strings by the Data Manager; any interpretation of such a string as, e.g., an INTEGER value is performed above the Data Manager interface. The advantage of such a scheme is that new data types can be introduced without any impact on the low-level components of the system. As an exercise, the reader may like to try working out suitable encodings for the other DB2 data types.

All stored fields are byte-aligned. There are no gaps between fields. Varying length data occupies only as many bytes as are needed to store the actual value.

Note: The foregoing describes the standard representation of a stored record. For any given table, however, the installation has the option of providing either or both of the following:

1. An "edit procedure" (EDITPROC), which will be given control every time a record is stored or fetched. On "store," the edit procedure can convert the standard representation for the record to any other form desired, and the record will be stored in that form. On "fetch," of course, the edit procedure must perform the opposite conversion.

2. One or more "field procedures" (FIELDPROCs). A field procedure is basically an edit procedure in the sense just described, but applies to an individual field rather than to an entire record. Field procedures were introduced into DB2 in conjunction with the GRAPHIC and VARGRAPHIC data types in order to facilitate (e.g.) the definition of installation-specific collating sequences for such data. However, they can be used with any string column of length less than 255 bytes (except columns to which dates, times, or timestamps are to be assigned and columns defined as NOT NULL WITH DEFAULT), and they can be used for any kind of data editing desired. There is a maximum of one FIELDPROC per field.

Thus, for example, the installation can decide to store data in a compressed or encrypted form; furthermore, it can make that decision on a table-by-table basis, or even on a field-by-field basis. Note, however, that there are many restrictions on edit and field procedures, including the following among others:

- They must be written in Assembler Language.
- They cannot invoke any operating system services involving supervisor calls; in particular, they cannot perform any I/O operations.
- They cannot perform any DB2 operations.

To return to the main thread of the discussion: Internally, records are addressed by "record ID" or RID. For example, all pointers within indexes are RIDs. RIDs are unique within the containing tablespace. Fig. 16.2 shows how RIDs are implemented. The RID for a stored record R consists of two parts, namely the page number of the page P containing R, and a byte offset from the bottom of P identifying a slot that contains, in turn, the byte offset of R from the top of P. This scheme represents a good compromise between the speed of direct addressing and the flexibility of indirect

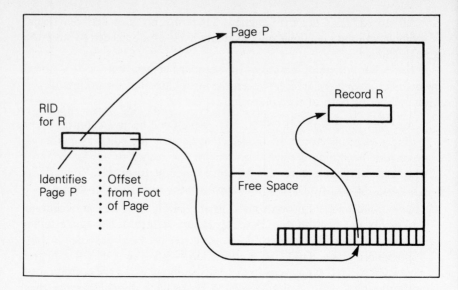

Fig. 16.2 Implementation of RIDs

addressing: Records can be rearranged within their containing page—e.g., to close up the gap when a record is deleted or to make room when a record is inserted—without having to change RIDs (only the local offsets at the foot of the page have to change); yet access to a record given the RID is fast, involving only a single page access.

Note: In rare cases it might involve two page accesses (but never more than two). This can happen if a varying length record is updated in such a way that it is now longer than it was before (i.e., the value in some varying length field has expanded), and there is not enough free space on the page to accommodate the increase. In such a situation, the updated record is placed on another ("overflow") page, and the original record is replaced by a pointer (another RID) to the new location. If the same thing happens again, so that the updated record has to be moved to still a third page, then the pointer in the original page is changed to point to this newest location.

We conclude our discussion of stored tables with a note on "validation procedures" (VALIDPROCs). A validation procedure resembles an edit procedure in that it is a procedure that can be specified by the installation for a given base table (maximum of one VALIDPROC per table). The validation procedure for a given table is given control each time a record of that table is INSERTed, UPDATEd, or DELETEd. The purpose of the procedure is to perform validation checks to ensure that the operation being performed is valid (and to reject it if not). Note, however, that validation procedures are subject to the same major restrictions as edit and field procedures; for example, they must be coded in Assembler Language.

16.5 INDEXSPACES

An indexspace is to an index what a tablespace is to a table. However, since the correspondence between indexes and indexspaces (unlike that between tables and tablespaces) is always one-to-one, there are no data definition statements for indexspaces per se; instead, the necessary indexspace parameters are specified on the corresponding index definition statements. Thus, for example, there is no CREATE INDEXSPACE; instead, the indexspace is created automatically when the corresponding index is created, via CREATE INDEX, and that CREATE INDEX can include such parameters as the name of the associated storage group, etc.

The pages in an indexspace are always 4K bytes in size. The unit for locking purposes can be less than one page, however (another difference from tablespaces); it can, for example, be a quarter-page (1024 bytes).

Like tablespaces, indexspaces can be reorganized and recovered independently. An indexspace that contains the (required) clustering index for a partitioned tablespace is itself considered to be partitioned; all other indexspaces are simple (nonpartitioned). A partition of a partitioned indexspace can be reorganized independently. Individual partitions can be associated with different storage groups.

16.6 INDEXES

Indexes in DB2 are based on a structure known as the *B-tree*. A B-tree is a multilevel, tree-structured index with the property that the tree is always *balanced;* that is, all leaf entries in the structure are equidistant from the root of the tree, and this property is maintained as new entries are inserted into the tree and existing entries are deleted. As a result, the index provides uniform and predictable performance for retrieval operations. Details of how this effect is achieved are beyond the scope of this book; however, Fig. 16.3 shows a simple example of what such an index might look like.

As you can see, the index consists of a root page, zero or more intermediate pages (at zero or more intermediate levels—there is one such intermediate level in the example), and a set of leaf pages. The leaf level contains an entry for each distinct value of the indexed field, giving the indexed field value and pointers (RIDs) to all records that contain that value for the indexed field; the leaf pages are chained together, so that they can be used for fast *sequential* access to the indexed data (in index sequence). Each level

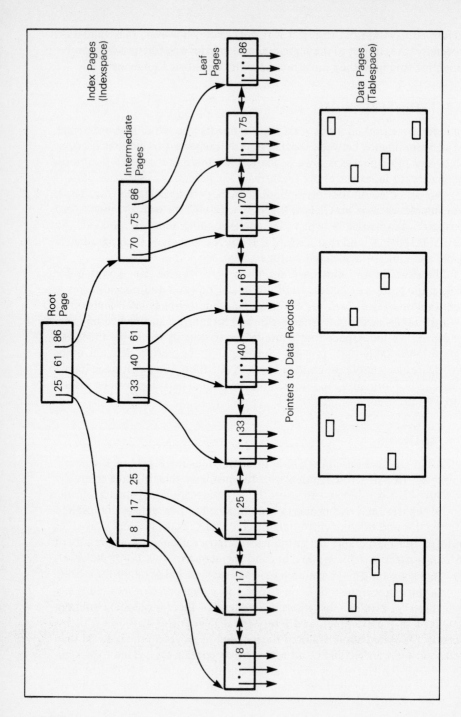

Fig. 16.3. Example of an index

above the leaf level, in turn, contains an entry (highest field value plus pointer) for every page of entries in the level below; thus the root page and intermediate pages together provide fast *direct* access to the leaf pages, and hence fast direct access to the indexed data also.

A given stored table can have any number of associated indexes, and thus any number of logical orderings imposed on it. (It always has exactly one physical ordering, of course. Also, if the installation follows our recommendation that every base table have a primary key, then every stored table will necessarily have at least one index, namely the primary index, as explained in Chapter 12).

To perform an exhaustive search on a table according to a given index, the Data Manager will access all records in the table in the sequence defined by that index ("index scan"); and since that sequence may be quite different from the table's physical sequence, a given data page may be accessed many times. (On the other hand, data pages not containing any records of the table will not be accessed at all.) It follows that exhaustive search via an index could potentially be much slower than exhaustive search via physical sequence ("tablespace scan")—unless the index concerned is a *clustering index:*

- A clustering index is one for which the sequence defined by the index *is* the same as, or close to, the physical sequence. (Note that "clustering" here refers to clustering within a single table, not cross-table clustering as described in Section 16.3.) The index is used to control physical placement of the indexed records—i.e., newly inserted records are physically stored such that the physical sequence of those records in storage closely approximates the logical sequence as defined by the index.

- If a table has any indexes at all, then *exactly one* is the clustering index for that table. As the previous paragraph suggests, that index should ideally be created before any data has been loaded into the table; it should probably be the *first* index created for the table.*

- If a table has a clustering index, then records must be loaded into that table via the load utility in clustering order (i.e., they must be sorted first). The loaded records will be stored in the tablespace (or partition, in the case of a partitioned tablespace) in order of arrival from left to right—i.e., in increasing address sequence—with periodic gaps to allow

---

*Once again, if the installation follows our recommendation that every table have a primary key, then every table will have at least one index, and hence every table will a fortiori have a clustering index. Note, however, that the clustering index and the primary index are not necessarily the same.

for future insertions. Gap size and frequency are determined by installation-specified "freespace" parameters.

- If a table has no indexes, then records can be initially loaded in any logical order; again they will be stored left to right, with gaps as determined by the installation-specified "freespace" parameter.

- Subsequent insertions to the table will be stored in a gap (if a clustering index exists and the record can be physically stored close to its logical position), otherwise at the right-hand end.

Clustering indexes are extremely important for optimization purposes: The optimizer will always try to choose an access path that is based on a clustering index, if one is available, and if clustering sequence is appropriate for the SQL request under consideration.

16.7 STORAGE GROUPS

A storage group is a named collection of direct access volumes, all of the same device type. Each tablespace and each indexspace (or each partition in the case of a partitioned tablespace or indexspace) normally has an associated storage group.* When storage is needed for the space or partition, it is taken from the specified storage group. Storage groups thus provide a means for the installation to control data separation and data affinity—for example, they can force two tables to be stored on different volumes—while at the same time they allow most of the details of allocating data sets, extents, etc., to be handled automatically by the system.

Within each storage group, spaces and partitions are stored using VSAM linear data sets (many data sets per space or partition, in general). DB2 uses VSAM for such things as direct access space management, data set cataloging, and physical transfer of pages into and out of main memory. However, space management within pages (i.e., VSAM control intervals) is handled by DB2, not by VSAM, and VSAM indexing is not used at all. Note that it is not possible to use the facilities of DB2 (e.g., the SQL language) to access nonDB2 VSAM data sets. However, the DB2/VSAM Transparency product (mentioned briefly in Chapter 3) does support the inverse function, namely VSAM I/O operations against DB2 data. This product is intended to assist in the process of migrating VSAM data into DB2 databases.

---

*For a given space or partition, the installation always has the option of not using a storage group at all. If it does not, then it must use VSAM's Access Method Services utilities to define, extend, and delete data sets as necessary. The details of this option are beyond the scope of this book.

16.8 CONCLUDING REMARKS

In this chapter we have presented a brief overview of the storage objects supported by DB2. As explained in Section 16.1, it is not our intent in this book to give all the details of the corresponding data definition statements; however, we mention the following points.

- The tablespace for a given table is specified in the CREATE TABLE statement for that table.

- The database for a given tablespace is specified in the CREATE TABLESPACE statement for that tablespace; the database for a given indexspace is implied by the table over which the index is defined (an indexspace must be part of the same database as the corresponding tablespace).

- Details of the partitioning (value ranges, etc.) for a partitioned tablespace are specified in the CREATE INDEX statement for the (required) clustering index. Details of the partitioning for the corresponding indexspace are also specified in that CREATE INDEX statement.

- The storage group for a given space or partition is specified in the statement (CREATE TABLESPACE or CREATE INDEX) that defines that space or partition.

- The volumes that make up a given storage group are specified in the CREATE STOGROUP statement that creates that storage group.

In addition to all of the above (and as mentioned in Section 16.1), DB2 provides a comprehensive system of defaults that are designed to make it easy to "get on the air." The full default mechanism is as follows:

- CREATE TABLE can specify a database instead of a tablespace. If it does, then DB2 will automatically create a tablespace within that database for the new table; that tablespace will automatically be dropped when the table is dropped. It is not even necessary to specify a database; if neither a database nor a tablespace is specified, DB2 will create a tablespace for the new table within the *default database,* which is a system database that is created for such purposes when the system is installed.

- If CREATE TABLESPACE does not specify a database, the new tablespace will be assigned to the default database.

- A storage group can be specified at any or all of the following levels:
  - the database level (in CREATE DATABASE)
  - the space level (in CREATE TABLESPACE and CREATE INDEX)

- the partition level (in the partition specification within CREATE TABLESPACE and CREATE INDEX)

If no storage group is specified at the partition level for a given partition, the storage group that applies to that partition is the storage group that applies to the containing space. If no storage group is specified at the space level for a given space, the storage group that applies to that space is the storage group that applies to the containing database. If no storage group is specified at the database level for a given database, the storage group that applies to that database is the *default storage group,* which is a storage group that is created for such purposes when the system is installed.

From all of the above, it follows that the data definition statements discussed in Chapter 5 are indeed adequate for "getting on the air." In most realistic situations, however, the installation will probably wish to exercise the tighter control that is possible without the use of defaults. The purpose of the defaults is primarily to allow users to learn to use the system quickly, rather than to serve as an appropriate set of specifications for a full production environment.

We conclude this section (and this chapter) with a brief mention of a couple of miscellaneous points, namely *buffer pools* and *catalog storage structures.*

1. First, bufferpools. The buffers in main storage are grouped together into a number of pools. A given space can use only one such pool; the buffer pool for a given space is specified via yet another parameter in the appropriate CREATE statement (as usual, of course, a default is assumed if the parameter is omitted). In this way, the installation can control to some degree the separation and affinity of data in main storage. For example, a given indexspace and its corresponding tablespace might be assigned to different buffer pools, thus increasing the likelihood that index entries and data records might be present in main storage simultaneously.

2. Second, catalog storage structures. It is obvious that the catalog is a critical component in the overall DB2 system. In particular, it needs very careful management on the part of DB2 to ensure that it does not become a performance bottleneck (because it is on the critical path for so many operations). For this reason, the catalog makes use of certain storage structures that are currently not available for ordinary user data. Those structures include hashing (DB2 Version 1 Release 1 only—but hashing is still used in Version 2 in the *directory*), parent/child links (i.e., pointer chains), and various additional kinds of physical clustering. It seems reasonable to expect that some or all of these structures will eventually be made available for ordinary user data also.

CHAPTER

·17·

Administration Facilities

17.1 INTRODUCTION

In this chapter we take a brief look at DB2's administration facilities. The facilities in question fall into two broad categories, facilities for database administration and facilities for system administration. We consider each in turn.

Database administration involves the design, implementation, and maintenance of individual DB2 databases and associated applications. (Note, therefore, that we are using the term "database administration" here to include the full range of development activities.) Two DB2 features that can assist with these tasks are the "DB2 Interactive" component (DB2I) and the EXPLAIN facility; they are discussed in Sections 17.2 and 17.3, respectively. Section 17.4 then goes on to discuss the various utilities provided for such functions as database recovery, database reorganization, etc.

System administration covers the installation, monitoring, tuning, control, and maintenance of the overall DB2 system itself. Section 17.5 dis-

cusses the system utilities that are used to assist in maintaining the Boot
Strap Data Set (BSDS), and Section 17.6 covers the service aids that can be
used to diagnose errors that might arise during DB2 operation. Last, Section 17.7 describes DB2's facilities for monitoring and controlling system
operation.

17.2   THE DB2 INTERACTIVE INTERFACE

Almost all of the function of DB2 is available online through the "DB2
Interactive" interface (DB2I). That interface provides, not only the ability
to execute SQL statements interactively and to invoke prewritten application programs,* but also, e.g., the ability to issue operator commands, the
ability to invoke database utilities, and the ability to prepare application
programs for execution (i.e., precompile and compile them, bind them, and
so on). With regard to this last point, in fact, preparing programs interactively via DB2I is the normal mode of operation (although of course it is
always possible to use batch if you prefer—see the end of this section).

Fig. 17.1 illustrates the TSO environment. In particular, it shows how
DB2I relates to TSO. As explained in Chapter 3, TSO supports both batch
and online DB2 applications: TSO batch applications execute under the
TSO monitor program directly, TSO online applications execute under the
control of the Interactive System Productivity Facility (ISPF), which is a
screen/dialog manager for TSO. DB2I itself is a TSO online application. It
provides (among other things) the ability to execute SQL statements interactively by means of a component called SPUFI ("SQL Processor Using File
Input"; the name SPUFI is usually pronounced "spoofy"). SPUFI is discussed in a separate subsection below.

The following is the sequence of events for invoking DB2I:

- Log on to TSO in the normal way and enter ISPF.
- From the ISPF primary option menu, select the "DB2I" option.
- The DB2I main menu will appear, offering the following options (see
  Fig. 17.2).
  - SPUFI
  - DCLGEN
  - program preparation
  - precompile

---

*Note, however, that programs invoked for execution via DB2I are TSO applica-
tions (DB2I runs under TSO); such programs must therefore not contain any IMS
or CICS calls (see Chapter 3).

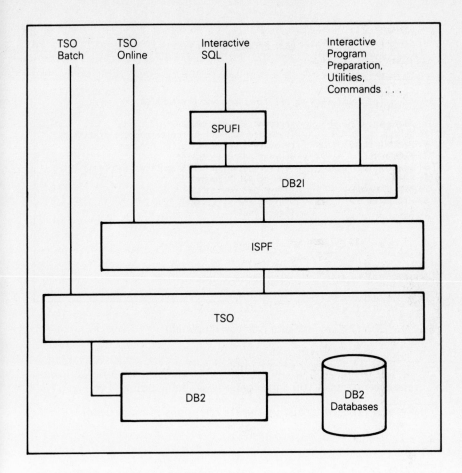

Fig. 17.1. The TSO environment

- bind/rebind/free
- run
- DB2 commands
- utilities

Selecting one of these options will lead you through a series of prompts and menus to perform the corresponding task. (As usual, of course, you will only be allowed to perform a given task if you have the necessary authorization for that task.) Each of those sets of prompts and menus is backed by a set of help and tutorial panels, so that in most

```
                      DB2I PRIMARY OPTION MENU
===>_


Select one of the following DB2 functions and press ENTER.

   1  SPUFI                   (Process SQL statements)
   2  DCLGEN                  (Generate SQL and source language declarations)
   3  PROGRAM PREPARATION     (Prepare a DB2 application program to run)
   4  PRECOMPILE              (Invoke DB2 precompiler)
   5  BIND/REBIND/FREE        (BIND, REBIND, or FREE application plans)
   6  RUN                     (RUN an SQL Program)
   7  DB2 COMMANDS            (Issue DB2 commands)
   8  UTILITIES               (Invoke DB2 utilities)
   X  EXIT                    (Leave DB2I)




   PRESS:   END to exit       HELP for more information
```

Fig. 17.2. The DB2I main menu (slightly simplified)

cases you should have no need of the printed manuals; most of the reference material you will require is available online. See Fig. 17.3.

We now proceed to discuss the DB2I options in more detail.

SPUFI

As explained above, SPUFI supports the interactive execution of SQL statements from a TSO terminal. The basic idea is that you can create a text file containing one or more SQL statements (using the ISPF editor), then execute that file of statements via SPUFI, and then use "ISPF Browse" to browse through the results of those statements (which will have been written to another text file). Note, therefore, that SPUFI is really a DP professional's tool, not an end-user's tool; *QMF* is the corresponding end-user facility (see Chapter 19). SPUFI is intended primarily for application programmers who wish to test the SQL portions of their programs or administrators who wish to perform SQL definitional operations (though in fact QMF can also be used to perform both of those functions).

Among other things, the SPUFI menus allow (or in some cases require) the user to specify the following parameters:

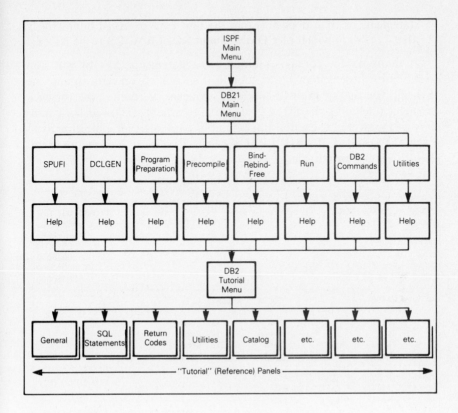

Fig. 17.3. DB2I menus and online documentation

- The file that is to contain the SQL statement(s); this file must already exist, though it may currently be empty.

- Whether that file is to be edited via the ISPF editor before it is ready to be executed (normally YES).

- The file that is to receive the result(s) from executing the SQL statement(s); this file need not already exist (if it does not, then SPUFI will create it).

- The isolation level (RR or CS); see Chapter 14.

- Whether "autocommit" is YES or NO (normally YES). YES means that SPUFI will automatically issue a COMMIT after execution of the statements in the input file if no errors have occurred, or a ROLLBACK otherwise. NO means either that the input file itself includes COMMIT statements or (if it does not) that the user is to be asked interactively after execution which of COMMIT and ROLLBACK is to be issued.

If the input file contains multiple SQL statements, SPUFI will stop execution of those statements as soon as it encounters an error in any one of them. The output file will contain a sequence of results, one for each statement (including the SQLCODE value returned), followed by a summary of the overall execution (including, in particular, an indication as to which of COMMIT and ROLLBACK occurred). Fig. 17.4 shows an example of a SPUFI output file.

```
BROWSE-- CJDATE.RESULT  -------------------------------------- COLUMNS 001 072
COMMAND INPUT ===>                                               SCROLL ===> PAGE
---------+---------+---------+---------+---------+---------+---------+-------
SELECT *                                                              00010000
FROM    P                                                             00020000
WHERE   WEIGHT IN ( 12, 16, 17 )                                      00030000
ORDER  BY P# ;                                                        00040000
---------+---------+---------+---------+---------+---------+---------+-------
P#      PNAME               COLOR   WEIGHT  CITY
---------+---------+---------+---------+---------+---------+---------+-------
P1      Nut                 Red        12   London
P2      Bolt                Green      17   Paris
P3      Screw               Blue       17   Rome
P5      Cam                 Blue       12   Paris
---------+---------+---------+---------+---------+---------+---------+-------
DSNE610I NUMBER OF ROWS DISPLAYED IS 4.
DSNE616I STATEMENT EXECUTION WAS SUCCESSFUL, SQLCODE IS 100.
---------+---------+---------+---------+---------+---------+---------+-------
---------+---------+---------+---------+---------+---------+---------+-------
DSNE617I COMMIT PERFORMED, SQLCODE IS 0.
---------+---------+---------+---------+---------+---------+---------+-------
```

Fig. 17.4. SPUFI output file (example)

DCLGEN

The DCLGEN menu allows the user to invoke the declarations generator program. As noted in Chapter 13, DCLGEN is a program that creates embedded SQL DECLARE TABLE statements and corresponding PL/I or COBOL structure declarations from table descriptions in the catalog. The output from DCLGEN is stored as a member of a partitioned data set, from which it can be copied into an application program by means of an embedded SQL INCLUDE statement.

Program Preparation

The program preparation menus allow the user to perform any or all of the following:

- precompilation
- compilation or assembly
- linkage editor processing
- bind processing
- program execution (TSO applications only)

All of the necessary parameters to the Precompiler, Bind, etc. can be supplied via the menus. Note that the source program itself must already have been created via an appropriate text editor, such as the ISPF editor.

Precompile

The PRECOMPILE menu is effectively just the "precompile" portion of the program preparation menu set. It allows the user to precompile an application program source module.

Bind/Rebind/Free

This menu allows the user to issue the BIND, REBIND, and FREE commands.

1. The BIND command creates an application plan from one or more Database Request Modules (DBRMs—see Chapter 2). The following parameters can be specified (among others):

- Whether the new plan is to replace an existing one ("replace BIND").
- The authorization ID that is to "own" the plan, if that ID is different from the ID of the user issuing the BIND command. This feature enables an individual user to bind a plan on behalf of some functional area (e.g., "the accounting department"), and thus make that plan available to all users within that area. See Chapter 11, Section 11.2.
- The isolation level (RR or CS) for the plan (see Chapter 14).
- Lock acquisition and release times for the plan (again, see Chapter 14).
- Whether the plan is to be "validated" at bind time or at run time. Validation is the process of checking that references to tables, columns, etc., are syntactically correct, that the tables, columns, etc., do exist, and that the would-be plan owner is authorized to execute the SQL

operations in the DBRM(s) being bound. Validation is normally performed at bind time. In some cases, however, it may not be possible to perform such checks at bind time; for example, the plan may include references to a table that does not yet exist (maybe the plan itself creates that table), or it may include operations for which the user does not yet have the required authority. In such cases runtime validation must be requested.

2. The REBIND command rebinds an existing plan. It differs from the "replace" version of the BIND command (see 1. above) in that its input is the SQL statements that were saved in the catalog when the plan was originally bound, not a set of DBRMs. "Replace BIND" would be used if the original SQL statements have been changed; by contrast, REBIND would be used after the physical structure of the database has changed sufficiently—for example, new indexes have been created—that a reevaluation of access strategy is warranted for the plan in question. It should also be used after RUNSTATS has been executed (see Section 17.4).

3. The FREE command drops an existing plan.

Run

The RUN menu is effectively just the "program execution" portion of the program preparation menu set. It allows the user to execute a previously prepared application program—provided that, as mentioned earlier, the program is a TSO application, not an IMS or CICS application.

Operator Commands

This menu allows the user to enter system operator commands such as START DATABASE, STOP DATABASE, etc.

Utilities

This menu allows the user to invoke various database utilities. The utilities in question are discussed in Section 17.4.

Bypassing DB2I

As mentioned in the introduction to this section, the use of DB2I is not mandatory. It is possible to invoke a DB2 application interactively without using DB2I by issuing the TSO command "DSN" (which invokes DB2), followed by the command

```
RUN PROGRAM ( program ) PLAN ( plan )
```

It is also possible to invoke a DB2 application in "TSO batch" mode through JCL statements that (a) specify the TSO Terminal Monitor Program (TMP) as the program to be run, and (b) pass the DSN and RUN commands as input to that program. Refer to Chapter 3 for a brief explanation of "TSO batch."

17.3 EXPLAIN

Officially, EXPLAIN is regarded as a statement of the SQL language; however, the function performed is much more in the nature of a utility, which is why we include it in this chapter. EXPLAIN allows the user to obtain information regarding the optimizer's choice of access strategy for a specified SQL statement. The information provided includes indexes used, details of any sorts that will be needed, and (if the specified statement involves any joins) the order in which tables will be joined and the methods by which the individual joins will be performed. Such information can be useful for tuning existing applications, also for determining how projected applications will perform. The syntax of EXPLAIN (somewhat simplified) is as follows:

```
EXPLAIN type FOR statement
```

Here "type" is PLAN or ALL (ALL has the same meaning as PLAN and is supported only for compatibility with SQL/DS), and "statement" is the SQL statement to be EXPLAINed (SELECT, INSERT, UPDATE, or DELETE—in practice, usually SELECT). The output from the execution of the EXPLAIN statement is placed into a table called *xyz*.PLAN_TABLE, which must already exist (*xyz* here is the authorization ID of the user issuing the EXPLAIN). Here is an example:

```
EXPLAIN PLAN FOR
        SELECT S.S#, P.P#
        FROM   S, P
        WHERE  S.CITY = P.CITY ;
```

When this EXPLAIN is executed, DB2 will place information regarding its implementation of the specified SELECT statement into the PLAN_TABLE of the user issuing the EXPLAIN. The user can then interrogate that table by means of ordinary SELECT statements in order to discover, for example, whether a particular index is being used or whether creating a new index might obviate the need for a sort.

Some additional points:

- The EXPLAIN statement includes a "query number" option by which the user can give a unique numeric identifier to each statement being

EXPLAINed. The query number is needed to distinguish in the PLAN_TABLE between the results of distinct EXPLAINs.

- The EXPLAIN output does *not* include the source form of the statement being EXPLAINed. Instead, users are recommended to save that source form (together with the appropriate query number) in a table of their own, for purposes of subsequent reference.

- EXPLAIN does not produce any output regarding additional operations that might be performed for referential integrity reasons. For example, if the statement to be EXPLAINed is a DELETE, there is nothing in the output regarding, e.g., any additional DELETEs caused by a CASCADE delete rule.

EXPLAIN output can also be produced when binding an application. If the option EXPLAIN (YES) is specified as a parameter to the BIND command, then EXPLAIN output will be produced for every SQL statement in the application plan being bound.

For more details of EXPLAIN—in particular, for details of the format of the PLAN_TABLE and guidance as to how to interpret its contents— the reader is referred to the IBM manuals.

17.4 DATABASE UTILITIES

The DB2 database utilities are all *online* utilities; that is, they can be invoked online (via DB2I), without having to stop execution of the DB2 system. They execute as regular MVS batch applications, using their own private interface to communicate with DB2 (i.e., they do not require the services of IMS/DC, CICS, or TSO). The necessary utility control statements to direct the operation of the specific utility in question must be created using a standard MVS editor and stored in a card image file before the utility is invoked. The necessary MVS job control (JCL) statements for the utility job can be created either via DB2I or by means of a DB2-provided CLIST called DSNU.

The main database utilities are as follows.

- *CHECK:* The CHECK utility can be used to perform certain checks on stored data (e.g., to check that a given index is consistent with the table it indexes). In particular, CHECK can be used to check a tablespace to see if there are any referential integrity violations. Any records it finds that contain an unmatched foreign key value can optionally be copied to an exception table, and optionally deleted as well. If any such records are found (and remain undeleted), the tablespace will now be in the "check pending" state. See the end of this section for an explanation of "check pending."

- *COPY:* The COPY utility creates a full or incremental backup copy (an "image copy") of a tablespace or partition. An incremental copy is a copy of just the data pages that have changed since the previous copy—full or incremental—was taken. Information about the copy is recorded in a DB2 catalog table called SYSCOPY. Information in SYSCOPY about image copies that are no longer required for recovery can be deleted using the MODIFY utility. *Note:* Certain operations, such as loading data (via the LOAD utility) into a tablespace with logging disabled, will place the tablespace in question into the "copy pending" state, meaning that a backup copy *must* be made before the data can be used.

- *LOAD:* The LOAD utility loads data from a sequential data set into one or more tables within one or more partitions of a specified tablespace. The tables in question can be initially empty or can contain existing data. Input rows that violate a uniqueness constraint (primary key or otherwise) will not be loaded.

  As indicated under the discussion of COPY above, LOAD can be run with logging enabled or disabled. Also, LOAD on a table that contains a foreign key can be run with referential integrity checking enabled or disabled. If checking is enabled, input rows that violate the referential constraint will not be loaded. If checking is disabled, a "check pending" condition will be set on the applicable tablespace (again, see below for a discussion of "check pending").

  Note: Input rows that fail a uniqueness check or violate a referential constraint can optionally be copied to a rejects file.

  The input data set for LOAD can consist of data unloaded from a VSAM data set, or from an IMS database, or from a DB2 or SQL/DS table. See the discussion of DXT in Part III of this book.

- *MERGECOPY:* The MERGECOPY utility merges a full copy and one or more incremental copies to produce an up-to-date full copy, or a set o˙ incremental copies to produce an up-to-date composite incremental copy (for a given tablespace or partition).

- *MODIFY:* The MODIFY utility is used to perform maintenance operations on recovery information in the DB2 catalog. It can, for example, be used to delete information from the SYSCOPY catalog table concerning image copies that are no longer required for recovery.

- *QUIESCE:* The QUIESCE utility is used to quiesce operations (temporarily) on a specified collection of tablespaces. The quiesced state corresponds to a single point in the log, so that the collection of tablespaces can subsequently be recovered as a unit (the quiesce point is recorded in the catalog in SYSCOPY). In particular, QUIESCE can be useful in establishing a "point of consistency" for a collection of tablespaces that are related via referential constraints, thus ensuring that subsequent recovery to that point will restore the data to a consistent state (see the discussion of RECOVER, below).

- *RECOVER:* The RECOVER utility uses the most recent full copy, any subsequent incremental copies, and any subsequent log data to recover one or more tablespaces, partitions, or pages after a media failure has occurred. RECOVER can also be used:

1. To perform "point-in-time" recovery by recovering from a specific image copy or recovering to a specific point in the log. Point-in-time recovery will set "check pending" on the applicable tablespace(s) unless recovery is to a point of consistency (established via QUIESCE—see above).

2. To rebuild one or more indexes or index partitions for a specific tablespace. Multiple indexes can be rebuilt on a single RECOVER invocation.

   The backup data sets (image copies, etc.) needed for a specific RECOVER invocation are automatically determined from the catalog (SYSCOPY table) and the Boot Strap Data Set (see Chapter 2).

- *REORG:* The REORG utility reorganizes a tablespace or indexspace (or tablespace or index partition) to reclaim wasted space and to reestablish clustering sequence (if applicable). The fact that a reorganization has been done is recorded in SYSCOPY.

- *REPAIR:* The REPAIR utility is used to "repair" stored data—for example, to set the byte string at some specific relative byte address within some specific page to some specific value. REPAIR can also be used to reset conditions such as "check pending."

- *REPORT:* The REPORT utility produces certain reports that are useful in connexion with managing the database recovery process. Specifically, it can be used to determine the image copies and archive log data sets required for a given tablespace recovery, or the collection of tablespaces that need to be recovered as a unit during point-in-time recovery in order to avoid a "check pending" condition.

- *RUNSTATS:* The RUNSTATS utility computes statistics on specified stored data (e.g., a specified tablespace or a specified index or a specified table and column(s)) and writes them to the system catalog. For details of the actual statistics computed, see the IBM manuals. Bind uses those statistics in its process of optimization. They can also be useful for determining when to reorganize a tablespace or index. RUNSTATS should be executed whenever a table has been loaded, an index has been created, a tablespace has been reorganized, or generally whenever there has been a significant amount of update activity on some table. It should then be followed by an appropriate set of REBINDs.

Note: As mentioned in Chapter 11, it is also possible to update certain statistics "manually" (i.e., via direct UPDATE on the relevant catalog columns); the only authority needed—rather surprisingly—is UPDATE authority on the column(s) to which the statistics apply. One reason for permitting such manual updating is to allow the database administrator to make the statistics on a test database match those on the corresponding production database, so that Bind will generate test application plans that genuinely resemble the ultimate production versions. However, this "manual statistics updating" facility should obviously be used sparingly and with extreme caution.

- *STOSPACE:* The STOSPACE utility gathers information regarding the amount of space allocated to a given set of tablespaces and indexes and stores that information in the DB2 catalog. Such information is useful for tracking disk space usage.

As indicated at the beginning of this section, all of the foregoing utilities execute while DB2 is active, and most are restartable in the event of a failure. Each invocation of a utility is associated with a *utility identifier,* which is used by DB2 to track the status of execution of the utility concerned. This status information is kept in a DB2 directory table called SYSUTIL and can be displayed using the DB2 DISPLAY UTILTY command. This command can, for example, be used to determine if a utility has abnormally terminated. The DB2 operator can also force the termination of a utility using the DB2 TERM UTILTY command. If as a result of a TERM UTILTY command DB2 determines that a tablespace or index may contain invalid data, it sets a "recover pending" condition, meaning that the tablespace or index must be recovered before it can be used.

Check Pending

Let T be a tablespace. As indicated above, certain operations will cause T to be placed in the "check pending" state. "Check pending" means that T either actually or potentially contains one or more unmatched foreign key values—i.e., foreign key values for which no target primary key value exists. The operations that set "check pending" are as follows:

- Actual detection of such a foreign key value via the CHECK utility;
- Defining a new foreign key for an existing nonempty table in T, via ALTER TABLE;
- LOAD or RECOVER utility operations, either on some referencing ta-

ble in T or on some target table that is referenced by some table in T, if such operations might possibly violate some referential constraint.

While T is in "check pending," data manipulation operations (SELECT, UPDATE, etc.) and COPY, REORG, and QUIESCE utility operations will not be accepted on T. Data definition operations will be accepted, however. The "check pending" condition can be reset either by the CHECK utility (presumably the normal case) or by the REPAIR utility.

17.5 SYSTEM UTILITIES

DB2 provides two system utilities for managing the Boot Strap Data Set (BSDS). The Boot Strap Data Set contains certain essential system control information—in particular, information having to do with the DB2 log; among other things, it includes a list of all log data sets (both active and archive). It also contains system-wide checkpoint information and "conditional restart" control records (see below).

The BSDS utilities are as follows.

- *CHANGE LOG INVENTORY:* This utility allows the contents of the BSDS to be modified. It can be used to add data sets to, or delete data sets from, the lists of active and archive log data sets. It can also be used to define data set passwords for the archive logs and the DB2 system catalog and directory, and to maintain "conditional restart" control records. "Conditional restart" refers to the process of restarting DB2 when a normal restart is not possible because part of the DB2 log has been damaged. BSDS conditional restart control records tell DB2 about the damaged log data so that it can avoid that part of the log during the conditional restart.

    Aside: Of course, conditional restart might lead to a loss of data integrity. This is where the DB2 service aids come into play (see Section 17.6); for example, the DSN1LOGP service aid could be used to determine the extent of the loss.

    The Change Log Inventory utility can be run only when DB2 is not active—i.e., it is an *offline* utility.
- *PRINT LOG MAP:* This utility is used to format and print the contents of the BSDS. It executes as a batch job and can be run when DB2 is active or inactive.

17.6 SERVICE AIDS

The DB2 service aids are batch utilities that can be run only when DB2 is not active. They are intended primarily for use in diagnosing certain error conditions, most details of which are beyond the scope of this book. We will limit our discussion to a brief overview of each aid. The main ones are as follows.

- *DSN1CHKR:* DSN1CHKR is a diagnostic aid used to check the correctness of the DB2 catalog and directory—in particular, to check that all internal pointers are valid. If it finds any errors, a formatted listing of the damaged pages can be produced. *Note:* Errors can be corrected using the REPAIR utility.

- *DSN1COPY:* DSN1COPY is used to copy DB2 data (tablespace or index) to a sequential data set, or vice versa. It can thus serve as a primitive export/import facility (i.e., to move data between DB2 systems). It can also be used to perform internal validity checking on the consistency of DB2 data.

- *DSN1LOGP:* DSN1LOGP is used to format and print DB2 system log information. It is intended to help in the diagnosis of particularly complex error situations—for example, to assist in determining the extent of the loss on a conditional restart, as suggested in Section 17.5. (Other, more complex examples could be given, but they are mostly beyond the scope of this text.)

- *DSN1PRNT:* DSN1PRNT is used to format and print the contents of tablespaces, indexes, image copies, and sequential data sets created by DSN1COPY.

17.7 MONITORING AND TUNING FACILITIES

DB2 provides several facilities for monitoring, tuning, and controlling DB2 system operation. In this section, we list some of the main ones and present a brief overview of their capabilities.

Instrumentation Facility

The DB2 Instrumentation Facility is responsible for gathering system diagnostic information, system-wide statistics, performance information, and accounting and audit data. This information can be written to an MVS Systems Management Facility (SMF) and/or Generalized Trace Facility (GTF) data set. The type and amount of data gathered is controlled by the DB2 START TRACE and STOP TRACE commands. Data produced by the Instrumentation Facility can be analyzed offline by a separate IBM product, the DB2 Performance Monitor (DB2PM). Reports produced by DB2PM include:

- graphical summaries of accounting and system statistics data
- processing time information (''transit time'') for SQL, Bind, utility, and command execution

- I/O summaries
- information on locking efficiency (number of deadlocks, number of waits, number of timeouts, etc.)
- a detailed trace of SQL statement execution

DB2 also provides an application program interface to the Instrumentation Facility that allows authorized applications (e.g., third-party online performance monitors) to access DB2 trace data, create user trace records, and issue DB2 operator commands. *Note:* This facility is not intended to be used as an automated operator interface, since it provides no means for dealing with unsolicited messages from DB2 (e.g., I/O error messages).

Resource Limit Facility

The DB2 Resource Limit Facility (RLF) is a "DB2 governor": It allows the installation to limit the amount of CPU time that can be consumed during the execution of dynamically bound SQL data manipulation statements— i.e., SELECT, INSERT, UPDATE, and DELETE statements that are bound at execution time, instead of at some earlier time. It applies to dynamically bound statements only, since the intent is basically to control ad hoc query usage rather than planned applications; the assumption is that planned applications are subject to (external) controls of their own anyway. *Note:* It is a little strange, however, that CPU time is the *only* resource that RLF pays any attention to; it would seem desirable to take numerous other factors into account, such as I/O's, tables being accessed, time of day, etc.

The CPU limits are defined by means of a special table (created and populated by means of SQL in the usual way) called a Resource Limit Specification Table (RLST). Any number of RLSTs can exist in the system simultaneously, but only one can be active at any given time. Operator commands are provided for starting and stopping the Resource Limit Facility and for specifying the RLST to be used. The CREATE TABLE for an RLST looks like this:

```
CREATE TABLE DSNRLSTxx
       ( AUTHID      CHAR(8) NOT NULL WITH DEFAULT,
         PLANNAME    CHAR(8) NOT NULL WITH DEFAULT,
         ASUTIME     INTEGER ) ;
```

where:

- xx can be any two alphanumeric characters.
- A UNIQUE index is required on the combination of AUTHID plus PLANNAME.
- AUTHID is the authorization ID to which the ASUTIME limit applies (blank means it applies to all IDs).

- PLANNAME is the plan to which the ASUTIME limit applies (blank means it applies to all plans).

- ASUTIME is the CPU time limit—i.e., the maximum number of MVS "CPU service units" permitted for the binding and execution of any single dynamically bound SQL statement (null means no limit, zero or a negative value means such SQL statements are not permitted at all). If the limit is exceeded, processing of the SQL statement is terminated (in the case of a noncursor operation, the effects on the database, if any, are undone), and a negative SQLCODE value is returned.

Here is an example of an RLST:

```
AUTHID     PLANNAME    ASUTIME
-------    --------    -------
CJDATE     QMF220         3000
CJWHITE    QMF220         3000
bbb        QMF220         1000
bbb        bbb             200
```

In this example, authorization IDs CJDATE and CJWHITE are limited to 3000 CPU units when entering a SQL statement through QMF (QMF220 is the name of the QMF plan). All other QMF users have a limit of 1000 CPU units. When entering dynamic SQL through any program other than QMF, all users (including CJDATE and CJWHITE) are subject to a limit of 200 units.

Note: Users holding SYSADM authority are not subject to any RLF constraints at all, regardless of what RLST happens to be in effect.

Initialization Parameters

During system startup DB2 loads a module known as DSNZPARM which contains parameters that control the operation of DB2. These parameters define such things as whether dual logging is in effect, the size of the database bufferpools, the size of log buffers, locking thresholds, and so forth. DB2 provides a set of macros which allow DB2 administrators to modify the contents of DSNZPARM to tailor and tune it to optimize DB2 operation.

DISPLAY Command

The DB2 DISPLAY command permits the operator to display information regarding DB2 "threads" (i.e., transactions, in our terminology, also known as *logical units of work*), databases, connected subsystems, applications waiting for or holding locks, and so forth.

PART

◆ III ◆

THE IBM RELATIONAL
PRODUCTIVITY FAMILY

CHAPTER

·18·

Related Products:
An Overview

18.1 INTRODUCTION

Up to this point in this book we have concentrated (for the most part) purely on the base DB2 product itself. Like most DBMSs, however, DB2 is accompanied by numerous auxiliary products—application development tools, database administration tools, end-user tools of various kinds, and so on. Such products are available both from IBM and from independent third-party vendors. We can expect to see a tremendous growth in this area over the next few years, given the success and widespread acceptance of DB2. In this part of the book we examine this area in some detail. The present chapter provides a general overview of the subject; Chapters 19–25 then go on to discuss certain specific products in depth.

It is obviously not possible in a book of this size to cover every product from every vendor in detail. We therefore limit detailed discussion to IBM's own products specifically (although we do at least mention some of the best-known competing products in passing, where appropriate). The IBM products are collectively known as *the IBM Relational Productivity Family*. At the heart of this family are four relational DBMSs:

- IBM DATABASE 2 (DB2) for the MVS environment
- Structured Query Language/Data System (SQL/DS) for the VM and VSE environments
- Operating System/400 (OS/400) Database Manager (supporting SQL/400) for the AS/400 environment
- Operating System/2 (OS/2) Extended Edition Database Manager for the OS/2 Extended Edition environment

DB2 is designed for both operational processing and end-user computing against large—possibly very large—centralized databases; SQL/DS and the OS/400 Database Manager are intended for lower-volume operational processing and end-user computing against smaller, perhaps departmental, databases. The OS/2 Extended Edition Database Manager is intended (among other things) for end-user processing of private copies of data extracted from centralized or departmental databases.

In addition to the base DBMSs, a variety of auxiliary products are available for each of the environments. Those auxiliary products can be broadly divided into the following categories:

- end-user tools
- application development tools
- copy management tools
- administration tools

The next four sections of this chapter (Sections 18.2–18.5) discuss each of these categories in turn and survey some of the available products in each category. Section 18.6 then offers a few comments on IBM's Systems Application Architecture (SAA) and future directions in this area.

One final preliminary remark before we delve into technical details: For obvious reasons, it is not really possible to include any Exercises or Answers sections in this part of the book. However, if the reader has access to any of the products described, then we strongly recommend at least trying out some of the examples discussed in the text. There is no substitute for genuine hands-on experience.

18.2   END-USER TOOLS

The simplicity and ease of use of relational systems such as DB2 make them particularly suitable for end-user computing: Users can get to the data directly and can develop simple applications on their own, instead of having to rely on the DP department to perform such functions for them. In other words, users are much more self-sufficient in a system like DB2, and the load on the DP department is accordingly much reduced. Of course, the feasibility of end-user computing is one of the reasons why relational systems provide much more productivity than nonrelational systems.

The functions that end-users need to be able to perform (and hence the end-user tools that are needed to support those functions) can be classified as follows:

1. *Query:* The ability to retrieve and update data in the database and produce reports and graphs accordingly

2. *Decision support:* The ability to perform statistical analysis and business planning based on data in the database

3. *Application development:* The ability to build simple customized applications for operating on the database

IBM provides two major products to support these requirements, namely Query Management Facility (QMF) and Application System (AS):

- Query Management Facility (QMF)

  QMF is a query tool for both DB2 and SQL/DS. It allows end-users to enter queries in either SQL or QBE ("Query-By-Example") and to produce a variety of reports and graphs from the results of those queries. It includes an application support interface that allows application programs to use QMF facilities also. QMF is discussed in Chapter 19. *Note:* The Query Manager product (an ad hoc query and report-writing system for the OS/2 Extended Edition Database Manager) resembles QMF in many respects.

- Application System (AS)

  AS provides facilities in all three of the areas mentioned above (query, decision support, application development), but IBM tends to emphasize its use for decision support. Like QMF, AS operates with both DB2 and SQL/DS; it also supports VSAM and sequential files. Queries can be entered in either SQL (for DB2 and SQL/DS only) or AS's own language. As with QMF, query results can be formatted into reports and graphs; the AS capabilities are more powerful than those of QMF but perhaps less user-friendly. AS decision support and business functions include project management, statistical analysis, financial planning, and text processing facilities. AS is discussed in Chapter 20.

Major third-party products supporting DB2 include FOCUS from Information Builders Inc., NOMAD2 from MUST Software International, and RAMIS from On-Line Software. These products compete primarily with AS. Other independent products include SAS, a statistics package from the SAS Institute, and Intellect, a natural language interface for both DB2 and SQL/DS, from Artificial Intelligence Corporation.

18.3 APPLICATION DEVELOPMENT TOOLS

As indicated in the previous section, end-user tools like AS and QMF can make significant contributions to productivity, because in many cases they can obviate the need to create application programs (in the traditional sense of that term) entirely. In most installations, however, there will still be some applications that are too complex to be dealt with by such tools and must therefore be handled by the DP department. Such applications can be created by means of either (a) a conventional programming language such as COBOL or PL/I, or (b) a suitable *application development tool.* The second of these alternatives, if feasible, is by far the preferred approach, for productivity reasons once again.

Aside: Before we go any further, a couple of editorial comments are necessary:

- First, by "application development tools" here we mean, primarily, tools that are intended for use by DP professionals rather than by end-users. Tools such as AS, by contrast, can be regarded as application development tools for the end-user.

- Second, application development tools are sometimes referred to as "fourth generation tools"—machine code, assembler language, and languages such as COBOL representing the first three generations—and the interface to such tools is accordingly sometimes called a "fourth generation language" (4GL). However, we choose not to adopt the 4GL terminology in this book, since it does not seem to have any very precise definition.

The marketplace trend is toward providing integrated application development tools that support the complete application development cycle, from requirements definition through to the final production cutover and maintenance of the application. These integrated tools are sometimes known as Computer-Aided Software Engineering (CASE) tools. They fall into two broad categories:

- Frontend ("upper CASE") analysis and design tools, which support requirements definition, data and process modeling, and database design

- Backend ("lower CASE") development tools, which support application program development and generation

Some vendors provide a single product that provides both upper and lower CASE facilities; however, most products cover just one of the two areas. Frontend tools are usually DBMS-independent and will therefore not be discussed further in this book (note, however, that several such tools do provide interfaces to backend tools that support DB2, and this fact could be an important consideration in selecting such a tool).

The backend tools, in turn, fall into three general types:

- Code or application generators, which create application modules or complete applications from a set of input specifications. Those specifications can sometimes have been created using a frontend CASE tool.

- Application development systems, which provide an integrated development environment for screen painting, application coding, application testing and debugging, etc.

- Expert system tools, which support the development of applications that make use of expert system technology.

IBM provides several backend application development products: Cross System Product (CSP), IMS Application Development Facility II (IMSADF II, or ADF for short), Expert System Environment (ESE), and Knowledgetool:

- Cross System Product (CSP)

  CSP is a complete application development system for MVS (TSO, CICS), VM, VSE, PC/DOS, and OS/2 applications (OS/400 support is scheduled for 1989). It provides a fully integrated environment for screen development, application coding, application testing and debugging, etc. CSP applications can process data stored in DB2, SQL/DS, and IMS databases, also in VSAM files. One advantage of CSP is that an application can be developed in one environment for execution in another; for example, an application could be developed and tested on SQL/DS under VM and then run on DB2 under MVS. CSP is discussed in Chapter 21.

- IMS Application Development Facility II (ADF)

  ADF is an application generator that creates IMS and CICS applications using ADF-supplied common modules and a set of rules defined by the application developer. The common modules support screen formatting, data entry and validation, database processing, etc. The rules determine the modules to be used and the databases to be accessed and updated. The generated applications can process data stored in IMS and DB2 databases, also in VSAM files. Exit routines can be written in a programming language such as COBOL or PL/I to supplement the ADF-supplied functions. ADF is discussed in Chapter 22.

- Expert System Environment (ESE)

  ESE is an expert system shell for developing knowledge-based applications for the MVS and VM environments. ESE applications can access DB2, SQL/DS (VM), and IMS databases.

- Knowledgetool

  Like ESE, Knowledgetool is used to build expert system applications. Instead of the high-level "shell" interface provided by ESE, Knowledgetool provides a PL/I-like language for application creation. Applications created via Knowledgetool can interface to other applications written in conventional languages such as COBOL and PL/I, and can access DB2, SQL/DS, and IMS databases.

  In addition to the foregoing, there are numerous nonIBM application development tools supporting access to DB2. Examples include APS from Sage Software, Pacbase from CGI Systems, Telon from Pansophic Systems, Transform from Transform Logic, Natural from Software AG, Mantis from Cincom Systems, IDEAL from Applied Data Research (now Computer Associates), IEF from Texam Instruments, ADS from Aion Corporation, and many others.

18.4 COPY MANAGEMENT TOOLS

End-users often need to perform some kind of analysis or other processing on data stored in an operational database on a central machine or in a shared end-user database on a departmental machine. Sometimes this processing cannot be done directly on the machine or database where the data is stored, either because the system in question does not have the right tools or because the nature of the required processing is such that it would interfere unduly with overall system performance (e.g., it requires the data to be "frozen" at some specific point in time). The solution in such a situation is to perform a "data extract"—i.e., make a copy of the required data and transfer it to a system (possibly a PC) where the processing can be supported. Copy management is the process of managing such data extracts.

IBM has three products supporting copy management:

- Data Extract (DXT)

  DXT allows data to be extracted from both relational and nonrelational databases and files into DB2 and SQL/DS tables.* It has two separate features, the *Relational Data Extract Feature* for extracting data from

---

*In IBM jargon the verb "extract" can take an indirect object of the form "into target," thus: "Extract (some data) *into* (some target)."

DB2 and SQL/DS databases, and the *General Data Extract Feature* for extracting data from IMS databases, VSAM and sequential files, and nonIBM data sources. Another product, the Data Extract Assist tool (DXTA), automates many of the steps required to use the General Data Extract Feature. DXT is covered in more detail in Chapter 23.

■ Host Data Base View (HDBV)

HDBV runs on an IBM PC that is connected via some communications link to a "host" machine running MVS or VM. It allows data to be copied to the PC from host files and databases. The host data required is specified by the PC user by means of SQL, prompt panels, or stored queries and procedures. The data is then retrieved via QMF or AS and copied down to the PC, where it can be accessed via any of several familiar PC products, such as Lotus 1–2–3 or dBase III. HDBV is discussed in Chapter 24. *Note:* Here and throughout this part of the book we take the term "PC" to include both the original IBM PC (or compatible machine) and the newer IBM Personal System/2 (PS/2), unless explicitly stated otherwise.

■ Enhanced Connectivity Facilities (ECF)

Like HDBV, ECF permits MVS and VM host data to be copied to a PC. ECF consists of a Requester program on the PC and a Server program on the host; the two communicate using a set of protocols known as the Server-Requester Programming Interface (SRPI). The Requester passes SQL statements generated by the PC user to the host Server, which uses those statements to extract data from DB2 or SQL/DS tables. Predefined DXT extract requests can also be executed through ECF. The user can also invoke host commands and programs from the PC and can use host disks, files, and printers as though they were connected to the PC. ECF is also discussed in Chapter 24.

Several third-party products also exist that compete with HDBV and ECF.

We conclude our brief discussion of copy management with a mention of IXF (Integration Exchange Format). IXF is an IBM standard self-defining file format. It is used as a basis for transferring data between programs, either user applications or IBM program products or both. IXF files can be created by QMF, AS, DXT, ECF, and Query.DL/I (a query tool for accessing IMS databases), and can be read by QMF, AS, and ECF.

18.5 ADMINISTRATION TOOLS

IBM provides several tools to assist with the administration of DB2 (see Chapter 17). Here we content ourselves with simply mentioning a few that were not discussed in that chapter and providing a brief summary of their capabilities. Please refer to the IBM manuals for more detailed information on the other products.

- The DB2 Performance Monitor (DB2PM) produces batch reports and online graphs showing DB2 performance, accounting, and audit data.

- The Data Base Migration Aid Utility (DBMAU) allows DB2 data, object, and authorization definitions to be moved between DB2 systems.

- The Data Base Relational Application Directory product (DBRAD) provides a set of database tables for defining application objects, user tables, programs, etc., together with the relationships between them. These tables form an application-oriented extension to the DB2 (or SQL/DS) catalog tables. DBRAD includes a reporting mechanism that uses these two sets of tables to produce (e.g.) where-used reports and impact reports about the effect of changing an object. Import facilities exist to import application information from application program copy libraries, the catalog tables, and CSP libraries (see Chapter 21). A model generator component can use the information stored in the DBRAD directory or the (DB2 or SQL/DS) catalog to generate application program data definitions and SQL data definition and manipulation statements. DBRAD is discussed in more detail in Chapter 25.

- *The IBM Information Repository:* IBM is known to have been developing an information repository product for several years, but at the time of writing the product remains unannounced and its content is still largely unknown. IBM has, however, stated what it perceives to be the "requirements" for such a repository and has discussed the broad architecture of the product in various forums. The following description is based on those statements from IBM.

  The main objective of the repository product will be to serve as a single source for information about data (or "metadata," as it is often called). The product will include three principal components:

  - Repository Manager, which will use DB2 to store the metadata. When DB2 distributed database support becomes available (see Chapter 26), the repository could span multiple DB2 systems; until that time, the repository will of course reside on a single system.

  - Public Interface, which will be a standard interface to the repository that will allow CASE tools (etc.) to retrieve and update repository information.

  - Frontend Interfaces, which will define and implement standard interfaces for those frontend tools (PF key settings, error codes, etc.).

IBM will convert existing tools such as CSP to use the repository and will provide new development tools as appropriate. It is likely that many of those new tools will run on workstations that operate in conjunction with the repository on the host. It is inevitable that many third-party tools will also support the repository.

It is perhaps worth mentioning that it is probably in the area of administrative tools that we can expect to see the most dramatic growth in the very near future. Already there are numerous products available from independent vendors, and IBM itself will no doubt also produce many more products of its own.

We close this section with a brief note on one more IBM product, the DB2/VSAM Transparency tool (though it is not exactly an administration tool per se). This product allows VSAM data to be moved into a DB2 database and then permits old VSAM applications to run unchanged against the migrated data. Also, of course, the migrated data is now available for use with all of the various tools mentioned earlier in this chapter.

18.6 THE IBM SYSTEMS APPLICATION ARCHITECTURE

As mentioned in the preface to the second edition of this book, IBM regards DB2 as a key member of its "Systems Application Architecture" (SAA) product set. SAA is intended to provide consistency across IBM's very diverse range of hardware and software offerings. It defines a set of common software interfaces, conventions, and protocols to be used by IBM's future program product offerings in the System/370 (TSO, CICS/MVS, IMS/DC, and VM/CMS), Application System/400 (OS/400), and PC (OS/2) environments. In this section we sketch the facilities of SAA very briefly, in order to provide some indication as to IBM's direction with regard to database management specifically.

SAA consists of four major components:

- *Common User Access* (interactive use of screens)
- *Common Programming Interface* (programming languages and services)
- *Common Communications Support* (communication protocols and services)
- *Common Applications* (application packages)

From a database standpoint, the most important piece of SAA is the Common Programming Interface. The Common Programming Interface, in turn, divides into components in two areas, namely languages and services. At the time of writing, the SAA languages are:

- C, COBOL, FORTRAN, RPG
- A procedure language based on the VM REXX language
- Application generation statements based on CSP

The main services components include:

- Database Interface (SQL)
- Dialog Interface based on the IBM PC EZ-VU product
- Presentation Interface similar to that in the IBM Graphical Data Display Manager product (GDDM)
- Query Interface based on (extensions to) QMF

Note in particular that SQL is defined as the common database interface (and of course DB2 is the provider of that interface for MVS). IBM's overall database strategy is thus clearly to provide SQL-based relational DBMSs with QMF- and CSP-like tools in all SAA environments. More recently, in fact, IBM has also added a *distributed SQL database* component to SAA, and has stated its long-term intent to permit SQL systems of all kinds to be able to participate (eventually) as partners in a heterogeneous distributed database system within SAA. See Chapter 26 for further discussion of this latter possibility.

C H A P T E R

·19·

Query Management Facility

19.1 INTRODUCTION

As explained in Chapter 18, Query Management Facility (QMF) is an ad
hoc query and report writing tool supporting end-user processing of data
stored in either DB2 (under MVS/TSO) or SQL/DS (under VM/CMS). We
focus in this book on the use of QMF with DB2, but most of the material
is equally applicable to its use with SQL/DS. *Note:* A separate version of
QMF for use with SQL/DS under VSE is also available, but that product
supports only a subset of the functions discussed in this chapter.

A report in QMF is the displayed (or printed) output from a QMF
query. QMF queries can be formulated in several different ways:

- By means of direct SQL statements;

- By means of a special *prompted query* interface, which allows users
  unfamiliar with SQL language details to construct certain SQL queries
  in a very simple manner;

- By means of a language called *Query-By-Example* (QBE). QBE is
  another relational language, comparable in some ways to SQL but

more user-friendly in certain respects. However, it is clear that, so far as QMF is concerned at any rate, IBM regards SQL as more important than QBE; we therefore do not discuss QBE in detail in this chapter, but instead defer such a discussion to an appendix (Appendix G). *Note:* The QBE language was previously supported by IBM as the interface to an "Installed User Program" (also called QBE) that ran on VM. However, QMF has nothing to do with that earlier product per se.

QMF reports are formatted in accordance with a set of report specifications called a *form*. When a given query is executed, the user has the option of specifying the corresponding form explicitly or of letting QMF create an appropriate *default* form. After viewing the report at the terminal, the user can revise the form and display the query output again in accordance with the revised version (without having to go back to the database to repeat the query). This cycle can be repeated as many times as necessary, until the user is satisfied. Thus a typical QMF session might go as follows (refer to Fig. 19.1).

1. The user constructs the query (any single SQL or QBE statement) in a QMF work area called QUERY.
2. The user issues RUN QUERY to execute the query in QUERY. The result is stored in another work area, called DATA (if it is too large to be kept entirely in main memory, it will be kept partly in an external "spill file").
3. QMF creates a default form for the result and displays the report accordingly. The form is kept in yet another work area, called FORM.
4. After inspecting the report, the user issues DISPLAY FORM to display the form in FORM, and proceeds to edit that form.
5. The user then issues DISPLAY REPORT to produce a revised report corresponding to the revised form. Note that it is not necessary to run the query again; the result has been kept in DATA, and DISPLAY REPORT uses the current FORM to format and display the current DATA.
6. Alternatively, the user can use DISPLAY CHART to display a chart or graph instead of a report (using the Interactive Chart Utility, ICU), or PRINT REPORT to obtain a hard copy.
7. Steps 4–6 are repeated as often as necessary.

Sections 19.2, 19.3, and 19.4 contain detailed discussions of query creation and execution, report formatting, and chart creation, respectively.

RUN QUERY, DISPLAY FORM, DISPLAY REPORT, DISPLAY CHART, etc., are examples of QMF *commands*. QMF allows a sequence

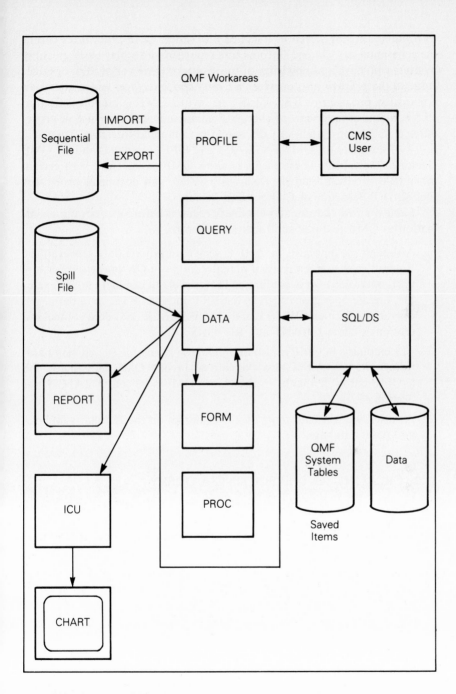

Fig. 19.1 QMF structure

of commands to be stored as a named *procedure.* QMF procedures permit the generation of "canned" production reports on a regular basis, possibly by users who have no knowledge of the details of QMF (or of SQL or QBE, come to that). QMF also provides a *Command Interface,* which allows an application program or TSO CLIST to invoke QMF commands. Section 19.5 contains an overview of the QMF commands and their use in procedures, and Section 19.6 briefly discusses the Command Interface. Then Section 19.7 discusses the QMF EXTRACT and ISPF commands and the QMF Document Interface. These facilities allow QMF to interface with certain other IBM products, namely DXT, ISPF/PDF, and document processors such as DCF (Document Composition Facility).

Finally, a few additional preliminary remarks before we start our examination of QMF features and facilities in depth:

1. Although the emphasis in QMF is very naturally on data retrieval, the "query" the user enters can actually be *any SQL operation* (or any QBE operation)—it is not limited to retrieval but can include, for example, update operations such as INSERT and DELETE, data definition operations such as CREATE and DROP TABLE, and data control operations such as GRANT and REVOKE.

2. The emphasis in QMF is also on *interactive execution* (again very naturally). However, it is also possible to invoke QMF as a batch job ("QMF batch"), thanks to the builtin QMF application BATCH (see Section 19.7).

3. As usual we will base most of our examples on the familiar suppliers-and-parts database.

19.2   CREATING AND EXECUTING A QUERY

Creating a New Query

After logging on to TSO and invoking QMF, the user is presented with the QMF *home panel* (Fig. 19.2). Like most QMF panels, this panel offers the user three possible actions:

- Press PF key 1 to get help, or
- Type a QMF command on the command line, or
- Press a PF key to execute a preassigned QMF command.

We now consider what is involved in creating a new query. Until further notice, we will assume that the query is to be constructed directly in SQL

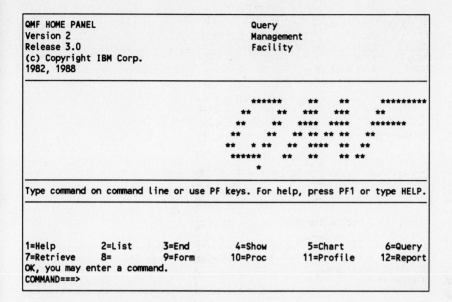

```
QMF HOME PANEL                       Query
Version 2                            Management
Release 3.0                          Facility
(c) Copyright IBM Corp.
1982, 1988

                              ******    **    **    *********
                              **   **   **   ***  ***   **
                              **   **   **  ****  ****  *******
                              **   **   ** ** ** **  **
                              **  * **  **  ****  **  **
                              ******    **    **    ** **
                                 *

Type command on command line or use PF keys. For help, press PF1 or type HELP.



1=Help        2=List      3=End      4=Show      5=Chart      6=Query
7=Retrieve    8=          9=Form     10=Proc     11=Profile   12=Report
OK, you may enter a command.
COMMAND===>
```

Fig. 19.2 The QMF home panel

(or QBE); we will discuss the prompted query case later in this section. First, the user types DISPLAY QUERY (or presses PF key 6). QMF responds by displaying a panel for entering the query. The user can then type the query (in either SQL or QBE), using the QMF full-screen editor. A sample query is shown in Fig. 19.3. *Note:* As mentioned in Section 19.1, all examples in this chapter will be based on SQL; examples of QBE can be found in Appendix G. Note that it is possible to switch dynamically between the two languages. The *default* language for any given user is defined in that user's "QMF profile," which is (typically) created by the *QMF administrator* but can be modified by the user at any time by means of appropriate QMF commands.

As already indicated, QMF queries can be created (and subsequently modified) using the builtin QMF full-screen editor. This editor provides simple commands for adding and deleting query lines, and is easy for a novice to learn and use. More experienced users who are familiar with more powerful editors can use one of those editors instead by issuing the QMF EDIT command. In this chapter, however, we restrict our attention for the most part to QMF's own editor.

QMF provides a DRAW command that can be used to assist in the process of constructing queries. DRAW "draws" a skeleton query on the

```
SQL QUERY                                                          LINE 1

SELECT     S.CITY, S.S#, SP.P#, SP.QTY
FROM       S, SP
WHERE      S.S# = SP.S#
ORDER BY   S.CITY, S.S#, SP.P#



*** END ***






1=Help       2=Run        3=End        4=Print     5=Chart      6=Draw
7=Backward   8=Forward    9=Form       10=Insert   11=Delete    12=Report
OK, cursor positioned.
COMMAND ===>                                         SCROLL ===> PAGE
```

Fig. 19.3. Sample QMF query (SQL)

screen for the table named in the DRAW command. For example, the command

```
DRAW S ( TYPE = SELECT )
```

will produce the following SELECT statement skeleton for the suppliers table (table S):

```
SELECT S#, SNAME, STATUS, CITY  -- S
FROM   S                        -- S
```

This skeleton query can now be edited to produce the query actually desired. *Note:* The "-- S" at the right-hand side of each of the two lines of the skeleton query is a comment.

Once the query has been created, the user can execute it by issuing RUN QUERY (or by pressing PF key 2). The result is displayed at the user's terminal using the default form constructed automatically by QMF. That form can be displayed by issuing DISPLAY FORM (or by pressing PF key 9). Figs. 19.4 and 19.5 show the report and the default form, respectively, for the query of Fig. 19.3.

The user can now edit the form, if desired, and then display a revised report corresponding to that edited form by issuing DISPLAY REPORT or by pressing PF key 12. (A detailed discussion of form editing is deferred to

```
REPORT                                      LINE 1      POS 1   79

   CITY              S#    P#          QTY
   ---------------   ----- ------  -----------
   London            S1    P1          300
   London            S1    P2          200
   London            S1    P3          400
   London            S1    P4          200
   London            S1    P5          100
   London            S1    P6          100
   London            S4    P2          200
   London            S4    P4          300
   London            S4    P5          400
   Paris             S2    P1          300
   Paris             S2    P2          400
   Paris             S3    P2          200




1=Help        2=           3=End       4=Print     5=Chart      6=Query
7=Backward    8=Forward    9=Form     10=Left     11=Right     12=
OK, this is the REPORT from your RUN command.
COMMAND ===>                                      SCROLL ===> PAGE
```

Fig. 19.4 Report for the query of Fig. 19.3

```
FORM.MAIN

COLUMNS:                   Total Width of Report Columns: 45
  NUM   COLUMN HEADING                    USAGE    INDENT   WIDTH   EDIT   SEQ
  ---   -------------------------------   -------  ------   -----   -----  ---
   1    CITY                                         2       15      C     1
   2    S#                                           2        5      C     2
   3    P#                                           2        6      C     3
   4    QTY                                          2       11      L     4
        *** END ***

PAGE:    HEADING ===>
         FOOTING ===>
FINAL:   TEXT ===>
BREAK1:  NEW PAGE FOR BREAK? ===> NO
         FOOTING ===>
BREAK2:  NEW PAGE FOR BREAK? ===> NO
         FOOTING ===>
OPTIONS :  OUTLINE? ===> YES          DEFAULT BREAK TEXT? ===> YES

1=Help      2=Check    3=End       4=Show        5=Chart       6=Query
7=Backward  8=Forward  9=         10=Insert     11=Delete     12=Report
OK, FORM is displayed.
COMMAND ===>                                      SCROLL ===> PAGE
```

Fig. 19.5 Default form for the query of Fig. 19.3

Section 19.3.) These two steps can be repeated as many times as necessary, until the user is satisfied with the result; the final report can then be printed by issuing PRINT REPORT, or by pressing PF key 4. For example, the command

```
PRINT REPORT ( WIDTH=132 LENGTH=65 DATETIME=YES PAGENO=YES )
```

will print the current report (i.e., the current contents of the DATA working area) on the printer specified in the user's QMF profile. Pages will be 132 characters wide and 65 lines deep, will contain the current date and time, and will be numbered.

It is also possible to direct the hard copy report to a different printer by means of the PRINTER option on the PRINT command. For example, to print the report on the printer called DEPT1, the following command could be used:

```
PRINT REPORT ( PRINTER = DEPT1 )
```

Saving and Reexecuting a Query

At any given time, the QMF working area includes at most five current "QMF items": one query, one result (DATA), one form, one procedure, and one profile (refer to Fig. 19.1). Thus, e.g., executing a new query will cause the current contents of DATA to be overwritten. However, any current item can be saved for later use by means of an appropriate SAVE command. For instance, the command

```
SAVE QUERY AS CITYQUERY ( SHARE = YES )
```

will save the current query as CITYQUERY (and will also make it available for use by other users, thanks to the option SHARE = YES; if the SHARE option were omitted, only the user saving the query would subsequently be able to execute it).

Saved queries can subsequently be executed by means of the RUN QUERY command. For instance, the command

```
RUN CITYQUERY ( FORM = CITYFORM )
```

will execute the saved query CITYQUERY, formatting the result in accordance with a form named CITYFORM.

The command LIST QUERIES can be used to display a list of saved queries. Options exist to limit the output to just those queries saved by a particular user and/or having a particular generic name. For example, the command

```
LIST QUERIES ( OWNER = ALL  NAME = CITY% )
```

will list all saved queries having "CITY" as the first four characters of their name. The user can then enter various QMF commands on the screen alongside any given query in the list. For example, if the user types the command DISPLAY against the query name CITYQUERY, QMF will bring that query into the QUERY working area, thereby making it the current query again.

Variables (i.e., parameters) are permitted in saved queries. For example, if the query

```
SELECT S#, SNAME
FROM    S
WHERE   CITY = &CITYNAME
```

is saved under the name CITYQUERY, it can be executed subsequently via the command

```
RUN CITYQUERY ( &CITYNAME = 'London' )
```

If the user forgets to supply a value for the &CITY variable, QMF will prompt for one.

Creating a Prompted Query

So far we have seen how QMF queries can be created using SQL statements directly. However, many end users are either not able or not inclined to learn all the complexities of SQL, and for such users some simpler kind of interface is desirable. The QMF *prompted query* facility provides such an interface: It allows queries to be constructed by means of a series of "pop-up" windows, which eliminate the need to know the syntax of SQL in detail and provide assistance in identifying the tables and columns to be accessed. The user's QMF profile indicates whether the prompted query facility is to be used.

Figs. 19.6, 19.7, and 19.8 (overleaf) show how the prompted query facility could be used to construct the SQL query already shown in Fig. 19.3. *Note:* Each window is selected from a master window (not shown).

- First, the required tables are specified, using the "Tables" window (Fig. 19.6). A list of known table names can be displayed if desired to help with this step.

- Once the table names (S and SP in the example) have been identified, the next step is to indicate how those tables are to be joined. This information is provided via the "Join Columns" window (Fig. 19.7), which displays the column names for each table, together with an associated column number in each case. The user indicates the columns over which the join is to be performed by means of those column numbers; in the

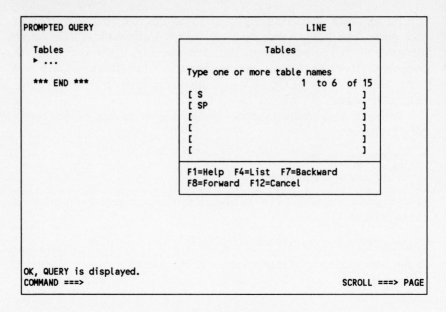

Fig. 19.6 Specifying the tables in a prompted query

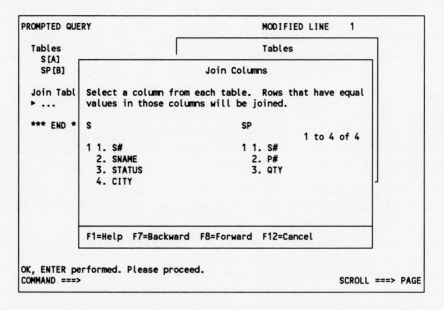

Fig. 19.7 Specifying the join columns in a prompted query

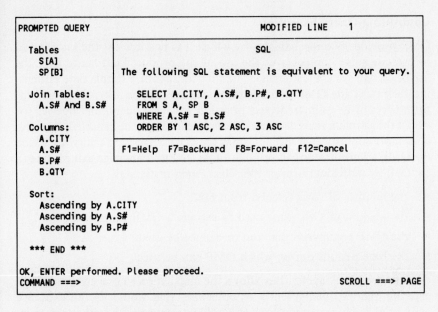

```
PROMPTED QUERY                              MODIFIED LINE    1

   Tables                              SQL
     S[A]
     SP[B]        The following SQL statement is equivalent to your query.

   Join Tables:          SELECT A.CITY, A.S#, B.P#, B.QTY
     A.S# And B.S#       FROM S A, SP B
                         WHERE A.S# = B.S#
   Columns:              ORDER BY 1 ASC, 2 ASC, 3 ASC
     A.CITY
     A.S#        F1=Help  F7=Backward  F8=Forward  F12=Cancel
     B.P#
     B.QTY

   Sort:
     Ascending by A.CITY
     Ascending by A.S#
     Ascending by B.P#

   *** END ***

OK, ENTER performed. Please proceed.
COMMAND ===>                                    SCROLL ===> PAGE
```

Fig. 19.8 The completed query and its SQL equivalent

example, we have specified that the join is taken over column 1 (S#) of table S and column 1 (S#) of table SP. *Note:* The "Join Columns" window assumes that the join is an equijoin. See Section 6.3 if you need to refresh your memory concerning the different types of join.

- Further windows (not shown) are used to specify the columns to be retrieved from the result of the join and the desired row sequence for the final output. Fig. 19.8 shows the completed query. It also shows the generated SQL version of the query (this information can be obtained by entering the command SHOW SQL).

The example does not illustrate the point, but the prompted query facility also allows scalar expressions to be specified as well as simple column names (for both the SELECT clause and the WHERE clause, in SQL terms). It also supports aggregate functions (SUM, AVG, etc.), arbitrarily complex "WHERE clause" conditions (involving AND, OR, etc.), and duplicate row elimination (DISTINCT). However, it does not support subqueries, GROUP BY, HAVING, or UNION; nor does it support operations other than retrieval (i.e., update, data definition, and data control operations are not supported).

Controlling Query Execution

QMF provides two mechanisms by which it is possible for the installation to exercise some control over the use of the product (and hence over the use of certain system resources). The first consists of a simple time estimating facility; if the QMF administrator requests this facility, QMF will inform users of its estimated execution time for each query, and queries for which the estimate exceeds some threshold can simply be canceled. The second, more sophisticated mechanism is the QMF *governor* facility, by which the QMF administrator can provide an Assembler Language exit routine to control, by individual user or user class, such matters as:

- the number of rows fetched from DB2
- the amount of CPU time used to execute a QMF command
- the QMF commands that can or cannot be used
- the time periods during which QMF can be used

The governor facility thus allows the installation to prevent users from entering queries, inadvertently or otherwise, that would use an excessive amount of some system resource or would interfere unduly with other activities in the system. A sample governor routine is provided with QMF that can be used to control the number of rows fetched and the amount of CPU time consumed.

Note: QMF query execution can also be controlled by means of the DB2 Resource Limit Facility (RLF), either as well as or instead of the QMF governor. Refer to Chapter 17 for details of RLF.

19.3   CREATING A REPORT

After composing and executing a query, the user can produce a tailored report from the result by means of a set of *form panels*. The starting point in this process is the default form produced by QMF when the query is first executed. That form can be displayed by issuing DISPLAY FORM (or by pressing PF key 9) after running the query; the effect is to display the form on a panel called FORM.MAIN (refer back to Fig. 19.5).

FORM.MAIN supports a set of basic formatting functions; more extensive formatting can be performed using additional form panels. We will first discuss the use of FORM.MAIN and then move on to describe the other panels. As already indicated, the default form we will be using as a basis for discussion is the one shown in Fig. 19.5 (the default form for the sample query of Fig. 19.3).

Basic Formatting

To demonstrate basic formatting, we will make some updates to the default form of Fig. 19.5. The modified form is shown in Fig. 19.9, and the resulting report (displayed by issuing DISPLAY REPORT or by pressing PF key 12) is shown in Fig. 19.10. By comparing Fig. 19.9 with the original default form (Fig. 19.5), we can see the effect of each of the major components of FORM.MAIN.

- COLUMN HEADING

The column headings on the default form are the same as the column names in the table, unless column labels are being used (see the discussion of the SQL LABEL statement in Section 9.3). Those headings can be changed to any name of up to 40 characters. An underscore starts a new line—i.e., it indicates that the rest of the heading (up to the next underscore) is to appear on the next line, centered beneath the portion on the previous line (up to nine lines are allowed in such a heading). In the example, the name CITY has been changed to City, and the names S#, P#, and QTY have been changed to the more meaningful names Supplier, Part, and Quantity, respectively.

```
FORM.MAIN

COLUMNS:              Total Width of Report Columns: 40
 NUM  COLUMN HEADING                        USAGE     INDENT  WIDTH  EDIT   SEQ
 ---  ------------------------------------- -------   ------  -----  -----  ---
   1  City                                  BREAK1    3       8      C      1
   2  Supplier                                        3       8      C      2
   3  Part                                            3       4      C      3
   4  Quantity                              SUM       3       8      L      4
      *** END ***

PAGE:    HEADING ===> Shipments by Supplier City - Date: &DATE
         FOOTING ===> Page: &PAGE
FINAL:   TEXT ===> *** Grand Total
BREAK1:  NEW PAGE FOR BREAK? ===> NO
         FOOTING ===> * Total for &1
BREAK2:  NEW PAGE FOR BREAK? ===> NO
         FOOTING ===>
OPTIONS: OUTLINE? ===> YES            DEFAULT BREAK TEXT? ===> YES

1=Help      2=Check   3=End       4=Show         5=Chart        6=Query
7=Backward  8=Forward 9=          10=Insert      11=Delete      12=Report
OK, cursor positioned.
COMMAND ===>                                      SCROLL ===> PAGE
```

Fig. 19.9 Modified form for the query of Fig. 19.3

```
Shipments by Supplier City - Date: 87/06/23

City       Supplier   Part   Quantity
--------   --------   ----   --------
London     S1         P1        300
           S1         P2        200
           S1         P3        400
           S1         P4        200
           S1         P5        100
           S1         P6        100
           S4         P2        200
           S4         P4        300
           S4         P5        400
                                --------
         * Total for London     2200

Paris      S2         P1        300
           S2         P2        400
           S3         P2        200
                                --------
         * Total for Paris       900
                                ========
       ***   Grand Total        3100
                                Page: 1
```

Fig. 19.10 Tailored report using the form of Fig. 19.9

- USAGE

USAGE codes determine how data columns are to be processed in producing the report. If no USAGE code is specified for a given column, values in that column are simply displayed without any special processing. The meanings of the various USAGE codes are as follows.

- OMIT means that the column is to be omitted from the report.
- BREAK*n* (*n* = 1 to 6) specifies that a *control break* is to occur each time a value change occurs in the indicated column. The main purpose of specifying control breaks is to let QMF compute and display subtotals (or similar partial results—see below) when the report is produced. In our example, a control break will occur each time the City value changes. Because USAGE for the the Quantity column has been specified as SUM, QMF will sum the Quantity values at each control break. Note that a request for subtotals automatically causes QMF to compute a grand total also.
- In general, BREAK1 signifies the most significant (major) control break column, BREAK2 the next most significant, and so on. QMF will reorder the report columns (but not the form columns) left to right in the order of significance of the control breaks. *Note:* The

original query must have included an appropriate ORDER BY specification for control breaks to make sense. See Fig. 19.3.

- BREAK*n*X is the same as BREAK*n,* except that the column is to be
  omitted from the report.
- The available "aggregate function" USAGE codes (with their mean-
  ings, where those meanings are not immediately obvious) are:
  — COUNT
  — FIRST
  — LAST
  — MAXIMUM
  — MINIMUM
  — SUM
  — CSUM (cumulative sum)
  — AVG
  — STDEV (standard deviation)
  — PCT (percentage of next subtotal)
  — CPCT (cumulative percentage of next subtotal)
  — TPCT (percentage of grand total)
  — TCPCT (cumulative percentage of grand total)
- The USAGE code GROUP causes one line of summary data to be
  displayed for each distinct value in the indicated column. (As with
  BREAK*n,* the data must be appropriately sorted for GROUP to
  make sense.) In our example, if we were to specify GROUP for the
  Supplier column (in addition to the BREAK1 and SUM codes already
  specified for the City and Quantity columns), the effect would be to
  group all rows for a particular supplier within a particular city together and to display a single line for that combination, giving the
  corresponding total quantity. The final result would thus look somewhat as follows (ignoring page headings and footings):

```
City       Supplier   Quantity
--------   --------   --------
London     S1             1300
           S4              900
                       --------
  * Total for London      2200
Paris      S2              700
           S3              200
                       --------
  * Total for Paris        900
                       ========
    *** Grand Total       3100
```

The Part column is automatically omitted from the report because no aggregate USAGE is specified for it.

- The USAGE code CALC*n* specifies that this is a "CALC column"— i.e., the results of "calculation*n*" are to be used as values for this column in the report. Calculations are defined using the FORM.CALC panel (see the subsection on "Advanced Formatting" at the end of this section). CALC columns can be added to a form by means of the QMF INSERT command. *Note:* Columns—any columns, not just CALC columns—can also be removed from a form by means of the QMF DELETE command.

- Finally, the USAGE code ACROSS can be used in conjunction with GROUP to produce a report in which each line of summary data for the GROUP column has an entry for each corresponding value of the ACROSS column. (As with BREAK*n* and GROUP, the data must be appropriately sorted for ACROSS to make sense.) For example, suppose we wanted to display quantity totals by city across all suppliers, as well as quantity totals for each individual supplier. By specifying ACROSS for Supplier and GROUP for City, the required result is produced:

```
                <------------- Supplier --------------->
                <- S1 ->  <- S2 ->  <- S3 ->  <- S4 ->  <-TOTAL->
     City       Quantity  Quantity  Quantity  Quantity  Quantity
     --------   --------  ---------  --------  --------  --------
     London        1300          0         0       900      2200
     Paris            0        700       200         0       900
                ========  =========  ========  ========  ========
                    1300        700       200       900      3100
```

Note: The suppliers-and-parts database does not permit the same supplier to appear in more than one city. The foregoing report is thus unrealistically simple. Nevertheless, the example does serve to illustrate the basic idea of "cross-summary" reporting.

- INDENT

INDENT specifies the number of blanks to appear between the indicated column and the one to its immediate left. All INDENT values in the example have been changed from 2 to 3.

- WIDTH

WIDTH specifies the width of the indicated column as it is to appear in the report (in terms of characters). In the example, the City, Supplier, Part, and Quantity widths have been changed from 15 to 8, 5 to 8, 6 to 4, and 11 to 8, respectively.

- EDIT

EDIT codes determine how column values are to be formatted. Codes C and L mean character and decimal, respectively. Other options permit numbers to be displayed in scientific (floating point) style or in a variety of fixed point styles (e.g., with currency symbols inserted, leading zeros suppressed, etc.). It is also possible to supply installation-defined exit routines to perform customized column value formatting. The reader is referred to the QMF manuals for details of all these possibilities. No changes were made to the EDIT codes in our example.

- SEQ

SEQ defines the order in which the columns are to appear in the displayed report. For example, if we changed the SEQ values to read 1, 3, 2, 4 (vertically), the columns would be displayed in the sequence City, Part, Supplier, Quantity (left to right). By default, the columns will appear in the left-to-right order specified in the SQL SELECT clause.

- PAGE HEADING, PAGE FOOTING, FINAL

PAGE HEADING and FOOTING define one line of heading and footing text to be produced on each page of the report. FINAL defines one line of text to be displayed on the final summary line (if any) of the report. Our example uses the variable &DATE to display the current date (in the format YY/MM/DD) in the heading text, and &PAGE to display the current page number in the footing text. The variable &TIME can also be used to display the current time in the format HH:MM.

- BREAK1

Two options are possible here, each specifying what is to be done when a control break occurs in the BREAK1 column. The first specifies whether a new page is to be started; the second specifies the text to be displayed on the corresponding summary line. Such text can include references to variables of the form &*n*. If it does, QMF will substitute the current value of column *n* before displaying the summary line. (The column number is shown under NUM on FORM.MAIN.) In the example, the variable &1 refers to column 1 on the form, and the current value of City will be displayed each time a control break on City occurs. *Note:* Variables can also be used in heading and footing text.

- BREAK2

BREAK2 is the same as BREAK1, mutatis mutandis. *Note:* There are no BREAK3, BREAK4, etc. options on FORM.MAIN; for information on how to code the text for control breaks 3 through 6, see the subsection "Advanced Formatting" at the end of the present section.

- OPTIONS

FORM.MAIN includes two further options, OUTLINE and DEFAULT BREAK TEXT. The example specifies an OUTLINE option of YES, which causes values to be displayed in a control break column only when the value changes; NO causes a value to be displayed on every line. The DEFAULT BREAK TEXT option specifies what is to happen when control breaks are used, but the user has not indicated any break footing text; YES causes a line of asterisks to be displayed, NO suppresses this default.

One final aspect of the form that should be mentioned is the line at the top showing "Total Width of Report Columns." This line gives the total report width, in characters. It cannot be changed directly, but is instead automatically updated by QMF every time a USAGE, INDENT, or WIDTH value is modified.

Advanced Formatting

The example discussed under "Basic Formatting" above gives some idea of how easy it is to use FORM.MAIN to produce a customized report. Sometimes, however, more sophisticated tailoring will be required. The form panels described in this subsection provide the necessary additional tailoring facilities. There are seven additional panel types, namely FORM.COLUMNS, FORM.PAGE, FORM.FINAL, FORM.BREAK*n*, FORM.DETAIL, FORM.CALC, and FORM.OPTIONS, with functions as follows:

- FORM.COLUMNS: Contains the same column information as FORM.MAIN, except that more column entries can be displayed on a single screen.

- FORM.PAGE: Allows multiple lines of heading and footing text (compared with just one on FORM.MAIN). Other options control text alignment and position, and the number of blank lines before and after the heading and footing.

- FORM.FINAL: Allows multiple lines of final report text and offers similar formatting options to FORM.PAGE.

- FORM.BREAK*n*: There are six of these panels, one for each of the six control break levels. Multiple heading and footing lines are allowed for each level; they are positioned using formatting options similar to those on FORM.PAGE. One further option controls whether column headings are to be repeated at each new control break.

- **FORM.DETAIL:**   Controls more precisely where retrieved data, constants, and calculated values (see FORM.CALC below) are to appear in the report. This form provides more flexibility in defining report layouts than the rather rigid FORM.MAIN panel does.

- **FORM.CALC:**   Allows the user to specify arithmetic and string operations to be performed on retrieved data. Each calculation is given a unique identifier so that it can be referenced in other FORM panels. A calculation with the identifier 5, for example, can be referenced on FORM.MAIN by specifying the USAGE code CALC5. This feature allows the result of the calculation to be included in the final report.

- **FORM.OPTIONS:**   Contains some fourteen different formatting options, controlling such matters as detail line spacing, line wrapping, final and break text width, the use of aggregate function names in column headings, automatic column reordering when using control breaks and grouping, page renumbering, column heading separators, and so forth.

These panels work in conjunction with FORM.MAIN to let the user construct more elaborate reports. Everything entered on FORM.MAIN is automatically reflected in a corresponding detailed form panel. Each of the detailed panels can be reached by selecting the appropriate PF key from FORM.MAIN (see the PF keys in Fig. 19.5 or Fig. 19.9).

19.4   CREATING A CHART

Section 19.3 explained what is involved in creating a QMF report. However, a report is only one way of displaying a query result; a chart or graph is another. QMF uses the Interactive Chart Utility (ICU) of the IBM Graphic Data Display Manager (GDDM) to create and display charts. Although most aspects of such charts are controlled by QMF, users can specify and save certain chart format options of their own in the ICU.

The QMF command syntax to display a chart is

```
DISPLAY CHART ( ICUFORM = name )
```

The chart is formatted and displayed in accordance with the chart format identified by "name"—either one of the builtin chart formats provided by QMF or a user-defined chart format previously saved in the ICU. For example, to display a pie chart using a QMF-provided format called PIE, the user would enter

```
DISPLAY CHART ( ICUFORM = PIE )
```

Similarly, to display a chart saved in the ICU with the name MYPIE, the command

```
DISPLAY CHART ( ICUFORM = MYPIE )
```

would be used.

As already indicated, several builtin ICU chart formats are provided by QMF to reduce the need for users to create and save their own chart formats. The builtin formats are BAR, PIE, LINE, TOWER, POLAR, HISTOGRAM, SURFACE, and SCATTER (these names are intended to be self-explanatory). By default, QMF formats data into a bar chart. This default format is stored under the name DSQCFORM in the ICU, and can be replaced by the user at any time.

To illustrate chart operation, we will use a modified version of the form in Fig. 19.9 (see Fig. 19.11), in which we have specified OMIT for the Supplier column and GROUP for the Part column. Executing the command DISPLAY CHART with this form will create the bar chart shown in Fig. 19.12.

The rules used by QMF for constructing charts are as follows:

- For report forms without any GROUP or BREAK*n* columns, the X-axis data is taken from the leftmost data column. For report forms

```
FORM.MAIN

COLUMNS:                  Total Width of Report Columns: 40
 NUM  COLUMN HEADING                    USAGE   INDENT  WIDTH  EDIT   SEQ
 ---  ----------------------------      ------  ------  -----  -----  ---
   1  City                              BREAK1    3        8     C     1
   2  Supplier                          OMIT      3        8     C     2
   3  Part                              GROUP     3        4     C     3
   4  Quantity                          SUM       3        8     L     4
      *** END ***

PAGE:    HEADING ===> Shipments by Supplier City - Date: &DATE
         FOOTING ===> Page: &PAGE
FINAL:   TEXT ===> *** Grand Total
BREAK1:  NEW PAGE FOR BREAK? ===> NO
         FOOTING ===> * Total for &1
BREAK2:  NEW PAGE FOR BREAK? ===> NO
         FOOTING ===>
OPTIONS: OUTLINE? ===> YES            DEFAULT BREAK TEXT? ===> YES

1=Help      2=Check    3=End      4=Show      5=Chart      6=Query
7=Backward  8=Forward  9=        10=Insert   11=Delete    12=Report
OK, cursor positioned.
COMMAND ===>                                    SCROLL ===> PAGE
```

Fig. 19.11 Form for displaying a bar chart

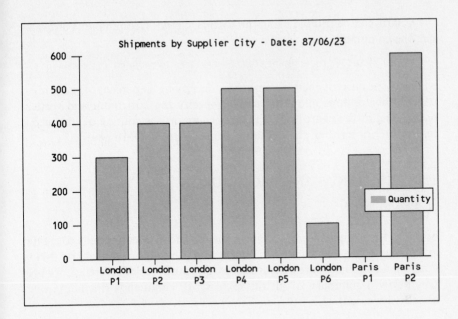

Fig. 19.12 Sample bar chart

that include one or more GROUP or BREAK*n* columns, as in our example, the X-axis data is taken from those columns.

■ The Y-axis data is taken from the remaining *numeric* columns of the report—i.e., the Quantity column, in our example.

■ The legend Quantity comes from the column heading of the Y-axis data column.

■ The chart heading is the same as the report heading.

It is important to realize that these four aspects of the chart format are completely defined by the QMF report form; they can be temporarily modified in the ICU for some specific purpose, but any such modifications will not be reflected in the chart when it is next displayed from QMF. Other aspects of the chart format, such as chart size, axis titles, data color, and the position, color, and size of the legend and titles, can be permanently modified, by making the desired changes and saving the modified format in the ICU under a new name. The modified format can then be used by specifying that new name in the QMF DISPLAY CHART command. If a QMF-provided chart format is used and not modified in any way, it does not have to be saved in the ICU.

Charts can be printed using the PRINT CHART command. For example, the command

```
PRINT CHART ( ICUFORM=PIE UNITS=PERCENT CWIDTH=80 CLENGTH=80 )
```

will print the current chart as a pie chart occupying 80 percent of the printed page. Other options allow the user to specify the horizontal and vertical positioning of the chart on the page and support the routing of the output to a printer other than the default one in the user's QMF profile.

19.5 COMMANDS AND PROCEDURES

Commands

So far in this chapter we have shown the use of QMF commands to create, execute, and save queries, and to display and print reports and charts. Many additional commands are also available. For purposes of reference, we present below a summary of all the main QMF commands (including ones already discussed):

- CONVERT: Translate a QBE, prompted, or SQL query into an executable SQL statement. All QMF variables are replaced by actual values. The converted query can be saved, exported, or transferred into an application program.

- DISPLAY: Display a query, form, report, chart, procedure, profile, or table. The table option provides a quick way to display some specified table (it is shorthand for coding and executing the SQL statement "SELECT * FROM table").

- DRAW: Create a skeleton query.

- EDIT: Edit a QMF procedure or SQL query, using an editor of the user's choice instead of the builtin QMF editor.

- ERASE: Erase a query, form, procedure, or table from the system (the table option is shorthand for coding and executing the SQL statement "DROP TABLE table").

- EXPORT: Transfer data, a query, form, procedure, table, report, or chart to a TSO data set (see Section 19.6).

- EXTRACT: Invoke DXT from the QMF environment (see Section 19.7).

- HELP: Get online information about using QMF.

- IMPORT: Transfer data, a query, form, table, or procedure from a TSO data set into QMF (see Section 19.6).

- ISPF: Invoke ISPF/PDF (see Section 19.7).
- LIST: List saved QMF items.
- PRINT: Print a query, form, report, chart, procedure, profile, or table.
- RESET: Clear the current panel.
- RETRIEVE: Retrieve and redisplay previously entered QMF commands.
- RUN: Execute a query or procedure.
- SAVE: Save the current query, form, procedure, profile, or data for future use (the data option is equivalent to executing the SQL statement "CREATE TABLE," followed by a statement to populate that newly created table).
- SET: Change the user profile without first displaying it.
- SHOW: Display the specified panel.
- TSO: Enter a TSO command or execute a QMF application (see Section 19.6).

Procedures

There will frequently be situations in which the same set of QMF commands needs to be executed repeatedly on some regular basis. In such a situation, it is obviously convenient to be able to execute the complete set via a single command. QMF therefore allows commands to be grouped together to form a QMF *procedure*. Such a procedure can be invoked by means of the QMF RUN command. Like queries, procedures are created using an editor; they can be saved for later reuse using the SAVE command, and—again like queries—can contain variables (i.e., parameters), values for which must be supplied when the procedure is executed.

Procedures must contain QMF commands only, and have no branching capability. They can optionally be run in batch, freeing the terminal for other work. The sample procedure below contains several of the commands discussed earlier in this chapter. *Note:* Lines beginning with a double hyphen are comment lines.

```
-- Run the stored query called CITYQUERY;
-- CITYNAME is a variable contained in CITYQUERY;
-- other variables are for use with the procedure itself:
--
RUN CITYQUERY ( FORM = &FORMN  &&CITYNAME = &CITY )
--
-- Create a new table containing the result data:
--
SAVE DATA AS &NEWTAB
```

```
--
-- Print report using a page length of 55 lines:
--
PRINT REPORT ( LENGTH = 55 )
```

The procedure can be saved by executing a SAVE command—for example:

```
SAVE PROC AS CITYPROC
```

—and can be executed using a RUN command. For example:

```
RUN CITYPROC ( &FORMN=CITYFORM &CITY='London' &NEWTAB=CITYDATA )
```

See also the discussion of QMF applications and the QMF Command Interface in Section 19.6.

19.6 APPLICATION SUPPORT FACILITIES

In addition to all of the end-user facilities discussed in this chapter so far, QMF also provides a set of facilities specifically intended for the professional programmer. Those facilities, known collectively as the *QMF application support facilities,* consist of:

- The QMF *Command Interface,* which allows application programs and TSO CLISTs to pass commands to QMF for execution. Those commands are executed in a similar fashion to those entered from the QMF command line or QMF procedures.

- *Installation-Defined Commands,* which make it possible for user-written applications to act as an extension of the QMF command set. Such commands can be invoked just like other QMF commands—i.e., from the QMF command line, from within QMF procedures, or through the QMF Command Interface.

- *PF Key Customization,* which can be used to reassign QMF commands to different PF keys and to add installation-defined commands to PF keys.

- *Application Support Commands,* which are a special set of commands for use by application programs. These commands make it possible for applications to behave just like QMF commands in their style of interaction with the end-user.

- *Externalized Items,* which allow applications to manipulate QMF items (e.g., QMF queries and forms) outside the QMF environment, using the QMF EXPORT and IMPORT commands.

We now briefly describe each of these facilities in turn.

The Command Interface

The Command Interface is a QMF-supplied program (DSQCCI) that can be invoked from a TSO CLIST or from a program written in APL, Assembler Language, COBOL, FORTRAN, or PL/I. Applications using the QMF Command Interface are initially invoked from QMF (interactive or batch) using the QMF TSO command. They can then in turn invoke the Command Interface, passing it a string representing the QMF command to be executed (see Fig. 19.13, overleaf).

The Command Interface is particularly useful in CLISTs, because CLISTs offer the branching and looping constructs not available in QMF procedures. For example, the CLIST statement

```
ISPEXEC SELECT PGM (DSQCCI)
        PARM (RUN CITYQUERY (FORM=CITYFORM &CITYNAME='London'))
```

invokes the Command Interface and requests QMF to execute the query CITYQUERY using the form CITYFORM (and the CITYNAME "London"). *Note:* ISPF services are used (ISPEXEC) because (as explained above) the application—i.e., the CLIST—is invoked from QMF, and QMF runs under ISPF.

The only information returned to the application is an indication of whether the command executed successfully; in the example above, the result of the query is not returned to the CLIST but is instead stored in the DATA workarea of the QMF session that invoked that CLIST (nor is any information displayed during the execution of the query at the QMF terminal that called the CLIST, incidentally). To access the output report from within the CLIST, it must be exported to a TSO data set and then read back from that data set. For example, the command

```
ISPEXEC SELECT PGM (DSQCCI) PARM (EXPORT REPORT TO CITYFILE)
```

exports the report to a data set called CITYFILE, which can now be read in the normal manner (the formats of exported QMF items are all fully documented in the QMF manuals). *Note:* Of course, there is no point in writing an application to execute a query unless further processing is to be done on the result of that query. As an illustration, the CLIST discussed above might go on to perform a more detailed analysis of the data in CITYFILE or produce a more complex report from that data.

QMF applications can also display ISPF information and data-entry panels during execution. Such panels can be made to have a similar appearance to the standard QMF panels.

As already stated, applications using the QMF Command Interface are invoked from QMF (interactive or batch), using the QMF TSO command.

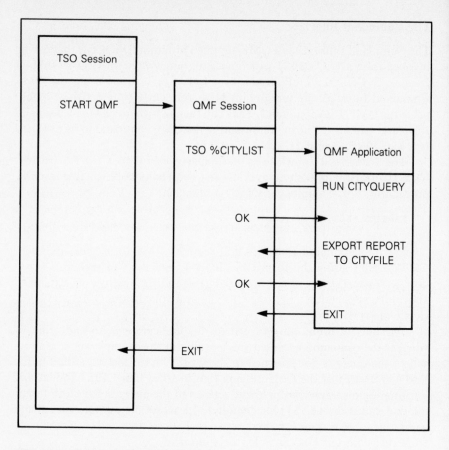

Fig. 19.13 QMF Command Interface

If the CLIST application discussed above is named CITYLIST, it can be invoked by means of the command

```
TSO %CITYLIST
```

This command can be made more memorable (i.e., more user-friendly) by giving it an appropriate *command synonym*. See the next subsection below.

Installation-Defined Commands

The process of invoking QMF procedures (via the RUN command) and applications (via the TSO command) can be considerably simplified by the introduction of *command synonyms*. Such synonyms constitute *installation-defined commands;* entries describing them are kept by QMF in a *command synonym table*. The specific synonym table to be used during a specific QMF session is defined in the user's QMF profile.

Each row in the synonym table consists of three components: verb, object (optional), and corresponding QMF command. For example:

Verb   Object   Command

```
COMPUTE  SHIPMENTS     TSO %CITYLIST PARM ('&ALL')
```

"COMPUTE SHIPMENTS" is a synonym for the indicated command; the verb is COMPUTE, and the object is SHIPMENTS. "PARM ('&ALL')" means that any additional information coded when entering the synonym is to be passed to the CLIST (i.e., CITYLIST). For example, if the user enters

```
COMPUTE SHIPMENTS ( FORM = CITYFORM  CITYNAME = 'London' )
```

the CLIST called CITYLIST is invoked and passed the text between the parentheses. This ability to pass text is useful for passing parameter values to an application that executes parameterized QMF queries.

Several synonyms can exist with the same verb, provided each has a different object. QMF's order of search for commands is:

1. Look in the synonym table for a verb/object match; if no match is found, or if no object was specified, then

2. Look in the synonym table for a verb match; if no match is found, then

3. Assume it is a QMF-supplied command.

Synonyms can be assigned to PF keys (see the next subsection).

PF Key Customization

Users can customize the PF key settings on QMF panels: Existing settings can be changed, and unassigned keys can be set, so that (in general) any key can be used for any QMF command or command synonym. The specific settings to be used during a specific QMF session are specified by an appropriate PF key table, which is defined in the user's QMF profile.

Application Support Commands

There are four special commands—INTERACT, MESSAGE, QMF, and STATE—that are specifically intended for use in QMF applications. They enable the application to carry out operations such as interrogating the QMF profile or passing a message out to the end-user via QMF.

- INTERACT

  Normally, as mentioned earlier, when a command is executed through the QMF Command Interface, no interactive communication takes place with the end-user. However, if the application is in fact being executed interactively (i.e., not in QMF batch), it can use the INTERACT command to perform such interactive communication. INTERACT invokes some other QMF command (such as EXPORT) and causes that command to display help, prompt, and status information to the end-user exactly as if it had been executed directly. For example, the following command—

  ```
  ISPEXEC SELECT PGM (DSQCCI)
              PARM (INTERACT EXPORT REPORT TO CITYFILE)
  ```

  —will not only execute the specified EXPORT command, but will also cause status information regarding that command to be displayed to the QMF end-user.

- MESSAGE

  QMF applications can issue their own messages to the QMF user by executing the MESSAGE command. This command can also be used in a QMF procedure. At the end of the CLIST application CITYLIST, for example, we might issue the command

  ```
  ISPEXEC SELECT PGM (DSQCCI)
              PARM (MESSAGE (TEXT='EXPORT COMPLETE'))
  ```

  to inform the user that the query was executed and the data exported successfully.

- QMF

  Normally, as explained earlier, when a command is issued, QMF searches the synonym table first to see if the command is installation-defined, before assuming it is QMF-supplied. There may be situations (to be avoided whenever possible) where an installation-defined command and a QMF-supplied command have the same name. To execute the QMF-supplied command in such a case, the synonym table search must be bypassed. The QMF command is provided for this purpose. For example, the command

  ```
  QMF RUN CITYPROC
  ```

  will execute the QMF-supplied RUN command, even if "RUN CITYPROC" is in fact a valid installation-defined command also.

- STATE

  The STATE command is used by a QMF application to retrieve information about the user's QMF profile settings. The command is executed though the Command Interface. It has no operands.

Externalized Items

The EXPORT and IMPORT commands let users transfer QMF items to and from TSO data sets. EXPORT allows DATA, FORM, PROC, QUERY, REPORT, and CHART items to be exported; it is useful for transferring items to other products for further analysis and/or modification outside the QMF environment. The IMPORT command allows DATA, FORM, PROC, and QUERY items to be imported; it is useful for importing externally created items, and for reimporting items that have been previously exported and then modified. In particular, EXPORT and IMPORT allow items to be moved from one QMF system to another.

Note 1: In addition to its own export/import file formats (see the QMF manuals for details), QMF also supports the transfer of data into and out of Integration Exchange Format (IXF) files. See Section 18.4 for a brief discussion of IXF.

Note 2: The EXPORT and IMPORT commands can also be applied to DB2 tables. A DB2 table can be exported to or imported from a TSO data set or an IXF file.

QMF-Supplied Applications

The facilities described in the body of this section permit DP professional users to build their own customized QMF applications. QMF also provides a number of *builtin* applications. We conclude this section by briefly summarizing the purposes of those applications:

- BATCH: Allows queries and procedures to be run in batch mode (QMF batch), rather than interactively.
- BUILDQ: Lets users build queries using prompt screens.
- DPRE: Displays reports as they would appear on a printer.
- ISPF: Invokes ISPF (see Section 19.7 for more details).

19.7 INTERFACING TO OTHER PRODUCTS

We have already seen in Section 19.6 how QMF can interface to other IBM products using the EXPORT and IMPORT commands. In this section we will look at additional ways of communicating with other products. The products in question are:

- Data Extract (DXT)
- Interactive System Productivity Facility/Program Development Facility (ISPF/PDF)
- Document processors such as Document Composition Facility (DCF)

Accessing DXT

As mentioned in Chapter 18, DXT is IBM's copy management tool for extracting data from operational files (VSAM and sequential) and databases (IMS, DB2, and SQL/DS) for loading into DB2 and SQL/DS tables. DXT provides a set of *end-user dialogs* for defining, modifying, and executing extract requests. These dialogs can be invoked from QMF using the QMF EXTRACT command. There are two ways of coding this command:

1. If the command is entered with no operands, the DXT main menu will be displayed. The user can then interactively create and/or edit a DXT request.

2. Alternatively, the command can include the name of an existing DXT extract request. For example, the command

   ```
   EXTRACT PART1
   ```

   will cause DXT to submit the extract request called PART1. In this case, there is no question of creating or editing the request before it is executed; the user is simply told that the request has been sent to DXT.

DXT is discussed in more detail in Chapter 23.

Using ISPF/PDF

ISPF/PDF is an application development tool for the TSO environment. Entering the QMF command

```
ISPF
```

will display the ISPF/PDF main menu, from which any of the ISPF/PDF options can be executed. Specific option panels can be invoked directly by entering the appropriate option number with the ISPF command as in the following example:

```
ISPF 3
```

Using the Document Interface

It is possible to embed a QMF report in a conventional text file by means of a special command (actually a macro) called GETQMF, which can be invoked from the appropriate text editor environment (e.g., the ISPF/PDF Editor environment). As an example, the command

```
GETQMF ASIS DSN MYFILE
```

causes the report stored in the data set named MYFILE to be embedded in the text file currently being edited (DSN stands for "data set name"). The ASIS option causes the report to be embedded "as is" (the alternative to ASIS is DCF—see below).

Here is another example:

```
GETQMF DCF USEQMF
```

The USEQMF option causes QMF to be invoked, thereby enabling the user to create the required report dynamically. The DCF option ("Document Composition Facility") causes SCRIPT/VS control words to be placed at the start and end, at each page eject, and at the heading and footing of each page in the generated report before it is embedded in the text file.

It is also possible to invoke an editor from QMF (via the EDIT command—see Section 19.5), use that editor to edit a file, and, as part of that editing process, invoke GETQMF to embed a QMF report in that file. In this case the GETQMF command must specify an existing QMF procedure to be executed to generate the report. For example:

```
GETQMF ASIS USEQMF MYPROC
```

The procedure MYPROC will be invoked (via the QMF Command Interface) to produce the required report.

19.8 CONCLUSION

In this chapter, we have presented a comprehensive survey of the capabilities of QMF. QMF provides a set of easy-to-use facilities by which end-users can create their own queries and produce reports and charts (graphs) from the results of those queries. It also provides a set of application support facilities and a set of interfaces to certain other IBM products, all of which can be useful to the DP professional in constructing highly customized applications that make use of the features of QMF. However, QMF is not a complete solution to the application development problem; it does not include any decision support tools or end-user application generation facilities, and its report-writing capabilities are fairly unsophisticated. If the installation has more demanding requirements—requirements that cannot be satisfied by QMF—then a product such as IBM's Application System (AS) must be used instead. AS is covered in the next chapter.

C H A P T E R

·20·

Application System

20.1 INTRODUCTION

Application System (AS) is an end-user query, decision support, and application development tool. Like QMF, it operates with both DB2 (under MVS/TSO) and SQL/DS (under VM/CMS); it also supports VSAM and sequential files, as well as "AS tables," i.e., files stored in AS's own format.* A PC version is also available. We focus in this book on the use of AS with DB2.

As shown in Fig. 20.1, AS consists of a central file system, an integrated set of application tools, and interfaces to external files and databases. The central file system, in turn, consists of:

- The AS data dictionary, which contains descriptions of all AS tables;
- AS data tables;

---

*Throughout this chapter we will take the unqualified term "table" to mean an AS table specifically. We will use the explicitly qualified term "DB2 table" when we need to refer to a table in a DB2 database.

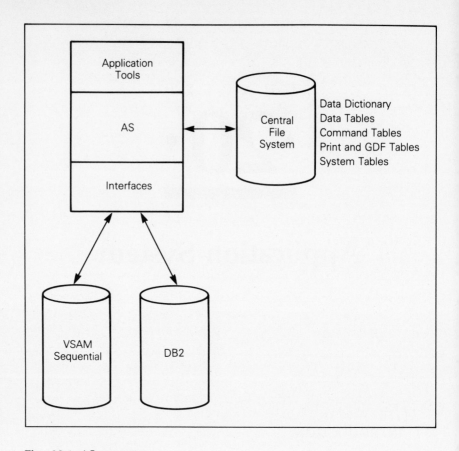

Fig. 20.1 AS structure

- User-created "command tables" containing AS commands or language statements;

- Print tables ("center files") and Graphics Data Format (GDF) tables containing print and graphic output; and

- Temporary system tables used to hold data and language statements created during the user session.

AS operation is controlled by commands or statements in the AS command language ("AS language statements"). Each individual AS tool has its own set of specialized commands; in addition, AS provides a set of generalized commands for common functions, such as exporting and importing data to and from other IBM products. The main AS tools and their functions are as follows:

Compose — to create text files and documents
Draw   — to build customized charts
Edit   — to create procedures for validating data
Image   — to define screens for data entry and display
Memo   — to write memos
Model   — to build company and financial models
Network — to manage a project plan
Procedure — to create canned AS procedures
Query   — to create AS or SQL queries
Report   — to format customized reports
Statistics — to perform statistical and forecasting functions
Tabulate — to perform data analysis
Update   — to update AS or DB2 tables

In general, the user can interact with an individual AS tool in three different modes, namely Command Mode, Conversational Mode, and Interactive Mode (though not all tools support all three).

1. In *Command Mode,* the user enters commands in the AS *command area.* The command area is located near the bottom of the terminal screen and is identified by a question mark ("?").

2. In *Conversational Mode,* AS conducts a dialog with the user to generate the required commands. These commands can then be modified, executed, or saved for later use.

3. In *Interactive Mode,* AS uses windowing facilities and PF keys to perform the required functions. Most tools that support this mode of operation will optionally produce an equivalent set of AS commands as output, which can then be modified, executed, or saved for later use.

Examples in this chapter show the use of all three modes.

Commands can be stored in command tables, which are created and modified using the AS language editor; this facility permits sets of commands to be saved for later use. All commands are checked by the language editor for syntax errors as they are entered (with the sole exception of SQL SELECT statements entered via the AS Query tool; such statements are not checked until they are executed).

The command for invoking an AS tool has the general form

```
tool  input-table, output-table
```

where:

- "tool" is the tool to be invoked;
- "input-table" identifies an existing input command table (an asterisk means no input); and

- ''output-table'' identifies an output command table (either an existing table whose contents are to be replaced or a new table to be created).

For example, the command

```
QUERY *,CITYQRY
```

invokes the Query tool and causes a new output command table to be created called CITYQRY. The user can now create and store a DB2 query (SQL SELECT statement) in that table. If no output table is specified (second argument left blank), AS will create a ''system table'' automatically, assigning it a system-generated name. At the end of the session, AS will ask the user which system tables are to be kept (if any).

The plan of the rest of the chapter is as follows.

- First, we consider the use of SQL with AS. (*Note:* To access DB2, the user can use either AS commands or SQL statements. If AS commands are used, AS will convert them into corresponding SQL statements. In this chapter we concentrate on SQL, for reasons of familiarity.) SQL statements can be entered and executed in AS by means of the AS QUERY and DB2 commands:

  - The QUERY command invokes the Query tool, which is used to enter and execute SQL SELECT statements (only). Once the required data has been retrieved, the Report and Draw tools can be used to produce tailored reports and charts from the retrieved data. Sections 20.2, 20.3, and 20.4 contain detailed discussions of query creation and execution, report formatting, and chart creation, respectively.

  - SQL statements other than SELECT are entered and executed using the DB2 command. Section 20.5 shows how this command can be used to perform data modification, data definition, and authorization operations.

- As already mentioned, AS commands can be stored in command tables. A command table can be regarded as a ''canned'' application or procedure that can be run on a regular basis, via the AS RUN command. Such procedures can vary in complexity considerably; simple procedures might be constructed by an end-user, but more complicated ones would typically be created by a person with programming skills. Sections 20.6 and 20.7 discuss the use of basic procedures and more complex procedures, respectively. Section 20.7 also looks at other AS application development facilities, including the AS Image and Edit tools, which are used to build data entry and validation applications.

- There are several ways of interfacing AS to other IBM products. For example, AS provides commands to allow the AS user to communicate with IBM's DXT and QMF products. Also, the IMPORT and EXPORT commands allow data to be transported between AS systems, and between AS and any other product that supports IBM's Integration Exchange Format (IXF). This subject is discussed in Section 20.8.

- Finally, AS also provides a variety of additional facilities: data analysis and statistics tools, a business planning facility, a project management feature, text processing tools, and an application preparation facility. A brief overview of these facilities is presented in Section 20.9.

20.2 CREATING AND EXECUTING A QUERY

After logging on to TSO and invoking AS, the user is presented with the AS Application Code screen (Fig. 20.2), which lists the "application codes" currently available to this user. An application code is really just shorthand for a list of AS table names; it identifies the set of tables that can be accessed under this particular code. From the Application Code screen, the user can either select one of the existing codes or create a new one. In the example, the code PART has been selected ("PART" has been typed in the command area). Any AS tables created during the AS session will now be associated with this application code.

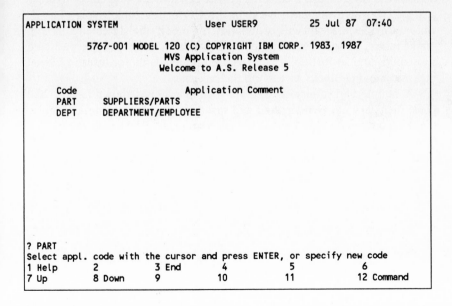

Fig. 20.2 The AS Application Code screen

In order to access DB2 from AS, the user must first issue an appropriate ATTACH command—for example:

```
ATTACH DB2, SYSTEM(DB2A)
```

This command will connect AS to the DB2 system named DB2A. Options on the ATTACH command permit the specification of such matters as the tablespace and database in which new DB2 tables are to be created, whether SQL LABELS are to be used as column titles in reports, and so forth. (One option in particular, DEFAULT, allows the user to specify that input tables are to be found, and output tables stored, in a certain default location if no other location is specified explicitly. For example, DEFAULT(DB2) means the default location is the DB2 system with which AS is in communication. DEFAULT(AS) is assumed if nothing else is specified.)

Once AS has been connected to the DB2 system, the user can perform DB2 operations—in particular, SQL SELECT statements. SELECT statements are created and executed via the AS Query tool, which is invoked via the QUERY command. For example:

```
QUERY *,CITYQRY
```

This command creates an output command table called CITYQRY and invokes the AS full-screen editor. The user can now use that editor to create a SELECT statement and save it in the CITYQRY table. *Note:* The AS editor provides a set of edit commands for modifying statements in command tables, merging in other command tables, searching for particular substrings, and so forth. Commands are also available for inserting, deleting, and moving blocks of text on the screen.

A sample SQL query entered via the AS editor is shown in Fig. 20.3. Once the query has been created and saved in the output command table,* the user can validate and execute it by issuing the RUN and VIEW commands; RUN passes the query to DB2 for validation and preparation (dynamic SQL PREPARE, etc.), VIEW causes the data to be retrieved. For example (assuming that the query has been saved in CITYQRY):

```
RUN CITYQRY
VIEW
```

The result is shown in Fig. 20.4.

---

*The query can be saved in the output command table by means of PF key 3. (It can also be saved and then immediately RUN by means of PF key 2.) A saved query can be made available to other users via the AS SHARE command; such privileges can subsequently be revoked via the AS WITHDRAW command.

```
QUERY *,CITYQRY                        Origin 1              4 Lines

SELECT    S.CITY, S.S#, SP.P#, SP.QTY                         00001
FROM      S, SP                                               00002
WHERE     S.S# = SP.S#                                        00003
ORDER BY  S.CITY, S.S#, SP.P#                                 00004




?
1                 2 Run        3 End        4 Print      5 Recall     6 Origin
7 Up              8 Down       9 Switch     10 Left      11 Right     12 Command
```

Fig. 20.3 Sample AS query (SQL)

```
VIEW     QUERY(CITYQRY)                            25 Jul 87   07:55
                                                                 1/1
CITY            S#      P#           QTY                      Action
London          S1      P1           300
London          S1      P2           200
London          S1      P3           400
London          S1      P4           200
London          S1      P5           100
London          S1      P6           100
London          S4      P2           200
London          S4      P4           300
London          S4      P5           400
Paris           S2      P1           300
Paris           S2      P2           400
Paris           S3      P2           200




?
1                 2 Input      3 End        4 Print      5 Recall     6 Top
7 Up              8 Down       9 Switch     10 Left      11 Right     12 Command
```

Fig. 20.4 Output for the query of Fig. 20.3

Note: The AS VIEW command typically does *not* retrieve the entire set of result rows all at once. Instead, what happens is the following. Initially, enough rows are fetched to fill the terminal screen; those rows are also kept in an internal file (in main storage if possible, otherwise in an AS table). Backward scrolling merely redisplays rows already retrieved. Forward scrolling retrieves more result rows if necessary and adds them to the internal file. (In contrast to the VIEW command, other AS commands do retrieve the entire set of result rows all at once.)

Parameters are permitted in saved queries. For example, if the query

```
SELECT S#, SNAME
FROM   S
WHERE  CITY = @1
```

is saved in the command table CITYQRY, it can be executed later using the commands

```
RUN CITYQRY, @PASS(''London'')
VIEW
```

Saving Query Results

The result of a query can be stored in an AS or DB2 table using the OUT and COPY commands in place of the VIEW command. For example, the commands

```
RUN CITYQRY
OUT CITYFILE
COPY
```

will create an AS table named CITYFILE and store the data in that table. (If the OUT command is omitted, the data will be stored in a system-generated table, and the user will be asked at the end of the session whether that table is to be kept.) Alternatively, the commands

```
RUN CITYQRY
OUT (DB2) CITYFILE
COPY
```

will create a DB2 table named CITYFILE and store the data there.

Query results can also be used as input to other AS tools such as Report, Draw, etc. (see Sections 20.3 and 20.4).

AS Language Queries

As stated in Section 20.1, the user can access DB2 using either AS commands or SQL statements. By way of example, we show an AS command version of the SQL query of Fig. 20.3.

```
IN (DB2) S
INCLUDE (DB2) SP(S#)
SEQUENCE CITY, S#, P#
VIEW CITY, S#, P#, QTY
```

The IN command identifies the DB2 suppliers table (table S) as the primary input table; the INCLUDE command joins the DB2 shipments table (table SP) to that primary table over matching supplier numbers; the SEQUENCE command defines the result row order; and the VIEW command defines the result columns and displays the result table.

Additional search conditions can be specified by means of the AS SELECT command (not the SQL SELECT statement!). For example, if we had specified

```
SELECT QTY > 300
```

between the INCLUDE and SEQUENCE commands (see above), the effect would have been to restrict the result to just those rows with a shipment quantity greater than 300. Alternatively, we could execute the IN–INCLUDE–SEQUENCE–VIEW statements as previously shown (to produce the result shown in Fig. 20.3), and then execute a SELECT and another VIEW—for example,

```
SELECT QTY > 300
VIEW S#, P#, QTY
```

—in which case the effect would be to produce a new set of output rows, derived from the previous output in accordance with the specified SELECT and VIEW statements.

Using AS commands instead of SQL statements does have a number of advantages:

1. The same commands can be used regardless of the type of table or file being accessed (DB2, VSAM, etc.).

2. The commands can be entered directly into the command area (it is not necessary to create a command table).

3. The AS SELECT statement supports *data browsing*. That is, the user can issue one query, look at the result, issue a SELECT (and VIEW) to refine the result further, etc. SQL does not provide a comparable facility.

20.3 CREATING A REPORT

Reports are defined and created by means of the AS Report tool. The data to be reported on can be an existing AS or DB2 table (identified by an IN command), or it can be the result of an AS query (produced by a RUN command). The report format is defined via one of the following:

1. AS language editor Report statements (Command Mode)
2. The conversational Report facility (Conversational Mode)
3. The interactive Report facility (Interactive Mode)

We briefly consider each in turn.

Command Mode

The AS language editor is invoked via the REPORT command. Report statements are entered and modified in a manner similar to that discussed in Section 20.2 for the Query component. For example, if the command sequence

```
RUN CITYQRY
REPORT *,CITYREP
```

is issued, AS will run the query stored in CITYQRY (as discussed in the previous section), then create an output command table called CITYREP. The user can now define a report to be produced from the result of the query by entering Report language statements into the CITYREP table, using the AS editor. (Some examples of Report language statements are discussed in the next subsection below.) The report can then be generated and displayed at the terminal using the RUN command:

```
RUN CITYREP
```

Conversational Mode

The Conversational Mode of operation is invoked by the ?REPORT command. For example, the command

```
?REPORT CITYREP
```

will start a question and answer dialog about the format of the required report. When the dialog is complete, AS will create a command table called CITYREP containing the required Report language statements. Those statements can then be executed by means of the RUN command in the usual way; alternatively, the statements can be edited, using Command Mode, to create a more customized report definition (in other words, Conversational Mode provides an easy way of generating an initial report definition for subsequent tailoring).

Fig. 20.5 shows an example of the use of Conversational Mode to define a simple report using the data retrieved via the query of Fig. 20.3. We have requested a display title (note that the title will include the page number and the current date and time); we have also requested AS to calculate subtotals (for numeric fields) each time the CITY value changes. The resulting report is shown in Fig. 20.6.

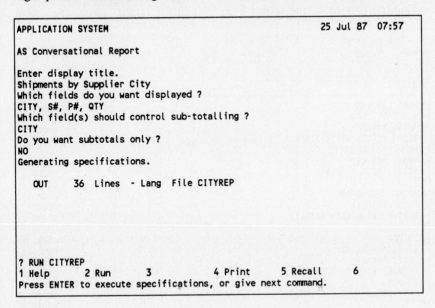

```
APPLICATION SYSTEM                              25 Jul 87  07:57

AS Conversational Report

Enter display title.
Shipments by Supplier City
Which fields do you want displayed ?
CITY, S#, P#, QTY
Which field(s) should control sub-totalling ?
CITY
Do you want subtotals only ?
NO
Generating specifications.

   OUT    36 Lines  - Lang  File CITYREP




? RUN CITYREP
1 Help      2 Run      3           4 Print     5 Recall     6
Press ENTER to execute specifications, or give next command.
```

Fig. 20.5 Defining a report using Conversational Mode

```
Page   1                 Shipments by Supplier City    25 Jul 87  08:03

CITY          S#     P#       QTY

London        S1     P1       300
              S1     P2       200
              S1     P3       400
              S1     P4       200
              S1     P5       100
              S1     P6       100
              S4     P2       200
              S4     P4       300
              S4     P5       400
                              -------
London                        2200

Paris         S2     P1       300
              S2     P2       400
              S3     P2       200
                              -------
Paris                         900
                              =======
                              3100
```

Fig. 20.6 Formatted report for the query of Fig. 20.3

The Report language statements created by AS in response to the dialog of Fig. 20.5 are shown in Fig. 20.7. The *format statements* F1, F2, etc., define the format of the report lines. When the report is run, the report

```
REPORT CITYREP                      Origin 1                    36 Lines

HEADING @PAGE                                                       00001
  PRINT F(1,0,'WHITE'),@PAGE,'Shipments by Supplier City',@DATE,@RUN TI 00002
  ME
  PRINT SKIP(1)                                                     00003
  PRINT F(2,0,'GREEN')                                             00004
*                                                                   00005
HEADING CITY,@PAGE                                                  00006
  PRINT SKIP(1)                                                     00007
  DEFINE !HEAD(A5)='PRINT'                                          00008
*                                                                   00009
DETAIL                                                              00010
  IF !HEAD='PRINT'                                                  00011
    LET !HEAD=' '                                                   00012
    PRINT F(4),CITY,S#,P#,QTY                                       00013
  IF NOT                                                            00014
    PRINT F(5)      ,S#,P#,QTY                                      00015
*                                                                   00016
TOTAL CITY                                                          00017
  PRINT F(6)                                                        00018
  PRINT F(8),LAST(CITY),TOTAL(QTY)                                  00019
*                                                                   00020
TOTAL                                                               00021
  PRINT SKIP(1)                                                     00022
  PRINT F(7)                                                        00023
  PRINT F(8),' '        ,TOTAL(QTY)                                 00024
  PRINT F(7)                                                        00025
*                                                                   00026
TOTAL @END OF PAGE                                                  00027
  PRINT SKIP(-1)                                                    00028
*                                                                   00029
F1: Page ####            &&&&&&&&&&&&&&&&&&&&&&&&&      DD MMM YY 00030
  #####
F2:CITY              S#     P#     QTY                              00031
F4:&&&&&&&&&&&&&& &&&&&& &&&&&& &&&&&&&                             00032
F5:              &&&&&& &&&&&& &&&&&&&                             00033
F6:                           -------                              00034
F7:                           =======                              00035
F8:&&&&&&&&&&&&&&           &&&&&&&                                 00036
                                                                    00037
1          2 Run     3 End      4 Hardcopy  5 Recall    6 Origin
7 Up       8 Down    9 Switch   10 Left     11 Right    12 Command
```

Fig. 20.7 Generated report statements

lines will be filled with data and displayed at the terminal as directed by the Report language PRINT statements. Observe that those PRINT statements include references to the format statements; for example, line 00025 includes a reference to the format statement F7.

Note: Output can be sent to an AS "center file" instead of to the terminal by replacing each PRINT statement by a CENTER statement (CENTER here meaning "DP Center"). Alternatively, the RUN command itself can specify that all PRINT statements are to be (logically) replaced by CENTER statements for the duration of this run only. For example:

```
RUN CITYREP,PRINT=CENTER
```

AS center files are printed using standard MVS facilities.

The reader is referred to the AS manuals for a more detailed discussion of AS Report statements.

Interactive Mode

Interactive Mode is a more powerful alternative to Conversational Mode. It allows many more formatting options and will frequently eliminate the need to use Report language statements entirely. As in Conversational Mode, a command table is generated to allow the user to modify the generated Report statements should such modification be required. A sample screen from Interactive Mode is shown in Fig. 20.8.

The big advantage of Interactive Mode is that users see the effects of their actions immediately. When the Report tool is invoked, the input data is displayed at the terminal. Pressing PF key 6 will display an option list, which can be used to display option windows to control the format of the report. Fig. 20.8 shows a *Column Detail* window, which can be used to modify such things as the column heading and width. In the example, we assume that a number of such modifications have already been made (compare the displayed report, partially visible behind the Column Detail window, with the earlier version shown in Fig. 20.6).

The option windows permit the user to specify:

- the overall layout and structure of each page
- the content and position of the top and bottom titles
- the columns required, their headings, width, and layout
- how data is to be totaled, subtotaled, and ordered

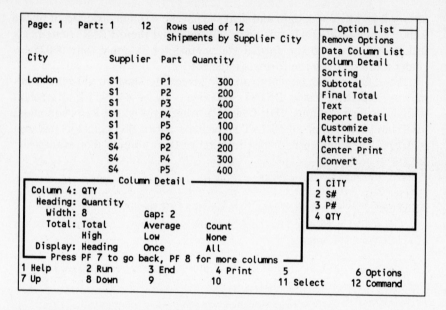

```
Page: 1   Part: 1      12   Rows used of 12         ─── Option List ───
                            Shipments by Supplier City  Remove Options
                                                        Data Column List
 City              Supplier  Part  Quantity             Column Detail
                                                        Sorting
 London            S1        P1       300               Subtotal
                   S1        P2       200               Final Total
                   S1        P3       400               Text
                   S1        P4       200               Report Detail
                   S1        P5       100               Customize
                   S1        P6       100               Attributes
                   S4        P2       200               Center Print
                   S4        P4       300               Convert
                   S4        P5       400
         ──── Column Detail ────                       ┌──────────────┐
  Column 4: QTY                                        │ 1 CITY       │
   Heading: Quantity                                   │ 2 S#         │
     Width: 8              Gap: 2                       │ 3 P#         │
     Total: Total          Average    Count            │ 4 QTY        │
            High           Low        None             │              │
   Display: Heading        Once       All              └──────────────┘
    ─── Press PF 7 to go back, PF 8 for more columns ───
 1 Help        2 Run       3 End        4 Print     5              6 Options
 7 Up          8 Down      9            10          11 Select     12 Command
```

Fig. 20.8 Defining a report using Interactive Mode

- the format, color, and font of any report component
- whether the report is to be printed on a system printer

More detailed formatting, to add procedural logic, for example, can be done by editing the generated command table. Again, the reader is referred to the AS manuals for further information.

20.4   CREATING A CHART

Section 20.3 explained what is involved in creating an AS report. Another way of presenting data is to use the AS Draw tool to create a chart or graph. The Draw tool uses the Presentation Graphics Facility (PGF) of the IBM Graphic Data Display Manager (GDDM) to display charts. The chart types supported by AS are TOWER, MAP, RADAR, PIE, SCATTER, LINE, SURFACE, HISTOGRAM, and MIXED (as with the analogous feature of QMF, these names are supposed to be self-explanatory). *Note:* The Interactive Chart Utility (ICU) of GDDM can also be used to construct and display charts. It is invoked using the AS ICU command. However, we do not discuss this latter facility here; instead, we restrict our attention to the AS Draw tool specifically.

Fig. 20.9 shows the Draw tool primary screen, which is displayed by means of the AS DRAW command. The user must enter the names of the input and output specification tables. These tables are a special type of command table used to store chart specifications; they cannot be edited by the AS language editor, but can be modified by the Draw tool. Other information entered on the primary screen includes the type of chart being produced—a bar chart (histogram) in our example—and the information (X- and Y-variables) to be plotted on the chart. Once this data has been entered, a "default chart" can be displayed by pressing PF key 2.

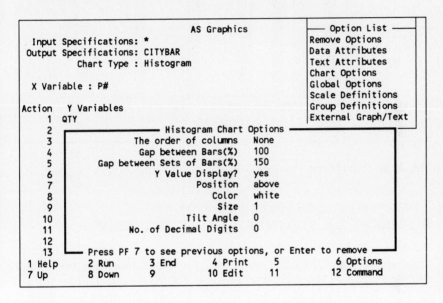

```
                        AS Graphics        ┌─── Option List ───┐
  Input Specifications: *                  │Remove Options
Output Specifications: CITYBAR             │Data Attributes
            Chart Type : Histogram         │Text Attributes
                                           │Chart Options
  X Variable : P#                          │Global Options
                                           │Scale Definitions
Action   Y Variables                       │Group Definitions
     1   QTY                               │External Graph/Text
     2        ┌──────── Histogram Chart Options ────────┐
     3        │          The order of columns    None   │
     4        │           Gap between Bars(%)    100    │
     5        │      Gap between Sets of Bars(%) 150    │
     6        │              Y Value Display?    yes    │
     7        │                    Position      above  │
     8        │                       Color      white  │
     9        │                        Size      1      │
    10        │                  Tilt Angle      0      │
    11        │          No. of Decimal Digits   0      │
    12        │                                         │
    13        └─ Press PF 7 to see previous options, or Enter to remove ─┘
 1 Help      2 Run      3 End       4 Print     5            6 Options
 7 Up        8 Down     9          10 Edit     11           12 Command
```

Fig. 20.9 Defining a bar chart

The default chart can be tailored using option windows in a manner similar to that discussed in Section 20.3 for tailoring AS reports (Interactive Mode). The option list is displayed by pressing PF key 6. Various option windows can then be selected to do the tailoring. Fig. 20.9 shows an example of a *Chart Options* window, which has been used to modify the spacing of the bars in the chart and to label the bars with Y-variable values. The resulting chart is shown in Fig. 20.10. This chart can be saved by first pressing the Enter key to display the PF key legends and then pressing PF key 5. Chart output is stored in AS Graphics Data Format (GDF) tables. These tables can be displayed using the AS REVIEW command. Chart output can also be directed to a printer by pressing PF key 4.

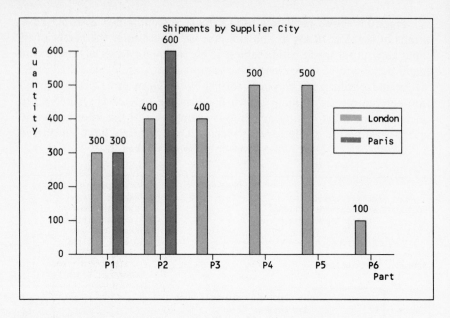

Fig. 20.10 Sample bar chart

20.5 USING SQL STATEMENTS OTHER THAN SELECT

We have seen in Section 20.2 that the AS Query tool can be used to enter and execute SQL SELECT statements. For SQL statements other than SELECT, AS provides the DB2 command. This command supports the use of SQL data modification, data definition, and authorization definition statements.

There are three ways to enter SQL statements with the DB2 command:

1. Using the AS command screen

   If the DB2 command is entered without any parameters, an empty screen is displayed (the AS command screen), which can be used to enter a single SQL statement. Once the statement has been entered, pressing PF key 3 will pass it to DB2 for execution.

2. From the AS command line

   In this mode the user types in the SQL statement as a parameter of the DB2 command. The statement is executed immediately. To create an index on column S# of the DB2 shipments table (table SP), for example, we could enter

```
DB2 CREATE INDEX XSPS ON SP ( S# )
```

on the AS command line.

3. From an AS procedure

   AS commands can be embedded in AS procedures. Therefore, any DB2 command (and hence any SQL statement supported by AS) can be included in such a procedure. Procedures are discussed in more detail in the next section.

AS provides several commands of its own that can be used in place of SQL statements. We have already seen (in Section 20.2) how the OUT and COPY commands can be used to create and populate a DB2 table. A brief summary of the AS commands that generate SQL statements other than SELECT is presented below (the SQL statements generated are also shown in each case):

- SHARE   — grant authority (GRANT)
- WITHDRAW — remove authority (REVOKE)
- OUT/COPY — create and populate a table (CREATE TABLE plus INSERT ... SELECT)
- CLEAR   — delete all rows (DELETE)
- PURGE   — delete a table (DROP)
- UPDATE   — insert, update, or delete data (see below)

The commands are all basically self-explanatory, except for the last one, UPDATE. The UPDATE command invokes the Update tool. We explain that tool by means of an example. Suppose we have an AS table SNEW containing a set of new supplier rows to be added to the DB2 suppliers table (table S). Suppose also that an AS command table called UPDSTMT already exists, containing Update language statements that specify exactly how the AS table SNEW is to be used to update the DB2 table S (see below for more details). That table will have been created via the UPDATE command, which invokes the AS editor and permits the creation and/or modification of Update language statements. Now consider the following AS commands:

```
IN (DB2) S, SNEW
MERGE S#
OUT (DB2) S
RUN UPDSTMT
```

These four AS commands have the following effect:

- The IN command specifies the DB2 table to be updated (table S) and the table that contains the updating information (SNEW). *Note:* SNEW is an AS table in our example, but in general it too could be a DB2 table.

- The MERGE command is used to pair the rows of the two tables based on matching values of column S.S# and column SNEW.S#.

- The OUT command indicates where the output is to be written.

- Finally, the RUN command causes the Update statements in the command table UPDSTMT to be executed. The effect is as follows:

  - AS reads each row of the SNEW table and uses it to access the S table.

  - For each SNEW row, if a match is found, it sets a special variable called @MATCH; if not, it sets a variable called @DETAIL.

  - These variables will be used in Update statements in the UPDSTMT command table to control the update process. For example, the statement

```
WHEN @MATCH
    PRINT 'Error :', S#, ' supplier already exists'
```

  tests the variable @MATCH; if it is set, the statement then displays an error message informing the user that the supplier number of the SNEW row already exists in the supplier table.

Update language statements can also be used to perform UPDATE and DELETE operations. In this case, the table that contains the updating information must include a column whose values indicate the rows to be UPDATEd or DELETEd. This column is referenced by Update language statements to control the UPDATE or DELETE operation. The reader is referred to the AS manuals for a more detailed discussion of the Update language.

20.6 PROCEDURES

A procedure—more precisely, a procedure table—consists of a named set of *generalized* AS commands (as opposed to the specialized AS commands used with each individual AS tool; refer back to Section 20.1 if you need to refresh your memory regarding the distinction between the two). Such procedures can be invoked by means of the AS RUN command. In this section we introduce the basic ideas of AS procedures; the next section then discusses some of the more sophisticated aspects of this facility.

Like other command tables, procedures are created using the AS language editor. To create a procedure called CITYPROC, for example, the user would enter the command

```
PROCEDURE *,CITYPROC
```

The statements constituting the procedure can now be created, using the AS editor. Here is a simple example:

```
/* CITYPROC procedure
*
* run the query called CITYQRY
RUN CITYQRY
*
* run the report called CITYREP
* redirect the output to an AS print file
RUN CITYREP,PRINT=CENTER
*
/* end of CITYPROC
```

Note: All lines in this procedure except the two RUN commands are comment lines. Comments prefixed by "*" are displayed at the terminal when the procedure is executed, comments prefixed by "/*" are not.

20.7 APPLICATION SUPPORT FACILITIES

In addition to its standard end-user tools, AS provides a set of *application support facilities* for extending its capabilities in a variety of ways:

- *AS Procedures:* The AS procedure language provides facilities for building complex applications.
- *Image Tool:* The Image tool is used to build tailored screens for data entry and display.
- *Edit Tool:* The Edit tool provides statements to validate data read from terminals and input tables.
- *Command Interface:* The command interface allows application programs to invoke AS facilities.

We briefly describe each of these facilities in turn.

AS Procedures

The previous section showed how simple AS procedures can be created and executed. More complex procedures can be created using the full AS procedure language (which is in effect a full-function programming language). Facilities provided include:

- arithmetic and logical expressions
- constants
- user and system variables
- branching and looping
- nested procedures
- arguments and parameters
- screen displays
- prompting
- PF key definition

Image Tool

Data entry screens are built using the Image tool. As with most AS tools, Image statements are entered using the language editor, invoked in this case by the IMAGE command. Facilities are provided to support the definition of screen attributes, field data types and lengths, default values, validity checks, and so forth, for data entered via the screen. *Note:* The Edit tool can be used to perform more extensive data validation (see below).

Edit Tool

The Edit tool uses procedural language statements for performing data validation checking. These checks can be made against data retrieved from both AS and DB2 input tables, also against data entered using AS Image screens. The validated data is stored in an AS or DB2 output table. The Edit tool is invoked using the EDIT command.

Command Interface

The AS command interface permits an application program to call AS to perform some AS operation and return the result(s) to the application. Such applications can be written in a conventional programming language such as COBOL or PL/I or in either the CMS REXX or TSO CLIST command language.

20.8 INTERFACING TO OTHER PRODUCTS

In this section, we take a brief look at how AS can interface to three specific IBM products:

- Data Extract (DXT)
- Query Management Facility (QMF)
- Interactive System Productivity Facility (ISPF)

We also briefly describe the AS EXPORT and IMPORT commands, which can be used to exchange data between AS systems and between AS and other products.

Accessing DXT

The AS facilities for interfacing with DXT directly parallel the analogous QMF facilities (see Section 19.7). Thus, the DXT end-user dialogs, which support the definition, modification, and execution of data extract requests, can be invoked from AS using the AS EXTRACT command (directly comparable to the QMF EXTRACT command). There are two ways of coding this command:

1. If the command is entered with no operands, the DXT main menu will be displayed. The user can then interactively create and/or edit a DXT request.
2. Alternatively, the command can include the name of an existing DXT extract request. For example, the command

   `EXTRACT PART1`

   will cause DXT to submit the extract request called PART1.

Using QMF

As explained in Chapter 18 (and amplified in Chapter 19), QMF is an end-user query and report writing tool for the DB2 and SQL/DS environments. The facilities of QMF are quite user-friendly but are not as sophisticated as those of AS. There may therefore be situations where the user wants to use QMF to do some initial work and then transfer the results into AS for more detailed processing. The AS QMF command is intended to support this style of operation. It uses the QMF Command Interface (see Section 19.6) to pass a command to QMF for execution. For example, the AS command

`QMF RUN QUERY CITYQUERY`

will request QMF to execute a QMF query named CITYQUERY.

Using ISPF

ISPF is a dialog manager for the TSO environment. If AS is started from ISPF, the AS user can invoke any ISPF dialog (using ISPEXEC), set and retrieve ISPF dialog variables, and use ISPF tables (using the AS IN and OUT commands).

IMPORT and EXPORT Commands

AS supports the export and import of IXF files, also files in AS "transportable format." AS transportable format is used to transfer information between AS systems. To export the AS table CITYDATA into a file named CITYTEMP, the following command could be used:

```
EXPORT CITYDATA, FILE(CITYTEMP) FORMAT(ASTRAN)
```

The keyword ASTRAN indicates that the exported file is to be in AS transportable format (the keyword IXF could be used instead to create a file in IXF format). The ASTRAN-format CITYTEMP file can then be reimported using the command:

```
IMPORT CITYTEMP, REPLACE, FORMAT(ASTRAN), RENAME(CITYDATA)
```

20.9   ADDITIONAL AS FACILITIES

As indicated in Section 20.1, AS provides an extensive set of additional facilities to assist with the following functions:

- data analysis and statistics
- business planning
- project management
- text processing
- application preparation

Each of these facilities is briefly described below.

Data Analysis and Statistics

SQL aggregate functions (SUM, AVG, etc.) can be used to perform very simple statistical analysis of data in DB2 tables. AS augments those functions with its Tabulate and Statistics tools.

1. The Tabulate tool is invoked by the TABULATE command. It performs various arithmetic functions in one, two, or three dimensions (e.g., it could be used to analyze the distribution of parts by supplier

city). The functions supported are total, percentage, average, low, high, and count.

2. The Statistics tool is invoked by the STATISTICS command. It provides a broad range of statistical and forecasting functions, including:

   - descriptive statistics
   - correlations
   - regression
   - time series analysis
   - parametric and nonparametric statistics
   - analysis of variance
   - cluster analysis
   - component analysis

   The tool can operate in Command, Conversational, and Interactive Mode. An interface is provided to the AS Draw tool for displaying results, doing curve-fitting, etc. AS or DB2 tables can be used for both input and output to the Statistics tool. Results from the analysis can also be used as input to other AS tools.

Business Planning

The AS business planning facility provides capabilities similar to those provided by PC spreadsheet tools. Models are constructed using AS Model language statements or by Interactive Mode (as available with the AS Report and Chart tools). Data entered into such models can be supplied from the terminal, read from an AS or DB2 table, or explicitly defined in the model. Output can be stored in an AS or DB2 table for use by other AS tools. There is also a direct linkage into the AS Chart tool.

Project Management

Project planning is performed using the AS Network and Project Management Cost tools. These tools can handle numerous planning functions, including time and risk analysis, progress reporting, project costing, and resource allocation. The project plan can be displayed as an arrow diagram or a precedence diagram. Both AS and DB2 tables can be used for input and output.

Text Processing

AS provides the Memo and Compose tools for text processing. The Memo tool is intended for small documents such as letters and memos. Document formatting is done using the WYSIWYG ("What You See Is What You Get") mode of operation common in most PC word processors. Formatting parameters, such as page width, color attributes, font type, etc., can be changed dynamically at any time. AS tables can also be used to substitute data into memo variables.

Longer and more complex documents can be created using the Compose tool. This tool uses language statements similar to those of IBM's Document Composition Facility (DCF). It supports the building of indexes and tables of contents, box drawing, figure lists, conditional processing, and so forth. Data from AS tables and tools can also be included in a document.

Application Preparation

The Application Preparation Facility (APF) is a simple application generator—i.e., it is a menu-driven tool that allows inexperienced users to build simple AS applications without having to learn AS commands. It uses a full-screen interface to prompt the user for the necessary application specifications: the screens to be used (e.g., for data entry), the tables to be accessed, the reports and charts to be produced, etc. However, the generated application cannot use the AS decision support facilities (statistics, business planning, etc.) discussed earlier in this section.

C H A P T E R

·21·

Cross System Product

21.1 INTRODUCTION

As explained in Chapter 18, IBM provides two principal DP professional application development tools for DB2, namely Cross System Product (CSP) and IMS Application Development Facility II (IMSADF II—ADF for short). We discuss CSP in this chapter and ADF in Chapter 22.

CSP consists of a set of DP professional tools for interactive application development and execution. It is called *Cross System* Product because it permits applications to be developed in one environment for execution in another; for example, a CSP DB2 application can be developed under TSO and executed under CICS. The environments supported by CSP are MVS (CICS, TSO), VM/CMS, SSX, and VSE (CICS), also PC/DOS, OS/2, and OS/400 (application execution only, not application development, in the case of these last three, at least at the time of writing).

CSP is really several products, not just one:

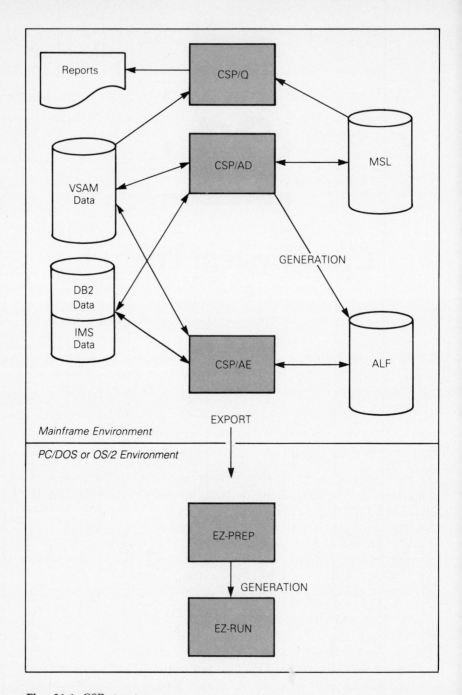

Fig. 21.1 CSP structure

- Cross System Product/Application Development (CSP/AD)
- Cross System Product/Application Execution (CSP/AE)
- EZ-PREP and EZ-RUN
- Cross System Product/Query (CSP/Q)

CSP applications are developed and tested using CSP/AD, and then executed under CSP/AE (see Fig. 21.1). Applications (more accurately, application *specifications*) are stored during development as members of a VSAM data set called the *Member Specification Library* (MSL), which can be thought of as a data dictionary for CSP. When the application has been fully developed, tested, and debugged, it must be "generated" for use in the relevant target environment. The generated form of the application is stored in another VSAM data set called the *Application Load File* (ALF). Export and import utilities exist to migrate MSL and ALF data sets from one CSP environment to another.

The EZ-PREP and EZ-RUN products support the generation and execution but not development) of CSP applications for use on a PC. Development of such applications must have been performed previously using CSP/AD in one of the mainframe environments mentioned above.

The last product in the set, CSP/Q, is a query and report-writing tool for VSAM and CMS data. Definitions of the files to be queried are kept in CSP/AD libraries. Queries are coded using language statements whose syntax is similar to that of SELECT in SQL; they can be saved for later reuse.

CSP applications can access a variety of different databases and files—DB2 tables, IMS databases, VSAM files, and so forth. However, EZ-PREP, EZ-RUN, and CSP/Q do not support DB2; we will therefore make no further mention of those components in this book, but will instead concentrate on the use of CSP/AD and CSP/AE specifically.

21.2 DEVELOPING CSP APPLICATIONS

CSP applications are built and tested using CSP/AD, which supports both DB2 and SQL/DS. Creating an application for SQL/DS is very similar to creating one for DB2; in fact, an application can be built and tested under SQL/DS (e.g., using VM/CMS) for execution under DB2 and vice versa. Fig. 21.2 illustrates the main components of a CSP application, namely record, map, and process definitions. *Note:* Each component has its own name and is stored as a separate member in the Member Specification Library.

- *Record definitions* specify the data to be retrieved and manipulated by the application. A record definition for processing DB2 data consists

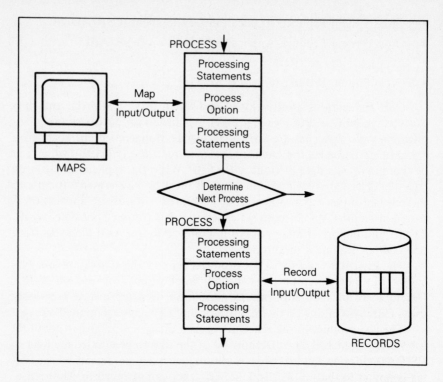

Fig. 21.2 CSP application components

of fields from one or more DB2 tables and is defined using CSP/AD's Record Definition screens. Existing DB2 definitions (for both base tables and views) can be retrieved from the DB2 catalog to help with the record definition process.

- *Map definitions* specify the screen and printer formats to be used by the application. The CSP/AD *screen painter* provides a set of Map Definition screens for defining such formats and for defining data "edit rules." Edit rules are used to validate data entered by the application user or to format data displayed to the application user (such data will be entered or displayed at execution time via the maps). For example, we might define a rule to verify that any value entered for a shipment quantity is greater than 99 (say).

- *Process definitions* specify the application processing logic. Among other things, they control the display of maps and the reading and writing of records. Processes are defined by means of the CSP/AD Application Definition and Application Process Definition screens. A process definition consists of:

- A *process option,* which specifies the major task (data access or map display) to be performed by the process, and

- A set of *processing statements,* which perform computations, control the execution flow from one process to the next, etc.

CSP/AD provides several process options for operating on DB2 data (most of which correspond to SQL operations in a fairly obvious manner). It also provides a wide range of processing statements.

Once the application definition is complete, testing can begin. During testing, all access to DB2 data is performed using dynamic SQL (described in Chapter 15). Trace information about the processing of SQL statements can be displayed to the application developer for debugging purposes. When the application has been fully tested and debugged, it can be generated for execution under CSP/AE. At this time, the developer must decide whether the application is to execute in "dynamic mode" or "static mode." Dynamic mode uses dynamic SQL (as in CSP/AD), static mode uses static SQL; static mode is more efficient, but of course requires additional steps during the generation process (to precompile and bind the SQL statements created by CSP/AD). When generation is complete, the application is ready for execution under CSP/AE (except that, if the CSP/AD and CSP/AE operating environments are not the same, utilities will have to be used to move the generated application to the target system).

We have now summarized all of the major tasks involved in developing CSP applications. Before we move on to discuss those tasks in detail, we briefly describe the layout of CSP/AD screens and indicate what is involved in communicating with CSP/AD via such screens. The Record Definition screen (see Fig. 21.3 for an example) can be regarded as typical of CSP/AD screens in general, and we will use it as the basis for our discussion.

The various parts of the screen have the following meanings and uses.

- Line 1 is the title line.

- Line 2 is used for messages from CSP/AD (diagnostics, etc.).

- Line 3 is the *command line* (strictly, *sub*command line). This is where the application developer enters CSP/AD commands to control the CSP/AD session. The CANCEL command, for example, cancels the current function, and the EXIT command exits from the current function.

```
EZEM11                    RECORD DEFINITION
EZE00087I New definition being created
==>
            PF3 = Exit  (or continue if new definition)
                    Record Name = SHIPREC
.................... RECORD SPECIFICATION .............................

 Organization  => 7
   1  Indexed
   2  Relative
   3  Serial           Default Key Item        =>
   4  Working Storage
   5  Redefined Record
   6  DL/I Segment
   7  SQL Row           Alternate Specification for =>

 ....Total Lines 00003  ..SQL Table Names(s)............................
    CREATOR ID:       TABLE NAME:      TABLE LABEL:
***                    TOP OF LIST
001 cjdate            s                T1
002 cjdate            sp               T2
003 cjdate            p                T3
***                    END OF LIST
```

Fig. 21.3 Sample CSP/AD Record Definition screen

- Line 4 specifies the PF (and other) keys that can be used to exit from the current display.

- Line 5 includes an identification of the object defined via the rest of the screen (where applicable).

- The rest of the screen is divided into a *fixed area* and a *scrollable area* (in general, though not all screens have both). Generally speaking, the fixed area is used to respond to CSP/AD prompts, and the scrollable area (from "TOP OF LIST" to "BOTTOM OF LIST") is used for entering record, map, and process definitions (etc.). The CSP/AD editor supports standard line-oriented editing commands for editing text within this latter area. The editor is context-sensitive, in that it recognizes invalid processing statements, unclosed IF statements, etc.

We now proceed to show what is involved in using CSP to build a SHIPMENT application that will use the suppliers-and-parts database to display information about part shipments for a given supplier. The input to the application is a supplier number; the output consists of the supplier number and city, plus part number, part city, and shipment quantity for all parts supplied by that supplier. We begin by examining the record definition for this application (Section 21.3).

21.3 RECORD DEFINITION

The process of defining a CSP application starts with the CSP/AD *Facility Selection* screen (not illustrated). Selecting option 2 ("Definition") on that screen brings us to the *Definition* screen (Fig. 21.4). That screen in turn permits us to invoke specific screens to define the various components—records, maps, and processes—that go to make up a CSP application. The normal procedure is to define the records first, then the maps, and finally the processes. In our example, therefore, we begin by selecting option 1 ("Record") on the Definition screen and entering a name, say SHIPREC, for the record we intend to define. This option leads us to the Record Definition screen already discussed briefly in the previous section (refer back to Fig. 21.3).

As indicated at the end of the previous section, the SHIPMENT application needs data from all three of the database tables S, SP, and P (S#, P#, and QTY from SP, S.CITY from S, and P.CITY from P). On the Record Definition screen, therefore, we specify option 7 ("SQL Row"), and enter the qualified names of these three tables (owner name plus table name) in the scrollable area created by selecting that option. The "labels" T1, T2, and T3 are generated automatically by CSP/AD; references to the tables

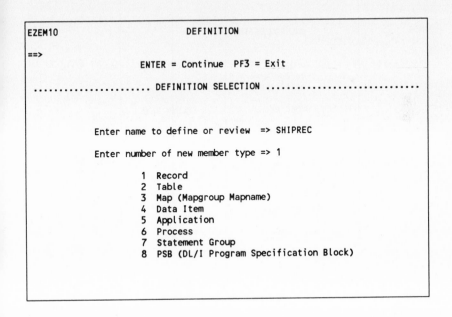

Fig. 21.4 CSP/AD Definition screen

on subsequent screens (e.g., in generated SQL statements) will use these unique labels instead of the qualified names.

One other entry on the Record Definition screen is relevant to DB2 applications (in general, though we do not use it in our example)—"Default Key Item." From the entries on the Record Definition screen, CSP/AD builds a set of SQL statements for accessing the required data. The field name specified in the Default Key Item entry (if any) is used to build a default search condition for those statements. We did not specify any such field name in our example because the search condition will be defined explicitly in a later stage of the record definition process (see below).

Once the required tables have been specified via the Record Definition screen, CSP/AD displays the SQL Row Definition screen (Fig. 21.5). This screen allows the developer to indicate which specific fields of those tables are needed. Most of the information displayed on this screen is obtained by CSP from the DB2 catalog. The READ ONLY specification is set to YES for every field, because multiple tables are involved—SHIPREC involves a join—and DB2 does not permit joins to be updated. *Note:* CSP/AD automatically creates a set of host variables with the same names as the DB2 fields (S#, SNAME, etc.). These variables are used in (e.g.) INTO clauses in generated SQL SELECT statements.

```
EZEM15                    SQL ROW DEFINITION

==>
  PF3 = Exit    PF4 = SQL Compare    PF10 = Scroll Left    PF11=Scroll Right
                        Record Name = SHIPREC
Total lines 0012 ........ DATA ITEM DEFINITION ...........................

*** NAME          TYPE  LENGTH DEC BYTES  READ SQL COLUMN NAME
***                                       ONLY
***                     TOP OF LIST
001 S#            CHA   00005      00005  YES  T1.S#
d02 SNAME         CHA   00020      00020  YES  T1.SNAME
d03 STATUS        BIN   00004      00002  YES  T1.STATUS
004 scity         CHA   00015      00015  YES  T1.CITY
d05 S#            CHA   00005      00005  YES  T2.S#
d06 P#            CHA   00005      00005  YES  T2.P#
007 QTY           BIN   00009      00004  YES  T2.QTY
008 P#            CHA   00006      00006  YES  T3.P#
d09 PNAME         CHA   00020      00020  YES  T3.PNAME
d10 COLOR         CHA   00006      00006  YES  T3.COLOR
d11 WEIGHT        BIN   00004      00002  YES  T3.WEIGHT
012 pcity         CHA   00015      00015  YES  T3.CITY
***                     END OF LIST
```

Fig. 21.5 CSP/AD SQL Row Definition screen

The following editing has been performed in Fig. 21.5.

- The "d" line editor command has been used to remove the fields not required for SHIPREC.

- The field names for S.CITY and P.CITY have been changed to SCITY and PCITY, respectively, to avoid ambiguity.

The developer is free to make other changes on the Row Definition screen—fields can be added or deleted, field definitions can be modified, and so forth. To ensure that everything matches the appropriate DB2 definitions, PF key 4 can be pressed to request a comparison with the DB2 catalog entries. Any discrepancies found will be displayed on a separate screen.

Finally, CSP/AD needs to know the SQL SELECT statement to be used to retrieve SHIPREC data from the database. This information is specified by means of the *SQL Row Record Definition* screen (see Fig. 21.6). CSP/AD generates a candidate SQL statement automatically, with appropriate SELECT and FROM clauses; if SHIPREC had been drawn from a single underlying table and if we had supplied an entry for the "Default Key Item" on the Record Definition screen, CSP/AD would also generate an appropriate WHERE clause. As it is, however, SHIPREC

```
EZEM16              SQL ROW RECORD DEFINITION
EZE006421 SQL syntax check has completed successfully
==>
 PF3 = File and exit PF4 = Reset to default statement PF5 = SQL syntax check
 Record  = SHIPREC
                                      Modified clause = YES
Total lines 0011 .... DEFAULT SELECTION CONDITIONS DEFINITION ..............

***                     TOP OF LIST
*** SELECT
***     T1.S#, T1.CITY,
***     T2.QTY,
***     T3.P#, T3.CITY
*** FROM
***     cjdate.s T1,
***     cjdate.sp T2,
***     cjdate.p T3
*** WHERE
010     t1.s# = t2.s# and
011     t2.p# = t3.p#
***                     END OF LIST
```

Fig. 21.6 CSP/AD SQL Row Record Definition screen

involves a join, and therefore we must enter the WHERE condition (the *selection condition*) explicitly. In the example, we have specified the "obvious" join of tables S, SP, and P over supplier numbers and part numbers.

21.4 MAP DEFINITION

Note: Maps in CSP have little to do with DB2 per se—they are concerned with operations on the terminal, not operations on the database. We therefore present only a very brief overview of the map definition process.

Maps provide the medium of communication between the CSP application and the user of that application (i.e., the end-user). They permit

(a) the application to display information to the end-user (typically information retrieved from the database), and

(b) the end-user to submit information to the application (typically information to be used for updating the database or for controlling retrieval from the database).

All the maps used in a given application are considered to belong to the same *mapgroup*. We will assume that the maps in our SHIPMENT example are called SHIP001, SHIP002, etc., and that together they constitute a mapgroup called SHIP. SHIP001 will be used to request a supplier number from the user; SHIP002 will be used to display corresponding output information back to the user. Let us consider what is involved in defining one of these maps, say SHIP002. We go through the following steps:

- Starting—as always—with the CSP/AD *Definition* screen (refer back to Fig. 21.4), we select option 3 ("Map"), specifying mapgroup SHIP and map SHIP002.

- We define the device or devices to be used to display the map on the *Map Definition – Device Selection* screen (not illustrated).

- We define the size of the map and its position on the display using the *Map Definition – Map Specification* screen (not illustrated).

- We use a series of *Map Definition* screens to define the map appearance, map variables, and associated edit rules (if any). The rest of this section describes the use of these Map Definition screens in more detail. For the sake of the example, we assume that the map we are defining (SHIP002) is to appear as shown in Fig. 21.7.

To define the SHIP002 layout, we use the CSP/AD screen painter and the Map Definition screen shown in Fig. 21.8. *Note:* The fields that make up a map are divided into constant fields and variable fields. Constant fields contain fixed text data; variable fields contain data that can be modified by

```
                    Shipment Information


        Supplier:                    Supplier City:

        Part:                        Part City:

        Quantity:
```

Fig. 21.7 Map SHIP002

```
EZEM22                   MAP DEFINITION

==>
                PF3 = Exit (or continue if new definition)
Total positions 079     Map Name = SHIP SHIP002      Positions 001 to 079
Total lines     024 ...        C(#) V(~) S(/)     ... Lines    001 to 014



                    #Shipment Information


        #Supplier:~    #              #Supplier City:~           #

        #Part:   ~     #                 #Part City:~            #

        #Quantity: ~   #


                                                                   #
```

Fig. 21.8 CSP/AD Map Definition: using the screen painter

the user or by the application. Fields are delimited in the map definition by special code or attribute bytes, which indicate properties of the field such as color, brightness, whether constant or variable, etc.

We explain Fig. 21.8 as follows.

- The application developer has entered the values for constant fields (the "Shipment Information" heading, etc.) and has used the "#" code to mark the position of those fields.

- The developer has also used the " ˜ " code* to mark the position of variable fields (to be used for data entry and display).

A code of "/" can also be used to left or right justify or center text on the map. Various screen painter commands can be entered on the subcommand line (Line 3 on the screen) to specify field attributes (color, protection, brightness, etc.), field positioning, text copying and modification, and so forth. For example, the screen painter command TEST displays (the current version of) the map as it would appear during execution.

Having defined the map layout, the developer must now specify names for the variable fields so that they can be referenced from within the application (see Fig. 21.9). CSP/AD automatically numbers each variable field

```
EZEM24                    MAP DEFINITION

==>
                   PF3 = Exit (or continue if new definition)
0001 <= Number of first field to name       Map Name = SHIP SHIP002
...................... VARIABLE FIELD NAMING ...........................
      NAME                    NAME                         NAME
   1  MSNO                 2  MSCITY                    3  MPNO
   4  MPCITY               5  MQTY                      6  EZEMSG

Total positions 079                          Positions 001 to 079
Total lines     024 ............................. Lines     007 to 014
      Supplier: 1                    Supplier City: 2

      Part:   3                        Part City: 4

      Quantity: 5


6
```

Fig. 21.9. CSP/AD Map Definition: variable field naming

---

*We remind the reader that in this book we use the tilde (˜) in place of the PL/I-style "not" symbol, for typographic reasons.

and displays an area for the developer to assign names corresponding to those numbers. In our example, we have specified field names MSNO, MSCITY, ..., and MQTY (respectively) for the five variable fields labeled Supplier, Supplier City, ..., and Quantity on the map. (The sixth field, EZEMSG, allows the application to display messages to the application user.)

Finally, the developer can specify edit rules for variable fields, using the screen shown in Fig. 21.10. Such rules are used to constrain the set of values that can legally be entered by the end-user and to control the format of values that are displayed to the end-user. Examples are shown in Fig. 21.10. A detailed discussion of all possible edit rule options is beyond the scope of this book, but most of them should be self-explanatory.

```
EZEM26                     MAP DEFINITION

==>
      ENTER = Edit changes ( or go to next variable field)  PF3 = Exit
 Field Name = MQTY      Map Name = SHIP SHIP002     Occurs =   Length = 4
 ................... VARIABLE FIELD EDIT DEFINITION ...................
 Data Type        => NUM       Description => number of parts shipped
  Justify         => LEF  Decimal Positions=>     Sign(NO,TRA,LEA) => NO
 Fill Character   =>       Zero Edit      => NO  Numeric Separator=> NO
 Fold             => NO   Currency Symbol => NO  Date Edit(1->11) =>
                                            Edit Error Message Numbers:
 Input Required   => NO                       Input Required Error=>
 Edit Routine     =>                          Edit Routine Error  =>
 Minimum Input    =>                          Minimum Input Error =>
 Minimum Value    =>                          Value Error         =>
 Maximum Value    =>                          Data Type Error     =>
 Total positions 079                            Positions 001 to 079
 Total lines     024 ............................ Lines     001 to 015

     Supplier: _____                  Supplier City: _____

     Part:      _____                 Part City: _____

     Quantity:  ****
```

Fig. 21.10 CSP/AD Map Definition: variable field edit definition

21.5 PROCESS DEFINITION

As explained in Section 21.2, a CSP application contains one or more named processes (refer to Fig. 21.11). The processes define the processing logic for the application. Processing logic involves displaying maps, reading and writing database data, performing computational operations, etc. A process consists of:

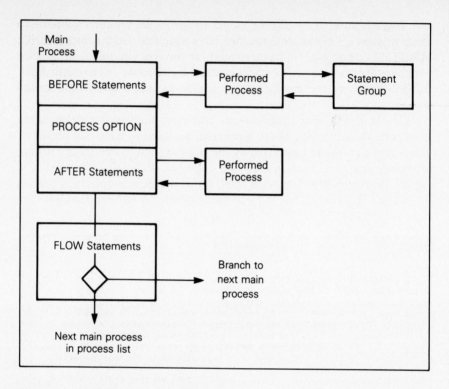

Fig. 21.11 Application process structure

(a) A single *process option,* which performs some specific task, typically involving a CSP record (database access) or a CSP map (terminal I/O); together with

(b) Zero or more *processing statements,* which perform various computational or flow-of-control functions.

Processing statements can appear *before* or *after* a process option (or both) and/or in a *flow section*. Statements appearing before the process option are typically used to clear fields on a map, or to specify data to be read from the database. Statements appearing after the process option are typically used to check data entered by the user, or to check return codes after performing database access. Statements appearing in a flow section are used to control the execution flow between the main processes of an application. *Note:* A main process can also invoke other processes by means of the PERFORM statement (see Fig. 21.11); a PERFORMed process can include BEFORE and AFTER statements, but no FLOW statements.

Processing statements can also be used to build common subroutines called *statement groups*. A statement group is invoked simply by specifying its name. Statement groups do not contain a process option.

In order to give some idea as to what is involved in process definition, let us first assume that the logical structure of our SHIPMENT application is as indicated by the following pseudocode:

```
do initialization ;
get supplier number from user using map SHIP001 ;
set up for database read loop ;
do until no more SHIPREC records for this supplier ;
   retrieve next SHIPREC record from database ;
   display SHIPREC record using map SHIP002;
end ;
```

The SHIPMENT application will use:

- A main process called MAIN001 to control the overall logic of the application;

- Processes GETSNUM and DISPDATA to get the supplier number and to display SHIPREC records at the terminal;

- Processes READIT and GETNEXT to set up for the database read and to read the SHIPREC records from the database.

As usual, the starting point for definition is the CSP/AD Definition screen (refer back to Fig. 21.4). This time, we choose option 5 ("Application"), specifying the application name SHIPMENT. After we have defined the type of application we are building (batch or online, for example), the *Application Definition* screen shown in Fig. 21.12 will be displayed. We then use this screen to define the main processes (known as the *process list*) for the application. The process list contains the name of each process, its processing option, the CSP map or record ("object") to be used by the processing option (if any), and a description of what the process does. We enter the name of the single main process, MAIN001, which will be invoked using the EXECUTE processing option. No object name is entered because MAIN001 does not use any CSP maps or records.

We can now enter the "s" Select Definition option on line 001 under the SEL column to display screens for entering the BEFORE, AFTER, and FLOW processing statements for MAIN001. After we have defined these statements (see the subsection "Processing Statements" below for the details), we use the "l" option to display the *Structure List* screen shown in Fig. 21.13. This screen shows the structure of SHIPMENT defined so far. It shows that MAIN001 invokes the lower level (LVL 002) processes GETSNUM, READIT, GETNEXT, and DISPDATA. The processing options, object names, and process descriptions for these lower level processes can now be entered on the screen as shown. Once this has been done, the

```
EZEM36                    APPLICATION DEFINITION

==>
            ENTER = File and continue    PF3 = File and exit
            PF4 = Display application structure
                       Application Name = SHIPMENT
Select Definition:  S = P+F+L   P = Processing   F = Flow   E = Edit Object
                    O = Object Selection        L = Structure List
Total lines 0001 ...... APPLICATION PROCESS LIST ..........................

SEL PROCESS     OPTION      OBJECT     ERROR    DESCRIPTION
***                      TOP OF LIST
001 MAIN001     EXECUTE                          main process
***                      END OF LIST
```

Fig. 21.12 CSP/AD Application Definition screen

```
EZEM37                        STRUCTURE LIST

==>
       ENTER = File and continue     PF3 = File and exit     PF4 = Refresh
                       Member Name = SHIPMENT
Select Definition:  S = P+F      P = Processing   F = Flow   E = Edit Object
                    O = Object Selection        Maximum Level => 002
Total lines 0005 ....... PROCESS AND GROUP LIST ..............

SEL NAME      LVL  OPTION     OBJECT    ERROR    DESCRIPTION
***                     TOP OF LIST
001 MAIN001   001  EXECUTE                        main process
002 GETSNUM   002  CONVERSE   SHIP001             get supplier number from user
o03 READIT    002  SETINQ     SHIPREC             set up for data retrieval
004 GETNEXT   002  SCAN       SHIPREC             read a row
005 DISPDATA  002  CONVERSE   SHIP002             display row data
***                     END OF LIST
```

Fig. 21.13 SHIPMENT application Structure List

"p" Select Definition option can be entered alongside each process name in turn to define the processing statements for the selected process. *Note:* Option "p" is used instead of option "s" because lower level processes do not have a flow section.

We are returned to the Structure List screen after defining the statements for each process. Pressing the PF 4 key on this screen will cause the screen to be refreshed with the latest process structure for the application.

To explain the process options and statements in more detail we will consider the process called READIT.

Process Options

The process option for READIT, namely SETINQ, corresponds in SQL terms to declaring a cursor for some specified query. This query will access the object of the process option, which we have specified as SHIPREC (see Fig. 21.13). In general, the process option can be any of the following (by way of explanation, we give an approximate SQL equivalent in each case):

- INQUIRY — retrieve a single table row
  (DECLARE CURSOR–OPEN–FETCH–CLOSE)
- UPDATE — retrieve a single row for update
  (DECLARE CURSOR FOR UPDATE–OPEN–FETCH)
- SETINQ — define a set of rows to be retrieved
  (DECLARE CURSOR)
- SETUPD — define a set of rows to be retrieved and updated
  (DECLARE CURSOR FOR UPDATE)
- SCAN — retrieve a row from a defined set
  (FETCH)
- REPLACE — update a retrieved row
  (UPDATE CURRENT)
- DELETE — delete a retrieved row
  (DELETE CURRENT)
- CLOSE — terminate processing of defined set
  (CLOSE)
- ADD — insert a single row
  (INSERT)
- EXECSQL — execute the specified SQL statement
  (any SQL statement other than SELECT)

In addition there are three process options that have no SQL equivalents (i.e., that have nothing to do with database access at all):

- EXECUTE — execute the specified process
- CONVERSE — display a map and edit the response from the user
- DISPLAY — display a map (no response from user)

As already stated, the object of the SETINQ process option in our example is SHIPREC. The SQL statement generated by CSP/AD for this combination of process option and object can be displayed and subsequently edited by means of the CSP/AD Application Definition screen shown in Fig. 21.14. This screen is displayed by entering the option "o" alongside the READIT process name on the Structure List screen for the SHIPMENT application (refer back to Fig. 21.13).

The SQL statement is initially generated by CSP/AD using the SHIPREC record defined earlier; we have tailored it for the READIT process by adding an extra search condition and an ORDER BY clause. The purpose of the extra search condition is to ensure that SHIPREC records are retrieved for the required supplier only.

```
EZEM3M                 APPLICATION DEFINITION
EZE00590I You may edit lines preceded by line numbers
==>
 PF3 = File and exit PF4 = Reset to default statement PF5 = SQL syntax check
 Process = READIT    Description = set up for data retrieval
 Option = SETINQ     Object      = SHIPREC    Modified statements = YES
Total lines 0012 ... OBJECT SELECTION: SQL STATEMENT DEFINITION ............
***                    TOP OF LIST
*** SELECT
002    T1.S#, T1.CITY,
003    T2.QTY,
004    T3.P#, T3.CITY
*** INTO
006    :S#, :SCITY, :QTY,
007    :P#, :PCITY
*** FROM
***    cjdate.s T1,
***    cjdate.sp T2,
***    cjdate.p T3
*** WHERE
010    t1.s# = t2.s# and
011    t2.p# = t3.p# and t1.s# = :s#
012 order by t3.p#
***                    END OF LIST
```

Fig. 21.14 SELECT statement for the READIT process

Processing Statements

The CSP/AD *Application Process Definition* screen shown in Fig. 21.15 is displayed as a result of selecting the "p" option on the Structure List screen (refer back to Fig. 21.13). The Application Process Definition screen allows us to specify the processing statements for the process under consideration. In the simple example shown, the BEFORE processing consists of a single MOVE statement to copy the supplier number entered by the user (via the map SHIP001) into the S# field of the SHIPREC record. The process option SETINQ will use the S# field to retrieve shipment information using the SHIPREC record. There are no AFTER processing statements.

A more complex example appears in Fig. 21.16, overleaf. That figure shows the processing statements for the MAIN001 process of the SHIPMENT application. This process has a processing option of EXECUTE, which simply causes the statements in the process to be executed (no map or record process is performed). There are no BEFORE processing statements. The AFTER processing statements control the flow of the lower level processes. *Note:* The example of Fig. 21.16 is intended to illustrate process definition in general terms, not to represent a totally realistic application. The statements shown are intended to be more or less self-explanatory.

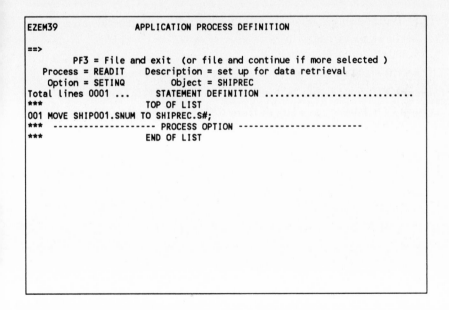

```
EZEM39              APPLICATION PROCESS DEFINITION

==>
        PF3 = File and exit  (or file and continue if more selected )
   Process = READIT    Description = set up for data retrieval
    Option = SETINQ          Object = SHIPREC
Total lines 0001 ...     STATEMENT DEFINITION ...........................
***                         TOP OF LIST
001 MOVE SHIP001.SNUM TO SHIPREC.S#;
***  ------------------- PROCESS OPTION -----------------------
***                         END OF LIST
```

Fig. 21.15 READIT process definition

```
EZEM39                  APPLICATION PROCESS DEFINITION

==>
        PF3 = File and exit  (or file and continue if more selected )
   Process = MAIN001   Description = set up for data retrieval
   Option = EXECUTE         Object =
Total lines 0010 ...     STATEMENT DEFINITION ............................
***                    TOP OF LIST
*** ------------------- PROCESS OPTION -----------------------
001 PERFORM GETSNUM ;     GET SUPPLIER NUMBER
002 SET SHIP002 ;         CLEAR DISPLAY
003 PERFORM READIT ;      SET UP FOR DATABASE READ
004 PERFORM GETNEXT ;     READ FIRST ROW
005 IF SHIPREC IS NRF ;   SUPPLIER NOT FOUND TELL USER
006   MOVE "INVALID SUPPLIER" TO EZEMSG;
007 ELSE
008   WHILE SHIPREC NOT NRF ;
008     PERFORM DISPDATA ; DISPLAY ROW
009     PERFORM GETNEXT ;  READ NEXT ROW
009   END ;
010 END ;
***                        END OF LIST
```

Fig 21.16 MAIN001 process definition

CSP processing statements fall into the following general categories:

- Computational statements:
  - arithmetic operations ($+$, $-$, $*$, $/$, rounding, remainder)
  - MOVE (move data between CSP objects and working storage)
  - RETRIEVE (retrieve data from CSP edit/reference tables)
  - SET (set a map, record, or field to a specific value)
- Conditional statements:
  - FIND (search for a matching value in a CSP edit/reference table and execute the associated statement group)
  - IF/ELSE/END (perform processing based on comparisons)
  - WHILE/END (conditionally repeat processing)
  - TEST (check status after map and record processing and execute appropriate processing statement group)
- Application linkage statements:
  - CALL (invoke another CSP or user-written application and return to the next statement in the calling process)

- TRANSFER (transfer control to another CSP or user-written application)
- Unconditional statements:
  - PERFORM (invoke the next lower level process and return to the next statement in the calling process or [optionally] to the flow section of a main process)
  - *statement group name* (invoke the named statement group)
  - *process name* (used in the flow section to transfer control to the named main process; by default, processing is performed in the order of the processes in the process list)
  - *function name* (invoke the specified CSP function)

21.6 TESTING AND GENERATING THE APPLICATION

The CSP/AD test facility is entered by selecting option 3 ("Test") on the main CSP Facility Selection screen. Two principal testing functions are provided:

- *Preprocessor:* Checks the syntax of the CSP processing statements used by the application.
- *Run:* Allows the developer to test application execution. A statement-level trace of the test run can be provided at the terminal. Also, stop points can be defined at which the test run is to pause.

As explained in Section 21.2, all processing during testing is performed using dynamic SQL. After the application is tested and debugged, it can be generated for production execution under CSP/AE by selecting option 4 ("Generation") on the main CSP Facility Selection screen. At this point, a choice must be made between static and dynamic SQL. In a production environment, at least, static SQL would normally be chosen; if it is, then CSP will generate an Assembler Language program containing the required SQL statements and will store it in the Application Load File. That program will contain certain CSP macros and must therefore be processed by the macro assembler, using the relevant CSP-supplied macro library. It can then be prepared for execution on DB2 by means of the standard DB2 program preparation procedures (see Chapter 17).

21.7 CSP UTILITIES

CSP provides many utilities to assist in the building and maintenance of CSP applications. From a DB2 perspective, the most important ones are the *MSL and ALF utilities* and the *CSP List Processor.*

- The MSL (Member Specification Library) utilities consist of a set of facilities for manipulating and backing up MSL members (record definitions, map definitions, and process definitions), as follows:
  - *Export and Import:*   Move MSL members to and from external files. These functions are used to move applications from one environment to another. A special form of external file, an *External Source Format* file, can be used to move application definitions to and from other application development products—for example, third-party CASE tools such as Excelerator from Index Technology.
  - *Print:*   List the components of a specified application, together with a cross-reference listing.
  - *Copy/Rename/Delete:*   Copy, rename, and delete MSL members.
- The ALF (Application Load File) utilities include analogous functions for manipulating ALF objects.
- The CSP List Processor produces a full screen listing of selected MSL members and allows any of the MSL utility functions (except Import) to be executed for a given member or list of members. It also produces a where-used list showing where members are used, allows a global change of all references to a specific member name, and permits individual members to be viewed and edited. The List Processor also supports application testing and application generation.

CHAPTER

·22·

Application
Development Facility

22.1 INTRODUCTION

ADF (Application Development Facility—or, to give it its full name, IMS Application Development Facility II, also known as IMSADF II) is an application generator for developing IMS and CICS applications that access data stored in IMS and DB2 databases (also in VSAM files). ADF provides a set of *modules* for performing common application tasks (e.g., database and file access, screen formatting, data editing and validating, etc.). These modules are used by an ADF *transaction driver* program (see Fig. 22.1) to perform the required application tasks in accordance with *rules* defined by the application developer. The purpose of the rules is to direct the execution of the driver program and to determine which modules are to be used and how they are to be executed. Many applications can be built entirely in terms of such rules. However, if the application has requirements beyond

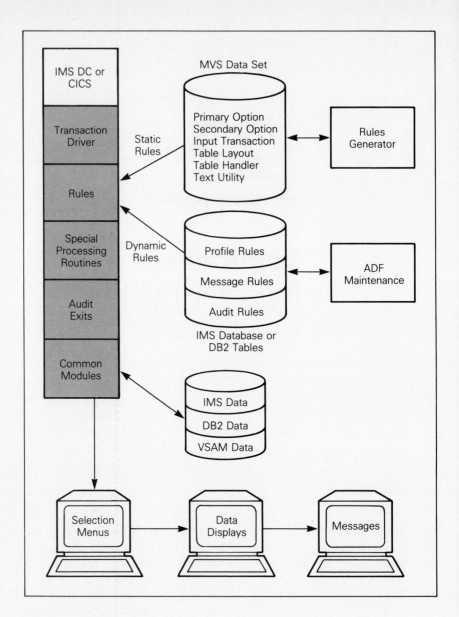

Fig. 22.1 ADF structure

the capabilities of the ADF-supplied rules and modules, special-purpose routines can written by the developer, in (e.g.) Assembler Language or COBOL, to supplement the standard modules.

ADF applications can be developed under TSO, using a set of interactive dialogs called Interactive ADF (IADF). IADF also provides facilities that allow the generated application to be tested under TSO (even though it is eventually destined to run under IMS or CICS). Alternatively, ADF applications can be developed directly under IMS or CICS. In this chapter we concentrate exclusively on this latter possibility. We also (of course) concentrate on applications that will access DB2.

As suggested by the first paragraph above, ADF applications can be characterized as *rules-driven.* ADF rules in turn can be divided into two kinds, static and dynamic.

- Static rules are used to specify database and file layouts and overall processing logic; they are defined by means of a batch *Rules Generator* program and stored in an MVS library data set. Interfaces exist between the Rules Generator and the DB2 catalog (and the IBM DB/DC Data Dictionary) to help in database layout definition. The Rules Documentation feature (RDOC) can be used to produce reports on the stored static rules.

- Dynamic rules are used to specify "dynamic" information—i.e., information that might change over the lifetime of the application, such as integrity constraints ("audit criteria"). There are three types of dynamic rule:

  - *Profile Rules,* which control the applications and operations a user is allowed to execute;

  - *Message Rules,* which specify messages to be sent to the user if, e.g., an audit rule is violated (see below);

  - *Audit Rules,* which control data format and content. Audit rules are formulated in a high-level audit language which supports logical branching, subroutine calls, table lookup, SQL statement execution, etc. Such rules can be invoked after accepting screen input, before issuing a database call, and before displaying screen output. Customized exit routines can be invoked to perform audit functions not directly supported by the facilities of the audit language.

Dynamic rules are defined interactively via ADF itself and are stored either in DB2 tables or in IMS databases (according to an installation option). Facilities are provided for displaying and modifying the stored dynamic rules.

22.2 DEVELOPING ADF APPLICATIONS

ADF applications can perform three types of processing: standard, special, and text.

- *Standard processing* is used to display and update rows in DB2 tables. This function is controlled entirely by rules—no conventional programming is required at all. The Rules Generator creates an Assembler Language program (containing static SQL) to perform the required SQL processing, and dynamically invokes the DB2 Precompiler and the Assembler and Linkage Editor. All of the ADF audit functions are available while the application is performing standard processing. If audit exit routines (coded by the developer) are used, they can request ADF to execute prebuilt SQL statements (defined to the Rules Generator) on their behalf, or they can themselves issue SQL statements (either static or dynamic) directly.

- *Special processing* is the execution of customized application routines to perform functions not supported by the ADF common modules. SQL statements can be invoked from such routines just as they can from audit exit routines (see "standard processing" above).

- *Text processing* supports the manipulation of text data stored in IMS databases. It is not supported for DB2 and will not be discussed further in this chapter.

Let us now consider what is involved in building the SHIPMENT application using ADF (the same example that we used in the previous chapter on CSP). For convenience, we repeat the description of the application here:

- The application uses the suppliers-and-parts database. Its purpose is to display information about part shipments for a given supplier. The input is a supplier number; the output consists of the supplier number and city, plus part number, part city, and shipment quantity for all parts supplied by that supplier.

To simplify the discussion, we will assume that the developer has already defined a DB2 view called SHIPVIEW that combines the required information into a single table:

```
CREATE VIEW SHIPVIEW ( S#, SCITY, P#, PCITY, QTY )
    AS SELECT S.S#, S.CITY, P.P#, P.CITY, SP.QTY
       FROM   S, SP, P
       WHERE  S.S# = SP.S#
       AND    SP.P# = P.P# ;
```

Note: It is not essential that a suitable view already exist; the join could be defined via ADF instead. However, details of this latter possibility are beyond the scope of this chapter.

We now consider the ADF rules required to build this application. As a basis for explaining those rules, we will examine the screens that will be encountered by an end-user in using the application after it has been built. There are four major steps involved.

1. First, the user's authorization must be checked. The user enters a user ID and project/group information on the ADF sign-on screen (not illustrated). The entered data is verified against the user's sign-on profile (originally created via an appropriate Profile rule).

2. After successfully signing on, the user is presented with the ADF *Primary Option Menu* (see Fig. 22.2), which contains a list of available options and "transaction modes." In the example, the user has specified option D ("transaction selection") and mode 6 ("retrieve"), together with the two-character identifier ("SH") of the transaction to be run. That identifier directs ADF to the *Input Transaction Rule* for the transaction, which specifies the database tables to be accessed (i.e., table SHIPVIEW, in our example) and the type of processing to be performed (e.g., conversational or batch).

Note: If the transaction identifier is not known, the user can press the

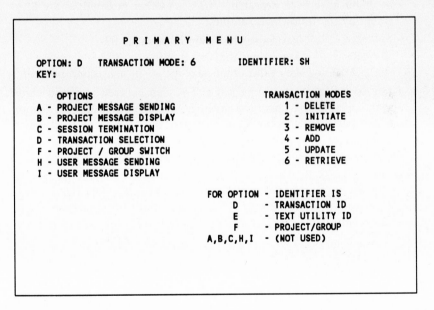

```
                P R I M A R Y   M E N U

    OPTION: D    TRANSACTION MODE: 6        IDENTIFIER: SH
    KEY:

        OPTIONS                          TRANSACTION MODES
    A - PROJECT MESSAGE SENDING              1 - DELETE
    B - PROJECT MESSAGE DISPLAY              2 - INITIATE
    C - SESSION TERMINATION                  3 - REMOVE
    D - TRANSACTION SELECTION                4 - ADD
    F - PROJECT / GROUP SWITCH               5 - UPDATE
    H - USER MESSAGE SENDING                 6 - RETRIEVE
    I - USER MESSAGE DISPLAY


                              FOR OPTION - IDENTIFIER IS
                                      D  - TRANSACTION ID
                                      E  - TEXT UTILITY ID
                                      F  - PROJECT/GROUP
                              A,B,C,H,I  - (NOT USED)
```

Fig. 22.2 ADF Primary Option Menu

enter key to request ADF to display the *Secondary Option Menu* (not illustrated), which shows a list of available transactions.*

3. ADF now invokes a *transaction driver* to process the requested transaction (namely, SHIPMENT). In general, the driver allows the user to retrieve and update data in the tables specified in the Input Transaction Rule; in our example, however, no updating is allowed because the table concerned (namely, SHIPVIEW) is a join view.

In order to perform a retrieval, the user must specify an appropriate "key selection" condition, using the ADF *Primary Key Selection Screen* (Fig. 22.3). *Note:* All tables accessed via ADF should have a unique primary key, defined as part of the *Table Layout Rule* for the table in question. For SHIPVIEW, the primary key is the combination (S#,P#).

The Primary Key Selection Screen supports two different key selection conditions, unique key search and generic key search:

- If the user enters a specific key value, the driver will use that value to retrieve and display the (unique) corresponding row.

- Alternatively, the user can specify a generic key search as illustrated by the example in Fig. 22.3. The generic key value "S2>" specifies a search for rows where the first two characters of the key value are greater than or equal to "S2." (*Note:* "S2>" is correct here!—not, as might have been expected, "S2<".) Other possibilities are illustrated by the following examples:

  S2<   —   key values less than or equal to S2
  S%   —   key values that begin with an "S"
  _2%   —   key values that have a "2" in the second position

  The special characters "%" and "_" can be used as "wild card" search characters, exactly as in the SQL LIKE predicate (see Section 6.2 in Part II of this book).

4. In the case of generic key search (only), key values for rows that satisfy the search condition are displayed on the ADF *Secondary Key Selection Screen* (see Fig. 22.4). The user can then display any individual row by specifying the appropriate row number in the SELECTION field. In the example, the user selects number "3", which causes the *Transaction Display Screen* shown in Fig. 22.5 to be displayed. (That screen is also dis-

---

*The reader is warned that the term "transaction" is used in ADF in the IMS or CICS sense, not in the sense of Part II of this book (where we defined it as a logical unit of work, terminated by COMMIT or ROLLBACK). A transaction in ADF is basically just the input from the terminal that causes some program to be invoked— in other words, it is an input message (loosely speaking).

```
             S H I P M E N T   S A M P L E   P R O B L E M

      P R I M A R Y   K E Y   S E L E C T I O N   S C R E E N

RETRIEVE                          TRANSACTION: SHIPMENT
OPTION:    TRX: 6SH   KEY:
     *** ENTER THE FOLLOWING KEY INFORMATION ***
   SUPPLIER SEARCH CONDITION S2>
```

Fig. 22.3 ADF Primary Key Selection Screen

```
     S E C O N D A R Y   K E Y   S E L E C T I O N   S C R E E N

RETRIEVE                          TRANSACTION: SHIPMENT
OPTION:    TRX: 6SH   KEY:  S2>
SELECTION: 3       *** ENTER A SELECTION NUMBER FROM THIS SCREEN ***
        SUPPLIER    PART
        NUMBER      NUMBER
   1   S2          P1
   2   S2          P2
   3   S3          P2
   4   S4          P2
   5   S4          P4
   6   S4          P5
```

Fig. 22.4 ADF Secondary Key Selection Screen

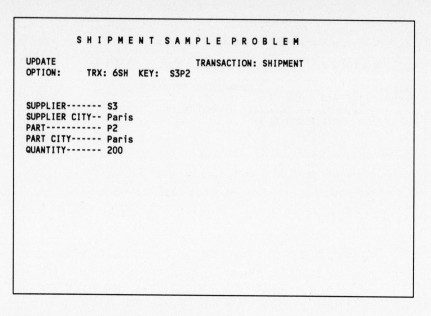

```
            S H I P M E N T   S A M P L E   P R O B L E M

    UPDATE                             TRANSACTION: SHIPMENT
    OPTION:      TRX: 6SH  KEY:  S3P2


    SUPPLIER-------  S3
    SUPPLIER CITY--  Paris
    PART-----------  P2
    PART CITY------  Paris
    QUANTITY-------  200
```

Fig. 22.5 ADF Transaction Display Screen

played if the user enters a unique key value on the Primary Key Selection
Screen.) If the data can be updated (it cannot, in our example, because the
data is retrieved from a join), the user can modify the displayed data by
overtyping. Of course, any updates made in this manner will be validated
in accordance with all applicable audit rules and audit exit routines.

Key values entered on a key selection screen are inserted into the
WHERE clause of SQL statements generated by the *Table Handler Rule*
for the table being accessed (each table must have such a rule; see Section
22.4).

This concludes our overview of ADF standard processing. Special processing routines are handled in the same way as standard processing routines,
except that the transaction identifiers listed on the Secondary Option Menu
will include "special processing" transactions.

We are now in a position to summarize the main tasks involved in
building a DB2 application with ADF:

1. Define the static rules:
   - Table Layout Rules
   - Table Handler Rules
   - Input Transaction Rules

Note: There are other rules that control the operation of the system as a whole (e.g., rules that specify the contents of the Primary and Secondary Option Menus), but for simplicity those rules are not included here.

2. Define the screen formats
3. Define the dynamic rules:
   - Profile Rules
   - Message Rules
   - Audit Rules (using high-level audit language)
4. Code and install any additional processing routines:
   - audit exit routines
   - special processing routines

A detailed discussion of all of the above steps is beyond the scope of this book; the reader is referred to the IBM manuals for more information. However, in order to give some idea as to how ADF supports DB2 specifically, the next three sections briefly discuss the static rules for the SHIPMENT application.

22.3 GENERATING THE TABLE LAYOUT RULE

The Table Layout Rule is defined by means of three Rules Generator statements:

- TABLE   —   to define the table layout
- COLUMN   —   to define the format of each column
- GENERATE   —   to generate the rule

Alternatively, if the DB2 catalog already contains a definition of the table in question, that definition can simply be extracted using the ADF RGLGEN utility. For the sake of the example, however, we will build the ADF SHIPVIEW table definition from scratch, as follows.

TABLE Statement:

```
TABLE ID=SV,TYPE=TBL,SQLNAME='SHIPVIEW',
      SQLIND=YES,SKSEGS=20,
      SKLEFT='SUPPLIER    PART',
      SKLEFT='NUMBER      NUMBER'
```

The first line defines the two-character ADF table identifier for the table ("SV") and gives the corresponding DB2 name. The SQLIND entry requests ADF to generate SQL indicator variables to handle nulls during processing. The SKSEGS entry specifies the number of rows to display on the Secondary Key Selection Screen. The SKLEFT entries specify the column heading text to be displayed on this latter screen.

COLUMN Statements:

Here are the COLUMN statements for two of the five columns of SHIP-VIEW (the supplier number and supplier city columns):

```
COLUMN ID=0001,SQLNAME='S#',KEY=YES,
       TYPE=C,LENGTH=005,SQLUPD=NO,
       SNAME='SUPPLIER SEARCH CONDITION'

COLUMN ID=0002,SQLNAME='SCITY',
       TYPE=C,LENGTH=015,SQLNULL=YES,SQLUPD=NO,
       SNAME='SCITY'
```

The first line of each statement defines the ADF identifier for the column and gives the corresponding DB2 name. "KEY = YES" (specified for S# but not SCITY) indicates that this column is a component of the primary key of the table. The second line contains "attribute information"—data type, column width, whether nulls are allowed, and whether the column is updatable. The last line specifies text to be used on the key selection screens.

GENERATE Statement:

```
GENERATE OPTIONS=TABL,TABLES=(SV)
```

The GENERATE statement translates the information from the TABLE and COLUMN statements into internal form and adds the generated rule to the ADF static rules library. The parameters are basically self-explanatory: OPTIONS = TABL specifies the rule type (a Table Layout Rule), and the TABLES entry specifies the ADF identifier of the table in question.

22.4 GENERATING THE TABLE HANDLER RULE

The GENERATE statement is also used to generate the Table Handler Rule for the SHIPMENT transaction:

```
GENERATE OPTIONS=TABH,TABLES=(SV),
         SQLCALL=(DSQCALL,KSELECT2)
         SQLUSER=YES
KSELECT3 SELECT   WHERE S# >= :S#.SW AND SCITY = :SCITY.SW
                  ORDER BY S#
&SQLENDS
```

The first line, as before, identifies the rule type and table identifier. The SQLCALL entry on the second line identifies certain predefined SQL func-

tions that are to be included in the generated rule (see below). The
SQLUSER = YES, KSELECT3, and &SQLENDS specifications are explained later.

The predefined ADF SQL functions fall into two categories, standard
and nonstandard. Standard functions are used in ADF standard processing—also possibly in special processing, audit processing, and audit exits.
Nonstandard functions are used in special processing, audit processing, and
audit exits only. The available functions are as follows. (In each case we
give the ADF function name, the function performed, and, by way of explanation, the SQL statements generated.)

1. *Standard functions:*

   CSELECT   —   retrieve a single row using the Primary Key Se-
   lection search condition
   (DECLARE CURSOR–OPEN–FETCH–
   CLOSE)

   CUPDATE   —   update a single row
   (DECLARE CURSOR–OPEN–FETCH–
   UPDATE–CLOSE)

   CDELETE   —   delete a single row
   (DECLARE CURSOR–OPEN–FETCH–
   DELETE–CLOSE)

   INSERT   —   insert a single row
   (INSERT)

   KSELECT1   —   retrieve rows using the Secondary Key Selection
   search condition, where that condition involves
   "<" or ">"
   (DECLARE CURSOR–OPEN–FETCH–
   CLOSE)

   KSELECT2   —   retrieve rows using the Secondary Key Selection
   search condition, where that condition involves
   "%" or "_"
   (DECLARE CURSOR–OPEN–FETCH–
   CLOSE)

   The SQLCALL entry "DSQLCALL" on the GENERATE statement is
shorthand for the combination "CSELECT, INSERT, CUPDATE,
CDELETE, KSELECT1."

2. *Nonstandard functions:*

   SELECT   —   retrieve a single row
   (SELECT)

| UPDATE | — | update a single row (UPDATE) |
| DELETE | — | delete a single row (DELETE) |

In addition to the predefined (standard and nonstandard) ADF SQL functions, users can define their own functions by specifying SQLUSER = YES on the GENERATE statement and immediately following that statement with a definition of the SQL function(s) required (terminated by the &SQLENDS statement). Those functions are then incorporated into the Table Handler Rule being generated. Our example shows a function named KSELECT3 that provides additional search conditions for use in Secondary Key Selection. (We deliberately do not explain all of the operands of KSELECT3 in full detail. See the IBM manuals for more information.) User functions can be used in Secondary Key Selection, audit processing, audit exits, and special processing routines.

Audit exit routines and special processing routines can invoke SQL functions via a special call to ADF. Alternatively, they can issue SQL statements (either static or dynamic) directly. The disadvantage of this latter approach is that the exits and routines must be separately processed by the DB2 Precompiler and Bind components, and separately maintained.

22.5   GENERATING THE INPUT TRANSACTION RULE

The last rule we discuss is the Input Transaction Rule for the SHIPMENT transaction:

```
GENERATE TRXID=SH,OPTIONS=CVALL,DBPATH=(SV),
        TRXNAME='SHIPMENT'
            .
            .
        *** screen format information for the  ***
        *** Transaction Display Screen omitted ***
```

For simplicity, we show only a portion of this rule definition (the omitted portion is chiefly concerned with screen formatting data for the Transaction Display Screen, Fig. 22.5). The transaction is a conversational transaction (CVALL option) with an identifier of "SH" (this was the identifier entered on the Primary Option Menu, Fig. 22.2). The table identifier on the DBPATH keyword, in our case SV, determines the table to be used for Primary Key Selection. The transaction name is SHIPMENT.

22.6   CONCLUSION

We conclude this chapter with a brief summary of the major differences between ADF and CSP (the subject of the previous chapter). ADF and CSP are both DP professional application development tools for DB2. However:

- ADF is less flexible than CSP.

- CSP is a complete application development system; ADF is merely an application generator.

- CSP allows an application to be developed in one environment and executed in another.

- ADF supports IMS/DC and CICS applications; CSP supports CICS, TSO, and CMS applications.

- ADF supports IMS databases (under IMS/DC and CICS) and DB2 databases; CSP supports IMS databases (under CICS) and DB2 and SQL/DS databases.

- CSP-like functions are included in IBM's Systems Application Architecture, SAA (see Chapter 18).

C H A P T E R
•23•

Data Extract

23.1 INTRODUCTION

Data Extract (DXT) is a program for extracting data from operational databases and files. The extracted data is in a suitable format for loading (via the appropriate load utility) into a DB2 or SQL/DS table on the same or a different computer system. DXT users can use either or both of the following:

- Relational Data Extract Feature (MVS, VM)
  —for extracting data from DB2 or SQL/DS databases
- General Data Extract Feature (MVS only)
  —for extracting data from IMS databases, VSAM or sequential files, or nonIBM data sources (e.g., nonIBM SQL databases)

In this chapter we first present an overview of both features; we then go on to discuss the relational feature in more depth. Details of the general feature are beyond the scope of this book; the reader is referred to the IBM manuals for more information.

The main components of DXT are as follows (refer to Fig. 23.1).

- End User and Administrative Dialogs
- Relational Extract Manager (REM)
- User Input Manager (UIM)
- Data Extract Manager (DEM)

Of these components, the End User and Administrative Dialogs constitute the DXT base product, the Relational Extract Manager constitutes the Relational Data Extract Feature, and the User Input Manager and the Data Extract Manager constitute the General Data Extract Feature.

End User and Administrative Dialogs

- The *End User* Dialogs allow users to submit existing extract requests or construct new ones. (*Note:* QMF and AS each provide commands to invoke these dialogs directly.) In the case of a new request, prompt screens allow the user to specify the source of the data, the specific data required (i.e., the selection criteria), and the target DB2 or SQL/DS table into which the extracted data is to be loaded. The data source is identified by selecting the required item(s) from a list of tables and "DXTVIEWs" (a DXTVIEW is a "flat file" view of fields that may be accessed from nonrelational files and databases). The source data and target table do not have to reside on the system where the dialog is executed.

- The *Administrative* Dialogs are used to define and maintain extract requests, to create DXTVIEW and other data descriptions, and to build information about the DB2 and SQL/DS tables accessible by individual users.

Relational Extract Manager (REM)

The REM is the component that performs the actual data extraction when the source is a DB2 or SQL/DS database. Thus, it extracts data from DB2 and SQL/DS tables in accordance with SQL extract requests generated by the DXT End User Dialogs. The extracted data is written to a sequential file or an IXF file or is placed in a spool file for routing back to the submitting location. The extract request can optionally invoke a batch job to load the extracted data into a DB2 or SQL/DS table, using the applicable load utility.

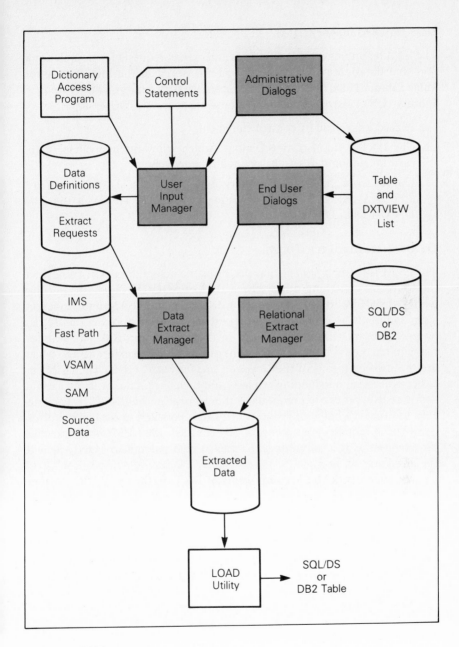

Fig. 23.1 DXT structure

User Input Manager (UIM)

The UIM maintains data descriptions and extract requests for nonrelational files and databases. Data descriptions are stored in the File Description Table Library (FDTLIB); extract requests are stored in the Extract Request Library (EXTLIB). There are three possible sources for UIM input:

1. A card image file of control statements
2. The DXT Administrative Dialogs, which allow the equivalent of the card image input file to be created interactively
3. Output from the DXT Dictionary Access Program (DAP), which creates data descriptions from existing information stored in the IBM DB/DC Data Dictionary

Data Extract Manager (DEM)

The DEM is the component that performs the actual data extraction when the source is something other than a DB2 or SQL/DS database. In other words, the DEM extracts data from IMS databases, VSAM and sequential files, and nonIBM data sources using extract requests stored in the Extract Request Library (EXTLIB). (*Note:* In the case of nonIBM data sources, the required data is extracted by means of user-supplied exit routines, which are specified by means of the *Generic Data Interface,* GDI.) The DEM can either process all outstanding requests and then terminate, or it can execute continuously, processing requests as they appear in the EXTLIB. Facilities exist to process a batch of requests in a single pass and to control the priority in which requests are processed. (By contrast, the REM simply executes each request as it is submitted.) Extracted data is handled exactly as with the REM.

So much for the basic components of DXT. In the rest of this chapter, we consider in some detail what is involved in using DXT to extract data from a DB2 table, basing our discussion (as usual) on the suppliers-and-parts database. We will first show how the End User Dialogs can be used to create and execute an extract request (Section 23.2), and then go on to discuss the facilities provided by the Administrative Dialogs for maintaining the DXT system (Section 23.3). Section 23.4 presents a brief conclusion.

23.2 CREATING AND EXECUTING AN EXTRACT REQUEST

In this section we consider what is involved in creating and executing a DXT request. By way of example, we create a request to extract supplier number, name, and city information for suppliers with status greater than 5. We begin with the main *DXT End User Dialogs* screen shown in Fig. 23.2. The

```
                        DXT END USER DIALOGS

Select ONE of the following options,
  or use the PF Keys:

    1      TABLES        - Display table and DXTVIEW
                           names available for extract
    2      COLUMNS       - Display  column  names  of
                           tables or DXTVIEWs selected
    3      CONDITIONS    - Specify conditions on the
                           columns
    4      JOIN          - Specify join condition if more
                           than one table or DXTVIEW selected
    5      TARGET        - Specify the target for loading
                           extracted data
    6      DB ACCESS     - Specify data base access information

    7      PROFILE REVIEW - Modify Profile settings

Available Commands:  Send, Save, Display, Status, Cancel, Reset, Check, Erase
PF 1=HELP      2=SEND      3=END      4=TABLES    5=COLUMNS   6=CONDTION
PF 7=BACKWARD  8=FORWARD   9=JOIN     10=TARGET   11=EXT LIST 12=ACCESS

OPTION ===> 1
```

Fig 23.2. Main DXT End User Dialogs screen

options on that screen lead us to further screens which allow us to specify all aspects of the request in detail. In general, to create a request we must do all of the following (refer to the figure):

- Select the names of the tables and/or DXTVIEWs from which data is to be extracted (Option 1, TABLES)

- Specify the columns to be extracted (Option 2, COLUMNS)

- Specify the search criteria to be used (Option 3, CONDITIONS)

- Specify the joining condition when extracting data from multiple tables or DXTVIEWs (Option 4, JOIN)

- Identify the target DB2 or SQL/DS table and the system on which it resides (Option 5, TARGET)

- Specify control information for the source and target systems (Option 6, DB ACCESS)

If the request already exists, we can execute it by selecting its name from the "extract list" obtained by pressing PF key 11. In our example, however, we want to create a new request, so we choose Option 1 (TABLES). That choice leads us to the *Select Tables/DXTVIEWs for Extract* screen (Fig. 23.3), which displays the name of each table or DXT-

```
┌─────────────────────────────────────────────────────────────────────────┐
│                  SELECT TABLES/DXTVIEWS FOR EXTRACT              ROW 1 OF 3 │
│                                                                            │
│ Enter an S under SELECT to select table(s) or dxtview(s) you wish to extract│
│ from. Remember to select items from the same LOCATION and of the same TYPE.│
│                                                                            │
│                                                                            │
│ SELECT  TABLE/DXTVIEW       CREATOR   LOCATION   TYPE    DESCRIPTION        │
│    S        NAME                                                           │
│                                                                            │
│ => S   S                    CJDATE    SANJOSE1   DB2     SUPPLIERS TABLE    │
│ =>     SP                   CJDATE    SANJOSE1   DB2     SUPPLIERS/PARTS TABLE│
│ =>     P                    CJDATE    SANJOSE1   DB2     PARTS TABLE        │
│ =>     EDUC                 DXT       SANJOSE2   DXT     IMS EDUCATION DB   │
│ **************************** BOTTOM OF DATA ****************************     │
│                                                                            │
│                                                                            │
│                                                                            │
│                                                                            │
│                                                                            │
│                                                                            │
│ PF 1=HELP       2=SEND      3=END       4=TABLES    5=COLUMNS   6=CONDTION  │
│ PF 7=BACKWARD   8=FORWARD   9=JOIN      10=TARGET   11=EXT LIST 12=ACCESS   │
│                                                                            │
│ COMMAND ===>                                              SCROLL ===> HALF  │
└─────────────────────────────────────────────────────────────────────────┘
```

Fig 23.3 DXT Select Tables/DXTVIEWs for Extract screen

VIEW we are allowed to access, the ID of its creator, the name of the system (i.e., node ID) on which it is located, its file type, and a short description of its use. (All of this information is maintained by the *DXT administrator* using the DXT Administrative Dialogs. See Section 23.3.)

According to Fig. 23.3, we are allowed to extract data from any or all of the suppliers (S), shipments (SP), and parts (P) tables, also from a DXTVIEW called EDUC (introduced purely for the sake of the example). We enter an "S" ("select") alongside the suppliers table name. Pressing PF key 5 will now display the *Select Columns and Specify Functions* screen (Fig. 23.4), which is used to specify the columns we want to extract. In our example, the screen contains a list of the columns of the supplier table. We select the S#, SNAME, and CITY columns by entering an "S" alongside those column names, and press PF key 6 to display the *Specify Conditions* screen (Fig. 23.5).

The screen in Fig. 23.5 lists the columns of the suppliers table with their data type and length. (The DXT Administrative Dialogs—again, see Section 23.3—allow the DXT administrator to obtain this information from the catalog tables for the DB2 source system, thereby making it possible for DXT to build the screen.) We want suppliers with status greater than 5, so we enter the appropriate search condition against the STATUS column; we

```
                    SELECT COLUMNS AND SPECIFY FUNCTIONS          ROW 1 OF 7
Do you wish to select ALL columns for extract, Yes or No?   ===> N


If not, enter an S under SELECT to select specific columns for extract
and enter any FUNCTIONs for the columns. Press HELP for a list of functions.

SELECT  FUNCTION COLUMN              TABLE              CREATOR
  S               NAME               NAME

=> S  =>        S#                   S                  CJDATE
=> S  =>        SNAME                S                  CJDATE
=>    =>        STATUS               S                  CJDATE
=> S  =>        CITY                 S                  CJDATE
***************************** BOTTOM OF DATA ******************************




PF 1=HELP      2=SEND      3=END      4=TABLES   5=COLUMNS  6=CONDITION
PF 7=BACKWARD  8=FORWARD   9=JOIN     10=TARGET  11=EXT LIST 12=ACCESS

COMMAND ===>                                           SCROLL ==> HALF
```

Fig 23.4 DXT Select Columns and Specify Functions screen

```
                        SPECIFY CONDITIONS                        ROW 1 OF 7
Specify the CONDITION field as operator followed by value(s). You may also use
the lines below for free formatted conditions. Press HELP key for syntax.

==>
==>

COLUMN              COLUMN   COLUMN    CONDITION
  NAME              TYPE     LENGTH

S#                  CHAR          5 =>
SNAME               CHAR         20 =>
STATUS              SMALLINT        => >5
CITY                CHAR         15 =>
***************************** BOTTOM OF DATA ******************************




PF 1=HELP      2=SEND      3=END      4=TABLES   5=COLUMNS  6=CONDTION
PF 7=BACKWARD  8=FORWARD   9=JOIN     10=TARGET  11=EXT LIST 12=ACCESS

COMMAND ===>                                           SCROLL ===> HALF
```

Fig 23.5 DXT Specify Conditions screen

then press PF key 10, which takes us to the *Name Target for Extract Output* screen. See Fig. 23.6.

To specify the extract target, we first give the "nickname" (CJW1 in our example) for the target system. Nicknames are intended to make it easy for the user to identify individual (source or target) systems. They are maintained by the DXT administrator. In general, a nickname is a shorthand for the combination of all of the following:

- System node ID
- File name: name of a file containing the job control (JCL) statements to be used in building the extract job stream
- File type: DXTVIEW (source systems only), DB2, SQL/DS, or IXF

After entering the nickname we specify:

- The target table name (SNEW)
- The target table owner (CJWHITE)
- Option "C" (create a new table)
- The mapping of source columns to target columns

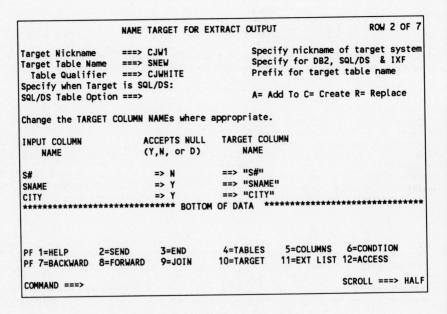

Fig 23.6 DXT Name Target for Extract Output screen

■   Whether nulls are allowed in the target columns (in the example, we have specified "nulls not allowed" for the S# column)

Once all this information has been entered, we press PF key 12 to reach the *Data Base Access* screen shown in Fig. 23.7.

The Data Base Access screen is in two parts. The top part is used to specify necessary control information to be used to access the source system (node ID, user ID, and password); this information will be used in constructing the data extract job stream. The bottom part (required only if the source system is SQL/DS) specifies similar information for the target system. (Remember that, in general, the source system, target system, and system running the DXT dialogs can all be different.) In practice, most of the information on the Data Base Access screen will be completed automatically using information supplied by the DXT administrator.

Our extract request is now complete. If we press PF key 2 the extract job will be submitted for execution. DXT will route the extract job to the source system, extract the data, and then route the extracted data to the target system. On the target system it will invoke the appropriate load utility and load the extracted data into the table specified. We will be notified when the data extract job completes and when the load of the target table is finished.

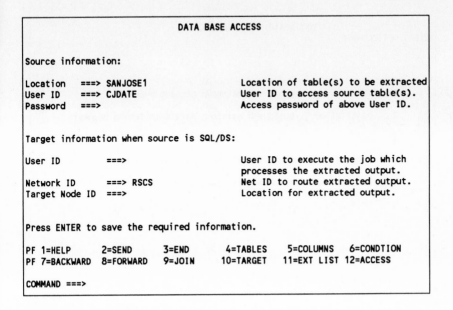

```
                            DATA BASE ACCESS


Source information:

Location    ===> SANJOSE1          Location of table(s) to be extracted
User ID     ===> CJDATE            User ID to access source table(s).
Password    ===>                   Access password of above User ID.



Target information when source is SQL/DS:

User ID          ===>              User ID to execute the job which
                                   processes the extracted output.
Network ID       ===> RSCS         Net ID to route extracted output.
Target Node ID   ===>              Location for extracted output.



Press ENTER to save the required information.

PF 1=HELP      2=SEND     3=END      4=TABLES    5=COLUMNS   6=CONDTION
PF 7=BACKWARD  8=FORWARD  9=JOIN     10=TARGET   11=EXT LIST 12=ACCESS

COMMAND ===>
```

Fig 23.7 DXT Data Base Access screen

23.3 USING THE ADMINISTRATIVE DIALOGS

The main DXT *Administrative Dialogs* screen is shown in Fig. 23.8. The dialogs support six different administration tasks:

- Build and maintain extract requests (Option 1, EXTRACT)

  This option allows the DXT administrator to build, maintain, and submit DXT requests. Facilities exist to check the status of submitted requests and to cancel them if required.

- Build and maintain data descriptions (Option 2, DESCRIPTION)

  The formats of files and databases to be accessed via the General Data Extract Feature are defined to DXT using this dialog. The dialog is also used to create DXTVIEWs for such files and databases.

- Build and maintain JCL statements (Option 3, JCL)

  The JCL job streams to execute the Data Extract Manager, the Relational Extract Manager, and the DB2 and SQL/DS load utilities are created and maintained using this dialog.

```
                          DXT ADMINISTRATIVE DIALOGS
SELECT OPTION ===>



        1    EXTRACT        Build and maintain extract requests.

        2    DESCRIPTION    Build and maintain data description requests.

        3    JCL            Build and maintain Job Control Language.

        4    PROFILE        Specify Dialogs processing options.

        5    ADMINISTER     End User Dialogs Administration.

        6    DXTA           Bridge to DXT Assist.



Press:   ENTER to select   END key to exit   HELP key for information
```

Fig 23.8 Main DXT Administrative Dialogs screen

- Specify dialog processing options (Option 4, PROFILE)

  Many of the options used in constructing extract job streams are obtained from the user's DXT profile. The DXT administrator uses this dialog to create and maintain such profiles.

- End User Dialogs administration (Option 5, ADMINISTER)

  The administrator uses this option to build the list of nicknames for each user and to construct a DXT table containing the table names and DXTVIEWs the user is allowed to access. A third option permits a job to be submitted to access the system catalog tables of DB2 and SQL/DS. This job extracts the data required to build the table and column information used by the End User Dialogs.

- Bridge to DXT Assist (Option 6, DXTA)

  This option provides a bridge to the DXTA ("DXT Assist") product. DXTA helps in building DXT descriptions of nonrelational source files and databases, in creating the definitions of the tables used to store extract results, and in creating the DXT control statements needed for the extract job streams.

23.4 CONCLUSION

Copy management is a complex task, particularly when extracting data from nonrelational files and databases. End-users will typically not set up and maintain their own copy management schemes, but will instead rely on the DP department to perform this function for them. The DXT Administrative Dialogs are designed to assist the DP department in this task. End-users can use the DXT End User Dialogs to code and submit extract requests to extract both relational and nonrelational data for loading into DB2 and SQL/DS tables. However, strict management of this process is required in practice.

CHAPTER

·24·

Micro-to-Mainframe Links

24.1 INTRODUCTION

It is widely recognized that, from the end-user's perspective, microcomputers tend to be much more responsive and much easier to use than their mainframe counterparts. This is why an increasing number of users prefer to use the PC for analyzing data, producing reports and graphs, etc. Frequently, however, the data to be analyzed or reported on resides in some central or departmental database on some other machine. The primary purpose of a micro-to-mainframe link product is to allow the user to extract the required data from that other machine and copy it down into a PC file or database (a process known as "downloading"), thereby making the data available for subsequent processing by a variety of PC tools.

A micro-to-mainframe link product involves two components, a requester program on the PC and a server program on the other machine (the "host"). The requester receives extract requests entered by the PC user and passes them to the server for processing. The server extracts the required

428 Micro-to-Mainframe Links

host data and passes it back to the requester. Conversion into the appropriate PC file format can be done either on the host or on the PC.

There are many micro-to-mainframe link products on the market that support access to DB2 on the host. In this chapter we describe two such products (both from IBM), namely Host Data Base View (HDBV) and Enhanced Connectivity Facilities (ECF). Each of these products allows data to be extracted from both VM and MVS hosts. For obvious reasons, however, we concentrate on the case where the host is running MVS (and DB2), and the data to be extracted resides in a DB2 database.

Note: As mentioned in Chapter 18, we generally take the term "PC" to include the IBM Personal System/2 as well as the original PC machine. Currently, HDBV and ECF both support PS/2 systems running PC/DOS but not OS/2. However, (a) OS/2 (Extended Edition) does include support for IBM's standard Server-Requester Programming Interface protocols (see Section 23.3), which means that micro-to-mainframe link systems can be written to run under OS/2, and (b) IBM has stated that it does intend to produce a version of ECF for the OS/2 environment (date of availability unknown at the time of writing).

24.2 HOST DATA BASE VIEW

Host Data Base View (HDBV) runs as a requester program on a standard IBM PC. The server function at the host is provided (typically) by QMF or AS. Data files created on the host by DXT can also be downloaded via HDBV. Communication between the PC and the host is performed using standard IBM PC communication facilities (details beyond the scope of this book); however, a User Communication Exit is also provided to allow the use of other (nonIBM) communication products. *Note:* The primary purpose of HDBV is of course to download data from the host to the PC. However, it does also permit files to be copied from the PC to the host ("uploading"), and it also allows the PC user to invoke procedures (e.g., EXECs or CLISTs) on the host.

In order to explain how HDBV works, we will consider an example of extracting data via QMF from the suppliers-and-parts database. (Refer to Chapter 19 if you need to refresh your memory regarding QMF.) When HDBV is first invoked, the HDBV *Main Menu* is displayed (Fig. 24.1). That menu allows us to:

- Extract data from host files and databases
- Reformat extracted data into several popular PC file formats (DIF, SYLK, WRK, WKS, SDF, etc.)
- Execute other PC programs (e.g., dBase III, Lotus 1-2-3) to process the reformatted data

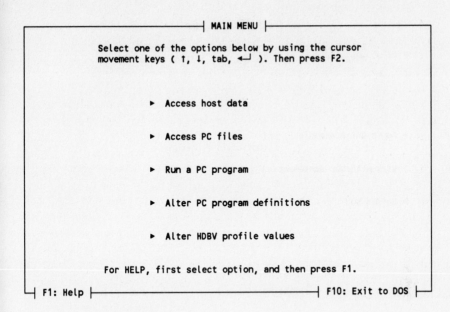

┤ MAIN MENU ├

Select one of the options below by using the cursor
movement keys (↑, ↓, tab, ↵). Then press F2.

► **Access host data**

► **Access PC files**

► **Run a PC program**

► **Alter PC program definitions**

► **Alter HDBV profile values**

For HELP, first select option, and then press F1.

F1: Help ├ ┤ F10: Exit to DOS

Fig. 24.1 HDBV Main Menu

- Add programs to the list of PC programs that can be invoked from HDBV
- Modify values in the HDBV profile (e.g., change the host operating system)

We wish to extract data from the host, so we select "Access host data," which causes the HDBV *Host Services Menu* (not shown) to be displayed. That menu allows us to choose the host product to be used for extracting the data. Choosing QMF brings us to the HDBV *QMF Services Menu* (Fig. 24.2), which offers three different ways of using QMF:

1. QMF procedure:

   The user can invoke a predefined QMF procedure already existing on the host. This method is useful if the user is not familiar with QMF or SQL. HDBV will display a list of available procedures on request.

2. SQL statement:

   The user can create and execute his or her own SQL statements directly. Those statements can be saved and later reused, with or without subsequent modification. *Note:* All SQL statements are supported—e.g., the HDBV user can perform updates on the host as well as retrievals (authorization constraints permitting, of course).

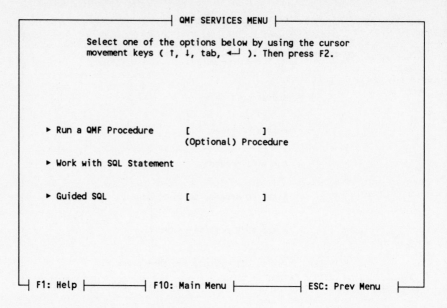

Fig 24.2 HDBV QMF Services Menu

3. Guided SQL:

HDBV can guide the user through a series of prompts and menus and hence create SQL statements on the user's behalf. From a displayed list of table names, the user selects the table from which data is to be extracted. Further options allow the user to specify the columns required, the search criteria, and the order in which data is to be returned. This method suffers from the limitation that the generated SQL statement cannot extract data from more than one table (though the table in question can be a view and might therefore involve multiple tables indirectly).

In our example, we will create our own SQL statement. Choosing "Work with SQL Statement" on the HDBV QMF Services Menu leads us to the HDBV *QMF SQL Entry Menu* (Fig. 24.3). We then enter the SQL request shown to extract supplier numbers, names, and cities for suppliers with status greater than 5. (*Note:* By entering a name in the "Statement Name" field and pressing PF key 6, we could save the statement for later use.) Then we press PF key 2 and HDBV passes the statement to QMF for execution.

HDBV will inform us when the query has finished and the data has been downloaded to the PC. We can then use the "Access PC files" option on the HDBV Main Menu (refer back to Fig. 24.1) to display the data for

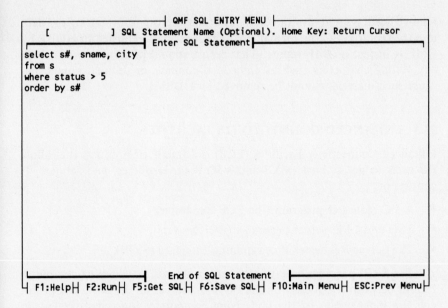

```
┤ QMF SQL ENTRY MENU ├
   [              ] SQL Statement Name (Optional). Home Key: Return Cursor
                  ┤ Enter SQL Statement├
select s#, sname, city
from s
where status > 5
order by s#




                      End of SQL Statement
┤ F1:Help├ F2:Run├ F5:Get SQL├ F6:Save SQL├ F10:Main Menu├ ESC:Prev Menu├
```

Fig. 24.3 HDBV QMF SQL Entry Menu

browsing or to reformat the extracted data. If we select the browse option, the result shown in Fig. 24.4 will be displayed. This screen can be used to

```
BROWSING : C:SUPPLIER.RPT              Line 1    of  7    Column 1    of 35
COMMAND ====>

    S#          SNAME        CITY
    --          -----        ----
    S1          Smith        London
    S2          Jones        Paris
    S3          Blake        Paris
    S4          Clark        London
    S5          Adams        Athens









1:Help 2:Cmd 3:← 4:→ 5:Block 6:Row 7:Col 8:Hide 9:Fields 10:Reform ESC:Exit
```

Fig 24.4 HDBV listing of extracted data

remove headings and unwanted blocks of data before reformatting the data into the required PC file format. (Note that the data returned to HDBV by QMF is in fact a QMF report. That report should preferably not include any editing characters such as embedded commas or decimal points, because such material cannot be removed by HDBV.)

24.3   ENHANCED CONNECTIVITY FACILITIES

Enhanced Connectivity Facilities (ECF) is a family of products that allow PC users to access host (MVS and VM) data, resources, and services. It consists of:

- A PC requester program (the ECF Requester)
- TSO and CMS server programs (ECF Servers)
- The Server-Requester Programming Interface (SRPI)

The SRPI provides a set of standard protocols for handling communications between a requester on the PC and a server on the host. The protocols are independent of the underlying communications environment; in fact, they are a subset of IBM's Advanced Program-to-Program Communications (APPC) architecture. The SRPI is provided with TSO/E and VM/SP on the host and with IBM 3270 emulation programs on the PC.

ECF provides three major sets of functions:

1. *Access to host data:*   Data can be downloaded from DB2, SQL/DS, and IMS databases, and from VSAM and sequential files.
2. *Access to host resources:*   Host disks, files, and printers can be accessed by PC users as though they were directly connected to the PC.
3. *Access to host services:*   PC users can directly invoke host EXECs, CLISTs, commands, and programs.

In order to facilitate a direct comparison with HDBV, we will first look at the ECF host data access functions. We will then move on to describe the ECF facilities for using host resources and services.

Accessing Host Data

Unlike HDBV, ECF has its own server program and does not require a separate product on the host to access host data. The PC user interacts with the ECF Requester using either commands or menus to specify extract requests. The ECF Requester routes those requests via the SRPI to the ECF Server on the host, which extracts the required data. The extracted data is then either stored in a host file or downloaded to the PC (whichever is specified by the user).

Consider what is involved in using ECF to perform the SQL extract request from Section 24.2: "Extract supplier number, name, and city for all suppliers with status greater than 5" (we deliberately use the same example as we did in our HDBV discussion). When ECF is first invoked, the *Cooperative Processing Services* menu is displayed (Fig. 24.5). From that menu, we can reach any of the services provided by ECF. We wish to extract host data, so we choose the "Use Database Services" option, which opens up the *Use Database Services* window shown in Fig. 24.6. *Note:* That figure also shows the *Use SQL Services* window, to be discussed below.

The *Use Database Services* window provides a menu offering two choices, "Use SQL Services" and "Use DXT Services." If DXT is chosen, the extract request must already have been created on the host; the ECF Requester can display a list of existing DXT requests from which one can be selected for batch execution. In our example, however, we wish to use SQL, so we choose the "Use SQL Services" option. A second window ap-

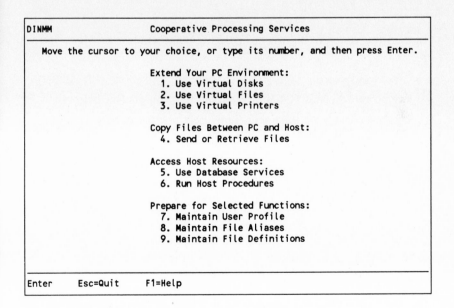

```
DINMM                  Cooperative Processing Services

  Move the cursor to your choice, or type its number, and then press Enter.

                       Extend Your PC Environment:
                         1. Use Virtual Disks
                         2. Use Virtual Files
                         3. Use Virtual Printers

                       Copy Files Between PC and Host:
                         4. Send or Retrieve Files

                       Access Host Resources:
                         5. Use Database Services
                         6. Run Host Procedures

                       Prepare for Selected Functions:
                         7. Maintain User Profile
                         8. Maintain File Aliases
                         9. Maintain File Definitions



  Enter       Esc=Quit      F1=Help
```

Fig. 24.5 ECF Requester: Cooperative Processing Services menu

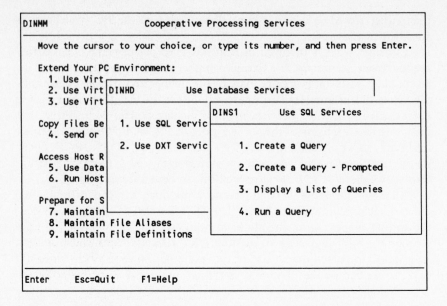

```
DINMM                    Cooperative Processing Services

  Move the cursor to your choice, or type its number, and then press Enter.

  Extend Your PC Environment:
     1. Use Virt┌──────────────────────────────────────────────────┐
     2. Use Virt│DINHD          Use Database Services               │
     3. Use Virt│             ┌──────────────────────────────────────────────┐
                │             │DINS1          Use SQL Services               │
  Copy Files Be│ 1. Use SQL Servic                                           │
     4. Send or │             │                                              │
                │ 2. Use DXT Servic  1. Create a Query                       │
  Access Host R│             │                                              │
     5. Use Data│             │    2. Create a Query - Prompted              │
     6. Run Host│             │                                              │
                │             │    3. Display a List of Queries              │
  Prepare for S│             │                                              │
     7. Maintain└─────────────     4. Run a Query                           │
     8. Maintain File Aliases                                               │
     9. Maintain File Definitions                                           │


Enter      Esc=Quit     F1=Help
```

Fig. 24.6 ECF Requester: Database Services and SQL Services menus

pears on the screen as shown in Fig. 24.6. That window provides options to:

- Create and execute SQL statements directly (much as with HDBV)
- Create and execute SQL statements using prompts (see below)
- Display saved SQL statements and select one for editing
- Execute a saved SQL statement

Note: As with HDBV, "SQL statement" here means *any* SQL statement—i.e., the PC user is not limited to retrievals only.

For the sake of the example, we choose Option 2, which takes us to the *Create a Query—Prompted* menu (Fig. 24.7). We enter the name of the table from which data is to be extracted, namely table S. *Note:* We could alternatively have entered an asterisk ("*"), which would cause ECF to access the DB2 catalog and display a list of tables we are allowed to use.

The Requester now displays a list of the columns in table S (see Fig. 24.8); this information is also obtained from the DB2 catalog. We can now indicate the columns to be extracted (S#, SNAME, and CITY), together with appropriate search criteria (STATUS > 5). If the data is to be returned in a particular sequence, pressing PF key 5 will open up a window

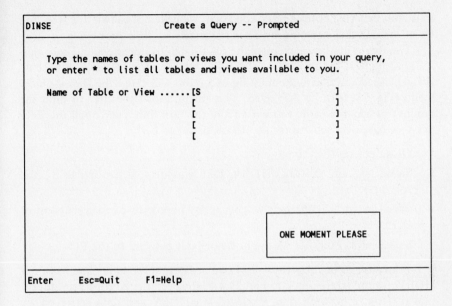

```
DINSE                    Create a Query -- Prompted

   Type the names of tables or views you want included in your query,
   or enter * to list all tables and views available to you.

   Name of Table or View ......[S                        ]
                               [                          ]
                               [                          ]
                               [                          ]
                               [                          ]




                                        ┌─────────────────────┐
                                        │                     │
                                        │  ONE MOMENT PLEASE   │
                                        │                     │
                                        └─────────────────────┘

 Enter      Esc=Quit      F1=Help
```

Fig. 24.7 ECF Requester: Create a Query—Prompted menu

```
DINSC                  List of Columns with Tables            18 Lines

   Do any of the following, and then press Enter:
   - to view detailed column information, type V to the left of column names
   - to select columns, specify output sequence numbers to the left
   - to omit columns from this list, type O to the left of column names
   - to limit the query results, type selection criteria

   When finished, press F4 to create the query statement

       Column Name      Owner    Name of Table/View Sort  Selection Criteria

 [1  ] S#               CJDATE   S                     [                    ]
 [2  ] SNAME            CJDATE   S                     [                    ]
 [o  ] STATUS           CJDATE   S                     [ > 5               ]
 [3  ] CITY             CJDATE   S                     [                    ]




 Enter      Esc=Quit      F1=Help     F4=Create Query   F5=Sort Sequence  PgUp
                                      F6=Expand Criteria                  PgDn
```

Fig. 24.8 ECF Requester: List of Columns with Tables menu

to permit ordering criteria to be specified; we have not shown this step, but let us assume that ordering by S# is requested.

The Requester now generates the required SQL statement and automatically displays it for review. At this point we can modify, save, or execute the generated statement. Requesting execution will cause the *Run a Query* menu (Fig. 24.9) to be displayed. This menu allows the user to limit the number of records to be retrieved from the host and also to tell the ECF Server where to place the result. Result data can be

■ Displayed on the screen

■ Saved in a PC file (like HDBV, ECF supports most popular PC file formats)

■ Saved in an IXF file on the host (see Chapter 18 for a discussion of IXF)

■ Saved in an ECF file on the host for later copying to the PC

The result of our request will of course contain the same data as in our HDBV example (refer back to Fig. 24.4). However, there is one very important difference between data retrieved via HDBV and data retrieved via ECF:

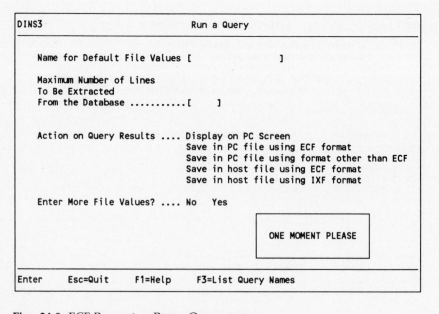

Fig. 24.9 ECF Requester: Run a Query menu

- For HDBV, extracted data is always in the form of a report. In other words, the data has been formatted at the host by the query product doing the extract.

- For ECF, on the other hand, extracted data is a copy of the data as extracted at the host; it does *not* contain any extraneous information such as headers, embedded punctuation marks, or the like.

So much for the host data access functions of ECF. We conclude this section by briefly describing the other two major ECF functions, namely the host resources and host services access functions.

Accessing Host Resources

Using ECF, PC users can use certain host resources—specifically, certain host devices and files—as if they were directly connected to the PC. Three types of such resources are supported:

- *Virtual disks* are used to store PC files (in PC format) on the host. This facility gives the PC user access to larger-capacity (and more reliable) disk storage. Most PC/DOS file and disk commands can be used with virtual disks.

- *Virtual printers* allow host printers to be used in the same manner as a PC printer.

- *Virtual files* are host files (in host format) that appear to the PC user as if they were stored on a PC disk. This facility allows PC users and programs to access host files without having to download them to the PC. It also allows the PC to share data with the host and/or other PCs. Many PC/DOS commands can be used to manipulate such files; ECF handles all necessary data and field conversions automatically.

Accessing Host Services

This ECF facility permits a PC user to execute VM EXECs, TSO CLISTs, and CMS and TSO commands and programs. Output results can be displayed on the PC screen or stored in PC files. Host functions requiring prompted input or full-screen output are not supported, however.

24.4 CONCLUSION

This completes our description of IBM's two micro-to-mainframe link products, HDBV and ECF. Each has its own particular strengths and weaknesses. HDBV provides a simple interface to IBM's mainframe query products (especially QMF and AS) by which host database and file data can be retrieved via those products and downloaded to the PC. It has the advantage that PC users can use tools and interfaces they may already have become familiar with on the host. ECF, on the other hand, contains a more general and more extensive set of functions; it provides a general architecture for cooperative processing between IBM PC and mainframe computers, and hence can be used as the basis for a variety of more specialized micro-to-mainframe link products. In fact, as mentioned in Chapter 3, HDBV itself can use the ECF facilities to access the host (though ECF is only one of several possible underpinnings for HDBV). ECF is likely to become increasingly important over the next few years.

CHAPTER

·25·

Data Base Relational Application Directory

25.1 INTRODUCTION

As explained in Chapter 9, descriptive information concerning DB2 objects such as base tables, views, etc., is recorded in the DB2 catalog. However, the DB2 catalog describes DB2 objects *only;* it does not contain any information about the use of such objects by application programs, nor about such programs themselves. In other words, it is not a full-function data dictionary. The subject of this chapter, Data Base Relational Application Directory (DBRAD), is not a full-function data dictionary either, but it does go further than the DB2 catalog in its support for dictionary-type functions. In particular, it provides a set of tables (logically an extension to the DB2 catalog) called the *DBRAD directory,** which allows administrators and ap-

---

*Not to be confused with the DB2 directory (see Chapter 2).

plication developers to record and manage information about applications—especially CSP applications—and their use of DB2 (and other) objects.

DBRAD supports DB2 in the MVS environment under both TSO and CICS. (A separate version of the product supports SQL/DS in the VM environment.) The main components of the MVS version are as follows (refer to Fig. 25.1).

- *Catalog Dialogs* (for querying and displaying DB2 catalog information)
- *Import Facilities* (for importing descriptors into the DBRAD directory from the DB2 catalog, COBOL and PL/I structure libraries, and CSP applications)
- *Directory Dialogs* (for querying, displaying, and updating DBRAD directory information)
- *Reports* (for reporting on DBRAD directory objects and their interrelationships)
- *Model Generator* (for creating "model" SQL statements, COBOL and PL/I structures, and VSAM and other definitions from DB2 catalog and DBRAD directory information)
- *Application Program Interface* (for updating DBRAD directory information from an application program)
- *Umbrella Dialogs* (for invoking other IBM tools such as DB2I, QMF, DBEDIT, and CSP)

Note: All of these components are supported under TSO. Only the Catalog and Directory Dialog components are supported under CICS.

Before we can describe the components of DBRAD in more detail, it is necessary to introduce a few basic concepts. First, every DBRAD object is uniquely identified by a 3-part name or "key" consisting of the name of the library the object belongs to, the type of the object, and the name of the object itself.* For example, a certain PL/I structure might be identified by the combination MYPLILIB (library name) plus RECORD (object type) plus EMPREC (object name). Note that every object is required to belong to some library. Libraries are used to group together objects that are logically related in some manner. For example, the set of all structures used in the same PL/I application would typically all belong to the same DBRAD library.

---

*An object can also be given an *alias* in addition to its 3-part library/type/name key. Such aliases can be user-defined or generated by the various directory import functions (see Section 25.4).

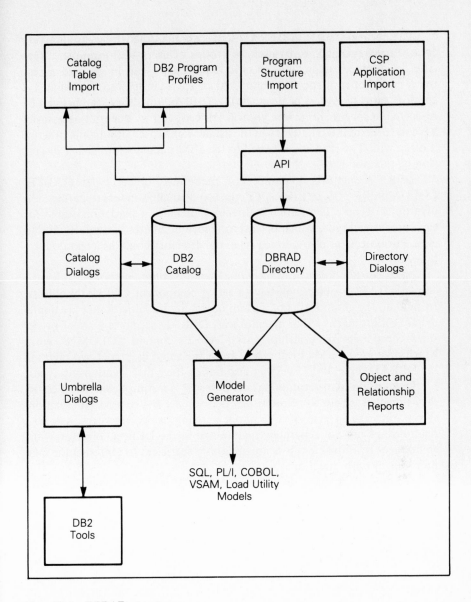

Fig. 25.1. DBRAD structure

The library concept in DBRAD serves among other things as an access control mechanism: Specific users or groups of users—for example, a specific development team or a specific department—can be granted access (read or write) to a specific library. Also, each library can be assigned a specific status (e.g., test or production). DBRAD directory searches can be restricted to specific libraries. *Note:* A DBRAD library does not necessarily have to correspond to a library in the usual MVS sense, although in practice it often will. The reader is referred to the IBM manuals for further discussion of this point.

DBRAD supports a number of predefined object types (TABLE, COLUMN, RECORD, LIBRARY, etc.). It also allows users to define their own object types. The DBRAD directory includes a predefined table for each predefined type, which is used to record attributes for objects of that type. For objects of user-defined type, the directory contains a text description only.

Next, certain objects can have one or more *component* objects; for example, a TABLE object will have a set of component COLUMN objects. In general, the components of a given object are the objects that are immediately subordinate to that given object. DBRAD supports a set of predefined component relationship types (TABLEs contain COLUMNs, etc.), which, like predefined object types, are represented by predefined tables in the DBRAD directory. Users can also define their own relationship types.

One last piece of terminology: If object *B* is a component of object *A,* then object *A* is said to be an *associate* of object *B.* An associate relationship is thus the inverse of a component relationship. However, associate relationships are not separately maintained in the DBRAD directory—the component relationship tables are obviously sufficient to represent the relationships in both directions.

We now move on to discuss each of the DBRAD components in turn.

25.2 CATALOG DIALOGS

The DBRAD Catalog Dialogs provide an easy way to explore the contents of the DB2 catalog. They are invoked by selecting the CD option on the DBRAD *Primary Option Menu* shown in Fig. 25.2. Selecting that option causes the DBRAD *Catalog Facility Home Panel* to be displayed. See Fig. 25.3. By way of illustration, we have included appropriate entries in that figure to request information for tables created by user CJDATE. *Note:* For DB2 tables, the DBRAD "library name" is usually just the DB2 authorization ID.

The effect of this request is to cause a list of all relevant tables to be displayed. From that list, we can request information about an individual

```
RAPRIM ---------------- DBRAD PRIMARY OPTION MENU ----------------------------
OPTION ===>
 5798-DZT (C) Copyright IBM Corp. 1987                     USERID   - DBRAD
 DBRAD Data Base Relational Application Directory          TIME     - 17:34
 DB2 Subsystem => TDB2      DBRAD System Id => 1 (1-9)      TERMINAL - 3278

 DBRAD Dialogs                     Application Development
 DD  Directory Dialogs            AD  CSP Application Development
 CD  Catalog Dialogs              AE  CSP Application Execution
                                   AU  CSP Application Utilities
                                   SM  CSP/DB2 Static Module Creation
 Database                          MU  CSP Message File Utility
 D   Database Interactive (DB2I)  MG  Model Generator
 DE  Database Edit (DBEDIT)       AS  Application System

 Reporting & Queries               Importing
 OR  Object Reports               SI  CSP Source Interface Utility
 RR  Relationship Reports         AI  CSP Application Import
 PP  DB2 Program Profile          PI  Program Structure Import
 Q   Query & Reporting Facility (QMF)  CT  Catalog Table Import
 QB  QMF Batch Procedures
                                   Program Development ( PD )
 Other                            0-7 ISPF/PDF Functions
 PA  DBRAD System Parameters      SD  Spool Display & Search Facility
```

Fig. 25.2 DBRAD Primary Option Menu

```
RACDCF1 ----------------- DBRAD CATALOG FACILITY -------------------------01
COMMAND ==>                                            SCROLL => PAGE
 5798-DZT (C) Copyright IBM Corp. 1987          RETRIEVE LIMIT => 0100
ENTER/MODIFY THE REQUIRED INFORMATION BELOW:

             CREATOR ====>  CJDATE          (AUTHID/USERID/GRANTEE)
                NAME ====>
                  IN ====>                  (Table Name or Database Name)
                TYPE ====>  T

WHERE TYPE IS ONE OF THE FOLLOWING:
    Z  VOLUME
    G  STOGROUP
    D  DATABASE
    R  TABLESPACE
    T  TABLE/VIEW
    V  VIEW
    S  SYNONYM
    I  INDEX
    C  COLUMN
    H  COLUMN HOMONYMS (REQUIRES NAME)
    P  PLANS
    A  AUTHORIZATIONS - USERS
    L  REVOKE OF AUTHORIZATIONS - IMPACT LIST
```

Fig. 25.3 DBRAD Catalog Facility Home Panel

table. In Fig. 25.4, we show the result of a request for information about table CJDATE.P (the parts table).

The panel displayed in response to our table request (i.e., Fig. 25.4) offers options ("commands") to display information about other related objects. Using the C command, for example, we could display details about each column of the table. The panel (not shown) used to display such detailed column information offers a *Column Homonym Search* facility, which produces a list of all tables that contain a column with the same name as the specified column. Fig. 25.5 shows a homonym listing for column name P#. The homonym search facility could be useful for (e.g.) checking consistency of column definitions across tables.

Returning to the table listing panel (Fig. 25.4), we see that another command option is A ("authorization"). If that option is selected, DBRAD will display a list of privileges held on the table, who granted them, and who holds them. DBRAD can also be requested to show the impact of revoking a particular privilege. Fig. 25.6 shows the effect of revoking ALL PRIVILEGES on the parts table from user CJWHITE. The report shows that CJWHITE has authorized USER1 and USER2 to access the parts table and that the revoke would remove these privileges.

```
RACDTB1 -------------------------- TABLE --------------------------------03
COMMAND ==>                                            SCROLL => PAGE
ENTER ONE OF THE FOLLOWING COMMANDS:           RETRIEVE LIMIT => 0100
  A - AUTH  S - SYNONYM  I - INDEX  V - VIEW  P - PLAN  U - UPDATEAUTH
  C - COLUMNS  B - BASETABLES  R - TABLESPACE  D - DATABASE
  CREATOR: CJDATE    NAME: P                    IN:
-----------------------------------------------------------------------
Table Type               : T
Database Name            : CJDDB
Table Space Name         : CJDTS
Number of Columns        : 5
Number of Pages (%)      : 1 (2)
Number of Rows           : 6
EDIT Procedure           :
VALID Procedure          :
Maximum Record Length    : 49
DBID/OBID                : 5/3
Label                    : PARTS
Remarks:


```

Fig. 25.4 Table listing for table P

```
RACDCH1 --------------------- COLUMN HOMONYMS ----------------------------06
COMMAND ==>                                                 SCROLL => PAGE
SELECT OBJECT(S) USING "S"                          RETRIEVE LIMIT => 0100

  CREATOR:          NAME: P#                IN:             0001 OF 0002
S TABLE                        COLTYPE  LENGTH DP NULL DEFAULT
------------------------------------------------------------------------
   CJDATE.P                    CHAR         6     N    N
   CJDATE.SP                   CHAR         6     N    N




```

Fig. 25.5 Column homonym listing for column name P#

```
RACDRS2 --------------------- REVOKE IMPACT LIST ----------------------------07
COMMAND ==>                                                 SCROLL => PAGE
                                                    RETRIEVE LIMIT => 0100

REVOKE ALL ON TABLE CJDATE.P    FROM CJWHITE  BY ALL          0001 OF 0002
LVL GRANTEE  TYPE  GRANTOR   DATE     TIME
------------------------------------------------------------------------
001 USER1    USER  CJWHITE   870916   19072981
001 USER2    USER  CJWHITE   870916   19075061
***************************** ((BOTTOM OF DATA)) *****************************B



```

Fig. 25.6 DBRAD Revoke Impact List

Another option provided by the Catalog Dialogs is the ability to display the SQL statements and access paths used by a particular application plan. The Program Profiles function, discussed in the next section, must be run before using this option.

25.3 IMPORT FACILITIES

DBRAD provides four facilities for importing object information into the DBRAD directory:

1. Catalog Table Import
2. DB2 Program Profile
3. Program Structure Import
4. CSP Application Import

Each of these facilities is invoked from the DBRAD Primary Option Menu (see Fig. 25.2). We discuss each in turn.

1. The DBRAD Catalog Table Import facility extracts table information from the DB2 catalog and stores it in the DBRAD directory as a TABLE object and a set of COLUMN objects. The component relationships between that table and its columns are also recorded.

Note: DB2 definitions must be imported into the DBRAD directory before the Directory Dialogs can be used to report on them. Analogous requirements apply to other definitions also, of course (e.g., CSP application definitions). This fact illustrates the important point that *the DBRAD directory is a passive information source, not an active one;* i.e., there is no guarantee that it contains the most recent version of the information. In particular, note the distinction between the Catalog Dialogs and the Directory Dialogs. The Catalog Dialogs do always operate in terms of the current state of the DB2 catalog. The Directory Dialogs, however, operate in terms of the current state of the DBRAD directory, which reflects the state of the DB2 catalog (and other information sources) *as of a specific time*—namely, the time when the information was imported into the directory.

2. The DB2 Program Profile facility analyzes information about an application plan in the DB2 catalog and produces a report showing the DBRMs, SQL statements, and access paths used by that plan, together with a list of authorized plan users. It also stores the SQL statements in a special DBRAD "SQL statements" table. That table is used by the Catalog Dialogs in responding to a request for the SQL statements and access paths used by a particular plan (see the end of Section 25.2).

The Program Profile facility also provides an option to store information in the DBRAD directory about the plan, DBRMs, SQL statements, and SQL references to COBOL and PL/I structures. That option must be selected if DBRAD is to be able to produce reports about the relationships between DB2 plans and application program objects. The option causes the following DBRAD objects to be created:

- TRANSACTION object for each DB2 plan
- PROGRAM object for each DBRM
- PROCESS object for each SQL statement
- RECORD object for each referenced COBOL or PL/I structure

All these objects are related together in the directory via appropriate component relationships.

3. The Program Structure Import facility is used to import COBOL and PL/I structures into the DBRAD directory from program source libraries. The facility creates RECORD and ITEM objects in the directory, but does not create any relationships between those objects and DB2 objects. Instead, such relationships must be created by means of the Directory Dialogs (see Section 25.4). Relationships can be created between records and their corresponding DB2 tables, and between items and their corresponding DB2 columns.

4. Finally, the CSP Application Import facility is (of course) used to import CSP application information. Surprisingly, the input to the import facility is not CSP's own "dictionary" (i.e., the Member Specification Library or MSL—see Chapter 21), but rather the output from the MSL Print utility. An advantage of this approach is that it allows the installation to consolidate MSLs. (Usually, when developing CSP applications, all programmers have their own MSL, and library control and maintenance can become cumbersome. DBRAD helps solve such problems.)

CSP Application Import creates the following DBRAD objects:

- APPLICATION object for each CSP application
- PROCESS object for each CSP process or statement group
- RECORD object for each CSP record, table, or SQL row
- MAP object for each CSP map
- ITEM object for each field in a CSP map or record

All these objects are related together in the directory via appropriate component relationships. The Directory Dialogs can be used to relate the CSP objects to the appropriate DB2 objects (tables, columns, plans).

Having discussed how objects are created by the various import functions, we can now move on to outline the facilities provided by DBRAD to query and report on such objects.

25.4 DIRECTORY DIALOGS

The DBRAD Directory Dialogs are used to query, display, and update information in the DBRAD directory. The dialogs are invoked by selecting the DD option on the DBRAD Primary Option Menu (refer back to Fig. 25.2). The DBRAD *Directory Facility Home Panel* shown in Fig. 25.7 is then displayed.

Five commands are available from the home panel:

- *Object Search:*   Display a list of objects that satisfy some specified search condition
- *Object Details:*   Display the attributes of some object
- *Object Components:*   Display the components of some object
- *Relationship Details:*   Display relationship information for some object
- *Object Associates:*   Display the associates of some object

Space does not permit us to discuss all of these commands in detail here. We content ourselves with a single example, namely a query to produce a "where-used" listing for a specified object. As shown in Fig. 25.7, we enter the "A" command ("object associates"), specifying the object as

```
RADDDF1 ----------------- DBRAD DIRECTORY FACILITY ----------------------01
COMMAND ==> A                                               SCROLL => PAGE
5798-DZT (C) Copyright IBM Corp. 1987              RETRIEVE LIMIT => 0100
ENTER ONE OF THE FOLLOWING COMMANDS:
    S  OBJECT SEARCH    C  OBJECT COMPONENTS   A   OBJECT ASSOCIATES
    O  OBJECT DETAILS   R  RELATIONSHIP DETAILS


ENTER/MODIFY THE REQUIRED INFORMATION BELOW

OBJECT: LIB ====> CJDMSL
        NAME ===> P#                      ALIAS =>
        TYPE ===> ITEM                    (RECORD,ITEM,FILE,PSB,TABLE,COLUMN)
                                          (PROGRAM,APPL,PROCESS,MAP,REPORT)
                                          (SYSTEM,JOB,TRAN) (INCLUDE,ALF)
                                          (LIBRARY (OR OTHER USER TYPES))

RELATIONSHIPS ==>                         (COUNT COMPONENTS,ASSOCIATES, OR BOTH)

RELATED: TYPE ==>
         NAME ==>
         SID ==>
         LIB ==>
```

Fig. 25.7 DBRAD Directory Facility Home Panel

type ITEM, name P#, in library CJDMSL. The result of the query is shown in Fig. 25.8. The result shows that only one object, the SHIPREC record, uses the specified item.

In general, directory queries can be specified using a full or partial object key (library name, object type, object name). Partial keys can be specified in the same way as the argument to the SQL LIKE predicate (see Chapter 6)—the special characters "%" and "_" can be used to represent any sequence of zero or more characters and any single character, respectively. Queries can also be performed on the basis of object aliases.

As well as retrieving information, the Directory Dialogs can also be used to insert, delete, and update individual objects and relationships. The details are beyond the scope of this book.

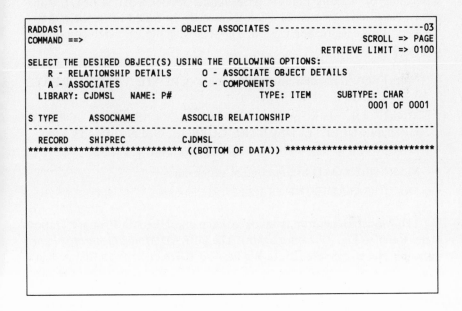

```
RADDAS1 -------------------- OBJECT ASSOCIATES ----------------------------03
COMMAND ==>                                               SCROLL => PAGE
                                                   RETRIEVE LIMIT => 0100
SELECT THE DESIRED OBJECT(S) USING THE FOLLOWING OPTIONS:
    R - RELATIONSHIP DETAILS      O - ASSOCIATE OBJECT DETAILS
    A - ASSOCIATES                C - COMPONENTS
  LIBRARY: CJDMSL   NAME: P#                 TYPE: ITEM     SUBTYPE: CHAR
                                                            0001 OF 0001
S TYPE      ASSOCNAME        ASSOCLIB RELATIONSHIP
---------------------------------------------------------------------------
  RECORD    SHIPREC          CJDMSL
**************************** ((BOTTOM OF DATA)) *****************************
```

Fig. 25.8 Where-used listing for the P# item

25.5 REPORTS

The DBRAD reporting facilities produce reports from directory information. Two types of report can be produced:

- *Object Reports,* which show the attributes of specified objects
- *Relationship Reports,* which show the associates and components of specified objects

These reporting facilities are invoked directly from the DBRAD Primary Option Menu (see Fig. 25.2 again).

25.6   MODEL GENERATOR

The DBRAD Model Generator uses table definitions in the DB2 catalog, or table and record objects in the DBRAD directory, to create "model" statements of various kinds—for example, model SQL SELECT statements. Such model statements can then easily be edited to fit the requirements of some specific application. The following models can be produced, among others:

- Model SQL data definition statements (CREATE TABLE, CREATE VIEW, CREATE INDEX, etc.)
- Model SQL data manipulation statements (SELECT, INSERT, UPDATE, DELETE, DECLARE CURSOR, OPEN, FETCH, etc.)
- Model COBOL and PL/I structure declarations
- Model DB2 LOAD utility control statements
- Model VSAM DEFINE CLUSTER statements

The Model Generator is invoked from the DBRAD Primary Option Menu (refer to Fig. 25.2 once again). The DBRAD *Model Generator Panel* is then displayed (see Fig. 25.9). We have specified options on that panel to request the generation of a model SQL SELECT statement against the parts table (P), suitable for embedding in a PL/I program. We have also specified that the DB2 catalog (rather than the DBRAD directory) should be used as the source for the necessary descriptor information. *Note:* The DBRAD directory might be used for tables that have been dropped from DB2 but not deleted from the DBRAD directory. Indeed, the directory might be used in such a case to construct a model CREATE statement that would permit the dropped table to be created again.

The generated SELECT statement corresponding to the specifications of Fig. 25.9 is shown in Fig. 25.10. As that figure indicates, one interesting feature of the model generator is that it will include comments in the generated statements regarding any available indexes on the referenced table(s).

```
RAMG00----------------- DBRAD MODEL GENERATOR ------------------------------
COMMAND ===>

ENTER/MODIFY THE REQUIRED INFORMATION BELOW

  SOURCE     => C        (D,C - Details from the Directory or DB2 Catalog)
  OUTPUT     => MODEL

  QUALIFIER  => CJDATE    (LIBRARY or AUTHID)
  NAME       => P
  TYPE       =>           (REC or TAB - for Directory Object)

  MODEL      => SELECT    Model Type:              SYSTEM  => DB2
                          Records - STRUCT,VSAM
                          Tables  - DML CURSOR,FETCH,SELECT,INSERT,UPDATE,DELETE
                                    ALL HOSTVAR,DECLARE, and DML List
                                    DDL SG,DB,SPACE,TABLE,LABELS,INDEX,VIEW
                                    LOAD

  LANGUAGE   => P      (C,P,S - COBOL,PLI,SQL)
  INDICATORS => N      (Y,N - Indicator Variables)
  QUALIFIED  => N      (Y,N - Variables qualified by structure name)
  GLOBALS    => N      (Y,N - Variables in Global pool)
  TABLE TYPE => A      (A,T,V - Select Table Type - ALL, TABLE, VIEW)
```

Fig. 25.9 DBRAD Model Generator Panel

```
EDIT ---- CJDATE.MODEL -------------------------------------- COLUMNS 001 072
COMMAND ===>                                                 SCROLL ===> CSR
RAIS002  A NEW SEQUENTIAL DATASET WAS CREATED.
000001         /*****************************************************/
000002         /* SELECT FOR CJDATE.P                              */
000003         /*****************************************************/
000004           SELECT_P: PROCEDURE;
000005             EXEC SQL
000006               SELECT
000007                 P#,PNAME,COLOR,WEIGHT,CITY
000008               INTO
000009                 :P#,:PNAME,:COLOR,:WEIGHT,:CITY
000010               FROM CJDATE.P
000011        /*  ** NOTE: THE WHERE COLUMNS MUST BE CHECKED */
000012        /*  FOR APPLICATION CONTEXT SUITABILITY.     */
000013        /*  INDEXED BY CJDATE.XP                     */
000014        /*  RULES  CLUSTERED UNIQUE                  */
000015               WHERE
000016                 P#=:P#
000017             ;
000018             END SELECT_P;
```

Fig. 25.10 Model SQL SELECT statement for the parts table

25.7 APPLICATION PROGRAM INTERFACE

DBRAD provides an Application Program Interface (API) to allow user application programs to update information in the DBRAD directory. The interface does not, however, support read access. Read access could be achieved by direct use of SQL SELECT statements against the directory tables.

Several DBRAD functions use this interface. One example is the DBRAD *Batch Load* facility, which allows most of the online functions we have discussed in this chapter so far to be executed in batch mode.

25.8 UMBRELLA DIALOGS

The DBRAD Umbrella Dialogs constitute the last major set of DBRAD facilities. They permit the DBRAD user to invoke other IBM tools, such as QMF and AS, without leaving the DBRAD environment. The Primary Option Menu in Fig. 25.2 shows several options for invoking such tools. *Note:* That menu can be tailored to suit the tools installed on a particular DB2 system.

25.9 CONCLUSION

As we have seen, the DBRAD directory extends the DB2 catalog to allow more application-oriented information to be recorded and tracked. It consolidates much of the information used by many of the separate IBM products that support DB2 (most notably CSP; DBRAD allows CSP users to consolidate distinct MSL libraries and to relate MSL information to the DB2 objects used by CSP applications). Although intended primarily as a tool to help integrate DB2 and CSP, it offers significant function for non-CSP users as well.

PART

IV

FUTURE
DIRECTIONS

CHAPTER

$\cdot 26 \cdot$

Distributed
Database Support

26.1 INTRODUCTION

In the preceding three parts of this book we have presented a detailed description of DB2, a state-of-the-art relational DBMS, and some of its major
companion products. Our description has generally been at the level of DB2
Version 2 Release 1 (DB2 V2.1 for short). To review briefly, the following
topics have been covered (among others):

- system structure
- operating environments
- basic objects and operators
- data definition
- data manipulation

- the catalog
- views
- security and authorization
- integrity
- application programming
- transaction management
- storage structure
- system and database administration
- end-user tools (QMF, AS)
- DP professional tools (CSP, ADF, DBRAD)
- data extract (DXT)
- PC link products (HDBV, ECF)

In October 1988 (in fact, only a matter of days after DB2 V2.1 became generally available), IBM announced DB2 Version 2 Release 2 (DB2 V2.2). The most significant feature of DB2 V2.2—scheduled for general availability in the third quarter of 1989—is that it provides some preliminary support for *distributed database*. In a simultaneous announcement, IBM also added certain distributed database capabilities to its Systems Application Architecture ("Distributed Relational Data in SAA"). In this, the final chapter of this book, we examine the significance of these announcements. Section 26.2 discusses the basic concepts of distributed database, with special reference to the corresponding features of SAA; Section 26.3 then presents a preliminary description of the relevant facilities of DB2 V2.2. By way of an overall conclusion, Section 26.4 then speculates on certain further possible functional enhancements that might find their way into DB2 V2.2 by the time it becomes generally available.

26.2   DISTRIBUTED DATABASE IN SAA

In this section we explain some of the basic ideas behind distributed database in general, and then discuss what distributed database means in SAA terms specifically. Of course, distributed database is a big topic in its own right; the discussions that follow are necessarily at a rather superficial level only.

We begin with a (very loose) working definition: A *distributed database system* is a system involving multiple computer sites connected together in some kind of communications network, in which:

(a) Each site is a database system site in its own right, with its own local stored data, its own local DBMS, its own local lock manager, its own local recovery log, and so forth;

(b) Users (both end-users and application programmers) can access data anywhere around the network exactly as if the data were all stored at the user's own site.

Thus, a *distributed database* is a kind of virtual object, consisting of data that is physically stored at multiple distinct sites, and a *distributed DBMS* is a kind of partnership among multiple distinct single-site DBMSs operating at multiple distinct sites. Again, of course, these definitions are still very loose. The key point, however, is that from the user's perspective a distributed database behaves for data manipulation purposes exactly as if it were *not* distributed, i.e., as if it were a local database stored in its entirety at the user's own local site. Users are isolated (logically speaking) from all details of the physical distribution.

The advantages of a distributed database system include the following (in general—but note that most of these do *not* fully apply to DB2 V2.2 or SAA in its present form):

1. *Location independence* (also known as location transparency): As just explained, users and user programs do not have to know where data is stored. As a result, data can be moved from one site to another in response to changing patterns of usage, without necessitating any rewriting of application programs.

2. *Capacity and performance:* Transaction volumes and database size are essentially unlimited because the network can grow to any size, again without necessitating the rewriting of application programs. Throughput is increased because of the parallelism inherent in the system structure. Response times can be reduced by placing data at the site at which it is most frequently used.

3. *Incremental growth:* Individual sites can be added, upgraded, and replaced in a transparent and nondisruptive fashion. Existing applications will continue to work after a nondistributed system has evolved into a distributed one; they will also continue to work as the distributed system itself evolves and new sites are added and/or data is redistributed across existing sites.

4. *Application portability:* Applications can be developed on one machine and can then run unchanged on another. Applications can easily be moved from one site to another around the network.

5. *Improved productivity:* As a consequence of the previous points,

users have universal and uniform access to data throughout the network. Data manipulation operations (SELECT, INSERT, UPDATE, DELETE, plus cursor-based operations and COMMIT and ROLLBACK) work against the distributed database exactly as if it were an ordinary local database. Application programs (both user-written applications and the IBM-provided frontend subsystems QMF, AS, etc.) therefore also operate exactly as if the database were purely local.

6. *Local autonomy:* Despite the fact that data is universally accessible as explained in the previous paragraph, local sites can still maintain control (for security and integrity and performance purposes) of data that logically belongs to them—they do not have to relinquish such control to some remote "master" site. Also, local applications (i.e., applications that do not need access to remote data) remain truly local; they are not penalized in any way by the fact that their local data is now accessible to remote sites. (In particular, applications that ran before the system became distributed will continue to run afterwards.)

7. *System independence:* In general, users and user programs should be independent of the underlying machines, operating systems, and network protocols. Such independence is certainly not fully available today, but it is IBM's ultimate intent to provide full distributed database support across the complete range of SAA environments—i.e., to allow DB2 sites, SQL/DS sites, OS/400 sites, and OS/2 Extended Edition sites all to participate as partners in a distributed system and together to present a "single-system image" to the user.

Let us turn now to SAA specifically. In a document entitled *Introduction to Distributed Relational Data,* dated September 1988, IBM defines four levels of "distributed relational data access," of which however only two (numbers 2 and 3 below) are currently included in SAA and supported (partially) by DB2 V2.2:

1. Remote request
2. Remote unit of work
3. Distributed unit of work
4. Distributed request

We explain these four levels as follows.

1. *Remote request* means that an application at one site X can send an individual database request (i.e., SQL statement) to some remote site Y for execution. That request is executed *and committed* (or rolled back) entirely at site Y. The original application at site X can subsequently

send another request to site Y (or possibly to another site Z), regardless of whether the first request was successful or unsuccessful.

ECF (see Chapter 24) is an example of a product that supports remote requests. For example, under ECF, a user on a PC can perform a SQL operation (possibly even an update) on data that is stored on a mainframe. However, remote request support is not a part of SAA and is not implemented in DB2 V2.2.

2. *Remote unit of work* means that an application at one site X can send all of the database requests in a given "unit of work" (i.e., a transaction, in our terms—in other words, a logically related set of SQL statements) to some remote site Y for execution. The database processing for the transaction is thus executed in its entirety at site Y; however, site X decides whether the transaction is to be committed or rolled back.

   Support for remote unit of work is included in SAA and is provided (partially) by DB2 V2.2. More details are given in the next section.

3. *Distributed unit of work* means that an application at one site X can send some or all of the database requests in a given unit of work (transaction) to one or more remote sites Y, Z, ..., for execution. The database processing for the transaction is thus spread across multiple sites, in general; each individual request is still executed in its entirety at a single site, but different requests can be executed at different sites. However, site X is still the cooordinating site, i.e., the site that decides whether the transaction is to be committed or rolled back.

   As with the previous level (remote unit of work), support for distributed unit of work is included in SAA and is partially provided by DB2 V2.2 (in fact, of course, remote unit of work is just a special case of distributed unit of work, so that a system that supports the latter will a fortiori support the former also). Again, for more details see the next section.

4. *Distributed request* is really the only level that approaches what is commonly accepted (in the research world, at least) as true distributed database support. Distributed request means everything that distributed unit of work means, *plus* it permits individual database requests (SQL statements) to span multiple sites—for example, a request originating from site X might ask for a join to be performed between a table at site Y and a table at site Z. Note that it is only at this level that the system can be said to be providing genuine location independence; in all three previous cases, users do have to have *some* knowledge regarding the physical location of data.

   This level is not part of SAA at this time and is not supported by DB2 V2.2.

One closing comment: The IBM terminology for levels 3 and 4 is slightly confusing, inasmuch as the term "distributed request" (level 4) intuitively suggests—at least to this writer—a *lower,* not higher, level of functionality than "distributed unit of work" (level 3). Actually, the difference between the two levels is analogous to the difference between many-to-one and many-to-many relationships: At level 3, many SQL statements are executed (in toto) at one site, but different statements can be executed at different sites; at level 4, parts of each SQL statement are executed at many sites, and each site executes parts of many SQL statements. Better terms might have been "partitioned unit of work" (for level 3, where the unit of work is partitioned, on a statement-by-statement basis, among several sites) and "distributed unit of work" (for level 4, where the unit of work truly is distributed, with no holds barred).

26.3 DISTRIBUTED DATABASE IN DB2 V2.2

Overview

The distributed database support in DB2 V2.2 provides DB2-to-DB2 access only—it is not possible, for example, to have a single distributed transaction that accesses a mixture of DB2 and SQL/DS data. Within a given transaction, each SQL statement must be wholly executed at one DB2 site; however, different SQL statements can be executed at different sites. (By "SQL statement" here, of course, we mean a SQL *data manipulation* statement.) DB2 V2.2 thus supports the SAA "distributed unit of work" capability (and hence the SAA "remote unit of work" capability also)—with the following major restrictions:

- All update operations in the transaction (INSERTs and/or UPDATEs and/or DELETEs), if any, must be performed at the same site.

- Furthermore, if the transaction is executing under IMS or CICS, then the single site at which all updates are performed must be the *local* site—i.e., the site at which the transaction first started execution. Note, however, that the update site can optionally be remote under TSO or the Call Attach Facility (and, of course, different transactions can have different remote update sites in this case).

Some Technical Details

We now address certain technical aspects of DB2 V2.2's distributed database support in a little more detail.

1. *General:* DB2 V2.2's distributed database support is provided by a new DB2 component, the Distributed Data Facility (DDF), which operates

in its own MVS address space. Intersite communication is performed using the Advanced Program-to-Program Communication (APPC) facilities of VTAM; each DB2 site acts as a VTAM "logical unit." Each site has a unique *location name* of 16 characters.

2. *Data naming:* If the system is truly to provide location independence, then users must continue to refer to data (i.e., tables) exactly as if the data were local, regardless of where the data is physically stored. The following is a sketch of how table naming works in DB2 V2.2.

- First, each table in the entire distributed system has a globally unique 3-part name, made up as follows—

```
location . user . name
```

—where "location" is the name of the site to which the table really belongs, "user" is an authorization ID at that site, and "name" is the table's regular unqualified name (the second and third of these components constitute an ordinary 2-part name as in DB2 systems prior to V2.2—see Chapter 5).

- Second, users *can* refer to tables directly by their 3-part name. However, to do so would clearly compromise the objective of location independence. Instead, users will normally use an *alias*. An alias is a simple (1-part) name for a table, introduced by means of a new SQL statement, CREATE ALIAS. For example:

```
CREATE ALIAS SUPPLIERS FOR SARATOGA.CJDATE.S ;
```

Users at the site at which the alias was created can refer to the name SUPPLIERS in SQL data manipulation statements exactly as if it identified a local table. For example:

```
SELECT  S#, CITY
FROM    SUPPLIERS
WHERE   STATUS > 5 ;
```

DROP ALIAS is also supported, of course.

It can be seen that an alias is rather like a synonym (see Chapter 9). The difference is, however, that aliases are *public,* in the sense that they are available to every user at the site at which they are defined, whereas synonyms are private to the user who defines them. Aliases are registered in the SYSTABLES table in the catalog—that is, SYSTABLES includes a row for each alias known at the site, showing the alias as a recognized table name and giving (among other things) the corresponding 3-part name for that alias.

3. *Authorization:* Authorization is another area that requires extended consideration in the distributed environment. If user U*x* operating at site X

is to be allowed to operate on data belonging to some user at site Y, then user U*x* must somehow be known at site Y so that the owner of the data in question can grant the appropriate access privileges to that user U*x*. DB2 V2.2 therefore supports the concept of "authorization ID translation," which works as follows (in outline).

- First, user U*x* at site X is allocated another authorization ID, U*y* say, at site Y. The owner of the data at site Y can now issue an appropriate GRANT operation:

  `GRANT .... ON ... TO Uy ;`

- Second, a special system table at site X called SYSUSERNAMES maps authorization IDs known at that site to authorization IDs at other sites. In the example, SYSUSERNAMES at site X would include a row indicating that authorization ID U*x* (at that site) corresponds to authorization ID U*y* at site Y. The SYSUSERNAMES table is kept in a special database at site X, the *Communications Database* (CDB), and is maintained using ordinary SQL statements. *Note:* The CDB serves a variety of other purposes as well, purposes that are however beyond the scope of this chapter at this time.

- When a SQL request is submitted to site Y from site X on behalf of user U*x,* the system will send the authorization ID U*y* along with that request. Authorization checking will then be done at site Y. (Note, therefore, that—unlike the situation today, in which, by definition, all requests are purely local—authorization checking for remote requests is always done at run time, not ahead of time as part of a totally separate Bind step. In fact, as we shall see in a moment, there *is* no totally separate Bind step for remote requests.)

- An extended form of GRANT TO PUBLIC is supported:

  `GRANT ... TO PUBLIC AT ALL LOCATIONS ;`

  An analogous form of REVOKE is also supported.

  4. *Data definition:* The existing SQL data definition statements are unaffected by DB2's distributed database support. There are a couple of limitations, however, namely as follows:

- It is not possible to define a view that spans sites (because, of course, no SQL data manipulation statement is allowed to span sites).

- It is not possible to define a foreign key at one site that references a primary key at another site, for essentially the same reason.

The statements CREATE and DROP ALIAS (which might be regarded as data definition statements) have already been mentioned. It is also possible to COMMENT ON an alias and LABEL an alias (refer to Chapter 9 for a brief description of comments and labels).

5. *Data manipulation:*   The existing SQL data manipulation statements are unaffected by DB2's distributed database support (indeed, that is the whole object of the exercise). There is one point to be made, however, regarding implementation: Requests for access to remote data are always processed by dynamic bind—that is, the optimization and plan generation functions (etc.) are always performed at run time, not ahead of time in a separate Bind step. (*Local* requests, by contrast, are still bound ahead of time as in DB2 today.)

6. *Application programming:*   Consider an application at site X that is using a cursor to run through a set of records that are physically stored at site Y. If each individual FETCH causes just one row of data to be transmitted across the communications network, the total overhead for retrieving all of the data is likely to be extremely high (it is well known that record-at-a-time access across a communications network is generally a bad idea).

Because of this problem, DB2 V2.2 uses *block FETCH* wherever possible; that is, it batches up the records to be retrieved into blocks of say 100 records each, and only physically transmits a new block when the current block is exhausted. Block FETCH is used whenever it can be guaranteed that no UPDATE CURRENT or DELETE CURRENT operations will be applied to the cursor (if UPDATEs or DELETEs are done, it unfortunately becomes necessary to keep the two sites X and Y "in synch," and block FETCH therefore cannot be used). Regardless of whether block FETCH is used or not, of course, the effect from the programmer's point of view is still as if each FETCH retrieves a single row; the block transmission is only from the system buffer at site Y to the system buffer at site X and is generally "transparent to the user."

How then does DB2 know whether to use block FETCH or not? First, the programmer can explicitly specify that no UPDATEs or DELETEs will be applied to a given cursor by means of a new clause, FOR FETCH ONLY, in the cursor declaration. For example:

```
EXEC SQL DECLARE W CURSOR FOR
                 SELECT S#, CITY
                 FROM    SUPPLIERS
                 WHERE   STATUS > 5
                 ORDER   BY S#
            FOR FETCH ONLY ;
```

If FOR FETCH ONLY is not specified but FOR UPDATE OF ... is specified instead, DB2 obviously will not use block FETCH. But what if neither is specified? It might still be the case that DELETE CURRENT operations will be applied to the cursor (recall that there is no such thing as a "FOR DELETE" clause). In this case, DB2 can still tell whether the cursor can possibly *permit* such operations, by examining the form of the cursor declaration itself; for example, the presence of a GROUP BY clause means that such operations cannot be permitted (refer to the end of Section 13.4 for details). If such operations are not permitted, DB2 will still use block FETCH. Otherwise, it will not.

7. *Administration:* Certain DB2 administration facilities are also extended in the distributed environment. For example, the Resource Limit Facility is extended to cover time spent on remote requests as well as local ones, and the Instrumentation Facility is extended to support accounting operations at multiple sites. For more details, see the IBM manuals.

26.4   OTHER POSSIBLE DEVELOPMENTS

In this final section, we offer a few speculations regarding possible additional features that might conceivably find their way into DB2 V2.2 by the time it becomes generally available (recent releases of both DB2 and SQL/DS have tended to include functions in the version that became generally available that were not included in the original announcement from IBM, and it would not be particularly surprising if the same were true of DB2 V2.2). Please note, however, that these speculations *are* only speculations and are not based on any kind of inside knowledge. They are merely "educated guesses."

First, concerning distributed database specifically, it is possible that support for *snapshots* might be included (indeed, snapshots would be useful in the nondistributed environment also). Snapshots were implemented in R*, the distributed version of the System R prototype built in IBM Research in San Jose, California. Briefly, a snapshot is a named derived table, like a view. Unlike a view, however, a snapshot is "real," not virtual—i.e., it is represented by its own distinguishable stored data. Here is an example:

```
CREATE SNAPSHOT SC ( S#, CITY )
    AS SELECT S#, CITY
       FROM   S
       REFRESH EVERY DAY ;
```

Creating a snapshot is much like executing a query, except that the result of that query is stored in the database under the specified name (SC in the example). The definition of the snapshot and the time of its creation are saved in the system catalog, and periodically (EVERY DAY in the example) the snapshot is "refreshed"—i.e., its current value is discarded, the query is reexecuted, and the result of that reexecution becomes the new value.

The usefulness of snapshots in general is that (to some extent) they provide a means for automating the copy management task (refer back to Chapter 23 for a discussion of copy management). In the distributed context specifically, snapshots provide an additional benefit: They provide a way of creating multiple copies of certain data and storing those copies multiple times, at multiple different sites. Retrieval operations can then be directed (transparently) to the nearest snapshot, instead of always having to go to the single "master" copy; in many cases, the effect will be to replace an otherwise remote access by a purely local one. (Update operations, on the other hand, will probably always have to go to the "master" data; however, it is frequently the case—at least for certain kinds of data—that retrievals outnumber updates by orders of magnitude.) Of course, the snapshots would only be as current as the most recent refresh, but for many applications that would not be a major concern.

Here are some other examples of function we might expect to see in DB2 V2.2 (again, all of these would be useful in both the distributed and the nondistributed environments):

- Preliminary support for domains
- Support for outer join
- Support for certain updates on certain join views
- Removal of UNION restrictions (e.g., UNION allowed in subqueries and in view definitions)
- Explicit support for set intersection and set difference operations (such support is not strictly necessary, since these functions can be simulated in existing SQL anyway—see Appendix B—but symmetry suggests that it might be nice to have them)
- Support for certain integrity checks on base tables, along the lines of the CHECK clause in the SQL standard (see Appendix F)
- Support for other missing features of the SQL standard, such as the INDICATOR keyword (used to mark an indicator variable) and the ESCAPE clause (used to disable the special interpretation given to the percent and underscore characters on a LIKE comparison)

APPENDIXES

APPENDIX

Advantages of DB2

A.1 INTRODUCTION

If the advantages of a relational system such as DB2 must be summed up in a single word, that word is *simplicity*—where by "simplicity" we mean, primarily, simplicity for the user. Simplicity, in turn, translates into *usability* and *productivity*. Usability means that even comparatively unskilled users can use the system to do useful work; that is, end-users can frequently obtain useful results from the system without having to go through the potential bottleneck of the DP department. Productivity means that both end-users and DP professionals can be more productive in their day-to-day activities; as a result, they can between them make significant inroads into the well-known application backlog problem (see Section A.7 below). In this appendix we discuss the advantages of a system like DB2 in some detail.

A.2   SOUND THEORETICAL BASE

The first point is that relational systems are based on a formal theoretical foundation, the *relational model* (discussed in detail in Appendix B). As a result, they behave in well-defined ways; and (possibly without consciously realizing the fact) users have a simple model of that behavior in their mind that enables them to predict with confidence what the system will do in any given situation. There are (or should be) no surprises. This predictability means that the user interfaces are easy to document, teach, learn, use, and remember.

Note: It cannot be denied that most systems today, even relational systems, do nevertheless display rather ad hoc and unpredictable behavior in some areas. As an example, consider the treatment of view updating in DB2, which does display a certain amount of unpleasant arbitrariness (see Section 10.4). But such arbitrariness tends to occur precisely at those points where the implementation has departed from the underlying theory. For example, a crucial component of the relational model is the concept of *primary key* (see Appendix B). However, DB2 does not fully support that concept,* and it is that omission that is the direct cause of the arbitrariness just referred to. DB2 is not the sole offender in this regard, of course—similar criticisms apply to most other systems at the time of writing—but it does serve to illustrate the undesirable consequences of disregarding the prescriptions of the underlying model.

Incidentally, we remark in passing that many critics of relational systems in the past have actually objected to the fact that they are based on theory! The objection seems to be that only theoreticians are capable of understanding, or need to understand, something that is based on theory. Our own position is exactly the opposite: Systems that are not based on theory are usually very difficult for *anyone* to understand. It cannot be stated too strongly that "theoretical" does *not* mean "not practical." On the contrary, considerations that are initially dismissed as being "only theoretical" (sic) have a nasty habit of becoming horribly practical a few years later on.

A.3   SMALL NUMBER OF CONCEPTS

The relational model is notable for the small number of concepts it involves. As pointed out in Section 8.5, all data in a relational database is represented in one and only one way, namely as column values within rows of tables,

---

*This remark is still true, even with DB2 Version 2.

and hence only one operator is needed for each of the four basic manipulative functions (retrieve, change, insert, delete). For exactly the same reason, fewer operators are also needed in a relational system for all the other functions—data definition, security and authorization control, integrity control, etc.—that are required in a general-purpose DBMS. In the case of authorization specifically, it is the simplicity and regularity of the data structure that makes it possible to define such a sophisticated data protection mechanism (one in which, as was shown by the examples of Chapter 11, value-dependent, value-independent, context-dependent, and other constraints can be easily defined and conveniently enforced).

A separate but related point is the following: In the relational model, distinct concepts are cleanly separated, not bundled together. By contrast, the parent-child (or owner-member) link construct found in hierarchic and network systems bundles together several fundamentally distinct notions: It is simultaneously a representation of a one-to-many relationship, an access path (or collection of access paths), a mechanism for enforcing certain integrity constraints, and so on. As a result, it becomes difficult to tell exactly what purpose a given link is serving (and it may be used for a purpose for which it was not intended). For example, a program may come to rely on an access path that is really a side effect of the way the database designer chose to represent a certain integrity constraint. If that integrity constraint needs to be changed, then the database will have to be restructured, with a strong likelihood that the program will then have to be rewritten—even if that program is completely uninterested in the integrity constraint per se.

A.4 SET-LEVEL OPERATORS

Relational data manipulation operations (such as SELECT, UPDATE, etc., in SQL) are *set-level* operations. This fact means that users simply have to specify *what* they want, not *how* to get to what they want. For example, a user needing to know which parts are supplied by supplier S2 can simply issue the SQL query:

```
SELECT P#
FROM   SP
WHERE  S# = 'S2' ;
```

DB2 decides how to "navigate" through the physical storage structure on the disk in order to respond to this query. (For this reason, as mentioned in Chapter 1, systems such as DB2 are frequently described as "automatic navigation" systems. By contrast, systems in which users have to do that navigation for themselves are described as "manual navigation" systems.) By taking this burden off the user's back, DB2 is freeing the user to concentrate on solving the real problem—i.e., on finding an answer to the query, in the case at hand, and using that information for whatever purpose it is needed in the outside world. In the case of end-users, in fact, it is automatic navigation that makes it possible for the user to use the system in the first place. It is not difficult to find a simple DB2 query for which an equivalent COBOL program would be ten or twenty pages long, and writing such a program would be out of the question for most users (and maybe not worth the effort involved even when not).

Furthermore, application programmers can take advantage of the automatic navigation feature of the system as well, just as end-users can. Application programmers too can be more productive in a system like DB2.

A.5 THE DUAL-MODE PRINCIPLE

In DB2 the same language, namely SQL, is used for both programming and interactive access to the database. This fact has two immediate consequences:

1. Different categories of user—system and database administrators, application programmers, end-users from any number of different backgrounds—are all "speaking the same language" and are thus better able to communicate with one another. It is also easy for one person to switch between categories—e.g., to perform data definition (administrative) functions on one occasion and ad hoc query (end-user) functions on another.

2. Application programmers can easily debug the database portions of their programs (i.e., the embedded SQL statements) through one of the DB2 interactive interfaces (e.g., DB2I or QMF). Those interfaces thus serve as a powerful and convenient program debugging aid.

A.6 DATA INDEPENDENCE

Data independence is the independence of users and user programs from details of the way the data is stored and accessed. It is critically important for at least two reasons:

1. It is important for application programmers because, without it, changes to the structure of the database would necessitate corresponding changes to application programs. In the absence of such independence, one of two things happens: Either it becomes almost impossible to make required changes to the database because of the investment in existing programs, or (more likely) a significant portion of the application programming effort is devoted purely to maintenance activity—

maintenance activity, that is, that would be unnecessary if the system had provided data independence in the first place. Both of these factors are significant contributors to the application backlog problem mentioned in the introduction to this appendix.

2. It is important for end-users because, without it, direct end-user access to the database would scarcely be possible at all. Data independence and very high level languages such as SQL go hand in hand.

Of course, data independence is not an absolute—different systems provide it in differing degrees. To put this another way, few systems, if any, provide no data independence at all; it is just that some systems are more data-dependent than others. Furthermore, the term "data independence" really covers two somewhat distinct notions, namely physical data independence (i.e., independence of the physical arrangement of the data on the storage medium) and logical data independence (i.e., independence of the logical structure of the data as tables and fields). DB2 is fairly strong on both aspects, though there is undoubtedly still room for improvement in both areas (for example, it is unfortunate that the logical notion of enforcing uniqueness is bundled with the physical notion of an index). Basically, DB2 provides physical data independence by virtue of its automatic navigation and automatic bind features (see Section 2.5 if you need to refresh your memory concerning "automatic bind"), and logical data independence by virtue of its view mechanism (see Section 10.5 for details).

A.7 EASE OF APPLICATION DEVELOPMENT

DB2 facilitates the application development process in a variety of significant ways:

1. First, as discussed in Chapter 18, the availability of the DB2 frontend products—QMF and AS in particular—means that it may not be necessary to develop an application program (in the traditional sense of the term) at all. The importance of this point can scarcely be over-emphasized.

2. Second, the availability of CSP and ADF (see Chapters 21 and 22) means that if specialized applications are needed, then they can be developed quickly and easily, still without any programming in the conventional sense.

3. Third, the high degree of data independence provided and the high level of the DB2 application programming interface (embedded SQL) together mean that when it *is* necessary to write a conventional program, then that program is easier to write, requires less maintenance, and is

easier to change when it does require maintenance, than it would be in an older, nonrelational system.

4. Last, and largely as a consequence of the previous three points, the application development cycle can involve a great deal more *prototyping* than it used to: A first version can be built and shown to the intended users, who can then suggest improvements for incorporation into the next version, and so on. As a result, the final application should do exactly what its users require it to. The overall development process is far less rigid than it used to be, and the application users can be far more involved in that process, to the benefit of all concerned.

A.8   DYNAMIC DATA DEFINITION

We have already discussed the advantages of dynamic data definition at some length in Chapter 5 (Section 5.5), and we will not repeat the arguments here. However, we make one additional point: The ability to create new definitions at any time without having to bring the system to a halt is really only part of a larger overall objective, which is to eliminate the need for *any* planned system shutdown. Thus, for example, utilities can be invoked from an online terminal, and they can run in parallel with production work; it is possible, for example, to take an image copy of the database even while transactions are simultaneously updating it. Ideally, the system should have to be started exactly once, when it is first installed, and should then run "forever." (We are not claiming that this objective has yet been fully achieved.)

A.9   EASE OF INSTALLATION AND EASE OF OPERATION

DB2 is designed to be as easy to install and easy to operate as possible. Various features of the system, some of them touched on in previous sections of this appendix, contribute to the achievement of this objective. Details of such features (other than details already given in the body of the text) are beyond the scope of this book, but it is worth pointing out explicitly one very important consequence of them, namely the following: It requires only a comparatively small population of DP professionals (system and database administrators, system programmers, system operators) to provide DB2 services to a very large population of users (application programmers and end-users). DB2 is an extremely cost-effective system.

A.10   SIMPLIFIED DATABASE DESIGN

Database design in a relational system is easier than it is in a nonrelational system for a number of reasons (though it may still involve some difficult decisions in complex situations):

- First, the decoupling of logical and physical levels means that logical and physical design problems can be separately addressed.

- Second, at the logical level, the data structure is just about as simple as it can possibly be.

- Third, there are some sound principles (basically the principles of *normalization*) that can be brought to bear on the logical design problem.

- Last, the dynamic data definition feature and the high degree of data independence (again) mean that it is not necessary to do the entire design all at once, and neither is it so critical to get it right first time.

A comprehensive logical design methodology that uses a combination of the principles of normalization with a top-down (entity-based) approach is described in the book *Relational Database: Selected Writings,* by C. J. Date (Addison-Wesley, 1986).

A.11 INTEGRATED CATALOG

As explained in Chapter 9, the DB2 catalog is completely integrated with the rest of the data, in the sense that it is represented in the same way (i.e., as tables) and can be queried in the same way (i.e., via SQL). In other words, there are no artificial and unnecessary distinctions between catalog data and other data, or between data and "data about the data" (or "metadata," as it is sometimes called). This integration brings with it a number of benefits, among them the following:

1. Looking something up in the database and looking something up in the catalog are one and the same process. To see the advantage here, consider the analogy of looking something up in a book and looking something up in the table of contents for that book. It would be very annoying if the table of contents appeared somewhere other than in the book itself, in a format that required some different manner of access (for example, if the table of contents was in Spanish and was stored on a set of 3-by–5 cards, while the text of the book itself was in English). The role of the catalog with respect to the database is precisely similar to that of the table of contents with respect to a book.

2. The process of creating generalized (i.e., metadata-driven) application programs is considerably simplified. For example, consider what is involved in creating a generalized data entry application, which accepts as initial input the name of a table and then displays the names and data types of the columns of that table on the screen, so that the end-user can proceed to enter data for rows of that table. The ability to access the catalog is clearly crucial to such an application.

A.12 SQL SUPPORT

DB2 supports (a dialect of) the industry standard relational language SQL. SQL can be used:

- For data definition, data manipulation, and data control operations in the basic DB2 DBMS
- For ad hoc query access to the database (QMF, AS)
- For defining the data to be reported on (QMF, AS)
- For defining the data to be graphed (QMF, AS)
- For defining the data to be downloaded to a PC (HDBV, ECF)
- For programmed access to the database via one of the DB2-supported programming languages (APL, BASIC, C, COBOL, FORTRAN, PL/I, or Assembler Language)

As the industry standard, SQL provides a potential base for intersystem communication: A DB2 site might one day be able to communicate across a communications network, not only with other DB2 sites (indeed, IBM is already committed to providing this level of communication in DB2 Version 2 Release 2), but with any site that supports a system of any kind that supports the same SQL interface. Such intersystem communication could in turn eventually provide the basis for full heterogeneous distributed database support (i.e., distributed database support across disparate DBMSs—see Section 26.2).

Finally, DB2 support for SQL also raises the possibility of running third-party, SQL-based applications software on top of the DB2 DBMS.

A.13 PERFORMANCE

Critics of relational systems have traditionally always focused on the performance question. Ever since the first prototypes were built in the early 1970s, relational systems have suffered from the stigma of being (allegedly) poor performers. Even today, when relational systems are completely dominating the database marketplace, the claim is still heard in some quarters that they will never be able to compete in terms of performance with older, nonrelational systems such as IMS. The truth, however, is quite otherwise. The fact is, performance is (at least potentially) a *strength* of relational systems! And DB2 stands out as a shining example of a relational product that is finally giving the lie to those old reactionary claims.

This is not the place to get into a detailed discussion of the performance specifics of DB2 per se. DB2 performance is, of course, a big subject in its own right—an entire book could be written about it, and probably will be.

Here we merely content ourselves with a reference to the performance figures quoted in the preface to the third edition of this book (throughput of several hundreds of transactions per second on a large IBM mainframe, which is more than adequate for all but the most demanding of application environments). For more details, the reader is referred to the relevant IBM manuals.

A.14 EXTENDABILITY

Ever since Codd published his original paper in 1970 on the relational model, the vast majority of research in database technology (easily more than 90 percent) has been founded upon a relational base. As a consequence, users of today's relational systems should be in a better position to take advantage of the fruits of that research as and when they appear (where by "better" we mean, of course, "better than if they were users of some other kind of system").

APPENDIX

◆ B ◆

The Relational Model

B.1 INTRODUCTION

DB2 is a relational DBMS ("relational system" for short). The purpose of this appendix is to explain exactly what that statement means. Basically, a relational system is a system that is constructed in accordance with the relational *model* (or at least the major principles of that model); and the relational model is *a way of looking at data*—that is, a prescription for how to represent data and how to manipulate that representation. More specifically, the relational model is concerned with three aspects of data: data *structure,* data *integrity,* and data *manipulation.* We examine each of these in turn (in Sections B.2, B.3, and B.4, respectively), and then consider the question of what exactly it is that constitutes a relational *system* (in Section B.5).

A few preliminary remarks before we start getting into details:

1. First, in this appendix we will (for the most part) be using formal relational terminology. For convenience, Fig. B.1 repeats from Chapter 1 certain major relational terms and their informal equivalents.

Formal relational term	Informal equivalents
relation	table
tuple	record, row
attribute	field, column
primary key	unique identifier

Fig. B.1 Some terminology

2. It should also be pointed out that the treatment of the relational model in this appendix is necessarily somewhat terse and superficial, for reasons of space. A more extensive and tutorial treatment can be found in the book *An Introduction to Database Systems: Volume I,* by C. J. Date (4th edition, Addison-Wesley, 1986).

3. Finally, we should also make the point that the relational model is not an entirely static thing, but rather has evolved (and continues to evolve) over time. The version described in this appendix might be called the "original" or "basic" model; however, many new features have been added since that original version was first defined. This appendix is concerned only with the original version.

B.2   RELATIONAL DATA STRUCTURE

The smallest unit of data in the relational model is the individual data value. Such values are considered to be *atomic*—that is, they have no internal structure so far as the model is concerned. A *domain* is the set of all possible data values of some particular type. For example, the domain of supplier numbers is the set of all valid supplier numbers; the domain of shipment quantities is the set of all integers greater than zero and less than 10,000 (say). Thus domains are *pools of values,* from which the actual values appearing in attributes (columns) are drawn. The significance of domains is as follows: If two attributes draw their values from the same domain, then comparisons—and hence joins, unions, etc.—involving those two attributes probably make sense, because they are comparing like with like; conversely, if two attributes draw their values from different domains, then comparisons (etc.) involving those two attributes probably do not make sense. In SQL terms, for example, the query

```
SELECT  P.*, SP.*
FROM    P, SP
WHERE   P.P# = SP.P# ;
```

probably does make sense, whereas the query

```
SELECT  P.*, SP.*
FROM    P, SP
WHERE   P.WEIGHT = SP.QTY ;
```

probably does not. (DB2, however, has no notion of domains per se. Both of the foregoing SELECT statements are legal in DB2.)

Note that domains are primarily conceptual in nature. They may or may not be explicitly stored in the database as actual sets of values. But they should be specified as part of the database definition (in a system that supports the concept at all—but most systems currently do not); and then each attribute definition should include a reference to the corresponding domain. A given attribute may have the same name as the corresponding domain or a different name. Obviously it must have a different name if any ambiguity would otherwise result (in particular, if two attributes in the same relation are both based on the same domain; see the definition of relation below, and note the phrase "not necessarily all distinct").

We are now in a position to define the term "relation." A *relation* on domains D1, D2, ..., Dn (not necessarily all distinct) consists of a *heading* and a *body*. The heading consists of a fixed set of *attributes* A1, A2, ..., An, such that each attribute Ai corresponds to exactly one of the underlying domains Di ($i = 1,2,...,n$). The body consists of a time-varying set of *tuples,* where each tuple in turn consists of a set of attribute-value pairs (Ai:vi) ($i = 1,2,...,n$), one such pair for each attribute Ai in the heading. For any given attribute-value pair (Ai:vi), vi is a value from the unique domain Di that is associated with the attribute Ai.

As an example, let us see how the supplier relation S measures up to this definition (see Fig. 1.2 in Chapter 1). The underlying domains are the domain of supplier numbers (D1, say), the domain of supplier names (D2), the domain of supplier status values (D3), and the domain of city names (D4). The heading of S consists of the attributes S# (underlying domain D1), SNAME (domain D2), STATUS (domain D3), and CITY (domain D4). The body of S consists of a set of tuples (five tuples in Fig. 1.2, but this set varies with time as updates are made to the relation); and each tuple consists of a set of four attribute-value pairs, one such pair for each of the four attributes in the heading. For example, the tuple for supplier S1 consists of the pairs

```
( S#      : 'S1'     )
( SNAME   : 'Smith'  )
( STATUS  : 20       )
( CITY    : 'London' )
```

(though it is normal to elide the attribute names in informal contexts). And of course each attribute value does indeed come from the appropriate underlying domain; the value S1, for example, does come from the supplier number domain D1. So S is indeed a relation according to the definition.

Note carefully that when we draw a relation such as relation S as a table, as we did in Fig. 1.2, we are merely making use of a convenient method for representing the relation on paper. A table and a relation are not really the same thing, though for most of this book we have assumed that they are. For example, the rows of a table clearly have an ordering (from top to bottom), whereas the tuples of a relation do not (the body of a relation is a mathematical *set,* and sets do not have any ordering in mathematics). Likewise, the columns of a table also have an ordering (from left to right), whereas the attributes of a relation do not.

Notice also that the underlying domains of a relation are "not necessarily all distinct." Many examples have already been given in which they are not; see, e.g., the result relation in Example 6.3.1 (Chapter 6), which includes two attributes both defined on the domain of city names.

The value *n* (the number of attributes in the relation, or equivalently the number of underlying domains) is called the *degree* of the relation. A relation of degree one is called *unary,* a relation of degree two *binary,* a relation of degree three *ternary,* ..., and a relation of degree *n n-ary.* In the suppliers-and-parts database, relations S, P, and SP have degrees 4, 5, and 3, respectively. The number of tuples in the relation is called the *cardinality* of that relation; the cardinalities of relations S, P, and SP of Fig. 1.2 are 5, 6, and 12, respectively. The cardinality of a relation changes with time, whereas the degree does not.

B.3 RELATIONAL DATA INTEGRITY

One important consequence of the definitions in the previous section is that *every relation has a primary key.* Since the body of a relation is a set, and sets by definition do not contain duplicate elements, it follows that (at any given time) no two tuples of a relation can be duplicates of each other. Let R be a relation with attributes A1, A2, ..., An. The set of attributes K = (Ai,Aj,...,Ak) of R is said to be a *candidate key* of R if and only if it satisfies the following two time-independent properties:

1. *Uniqueness:*

   At any given time, no two distinct tuples of R have the same value for Ai, the same value for Aj, ..., and the same value for Ak.

2. *Minimality:*

   None of Ai, Aj, ..., Ak can be discarded from K without destroying the uniqueness property.

Every relation has at least one candidate key, because at least the combination of all of its attributes has the uniqueness property. For a given relation, one candidate key is designated as the *primary* key; the remaining candidate keys (if any) are called *alternate* keys. *Note:* The rationale by which one candidate key is chosen as the primary key (in cases where there is a choice) is outside the framework of the relational model per se. In practice the choice is usually straightforward.

Example: Suppose that supplier names and supplier numbers are both unique (at any given time, no two suppliers have the same number or the same name). Then relation S has two candidate keys, S# and SNAME. We choose S# as the primary key; SNAME then becomes an alternate key.

Continuing with the example, consider attribute S# of relation SP. It is clear that a given value for that attribute, say the supplier number S1, should be permitted to appear in the database only if that same value also appears as a value of the primary key S# of relation S (for otherwise the database cannot be considered to be in a state of integrity). An attribute such as SP.S# is said to be a *foreign key.* In general, a foreign key is an attribute (or attribute combination) of one relation R2 whose values are required to match those of the primary key of some relation R1 (R1 and R2 not necessarily distinct). Note that a foreign key and the corresponding primary key should be defined on the same underlying domain.

We can now state the two integrity rules of the relational model. *Note:* These rules are *general,* in the sense that any database that conforms to the model is required to satisfy them. However, any specific database will have a set of additional specific rules that apply to it alone. For example, the suppliers-and-parts database may have a specific rule to the effect that shipment quantities must be a multiple of 100, say. But such specific rules are outside the scope of the basic relational model per se.

1. *Entity integrity:*

   No attribute participating in the primary key of a base relation is allowed to contain any nulls.

2. *Referential integrity:*

   If base relation R2 includes a foreign key FK matching the primary key PK of some base relation R1, then every value of FK in R2 must either (a) be equal to the value of PK in some tuple of R1 or (b) be wholly null (i.e., each attribute value participating in that FK value must be null). R1 and R2 are not necessarily distinct.

   (A couple of asides: First, a *base relation* corresponds to what we have been calling a base table in the body of this book; i.e., it is an autonomous, named relation. See Chapter 5 for further discussion. Second, although the two rules are framed in terms of nulls, we do not necessarily assume the rather peculiar kind of null found in SQL today.)

The justification for the entity integrity rule is as follows:

1. Base relations correspond to entities in the real world. For example, base relation S corresponds to a set of suppliers in the real world.

2. By definition, entities in the real world are distinguishable—i.e., they have a unique identification of some kind.

3. Primary keys perform the unique identification function in the relational model.

4. Thus, a primary key value that was null would be a contradiction in terms—in effect, it would be saying that there was some entity that had no known *id*entity. An entity that cannot be identified is a contradiction in terms. Hence the name "entity integrity."

To put it another way: *In a relational database, we never record information about something we cannot identify.*

As for the second rule ("referential integrity"), it is clear that a given foreign key value must have a matching primary key value in some tuple of the referenced relation if that foreign key value is nonnull. Sometimes, however, it is necessary to permit the foreign key to accept nulls. (We remark, however, that nulls in a foreign key position are likely to be of the "value does not exist" variety, rather than the "value unknown" variety.) For example, suppose that in a given company it is legal for some employee to be currently assigned to no department at all. For such an employee, the department number attribute (which is a foreign key) would have to be null in the tuple representing that employee in the database.

B.4   RELATIONAL DATA MANIPULATION

The manipulative part of the relational model consists of a set of operators known collectively as the *relational algebra,* together with a relational assignment operator which assigns the value of some arbitrary expression of the algebra to another relation. We discuss the algebra first.

Each operator of the relational algebra takes either one or two relations as its input and produces a new relation as its output. Codd originally defined eight such operators, two groups of four each: (1) the traditional set operations union, intersection, difference, and Cartesian product (all modified slightly to take account of the fact that their operands are relations, as opposed to arbitrary sets); and (2) the special relational operations select, project, join, and divide. The eight operations are shown symbolically in Fig. B.2. We give a brief definition of each operation below; for simplicity, we assume in those definitions that the left-to-right order of attributes within a relation *is* significant—not because it is necessary to do so, but because it simplifies the discussion.

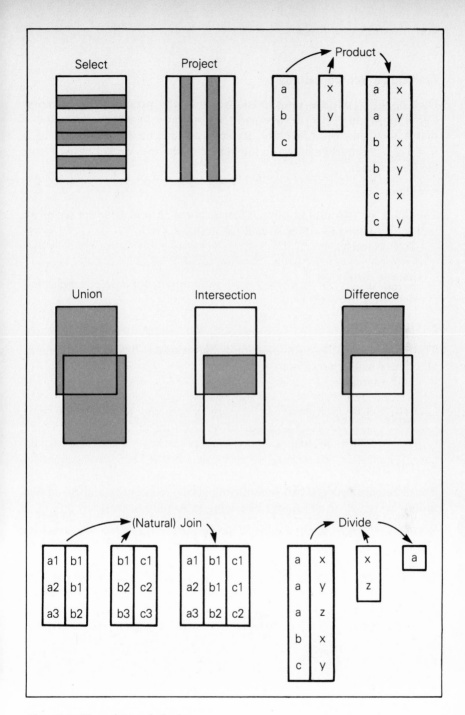

Fig. B.2 The relational algebra

Traditional Set Operations

Each of the traditional set operations takes two operands. For all except Cartesian product, the two operand relations must be *union-compatible*— that is, they must be of the same degree, n say, and the ith attribute of each $(i = 1,2,...,n)$ must be based on the same domain (they do not have to have the same name).

- Union

The union of two (union-compatible) relations A and B is the set of all tuples t belonging to either A or B (or both).
   SQL example:

```
SELECT S.S# FROM S
UNION
SELECT SP.S# FROM SP ;
```

- Intersection

The intersection of two (union-compatible) relations A and B is the set of all tuples t belonging to both A and B.
   SQL example:

```
SELECT S.S# FROM S
WHERE  EXISTS
       ( SELECT SP.S# FROM SP
         WHERE  SP.S# = S.S# ) ;
```

- Difference

The difference between two (union-compatible) relations A and B—in that order—is the set of all tuples t belonging to A and not to B.
   SQL example:

```
SELECT S.S# FROM S
WHERE  NOT EXISTS
       ( SELECT SP.S# FROM SP
         WHERE  SP.S# = S.S# ) ;
```

- Product

The product of two relations A and B is the set of all tuples t such that t is the concatenation of a tuple a belonging to A and a tuple b belonging to B.
   SQL example:

```
SELECT S.*, SP.*
FROM   S, SP ;
```

Special Relational Operations

- Selection (also known as restriction)

Let *theta* represent any valid scalar comparison operator (for example, $=$, $\sim =$, $>$, $> =$, etc.). The theta-selection of relation A on attributes X and Y is the set of all tuples *t* of A such that the predicate "*t*.X *theta t*.Y" evaluates to *true*. (Attributes X and Y should be defined on the same domain, and the operation *theta* must make sense for that domain.) A constant value may be specified instead of attribute Y. Thus, the theta-selection operator yields a "horizontal" subset of a given relation—that is, that subset of the tuples of the given relation for which a specified predicate is satisfied. *Note:* "Theta-selection" is often abbreviated to just "selection." But note that "selection" is not the same as the SELECT operator of SQL.
SQL example:

```
SELECT  S.*
FROM    S
WHERE   CITY ~= 'London' ;
```

- Projection

The projection operator yields a "vertical" subset of a given relation—that is, that subset obtained by selecting specified attributes and then eliminating redundant duplicate tuples (if any) within the attributes selected.
SQL example:

```
SELECT  DISTINCT P.COLOR, P.CITY
FROM    P ;
```

- Join

Let *theta* be as defined under "Selection" above. The theta-join of relation A on attribute X with relation B on attribute Y is the set of all tuples *t* such that *t* is the concatenation of a tuple *a* belonging to A and a tuple *b* belonging to B and the predicate "*a*.X *theta b*.Y" evaluates to *true*. (Attributes B.X and B.Y should be defined on the same domain, and the operation *theta* must make sense for that domain.)
SQL example:

```
SELECT  S.*, P.*
FROM    S, P
WHERE   S.CITY > P.CITY ;
```

If *theta* is equality, the join is called an equijoin. It follows from the definition that the result of an equijoin must include two identical attributes. If one of those two attributes is eliminated (which it can be via projection), the result is called the *natural* join. The unqualified term "join" is usually taken to mean the natural join.

- Division

In its simplest form (which is all that we consider here), the division operator divides a relation of degree two (the dividend) by a relation of degree one (the divisor), and produces a result relation of degree one (the quotient). Let the dividend (A) have attributes X and Y, and let the divisor (B) have attribute Y. Attributes A.Y and B.Y should be defined on the same domain. The result of dividing A by B is the relation C, with sole attribute X, such that every value *x* of C.X appears as a value of A.X, and the pair of values (*x,y*) appears in A for *all* values *y* appearing in B.

SQL example:

```
SELECT DISTINCT SPX.S# FROM SP SPX
WHERE  NOT EXISTS
      ( SELECT P.P# FROM P
        WHERE  NOT EXISTS
              ( SELECT SPY.* FROM SP SPY
                WHERE  SPY.S# = SPX.S# AND SPY.P# = P.P# ) ) ;
```

Here we are assuming for simplicity that (a) relation SP has only two attributes, namely S# and P# (we are ignoring QTY), and (b) relation P has only one attribute, namely P# (we are ignoring PNAME, COLOR, WEIGHT, and CITY). We divide the first of these two relations by the second and obtain a result, namely a relation with one attribute (S#) that lists supplier numbers for suppliers that supply all parts.

It is worth mentioning that this set of eight operations is not (and was never intended to be) a *minimal* set. A minimal set—i.e., a set of *primitive* operations—would be the set consisting of selection, projection, product, union, and difference; the other three operations can be defined in terms of those five. For example, the natural join is a projection of a selection of a product. In practice, however, those other three operations (especially join) are so useful that a good case can be made for supporting them directly.

Turning now to the relational assignment operation, the purpose of that operation is simply to allow the value of some algebraic expression—say a join—to be saved in some more or less permanent place. It can be simulated in SQL by means of the INSERT ... SELECT operation. For example, suppose relation XYZ has two attributes, S# and P#, and suppose also that it is currently empty (i.e., contains no tuples). The SQL statement

```
INSERT INTO XYZ ( S#, P# )
       SELECT S.S#, P.P#
       FROM   S, P
       WHERE  S.CITY = P.CITY ;
```

assigns the result of the SELECT (namely, a projection of a join) to the relation XYZ.

By way of conclusion, Fig. B.3 summarizes the major components of the relational model.

```
Data structure
    domains (values)
    n-ary relations (attributes, tuples)
    keys (candidate, primary, alternate, foreign)
Data integrity
    1. primary key values must not be null
    2. foreign key values must match primary key values (or be null)
Data manipulation
    relational algebra
        union, intersection, difference, product
        select, project, join, divide
    relational assignment
```

Fig. B.3 The relational model

B.5 RELATIONAL SYSTEMS

We are now (at last) in a position to define exactly what we mean by a *relational database management system* (relational DBMS, or relational system for short). The point is, *no* system today supports the relational model in its entirety (several come close, but most systems fall down on some detail or another—on domains if nowhere else). On the other hand, it would be unreasonable to insist that a system is not relational unless it supports every last detail of the model. The fact is, not all aspects of the model are equally important; some of course are crucial, but others may be regarded merely as features that are "nice to have" (comparatively speaking). We therefore define a system as relational—*minimally so*—if and only if it supports at least the following:

- Relational databases (i.e., databases that can be perceived by the user as tables, and nothing but tables);

- At least the operations select, project, and join of the relational algebra (without requiring any predefinition of physical access paths to support those operations).

Note carefully that a system does not have to support the select, project, and join operators *explicitly* in order to qualify as relational by this definition. It is only the functionality of those operators that we are talking about here. For example, DB2 provides the functionality of all three of those operators (and more besides) within the SELECT operator of SQL. More important, note that a system that supports relational databases but not these three operators does not qualify as a relational system under our definition. Likewise, a system that allows (say) the user to select tuples according to values of some attribute X only if that attribute X is indexed also does not qualify, because it is requiring predefinition of physical access paths.

We justify our definition as follows:

1. Although select, project, and join are less than the full algebra, they are an extremely useful subset. There are comparatively few practical problems that can be solved with the algebra that cannot be solved with select, project, and join alone.

2. A system that supports the relational data structure but not the relational operators does not provide the productivity of a genuinely relational system.

3. To do a good job of implementing the relational operators *requires* the system to do some optimization. A system that merely executed the exact operations requested by the user in a comparatively unintelligent fashion would almost certainly not have acceptable performance. Thus, to implement a system that realizes the potential of the relational model in an efficient manner is a highly nontrivial task.

DB2 is a relational system according to our definition (even though there are certain aspects of the relational model that it does not support). But there are a number of products on the market today that do not meet the criteria defined above. As we have tried to suggest, those criteria are useful as a means of drawing a sharp line between systems that are indeed genuinely relational and systems that are merely "relational-like." "Relational-like" systems do not truly provide the full benefits of the relational model. The distinction is thus worth making, as it ensures that the label "relational" is not used in misleading ways.

Note: The definition of "relational system" presented above was the definition in use in the early 1980s. For further discussion of what it means for a system to be relational—in particular, for a much more demanding definition, more appropriate to the late 1980s and the 1990s than the simple one given above—the reader is referred to Codd's forthcoming book, *The Relational Model for Database Management* (Addison-Wesley, 1989, to appear).

APPENDIX

$\cdot\;\mathbf{C}\;\cdot$

Date and Time Support

C.1 INTRODUCTION

The date and time support in DB2 is quite extensive (and quite complicated—unduly so, in this writer's opinion). Rather than discussing that support in full detail in the main part of the text, therefore, and thereby interfering with the overall flow of the presentation, it seemed better to relegate
any such discussion to some less obtrusive position in the book; hence this
appendix. *Note:* In order to make the appendix reasonably self-contained,
we do repeat some of the details (regarding, e.g., "date/time constants"
and date/time functions) from the body of the book.

One preliminary note on terminology: Throughout this appendix, we
use the term "date/time" to mean "date or time or timestamp." For example, the expression "date/time data types" means the three data types
DATE and TIME and TIMESTAMP, considered collectively.

C.2 DATA TYPES

As indicated at the end of the previous section, there are three date/time data types in DB2:

DATE
    Date, represented as a sequence of eight unsigned packed decimal digits (*yyyymmdd*), occupying four bytes; permitted values are legal dates in the range January 1st, 1 A.D., to December 31st, 9999 A.D., inclusive

TIME
    Time, represented as a sequence of six unsigned packed decimal digits (*hhmmss*), occupying three bytes; permitted values are legal times in the range midnight to midnight, i.e., 000000 to 240000, inclusive

TIMESTAMP
    "Timestamp" (combination of date and time, accurate to the nearest microsecond), represented as a sequence of 20 unsigned packed decimal digits (*yyyymmddhhmmssnnnnnn*), occupying ten bytes; permitted values are legal timestamps in the range 00010101000000000000 to 99991231240000000000, inclusive

By the term "legal dates" in the foregoing, we mean that DB2 will not permit invalid dates such as 19840431 ("April 31st, 1984") or 19870229 ("February 29th, 1987"). Similarly for times and timestamps, of course.

C.3 CONSTANTS

As explained in Chapter 4, strictly speaking there is no such thing as a date/time constant. Instead, there are *interpreted character string constants*. If a character string constant appears in a context that requires a date/time value,* then that character string will be interpreted as a date/time value, provided of course that it is of the appropriate form (a conversion error will occur if it is not). We will use the term "date/time string" to refer to a character string that represents a legal date/time value.

"Date/time string" constants, then, take the following forms (except as noted below):

---

*More generally, of course, any character string *expression* can appear in such a context (see Section C.6).

date string	Written as a character string constant of the form *mm/dd/yyyy,* enclosed in single quotes

Examples: `'1/18/1941'`
`'12/25/1989'`

time string	Written as a character string constant of the form *hh:mm* AM or *hh:mm* PM, enclosed in single quotes

Examples: `'10:00 AM'`
`'9:30 PM'`

timestamp string	Written as a character string constant of the form *yyyy-mm-dd-hh.mm.ss.nnnnnn,* enclosed in single quotes

Examples: `'1990-4-28-12.00.00.000000'`
`'1944-10-17-18.30.45'`

Note: Actually, several different date/time string formats are supported: US style (USA), European style (EUR), International Standards Organization style (ISO), Japanese Industrial Standard Christian Era style (JIS), and installation-defined (LOCAL). A variety of methods (installation options, Precompiler options, etc.) are available for specifying the particular style to be used in any particular context. In this appendix we will always assume US style, barring any explicit statement to the contrary. As pointed out in Chapter 4, a peculiarity of US-style time string constants is that they do not include a seconds component. Nevertheless, the internal representation of a time value always does include such a component.

To repeat some syntactic details from Chapter 4: Leading zeros can be omitted from the month and day portions of a date or timestamp string constant and from the hours portion of a time or timestamp string constant. The seconds portion (including the preceding colon or period) can be omitted entirely from a time string constant (in fact, it must be so omitted in US style); an implicit specification of zero is assumed. Trailing zeros can be omitted from the microseconds portion of a timestamp string constant; the microseconds portion (including the preceding period) can also be omitted entirely, in which case an implicit specification of zero is assumed.

C.4 COLUMN DEFINITIONS

Date/time column definitions of course use the conventional DB2 syntax—

```
column data-type [ NOT NULL [ WITH DEFAULT ] ]
```

—where "data-type" is DATE or TIME or TIMESTAMP. As mentioned in Section C.2, date/time values are represented internally as unsigned sequences of packed decimal digits, 2 digits to a byte, with a width of 4 bytes (DATE), 3 bytes (TIME), or 10 bytes (TIMESTAMP).

Default values for columns defined WITH DEFAULT are the value of CURRENT DATE or CURRENT TIME or CURRENT TIMESTAMP, as applicable (see Section C.7). Note, therefore, that if table T has a date/time column C defined WITH DEFAULT, then two consecutive INSERTs to T that both omit a value for C will cause two different values to be placed in the C position. This feature could be useful in situations in which there is no "natural" primary key—for example, given a table of temperature readings, which are not necessarily (or naturally) all distinct, we might define a TIMESTAMP column WITH DEFAULT to act as the primary key:

```
CREATE TABLE TEMP_READINGS
     ( READING_TIME   TIMESTAMP NOT NULL WITH DEFAULT,
       READING        DECIMAL(4,1),
       PRIMARY KEY ( READING_TIME ) ) ;
```

In effect, DB2 will then generate unique primary key values automatically (assuming of course that no explicit value is ever specified by the user on INSERT). Note, however, that a UNIQUE (primary) index will still be required on READING_TIME.

Note: The foregoing explanation of default values tacitly assumed that the column in question was defined via CREATE TABLE, not ALTER TABLE. The explanation requires some slight revision in the ALTER case. For rows inserted into the table after the ALTER is executed, the CURRENT defaults apply as discussed above. For rows already existing in the table at ALTER time, however, the defaults are defined as follows:

```
*  DATE        --   '01/01/0001'

*  TIME        --   '00:00 AM'

*  TIMESTAMP   --   '0001-01-01-00.00.00.000000'
```

The reason for the difference has to do with the way adding columns via ALTER TABLE is implemented in DB2. As explained in Chapter 5, existing rows are not physically extended at ALTER time. Instead, DB2 simply materializes the necessary default value (for the field in question) each time such a row is retrieved. Materializing a (different) "current" value on each retrieval would obviously be inappropriate.

C.5 DURATIONS

DB2 supports the notion of a *duration*. A duration is an interval of time, such as "3 years" or "90 days" or "5 minutes 30 seconds." For example, subtracting the time "9:00 AM" from the time "10:15 AM" yields the duration "1 hour 15 minutes." *Note carefully, however, that there is no dura-tion data type.* Instead, durations are *interpreted decimal integers.* For ex-ample, suppose we are given the following data definition:

```
CREATE TABLE T
     ( ... ,
         START_TIME   TIME,
         ... ,
         WAIT_TIME   DECIMAL(6),
         ... ) ;
```

Now consider the expression:

```
START_TIME + WAIT_TIME
```

If START_TIME and WAIT_TIME happen to have the values "9:00 AM" and 50000, respectively, then this expression will evaluate to "2:00 PM"; in other words, the value 50000 will be interpreted to mean "5 hours." Likewise, if they have the values "9:00 AM" and −50000, respec-tively, then the expression will evaluate to "4:00 AM."

It follows from the foregoing that durations can be stored in the data-base, but only in the form of DECIMAL values. DB2 is not aware that the column in question (i.e., WAIT_TIME, in the example) is really being used to hold duration values.

Durations are of two basic kinds, date durations and time durations. A third kind, "microsecond durations," also exists but seems to have no official classifying name; see the discussion of "labeled durations" below.*

- A date duration is a signed decimal integer of 8 digits (5 bytes) of the form *yyyymmdd,* where *yyyy* is the number of years (0–9999), *mm* is the number of months (0–99), and *dd* is the number of days (0–99).

- A time duration is a signed decimal integer of 6 digits (4 bytes) of the form *hhmmss,* where *hh* is the number of hours (0–99), *mm* is the num-ber of minutes (0–99), and *ss* is the number of seconds (0–99).

- A "microsecond duration" is a signed decimal integer of 6 digits (4 bytes) of the form *nnnnnn,* representing *nnnnnn* microseconds.

Note that a duration such as "90 days" or "25 hours" is legal; i.e., "days" is not restricted to a maximum of 31, nor "hours" to a maximum of 23 (etc.). To return to the example discussed earlier: If START_TIME

---

*Note that there is no such thing as a "timestamp duration." This omission is due to the following combination of facts: (a) Durations are intended primarily for use in date/time arithmetic; (b) timestamps are represented as 20-digit decimal numbers with an assumed decimal point six digits from the right; (c) DB2 cannot perform DECIMAL(20,6) arithmetic.

and WAIT_TIME have the values "9:00 AM" and 250000, respectively, then the expression

```
START_TIME + WAIT_TIME
```

evaluates to "10:00 AM"; the overflow in the hours position is ignored (see Section C.8).

Since "duration" is not really a data type but is instead just an interpreted decimal integer, there is strictly speaking no such thing as a "duration constant." Instead, decimal integers (of the appropriate format) can be used, as in (e.g.) the expression

```
START_TIME + 050000.
```

(Note that the decimal constant must have *exactly* the right precision and scale.)

However, DB2 does also include the notion of a *labeled duration*. Labeled durations are a special kind of scalar expression, whose value is a decimal integer that is to be interpreted as a duration (date or time or "microsecond"). Such expressions can be used to play the role of "duration constants" (among other things). Labeled durations take the form "n units", where "n" is any numeric expression (it is converted to a decimal integer if necessary), and "units" is any of the following:

```
YEAR[S]
MONTH[S]
DAY[S]
HOUR[S]
MINUTE[S]
SECOND[S]
MICROSECOND[S]
```

Examples:

```
3 YEARS
90 DAYS
1 MINUTE
47 MICROSECONDS
```

Of the seven possible "units" specifications listed above, the first three identify the duration as a date duration, the next three as a time duration, and the last one as a "microsecond duration" (not an official DB2 term). *Note:* Observe that date durations in general involve years *and* months *and* days, but *labeled* date durations involve years *or* months *or* days (not a mixture). Similarly, time durations in general involve hours *and* minutes *and* seconds, but labeled time durations involve hours *or* minutes *or* seconds, not a mixture.

Note: The IBM manuals classify durations differently, into date, time, and labeled durations (i.e., a labeled duration is not the same thing as either a date duration or a time duration). This classification is somewhat counter-intuitive, however, since a labeled duration clearly does represent a "duration" (in the ordinary English sense) of years or days or hours or ... (etc.). In this appendix we will stay with our own classification.

Here are some examples of the use of labeled durations:

```
UPDATE T
SET    START_TIME = START_TIME + 15 MINUTES
WHERE  ... ;

SELECT ...
FROM   T
WHERE  END_TIME < START_TIME + 1 HOUR + 30 MINUTES ;

UPDATE SCHEDULE
SET    FINISH = FINISH + :SLIPPAGE MONTHS
WHERE  ... ;
```

SLIPPAGE here is a (numeric) host variable.

Note finally that the *only* context in which a labeled duration can appear is in an expression involving infix " + " or " − ", in which one operand is the labeled duration in question and the other is a date/time value. See Section C.8 for further discussion.

C.6 CONVERSIONS

DB2 includes a number of scalar builtin functions for performing explicit conversions involving date/time data.

Extraction of Date/Time Components:

- YEAR, MONTH, DAY:

  Convert the year or month or day portion (as applicable) of a specified date or timestamp or date duration to a binary integer.

- HOUR, MINUTE, SECOND:

  Convert the hours or minutes or seconds portion (as applicable) of a specified time or timestamp or time duration to a binary integer.

- MICROSECOND:

  Converts the microseconds portion of a specified timestamp to a binary integer.

Examples:

```
MONTH ( END_DATE )
DAY ( DEPART - ARRIVE )
SECOND ( CURRENT TIME )
```

Conversions To/From Other Data Types:

- DATE, TIME, TIMESTAMP:

  Convert a specified scalar value to a date or time or timestamp (as applicable). In the case of TIMESTAMP, the scalar value can be specified as a pair of values, representing a date and a time, respectively.

- CHAR

  Converts a specified date/time value to its character string representation in USA, EUR, ISO, JIS, or LOCAL format (as specified either by an argument to the function or, if that argument is omitted, either by the DATE Precompiler option or by the DATE FORMAT installation option).

- DAYS

  Converts a specified date or timestamp to a binary integer, representing the number of days since December 31st, 1 B.C. (Note that there is no "0 B.C."; December 31st, 1 B.C., is immediately followed by January 1st, 1 A.D.)

Examples:

```
DATE ('6/7/87')
TIME ( CURRENT TIMESTAMP )
CHAR ( START_DATE, USA )
DAYS ( '1/18/1941' )
```

Implicit Conversions:

In certain circumstances DB2 will also perform implicit date/time conversions:

(a) If a character string value occurs in a position where the language requires a date/time value, then the string will be interpreted as a date/time if possible.

(b) If a decimal value occurs in a position where the language requires a duration, then the decimal value will be interpreted as a duration if possible.

(c) If a date/time value occurs in a position where the language requires a character string value, then the date/time will be converted to its character string representation.

Examples:

```
1. UPDATE T
   SET    START_DATE = :XM || '/' || :XD || '/' || :XY
   WHERE  ... ;
```

Here XM, XD, and XY are character string variables of two, two, and four characters, respectively. The character string expression is evaluated and then interpreted as a date string.

```
2. UPDATE T
   SET    START_TIME = START_TIME + 050000.
   WHERE  ... ;
```

In this example the decimal value is interpreted as a time duration of 5 hours.

```
3. SELECT START_DATE
   INTO   :HOST_CHAR_FIELD
   FROM   T
   WHERE  ... ;
```

Here START_DATE will be converted to its character string representation.

Note, however, that DB2 does not always permit a date/time value to appear in place of a character string value (Case (c) above). For example, the argument to LIKE is required to be a string—it cannot be a date/time value. On the other hand, the converse situations (Cases (a) and (b)) are apparently always legal—that is, a character string or decimal value can always appear in place of a date/time value or duration, respectively—although actually even this is not totally clear from the documentation. In fact, the precise rules as to exactly what is permitted do not seem to be very well defined. On the whole, the best practice would seem to be to avoid implicit conversions by always using the explicit functions DATE (etc.). We refer the reader to the IBM manuals for further clarification.

There are no implicit conversions between dates and timestamps, or times and timestamps, or dates and times.

C.7 SPECIAL REGISTERS

DB2 supports a number of date/time "special registers" (as explained in Chapter 4, this is the official DB2 term, although "zero-argument builtin scalar functions" would be closer to the mark). The date/time special registers are CURRENT TIMEZONE, CURRENT DATE, CURRENT TIME, and CURRENT TIMESTAMP. A reference to one of these registers returns a scalar value, as follows:

- CURRENT TIMEZONE

  Returns a time duration representing (typically) the displacement of the local time zone from Greenwich Mean Time (GMT).* The value re-

---

*The actual value of CURRENT TIMEZONE is established by an installation-defined MVS system parameter.

turned by each of CURRENT DATE, CURRENT TIME, and CURRENT TIMESTAMP (see below) is based on a reading of the CPU clock, incremented in each case by the value of CURRENT TIMEZONE. In the case of Pacific Standard Time, for example, if the CPU clock is set to GMT and CURRENT TIMEZONE to "−8 hours," then CURRENT DATE, CURRENT TIME, and CURRENT TIMESTAMP would each return the true local value. If, on the other hand, the CPU clock is in fact set to the local value, then CURRENT TIMEZONE should probably be set to zero.

- CURRENT DATE

  Returns the current date, i.e., the date "today" (but see CURRENT TIMEZONE above).

- CURRENT TIME

  Returns the current time, i.e., the time "now" (but see CURRENT TIMEZONE above).

- CURRENT TIMESTAMP

  Returns the current timestamp, i.e., the date "today" concatenated with the time "now" (but see CURRENT TIMEZONE above).

When any given SQL data manipulation statement is executed, all references to CURRENT DATE and/or CURRENT TIME and/or CURRENT TIMESTAMP are based on a single reading of the local clock. Thus, for example, the WHERE clause "WHERE CURRENT TIME = CURRENT TIME" is always guaranteed to evaluate to *true*.

C.8 EXPRESSIONS

The infix arithmetic operators " + " and " − " (only) can be used with date/times. For example, a date and a date duration can be added to yield another date. The reader is warned, however, that not all operations that would appear to make sense are in fact permitted. Here is a complete list of the legal possibilities in DB2:

First operand	Operator	Second operand	Result
date	+	date duration	date
date duration	+	date	date
date	−	date	date duration
date	−	date duration	date

time	+	time duration	time
time duration	+	time	time
time	−	time	time duration
time	−	time duration	time
timestamp	+	duration	timestamp
duration	+	timestamp	timestamp
timestamp	−	duration	timestamp

In other words:

- For addition (infix " + ")
  - if one operand is a date, the other must be a date or date duration
  - if one operand is a time, the other must be a time or time duration
  - if one operand is a timestamp, the other must be a duration
- For subtraction (infix " − ")
  - if the first operand is a date, the second must be a date or date duration
  - if the first operand is a time, the second must be a time or time duration
  - if the first operand is a timestamp, the second must be a duration
  - if the second operand is a date, the first must be a date
  - if the second operand is a time, the first must be a time

Note in particular that it is not legal to subtract one timestamp from another. It might reasonably be argued that such an operation does make sense and should yield a timestamp duration, but—as explained in Section C.5—DB2 does not support timestamp durations.

Labeled durations are subject to an additional (and very major) constraint, namely as follows: They are permitted *only* as operands of infix " + " or " − ", and *only* if the other operand is a date/time value—*not* another duration (labeled or otherwise). Thus the following operations are all *** ILLEGAL *** if either of the duration operands is labeled (the "Result" column thus shows what might be expected in each case, *not* what DB2 will actually produce).

First operand	*Operator*	*Second operand*	*"Result"*
date duration	+	date duration	date duration
date duration	−	date duration	date duration
time duration	+	time duration	time duration
time duration	−	time duration	time duration
microsec duration	+	microsec duration	microsec duration
microsec duration	−	microsec duration	microsec duration

The aggregate functions COUNT, MAX, and MIN (but not SUM or AVG) can be applied to date/time arguments; the result is an integer for COUNT, a date/time value of the appropriate type for MAX and MIN.

Examples:

Note that some of the following expressions are not legal. We leave it as an exercise for the reader to determine why not.

```
DATE ('8/17/1972') - DATE ('10/28/1969')
DATE ('8/17/1972') -      '10/28/1969'
     '8/17/1972'  - DATE ('10/28/1969')
     '8/17/1972'  -      '10/28/1969'           *** ILLEGAL ***

START_DATE +   1 YEAR   + 6 MONTHS
1 YEAR     +   6 MONTHS + START_DATE            *** ILLEGAL ***
               1 YEAR   + 6 MONTHS              *** ILLEGAL ***
( START_DATE + 1 YEAR ) + 6 MONTHS
START_DATE + ( 1 YEAR   + 6 MONTHS )            *** ILLEGAL ***
START_DATE +   6 WEEKS                          *** ILLEGAL ***
START_DATE +   4 HOURS                          *** ILLEGAL ***

START_TIME + WAIT_TIME
START_TIME + HOUR(WAIT_TIME) HOURS
START_TIME + 120000.
TIME('9:00 AM')  + 120000.
'9:00 AM'  + 120000.                            *** ILLEGAL ***
9 HOURS    + 120000.                            *** ILLEGAL ***

CURRENT TIMESTAMP + 1 SECOND + 500000 MICROSECONDS
CURRENT TIME - CURRENT TIMEZONE
ETA - ( CURRENT TIME - CURRENT TIMEZONE )
```

Date/time arithmetic is performed in accordance with the calendar and permissible date/time values. Thus, for example, the expression

```
DATE('5/31/1988') + 1 MONTH
```

yields the result "6/30/1988" (*not* "6/31/1988"—i.e., "June 30th, 1988," not "June 31st, 1988"). On the other hand, the expression

```
DATE('6/30/1988') - 1 MONTH
```

yields the result "5/30/1988" (not "5/31/1988"—i.e., "May 30th, 1988," not "May 31st, 1988"). In other words, the expression

```
DATE('5/31/1988') + 1 MONTH - 1 MONTH
```

does not yield "5/31/1988"! More generally, if we add a date duration *d* to some date and then subtract that same duration *d* from the result, we are not guaranteed to end up with the date we started with. By contrast, the expression

```
DATE('5/31/1988') + 30 DAYS - 30 DAYS
```

will indeed yield "5/31/1988"—i.e., we do end up with the date we started with in this case.

Another potential trap for the unwary is illustrated by the following example: What is the value of each of the following two expressions? We leave the details as an exercise for the reader. (Hint: Which value is the greater?)

```
TIME('9:00 AM') + 000100.
TIME('9:00 AM') + 000099.
```

Date/time arithmetic can cause overflow or underflow. The rules are as follows (for brevity, we use the term "overflow" to include both overflow and underflow):

- For dates:
  - overflow in the days position affects the months
  - overflow in the months position affects the years
  - overflow in the years position is an error
- For times:
  - overflow in the seconds position affects the minutes
  - overflow in the minutes position affects the hours
  - overflow in the hours position is ignored
- For timestamps:
  - same as above, except that overflow in the hours position affects the days

C.9 ASSIGNMENTS

Assignments occur on database update and retrieval operations. We consider the DATE data type first. On update:

- If the source is of type DATE, the target must be either of type DATE or of type character string. In the latter case, the date is implicitly converted to its string representation (a date string).

- If the target is of type DATE, the source must be either an expression that evaluates to a date or a character string that can legally be interpreted as a date (a date string). In the latter case, the string is implicitly converted to a date.

On retrieval:

- If the source is of type DATE, the target must be of type character string. The date is implicitly converted to its string representation (a date string).

Analogous rules apply to TIMEs and TIMESTAMPs, of course.

The fact that character strings are considered to be compatible with date/times for assignment purposes permits us to transfer date/time values to and from and programs written in languages such as PL/I that do not support any date/time data types.

Note that it is not possible to assign a value to an individual component (such as the days portion) of a date/time value. Note too that there are no explicit assignment rules for durations, because there is no duration data type; a "duration assignment" is merely a special kind of numeric assignment.

Examples:

```
SELECT  START_DATE
INTO    :HOST_CHAR_VBLE
FROM    T
WHERE   ... ;

INSERT
INTO    T ( ..., START_TIME, ... )
VALUES  ( ....., '10:30 AM', ... ) ;

UPDATE T
SET     START_TIME = :HOST_CHAR_VBLE + 25 MINUTES
WHERE   ... ;
```

An example of a "duration assignment":

```
UPDATE T
SET     WAIT_TIME = 030000.
WHERE   ... ;
```

Note that in this example no harm would result if the leading zero and the decimal point were dropped from the constant; DB2's ordinary numeric conversion rules would take care of everything satisfactorily.

C.10   COMPARISONS

Comparisons can be performed between

(a) a DATE, TIME, or TIMESTAMP value, on the one hand, and

(b) either another value of the same type or a character string that can legally be interpreted as a value of the same type (i.e., an appropriate date/time string), on the other.

Comparisons are performed in accordance with chronologic ordering. Note that the fact that character strings are considered to be compatible with date/times for comparison purposes permits us to compare date/time val-

ues with values from programs written in languages such as PL/I that do
not support any date/time data types. Note too that there are no explicit
comparison rules for durations, because there is no duration data type; a
"duration comparison" is merely a special kind of numeric comparison.

Examples:

```
SELECT ...
FROM    T
WHERE   START_TIME > '9:00 AM'
AND     END_TIME   < '5:00 PM' ;

SELECT ...
FROM    FLIGHTS
WHERE   ETA > CURRENT TIME - CURRENT TIMEZONE ;
```

Here is an example of a "duration comparison":

```
SELECT ...
FROM    T
WHERE   START_TIME - END_TIME < 080000. ;
```

And here are two examples involving date/time functions:

```
SELECT ...
FROM    T
WHERE   MINUTE ( START_TIME ) = 0 ;

SELECT ...
FROM    T
WHERE   HOUR ( START_TIME ) NOT BETWEEN 9 AND 17 ;
```

One possible surprise that can occur in connexion with TIME and
TIMESTAMP comparisons is the following: A time value (*hhmmss*) of
240000 is considered to be greater than a time value of 000000, even though
logically they both represent the same time (i.e., midnight). Note that these
two representations are both legal; refer back to Section C.2.

APPENDIX

Syntax of SQL Data Manipulation Operations

D.1 INTRODUCTION

We present a simplified BNF grammar for the four data manipulation operations of SQL (SELECT, INSERT, UPDATE, and DELETE) described in this book. The grammar makes use of the following convenient shorthand:

- If "xyz" is a syntactic category, then "xyz-commalist" is a syntactic category consisting of a list of one or more "xyz"s in which each pair of adjacent "xyz"s is separated by a sequence of characters consisting of zero or more spaces, followed by a comma, followed by zero or more spaces.

  We also make use of some simplifying abbreviations, namely "exp" for expression, "ref" for reference, and "spec" for specification. The following are terminal categories with respect to this grammar (i.e., they are not defined further in the production rules):

```
identifier
constant
integer
```

Note: Aspects of the four statements not described in the body of the book (e.g., the comparison operators > ANY, = ALL, etc.) are ignored. In the interests of clarity and brevity, moreover, the grammar does not accurately reflect all of the syntactic limitations of SQL but is instead rather permissive, in the sense that it allows the generation of certain constructs that are not legal in SQL. For example, it allows the argument to an aggregate function such as AVG to consist of a reference to another such function, which SQL does not permit (see Chapter 7, Section 7.4). It also makes no attempt to distinguish between the different types of scalar expression (numeric expressions, character string expressions, etc.). See Chapter 4, also Appendix C, for the details of such distinctions. (Our reason for making these simplifications is that SQL is a very context-sensitive language, and attempts to reflect context sensitivity in BNF tend to lead to a rather unwieldy set of production rules.)

D.2 BASIC ELEMENTS

```
table-spec
   ::=    table-ref [ range-variable ]

table-ref
   ::=    base-table | view

base-table
   ::=    [ user . ] identifier

user
   ::=    authorization-identifier

authorization-identifier
   ::=    identifier

view
   ::=    [ user . ] identifier

range-variable
   ::=    identifier

column-ref
   ::=    [ column-qualifier . ] column

column-qualifier
   ::=    table-ref
        | range-variable

column
   ::=    identifier
```

D.3 SCALAR EXPRESSIONS

```
scalar-exp
    ::=     scalar-term
        |   scalar-exp  +    scalar-term
        |   scalar-exp  -    scalar-term
        |   scalar-exp "||" scalar-term
```

Note: We show the concatenation operator "||" in quotes to avoid confusion with the vertical bar "|" which is used to separate alternatives in the grammar. The quotes are not part of the operator.

```
scalar-term
    ::=     scalar-factor
        |   scalar-term * scalar-factor
        |   scalar-term / scalar-factor

scalar-factor
    ::=     [ + | - ] scalar-primary

scalar-primary
    ::=     constant
        |   labeled-duration
        |   column-ref
        |   special-register
        |   scalar-function-ref
        |   aggregate-function-ref
        |   ( scalar-exp )

labeled-duration
    ::=     scalar-exp units

units
    ::=     YEAR[S]
        |   MONTH[S]
        |   DAY[S]
        |   HOUR[S]
        |   MINUTE[S]
        |   SECOND[S]
        |   MICROSECOND[S]

special-register
    ::=     USER
        |   CURRENT SQLID
        |   CURRENT TIMEZONE
        |   CURRENT DATE
        |   CURRENT TIME
        |   CURRENT TIMESTAMP

scalar-function-ref
    ::=     scalar-function ( scalar-exp-commalist )
```

```
scalar-function
    ::=     CHAR    | DATE        | DAY       | DAYS  | DECIMAL
        |   DIGITS  | FLOAT       | HEX       | HOUR  | INTEGER
        |   LENGTH  | MICROSECOND | MINUTE    | MONTH | SECOND
        |   SUBSTR  | TIME        | TIMESTAMP | VALUE | VARGRAPHIC
        |   YEAR
```

Note: Each of these scalar functions takes just a single scalar-expression argument, except (a) CHAR and TIMESTAMP, which take two, (b)

DECIMAL and SUBSTR, which take three, and (c) VALUE, which takes an arbitrary number (at least two).

```
aggregate-function-ref
    ::=     COUNT ( * )
        |   aggregate-function ( [ ALL ] scalar-exp )
        |   aggregate-function ( DISTINCT column-ref )

aggregate-function
    ::=     COUNT | SUM | AVG | MAX | MIN
```

D.4   SELECT-EXPRESSIONS

```
select-exp
    ::=     select-clause
            from-clause
        [ where-clause ]
        [ grouping-clause ]
        [ having-clause ]

select-clause
    ::=     SELECT [ ALL | DISTINCT ] select-spec

select-spec
    ::=     * | selection-commalist

selection
    ::=     table-ref . *
        |   scalar-exp

from-clause
    ::=     FROM table-spec-commalist

where-clause
    ::=     WHERE predicate

grouping-clause
    ::=     GROUP BY column-ref-commalist

having-clause
    ::=     HAVING predicate
```

D.5   PREDICATES

```
predicate
    ::=     predicate-term
        |   predicate OR predicate-term

predicate-term
    ::=     predicate-factor
        |   predicate-term AND predicate-factor

predicate-factor
    ::=     [ NOT ] predicate-primary

predicate-primary
    ::=     condition
        |   ( predicate )
```

```
condition
    ::=       compare-condition
            | between-condition
            | like-condition
            | in-condition
            | test-for-null
            | existence-test

compare-condition
    ::=       scalar-exp comparison scalar-exp
            | scalar-exp comparison ( column-select-exp )

comparison
    ::=      =  |  ~=  |  <>  |  <  |  ~<  |  <=  |  >  |  ~>  |  >=

column-select-exp
    ::=       column-select-clause
              from-clause
            [ where-clause ]
            [ grouping-clause ]
            [ having-clause ] ]

column-select-clause
    ::=       SELECT [ ALL | DISTINCT ] scalar-exp

between-condition
    ::=       column-ref [ NOT ] BETWEEN scalar-exp AND scalar-exp

like-condition
    ::=       column-ref [ NOT ] LIKE constant

in-condition
    ::=       scalar-exp [ NOT ] IN ( set-of-scalars )

set-of-scalars
    ::=       constant-commalist
            | column-select-exp

test-for-null
    ::=   column-ref IS [ NOT ] NULL

existence-test
    ::=       EXISTS ( select-exp )
```

D.6 STATEMENTS

```
statement
    ::=       select-statement
            | insert-statement
            | update-statement
            | delete-statement

select-statement
    ::=       union-exp [ ordering-clause ] ;

union-exp
    ::=       union-term
            | union-exp UNION [ ALL ] union-term

union-term
    ::=       select-exp
            | ( union-exp )
```

```
ordering-clause
  ::=    ORDER BY order-item-commalist

order-item
  ::=    ordering-column [ ASC | DESC ]

ordering-column
  ::=    column-ref | integer

insert-statement
  ::=    INSERT INTO table-ref [ ( column-commalist ) ]
                 source-values ;

source-values
  ::=    VALUES ( insert-item-commalist )
       | select-exp

insert-item
  ::=    constant | NULL | special-register

update-statement
  ::=    UPDATE table-spec
         SET column-assignment-commalist
       [ where-clause ] ;

column-assignment
  ::=    column = scalar-exp
       | column = NULL

delete-statement
  ::=    DELETE FROM table-spec [ where-clause ] ;
```

APPENDIX

◆ E ◆

DB2 Catalog Tables

In this appendix we present a brief summary of the tables that constitute the DB2 catalog, in order to give some idea of the control information that DB2 maintains therein and hence some idea of the kinds of SQL queries that are possible against the catalog. We remind the reader that all catalog tables have an "owner" of SYSIBM; the fully qualified name of the SYSTABLES table, for example, is SYSIBM.SYSTABLES.

- SYSCOLAUTH

  Shows which authorization IDs have UPDATE privileges on which columns of which tables.

- SYSCOLUMNS

  Contains one row for each column of each table (see Chapter 9).

- SYSCOPY

  Contains recovery information (see Chapter 17).

- SYSDATABASE

  Contains one row for each database.

- SYSDBAUTH

  Shows which authorization IDs have which privileges on which databases.

- SYSDBRM

  Contains one row for each DBRM (see Chapter 2).

- SYSFIELDS

  Contains one row for each column that has a FIELDPROC (see Chapter 16).

- SYSFOREIGNKEYS

  Contains one row for each column of each foreign key.

- SYSINDEXES

  Contains one row for each index (see Chapter 9).

- SYSINDEXPART

  Contains one row for each partition of each partitioned indexspace and one row for each simple indexspace (see Chapter 16).

- SYSKEYS

  Contains one row for each indexed column for each index (note that this has nothing to do with keys in the relational sense—the "keys" in question are "index keys," not necessarily primary or foreign keys.)

- SYSLINKS

  Contains one row for each parent/child link in the catalog (as explained at the end of Chapter 16, the catalog itself makes use of certain storage structures, including in particular parent/child links, that DB2 databases in general do not).

- SYSPLAN

  Contains one row for each application plan.

- SYSPLANAUTH

  Shows which authorization IDs have which privileges on which application plans.

- SYSPLANDEP

  Shows which application plans are dependent on which objects.

- SYSRELS

  Contains a row for each "relationship" (i.e., referential constraint).

- SYSRESAUTH

  Shows which authorization IDs have which privileges on which storage groups, tablespaces, and buffer pools.

- SYSSTMT

  Contains the source form of the SQL statements corresponding to the DBRMs listed in SYSDBRM (see above).

- SYSSTOGROUP

  Contains one row for each storage group.

- SYSSYNONYMS

  Contains one row for each synonym.

- SYSTABAUTH

  Shows which authorization IDs have which privileges on which tables.

- SYSTABLEPART

  Contains one row for each partition of each partitioned tablespace and one row for each simple or segmented tablespace (see Chapter 16).

- SYSTABLES

  Contains one row for each table (see Chapter 9).

- SYSTABLESPACE

  Contains one row for each tablespace.

- SYSUSERAUTH

  Shows which authorization IDs have which system privileges.

- SYSVIEWDEP

  Shows which views depend on which tables.

- SYSVIEWS

  Contains the source form of the SQL definition of each view.

- SYSVLTREE

  Contains the rest (if any) of the parse tree representation for each view (see SYSVTREE below).

- SYSVOLUMES

  Contains one row for each volume of each storage group.

- SYSVTREE

  Contains the first 4000 bytes of the parse tree representation for each view.

APPENDIX

◆ F ◆

Some Differences between DB2 and the SQL Standard

F.1 INTRODUCTION

In this appendix we summarize all known differences between the DB2 Version 2 dialect of SQL and the official ANSI/ISO standard dialect. For a thorough description of the standard version, the reader is referred to the book *A Guide to the SQL Standard,* by C. J. Date (2nd edition, Addison-Wesley, 1989).

In an attempt to structure the discussion, we divide what follows into three main sections: "Standard Features Not Supported in DB2," "DB2 Features Not Supported in the Standard," and "Incompatibilities" (features supported in both but treated differently). However, the assignment of topics to sections is sometimes a little arbitrary.

F.2 STANDARD FEATURES NOT SUPPORTED IN DB2

- The standard allows annotation (i.e., embedded comments, introduced by a double hyphen "--" and terminated by end-of-line) to appear within SQL statements. DB2 does not.

- DB2 does not support the NUMERIC data type.

- The standard supports user-defined default values. DB2 does not.

- UNIQUE constraints on CREATE TABLE are not supported in DB2 (instead, DB2 enforces uniqueness via UNIQUE indexes). PRIMARY KEY constraints are supported, but only by means of a separate PRIMARY KEY clause, not as part of an individual column definition.

- The REFERENCES specification (as part of an individual column definition) is not supported; FOREIGN KEY specifications are supported in DB2 only by means of a separate FOREIGN KEY clause. Foreign keys in DB2 are required to reference primary keys, not just candidate keys.

- DB2 does not support CHECK constraints on base tables (or columns thereof).

- DB2 does not support the REFERENCES privilege (it uses the ALTER privilege for the purpose instead).

- In DB2, if the argument to an aggregate function such as SUM includes DISTINCT, then the function reference must appear in isolation—i.e., it cannot be an operand in a larger arithmetic expression such as SUM(DISTINCT F) + 3. This restriction does not exist in the standard.

- The standard version of the LIKE condition includes an ESCAPE clause to permit the special interpretation given to the percent and underscore characters to be disabled. DB2 does not support this clause.

- The standard allows indicator variable references to be immediately preceded by the optional keyword INDICATOR. DB2 does not.

- DB2 does not allow indicator variables to appear in a WHERE or HAVING clause.

- The standard separates data definition operations from data manipulation operations. CREATE TABLE and CREATE VIEW (and GRANT) operations are specified as part of a "schema" by means of the *schema definition language.* All other standard SQL operations are specified as part of a "module" by means of the *module language.* DB2 has no notion of schemas or modules (in the sense of the standard) at all.

F.3   DB2 FEATURES NOT SUPPORTED IN THE STANDARD

- The standard does not allow any characters to appear in identifiers other than the uppercase letters A–Z, the digits 0–9, and the underscore character. DB2 allows the characters #, @, and $ to appear in an identifier wherever a letter can appear. DB2 also supports "delimited identifiers" (see the IBM manuals for details).

- DB2 allows consecutive underscore characters to appear in an identifier. The standard does not.

- The following DB2 data types are not supported in the standard:

```
VARCHAR (and LONG VARCHAR)
GRAPHIC
VARGRAPHIC (and LONG VARGRAPHIC)
DATE
TIME
TIMESTAMP
```

  The concept of "durations" also does not exist in the standard.

- The DB2 concept of system-defined default values does not exist in the standard; the specification NOT NULL WITH DEFAULT on CREATE (or ALTER) TABLE is a DB2 extension.

- Candidate keys must be defined to be NOT NULL in the standard but not in DB2. (*Primary* keys must be NOT NULL in both.)

- DB2's support for foreign keys includes (a) "constraint names" for foreign key constraints, (b) delete rules (CASCADE, SET NULL, and RESTRICT), and (c) support for constraint cycles. None of these items is included in the standard, except (implicitly) the RESTRICT delete rule. (*Note:* The DB2 support for primary and foreign keys is broadly but not totally compatible with the standards committees' longer-term proposals for extending the standard in this area.)

- DB2 allows a value of approximate numeric type (FLOAT, REAL, or DOUBLE PRECISION) to be assigned to an object of exact numeric type (SMALLINT, INTEGER, or DECIMAL). The standard does not.

- The standard does not include any date/time support at all. Thus everything discussed in Appendix C of this book is a DB2 extension.

- DB2 supports hexadecimal constants.

- DB2 supports a concatenate operator (||).

- The standard does not include any scalar builtin functions. Thus the functions discussed in Section 4.4 of this book (SUBSTR, LENGTH, etc., etc.) are all DB2 extensions.

- DB2 supports the scalar comparison operators $\sim =$, $\sim <$, and $\sim >$ as alternative representations of $<>$, $>=$, and $<=$, respectively.

- The standard SELECT statement is strictly a singleton SELECT—i.e., it retrieves a single row. Multiple-row retrieval must be done by means of a cursor. (The standard, not unnaturally, is oriented towards the use of SQL in application programs, rather than interactive SQL.)

- DB2 allows qualified references of the form "R.*" (where R is a range variable) in a SELECT clause. DB2 also allows references of the form "*" (or "R.*") in a SELECT clause to appear in conjunction with other items. Both of these possibilities are prohibited in the standard.

- In DB2, the commalist of constants in an IN condition (first format— see Example 6.2.8) must contain at least one constant; in the standard, it must contain at least two. DB2 also allows the argument to IN to be a single scalar expression, in which case the IN is interpreted as "$=$". This possibility was not discussed in the body of the book and is not included in the standard.

- UNION in the standard includes all the severe restrictions regarding "union-compatibility" that applied to DB2 Version 1, Releases 1 and 2. Those restrictions no longer exist in DB2.

- UNION (with or without ALL) is strictly a binary operation in the standard. That is, an expression such as *x* UNION *y* UNION *z* is not permitted; it must be replaced by one of the two expressions (*x* UNION *y*) UNION *z* or *x* UNION (*y* UNION *z*).

- DB2 supports the use of explicitly defined range variables in UPDATE and DELETE as well as in SELECT.

- The standard does not include any definition of catalog tables (SYSTABLES, SYSCOLUMNS, etc.).

- The standard does not support the COMMENT or LABEL statements.

- The standard does not support synonyms (CREATE SYNONYM, DROP SYNONYM).

- The only privileges defined in the standard are SELECT, INSERT, UPDATE (possibly column-specific), DELETE, REFERENCES (possibly column-specific), and ALL. As already noted in Section F.2, DB2 does not support the REFERENCES privilege; however, it does support numerous additional privileges (see the IBM manuals for details). In addition, the DB2 GRANT statement allows a commalist of table names (not just one, as in the standard) to be specified in the ON clause, and allows that commalist to be optionally preceded by the noiseword

TABLE (not permitted in the standard). DB2 also allows privileges to be REVOKEd (the standard does not include a REVOKE statement).

- The standard does not support the SET CURRENT SQLID statement.

- Certain restrictions on the use of view columns in the standard are relaxed in DB2. For example, if column C of view V is derived from an expression such as A + B, then in the standard an aggregate function reference of the form SUM (DISTINCT C) is (tacitly) illegal. In DB2, however, this restriction is relaxed if—and only if—the function reference appears within a statement that "meets certain special criteria" (this is the phrase used in the DB2 manuals). Details of those "special criteria" are beyond the scope of this appendix, however. The reader is referred to the DB2 manuals for more information.

- DB2's rules regarding view updatability (see Section 10.4) are slightly more permissive than those of the standard, as follows:

(a) In DB2, if a column of the view is derived from a constant or an expression that does not involve an aggregate function, then INSERT operations are not allowed, and UPDATE operations are not allowed on that column, but DELETE operations are allowed, and so are UPDATE operations on other columns. In the standard, such a view cannot be updated at all.

(b) In DB2, if the WHERE clause in the view definition includes a subquery *and the FROM clause in that subquery refers to the base table on which the view is defined,* then the view is not updatable. In the standard, a view cannot be updated if its definition involves any subquery whatsoever.

- The FOR UPDATE clause on a cursor definition is not included in the standard; nor is the FOR FETCH ONLY clause (the latter was added to DB2 in Version 2 Release 2).

- The SQLWARNING condition on WHENEVER is not included in the standard.

- The embedded SQL statement DECLARE TABLE is not included in the standard.

- The standard requires host variables that will be used within embedded SQL statements to be defined within an "embedded SQL declare section," bracketed by BEGIN and END DECLARE SECTION statements. DB2 does not have this requirement, except in the case of C.

- DB2 allows host variables to be elements of a structure, and also supports the use of structure variables where a commalist of scalars is required (e.g., in the VALUES clause on INSERT).

- The colon marker (":") on host variables can be omitted in DB2 in contexts where no ambiguity can arise (e.g., on the INTO clause in FETCH). It is always required in the standard.

- The SQL Communication Area (SQLCA) is not included in the standard, except for the single feedback parameter SQLCODE; there is therefore no INCLUDE SQLCA statement in the standard either. SQLCODE values are explicitly stated in the standard to be implementation-defined, except for the special values 0 and +100, so DB2 does conform to the standard in this respect even though other implementations will generate different SQLCODEs.

- The standard does not support an explicit LOCK TABLE statement.

- All dynamic SQL features—the statements PREPARE, DESCRIBE, and EXECUTE, the SQL Descriptor Area (SQLDA), the special INCLUDE statement for incorporating the SQLDA into host programs, the miscellaneous associated facilities (DECLARE STATEMENT, special form of OPEN, etc.)—are excluded from the standard.

- The standard does not include any ALTER or DROP statements at all. Therefore, the statements ALTER TABLE, DROP TABLE, and DROP VIEW are all DB2 extensions.

- The standard does not include any of the more "physical" data definition statements that are supported in DB2—CREATE/DROP INDEX, CREATE/DROP DATABASE, CREATE/DROP TABLESPACE, CREATE/DROP STOGROUP, etc. The standard also does not include any of the more "physical" operands on CREATE TABLE, such as EDITPROC, FIELDPROC, VALIDPROC, "IN tablespace," etc.

- As stated in Section F.2, DB2 has no notion of a schema per se. SQL definitional statements (like all other SQL statements) can be executed in DB2 both interactively and—in the form of embedded SQL—from within a program.

- DB2 supports partitioned tables. The standard does not.

- The standard does not support the EXPLAIN statement.

- The standard defines host language interfaces for COBOL, FORTRAN, Pascal, and PL/I (only). It also restricts the range of data types accessible from each of those languages; for example, INTEGER data is not accessible from PL/I in the standard (of course, this is probably an error in the standard). DB2 does not have such restrictions.

F.4   INCOMPATIBILITIES

- The standard and DB2 have different sets of reserved words.

- Authorization identifiers are limited to a maximum of 8 characters in DB2.

- String constants are varying length in DB2 but fixed length in the standard.

- In DB2, updates against a view V are checked against the check option (if any) specified for V and also against the check option (if any) specified for each view W (if any) on which V is defined. In other words, the check option is inheritable in DB2. This is not the case with the standard (nor was it with DB2, prior to Version 1 Release 3).

- The DB2 concept that there is an implicit WHENEVER statement for each condition—NOT FOUND, SQLERROR, also SQLWARNING—at the start of the program text, specifying CONTINUE in each case, is not supported in the standard.

- The standard does not explicitly permit the possibility that an error on retrieval might generate a null and set the indicator variable to -2. Whether it forbids it is unclear.

- The DB2 rules determining the binding of range variables to their corresponding table are not identical to those of the standard. The details are beyond the scope of this appendix; we merely observe that the behavior of DB2 may be unpredictable (and in some cases is certainly incorrect) if a FROM clause (a) mentions the same table twice and introduces an explicit range variable in one of the two mentions only (e.g., FROM S, S SX), or (b) mentions two tables and introduces explicit range variables for both, each having the same name as the other table (e.g., FROM S P, P S). The standard handles these cases (and all others like them) correctly.

- (Another illustration of the preceding point.) Suppose for the sake of the example that fields S.CITY and P.CITY (supplier city and part city) of the suppliers-and-parts database are renamed as S.SCITY and P.PCITY. Consider the following SELECT statement:

```
SELECT S#
FROM    S
WHERE   NOT EXISTS
     (  SELECT *
        FROM    P
        WHERE   PCITY = SCITY ) ;
```

This SELECT is valid in the standard but not in DB2 (the standard recognizes that the reference to SCITY is implicitly qualified by table name S, but DB2 does not; "correlated references" in DB2 are never unqualified).

- The keyword WORK in COMMIT and ROLLBACK is optional in DB2 but required in the standard. The COMMIT and ROLLBACK statements are illegal in DB2 under IMS batch, IMS/DC, and CICS.

- The standard requires all concurrent executions of interleaved transactions to be serializable (i.e., equivalent to some serial execution of those same transactions, running them one at a time). DB2 cannot provide such a guarantee if any of the transactions in question executes under CS isolation level.

A P P E N D I X

◆ G ◆

Query-By-Example

G.1 INTRODUCTION

As stated in Chapter 19, the Query Management Facility product (QMF) provides a Query-By-Example interface as well as a SQL interface. Query-By-Example (QBE) is a relational query language that is in some respects more "user-friendly" than SQL, at least for users who have no training in professional DP skills.* It is certainly true that SQL is more user-friendly than older languages such as DL/I (the IMS language), but it still assumes a certain amount of programming expertise; it is still basically a programming language in the traditional sense, albeit one at a very high level. QBE, by

---

*As explained in Chapter 19, the QBE language was previously supported by IBM as the interface to an "Installed User Program" product (confusingly also called QBE) running on the VM operating system. The reason for supporting the QBE language in QMF was presumably to wean away users of the old QBE product on to the new (and fully supported) QMF product.

contrast, is a language in which all operations are formulated simply by *making entries in empty tables on the screen*—in effect, by filling in forms. This "fill-in-the-blanks" style is very easy to learn and understand, and is frequently more attractive than the SQL style to users who have received little or no formal DP training. In this appendix, therefore, we present a short tutorial on QBE.

QBE (at least, the dialect of QBE supported by QMF) supports analogs of the SQL data manipulation operations SELECT, UPDATE, DELETE, and INSERT (but no others—data definition and data control operations, such as CREATE and GRANT, can be issued only via the SQL interface).* The operations available in QBE are P., U., D., and I., corresponding respectively to the SQL operations SELECT, UPDATE, DELETE, and INSERT. *Note:* "P." stands for "print," but it does not actually cause any printing to occur. The QMF PRINT command is provided for that purpose, as explained in Chapter 19.

The basic idea behind QBE is very simple, and is illustrated by the following example. Consider the query "Get supplier numbers for suppliers in Paris with status > 20" (Example 6.2.5 from Chapter 6). This query can be represented in QBE as follows:

```
S    | S# | SNAME   | STATUS   | CITY
-----|----|---------|----------|---------
     | P. |         |   > 20   | Paris
```

Explanation: First, by issuing the command DRAW S, the user causes QMF to display a blank version of table S (i.e., a version showing the table name and column names only, without any data values). Then the user constructs the query by typing entries in three positions in the body of that table, namely "P." in the S# position (to indicate the target of the query, i.e., the value(s) to be "printed" or displayed), and "> 20" and "Paris" in the STATUS and CITY positions (to indicate the condition(s) that those target values must satisfy).

It is also possible to specify "P." against the entire row, e.g., as follows:

```
S    | S# | SNAME   | STATUS   | CITY
-----|----|---------|----------|---------
P.   |    |         |   > 20   | Paris
```

---

*It is worth mentioning that some of the SQL features added to DB2 after the first release were exposed in the SQL interface of QMF but not the QBE interface. Examples of DB2 features omitted from the QBE interface are the scalar functions (e.g., SUBSTR, LENGTH, DATE), the ALL version of UNION, and date/time arithmetic operations. These omissions suggest that IBM now regards the QBE interface to QMF as a "second-class citizen."

which is equivalent to specifying "P." in every column position in the table:

```
S    | S#  | SNAME    | STATUS   | CITY     |
-----|-----|----------|----------|----------|
     | P.  | P.       | P. >20   | P.Paris  |
```

Note, incidentally, that character string values such as Paris can be specified without being enclosed in quotes. It is never wrong to supply the quotes, however, and sometimes they are required (e.g., if the string includes any blanks).

In the rest of this appendix we illustrate some of the highlights of the QBE interface by showing a number of further examples. For convenience we give references (where applicable) to the SQL versions of the examples in Chapters 6, 7, and 8. We do not however go into as much detail as we did with SQL. Before we get started, a couple of preliminary remarks:

- As stated in Chapter 19, the user's QMF profile specifies whether queries will be formulated in SQL or QBE. It is possible to switch dynamically between the two within a single QMF session.

- Editing commands are available to tailor blank tables on the screen by the addition or removal of columns and rows and by the widening and narrowing of columns. Tables can thus be edited to fit the requirements of whatever operation the user is trying to formulate; in particular, columns that are not needed for the operation in question can be eliminated. For example, in the first of the sample queries shown earlier, the SNAME column could have been eliminated:

```
S    | S#  | STATUS   | CITY     |
-----|-----|----------|----------|
     | P.  | > 20     | Paris    |
```

We shall usually not bother to show such details in what follows. However, we will frequently omit columns that are not needed to formulate the query under consideration.

G.2 RETRIEVAL OPERATIONS

G.2.1 Retrieval with Duplicate Elimination.   Get part numbers for all parts supplied, with redundant duplicates eliminated. (Example 6.2.2)

```
SP   | S#  | P#  | QTY |
-----|-----|-----|-----|
UNQ. |     | P.  |     |
```

"UNQ." stands for "unique" (corresponds to DISTINCT in SQL).

G.2.2 Retrieval with Ordering.

Get supplier numbers and status for suppliers in Paris, in ascending supplier number order within descending status order. (Extended version of Example 6.2.6)

```
S    |    S#     |  SNAME  |  STATUS  |  CITY
-----|-----------|---------|----------|--------
     | P.AO(2).  |         | P.DO(1). | Paris
```

"AO." stands for ascending order, "DO." for descending order. The integers in parentheses indicate the major-to-minor sequence for ordering columns; in the example, STATUS is the major column and S# the minor column.

G.2.3 Retrieval Involving OR.

Get supplier numbers and status for suppliers who either are located in Paris or have status > 20 or both. (Modified version of Example 6.2.5)

Conditions specified within a single row are considered to be "ANDed" together, as the examples so far have illustrated. To "OR" two conditions, they must be specified in different rows, as here:

```
S    |  S#  |  SNAME  |  STATUS  |  CITY
-----|------|---------|----------|---------
     | P.   |         |          | Paris
     | P.   |         |   > 20   |
```

Note: If a given supplier satisfies both of the conditions in this example, the corresponding supplier number will still appear only once in the output—in other words, redundant duplicate rows are automatically eliminated (as in UNION).

Another approach to this query makes use of what is known as a *condition box*. A condition box allows the specification of conditions of any degree of complexity. For example:

```
S    |  S#  |  SNAME  |  STATUS  |  CITY
-----|------|---------|----------|---------
     | P.   |         |   _ST    |  _SC

     |          CONDITIONS          |
     --------------------------------
      _SC = Paris OR _ST > 20
```

Explanation: _ST and _SC are "example elements." In fact, they are really *variables,* standing for the status and city, respectively, of some potential target supplier. The condition box specifies a predicate that those variables must satisfy in order that the corresponding target supplier appear among those retrieved. The name of an example element is arbitrary, except that it must begin with an underscore character.

Another editing command, DRAW COND, is provided to cause QMF to display a blank condition box. Conditions in a condition box can involve

AND, OR, NOT, IN (the simple list-of-values form only), LIKE, and NULL, very much as in SQL. (*Note:* IN, LIKE, and NULL can also be used in entries in a blank table as well as in a condition box.) But it is frequently just as easy to formulate queries without making use of a condition box, and we shall usually ignore the possibility from this point on.

G.2.4 Retrieval Involving Multiple Conditions on the Same Column ANDed Together. Get parts whose weight is in the range 16 to 19 inclusive. (Example 6.2.7)

P	P#	PNAME	COLOR	WEIGHT	WEIGHT	CITY
	P.			>= 16	<= 19	

Editing commands are used to add another column to the blank table and to name it WEIGHT before the query is formulated.

G.2.5 Retrieval of Computed Values. For all parts, get the part number and the weight of the part in grams. Weights are given in table P in pounds. (Example 6.2.3)

P	P#	WEIGHT		
	P.	_PW	P. 'Weight in grams ='	P. _PW * 454

G.2.6 Retrieving (Specified Fields from) a Join. Get all supplier-number/part-number combinations such that the supplier and part concerned are "colocated." (Example 6.3.4)

S	S#	CITY	P	P#	CITY			
	_SX	_CX		_PX	_CX	P.	_SX	_PX

Explanation: Three blank tables are needed for this query, one each for S and P (only relevant columns shown) and one for the result (no table name or column names may be specified). Notice how example elements are specified to link these three tables together. The entire query can be paraphrased:

"Display supplier-number / part-number pairs, SX / PX say, such that SX and PX are both located in the same city CX."

G.2.7 Joining a Table with Itself. Get all pairs of supplier numbers such that the two suppliers concerned are colocated. (Example 6.3.6)

S	S#	CITY			
	_SX	_CZ	P.	_SX	_SY
	_SY	_CZ			

A condition box can be used to specify the additional condition _SX < _SY, if desired (see Chapter 6 for a discussion of this point).

G.2.8 Retrieval Involving Existential Quantification. Get supplier names for suppliers who supply part P2. (Example 7.3.1)

S	S#	SNAME		SP	S#	P#
	_SX	P.			_SX	P2

The row in table SP is *implicitly* quantified by the existential quantifier "there exists." The query can be paraphrased:

> "Display supplier names for suppliers SX such that there exists a shipment showing supplier SX supplying part P2."

QBE thus (implicitly) includes an analog of EXISTS in SQL. Note, however, that it does *not* include any analog of NOT EXISTS. Thus, for example, a query such as "Get supplier names for suppliers who do *not* supply part P2" cannot be formulated in QBE, at least in the dialect implemented in QMF. The QMF dialect of QBE is therefore (unfortunately) strictly less powerful than the QMF dialect of SQL.*

G.2.9 Retrieval Involving an Aggregate Function. Get the total quantity of part P2 supplied. (Example 7.4.4)

SP	S#	P#	QTY	
		P2	_QX	P.SUM._QX

The following aggregate functions are supported: "CNT." (or "COUNT."), "SUM.", "AVG.", "MAX.", and "MIN.".

G.2.10 Retrieval Involving an Aggregate Function, with Grouping. For each part supplied, get the part number and the total shipment quantity for that part. (Example 7.4.7)

SP	S#	P#	QTY	
		G.P.	_QY	P.SUM._QY

"G." causes grouping (corresponds to GROUP BY in SQL).

G.2.11 Retrieval Involving an Aggregate Function, with Grouping and a Condition. Get part numbers for all parts supplied by more than one supplier. (Example 7.4.9)

---

*This statement is true quite apart from the fact that (as mentioned earlier in this appendix) certain features that were added to DB2 after its first release, such as date/time arithmetic, have been exposed in SQL but not in QBE.

```
SP  |   S#   |  P#  |      | CONDITIONS  |
----|--------|------|      |-------------|
    |   _SX  | G.P. |      | CNT._SX >1  |
```

The condition box can be used to formulate both WHERE-type conditions and HAVING-type conditions (in SQL terms).

G.2.12 Retrieval Involving Union. Get part numbers for parts that either weigh more than 16 pounds or are supplied by supplier S2 or both. (Example 7.5.1)

```
P   |  P# | WEIGHT |      SP  | S# |  P# |          |      |
----|-----|--------|      ----|----|-----|      ----|------|
    | _PX |  > 16  |          | S2 | _PY |       P. |  _PX |
                                                  P. |  _PY |
```

The QBE-style "union" always eliminates duplicates (there is no ALL option as there is with SQL).

G.3 UPDATE OPERATIONS

G.3.1 Single-Record Insert. Add part P7 (city Athens, weight 24, name and color at present unknown) to table P. (Example 8.2.1)

```
P   | P# | PNAME | COLOR | WEIGHT |  CITY  |
----|----|-------|-------|--------|--------|
I.  | P7 |       |       |   24   | Athens |
```

Note that "I." applies to the entire row and so appears beneath the table name.

G.3.2 Single-Record Update. Change the color of part P2 to yellow, increase its weight by 5, and set its city to null. (Example 8.3.1)

```
P   | P# | PNAME |  COLOR   | WEIGHT |  WEIGHT   |   CITY  |
----|----|-------|----------|--------|-----------|---------|
    | P2 |       | U.Yellow |  _WT   | U._WT + 5 | U.NULL  |
```

G.3.3 Multiple-Record Update. Set the shipment quantity to zero for all suppliers in London. (Example 8.3.3)

```
SP  |  S# | QTY  |      S   |  S# |  CITY  |
----|-----|------|      ----|-----|--------|
    | _SX | U.0  |          | _SX | London |
```

G.3.4 Multiple-Record Delete. Delete all shipments with quantity greater than 300. (Example 8.4.2)

```
  S    |  S#  |  P#  |   QTY
-----|----|----|--------
  D.   |      |      | > 300
```

"D.", like "I.", appears beneath the table name.

   This concludes our short tutorial on QBE. By way of practice, the reader is recommended to try producing QBE solutions to some of the exercises in Chapters 6–8.

APPENDIX

◆ H ◆

Bibliography

We present a short list of selected further reading (over and above the official DB2, QMF, etc., manuals, which are available from IBM).

M. M. Astrahan et al.: "System R: Relational Approach to Database Management." *ACM Transactions on Database Systems 1,* No. 2 (June 1976).

> The paper that first described the overall architecture of System R, the prototype forerunner of DB2 (and SQL/DS).

M. W. Blasgen et al.: "System R: An Architectural Overview." *IBM Systems Journal 20,* No. 1 (February 1981).

> Describes the architecture of System R as it became by the time the system had been fully implemented.

D. D. Chamberlin et al.: "A History and Evaluation of System R." *Communications of the ACM 24,* No. 10 (October 1981).

> Discusses the lessons learned from the System R prototype.

D. D. Chamberlin, A. M. Gilbert, and R. A. Yost: "A History of System R and SQL/Data System." *Proceedings of the 7th International Conference on Very Large Data Bases* (September 1981). Obtainable from ACM, IEEE, and INRIA.

Includes a description of the major differences between System R and SQL/DS (and, by extension, DB2).

Gabrielle Wiorkowski and David Kull. *DB2 Design and Development Guide* (Addison-Wesley, 1988).

A detailed guide to the use of DB2 in practice; describes proven strategies and techniques for designing and developing DB2 applications, with the emphasis on good performance. An ideal complement to the present book.

C. J. Date: "Dates and Times in IBM SQL: Some Technical Criticisms." *InfoDB 3,* No. 1 (Spring 1988).

An analysis and critical evaluation of the date and time support in DB2 (and SQL/DS), as described in Appendix C of the present book.

E. F. Codd: "A Relational Model of Data for Large Shared Data Banks." *Communications of the ACM 13,* No. 6 (June 1970). Reprinted in *Communications of the ACM 26,* No. 1 (January 1983).

This was the paper that (apart from some internal IBM documents) first proposed the ideas of the relational model.

E. F. Codd: "Relational Database: A Practical Foundation for Productivity." *Communications of the ACM 25,* No. 2 (February 1982).

The paper that Codd presented on the occasion of his receiving the 1981 Turing Award. The definition of "relational system" in Appendix B of this book is taken from this paper.

E. F. Codd: *The Relational Model for Database Management.* Addison-Wesley, 1989 (to appear).

Includes a more stringent definition of what it means for a system to be relational in the late 1980s.

American National Standards Institute: *Database Language SQL,* Document ANSI X3.135-1986. Also available as International Standards Organization Document ISO/TC97/SC21/WG3 N117.

The official SQL standard definition.

C. J. Date: *A Guide to the SQL Standard* (2nd edition, Addison-Wesley, 1989).

An indepth discussion of the SQL standard.

C. J. Date and Colin J. White: *A Guide to SQL/DS* (Addison-Wesley, 1989).

A companion to the present book.

C. J. Date: *A Guide to INGRES* (Addison-Wesley, 1987).

Another companion to the present book, describing another important relational product—INGRES, from Relational Technology Inc. (RTI).

Colin J. White: *A Guide to ORACLE* (Addison-Wesley, to appear).

Yet another companion book.

C. J. Date: *An Introduction to Database Systems: Volume I* (4th edition, Addison-Wesley, 1986); *Volume II* (1st edition, Addison-Wesley, 1983).

These two books between them provide the basis for a comprehensive education in most aspects of database technology. In particular, they include a very detailed treatment of the relational approach.

C. J. Date: *Relational Database: Selected Writings* (Addison-Wesley, 1986).

A collection of papers on various aspects of relational technology, including several on the SQL language and one (rather long) on a relational database design methodology that is directly applicable to DB2.

C. J. Date: "Referential Integrity and Foreign Keys. Part I: Basic Concepts; Part II: Further Considerations." To appear.

A comprehensive treatment of referential integrity, not just as implemented by IBM but in general terms.

APPENDIX

◆ I ◆

Abbreviations and Acronyms

We list below some of the more important abbreviations and acronyms introduced in the text, together with their meanings.

ADF	Application Development Facility
ALF	Application Load File (CSP)
ANSI	American National Standards Institute
API	application programming interface
AS	Application System
BNF	Backus-Naur Form
BSDS	Boot Strap Data Set
CASE	Computer-Aided Software Engineering
CICS	Customer Information Control System
CLIST	command list (TSO)
CS	cursor stability (isolation level)
CSP	Cross System Product

CSP/AD	CSP/Application Development
CSP/AE	CSP/Application Execution
DB/DC	database/data communications
DBA	database administrator
DBADM	database administration (privilege)
DBCTRL	database control (privilege)
DBMAINT	database maintenance (privilege)
DBMAU	DB2 Migration Aid Utility
DBMS	database management system
DBRAD	Data Base Relational Application Directory
DBRM	Database Request Module
DB2	IBM DATABASE 2
DB2I	DB2 Interactive
DB2PM	DB2 Performance Monitor
DCF	Document Composition Facility
DCLGEN	Declarations Generator
DDF	Distributed Data Facility
DEM	Data Extract Manager (DXT)
DXT	Data Extract
DXTA	DXT Assist
ECF	Enhanced Connectivity Facilities
EDITPROC	edit procedure
FIELDPROC	field procedure
GDDM	Graphic Data Display Manager
HDBV	Host Data Base View
I/O	input/output
IADF	Interactive ADF
IC/1	Info Center/1
ICU	Interactive Chart Utility
IMS	Information Management System
IMS/DB	IMS Database Manager
IMS/DC	IMS Data Communications Manager
IMSADF II	IMS Application Development Facility II (= ADF)
IRLM	IMS Resource Lock Manager
ISO	International Standards Organization
ISPF	Interactive System Productivity Facility
ISPF/PDF	ISPF Program Development Facility
IXF	Integration Exchange Format
MSL	Member Specification Library (CSP)
PF key	program function key
QBE	Query-By-Example
QMF	Query Management Facility
RDS	Relational Data System
REM	Relational Extract Manager (DXT)
RID	record ID
RR	repeatable read (isolation level)

S lock	shared lock
SAA	Systems Application Architecture
SPUFI	SQL Processor Using File Input
SQL	Structured Query Language
SQL/DS	Structured Query Language/Data System
SQLCA	SQL Communication Area
SQLDA	SQL Descriptor Area
SRPI	server-requester programming interface
SYSADM	system administration (privilege)
SYSOPR	system operation (privilege)
TIF	The Information Facility
TSO	Time Sharing Option
U lock	update lock
UIM	User Input Manager (DXT)
VALIDPROC	validation procedure
VSAM	Virtual Storage Access Method
WYSIWYG	what you see is what you get
X lock	exclusive lock

Index